MARKETING

MARKETING

Marketing

Geoff Lancaster

and

Paul Reynolds

First published 2004 by
PALGRAVE MACMILLAN
Houndmills, Basingstoke, Hampshire RG21 6XS and
175 Fifth Avenue, New York, N.Y. 10010
Companies and representatives throughout the world

PALGRAVE MACMILLAN is the global academic imprint of the Palgrave Macmillan division of St. Martin's Press, LLC and of Palgrave Macmillan Ltd. Macmillan® is a registered trademark in the United States, United Kingdom and other countries. Palgrave is a registered trademark in the European Union and other countries.

ISBN 0–333–98789–6

This book is printed on paper suitable for recycling and made from fully managed and sustained forest sources.

A catalogue record for this book is available from the British Library.

A catalog record for this book is available from the Library of Congress.

Editing and origination by Aardvark Editorial, Mendham, Suffolk

10 9 8 7 6 5 4 3 2 1
13 12 11 10 09 08 07 06 05 04

Printed and bound in Great Britain by
Creative Print & Design (Wales), Ebbw Vale

CONTENTS

LIST OF FIGURES AND TABLES

Figures

Tables

1 Development of the Marketing Concept

Most people have heard the term 'marketing' but few fully understand what the term really means. Many people tend to think of the term as synonymous with selling, but marketing is much more than that. Others regard marketing as advertising or public relations (PR). Again this is a very narrow and simplistic view of the subject. Marketing encompasses much more than selling and much more than advertising or PR. Marketing is a business function which utilises a range of well-developed management techniques but, as we shall see, it is also, and perhaps more importantly, an overall business philosophy which should permeate the entire business. Marketing as an organisational philosophy and activity is applicable to almost all types of organisation, whether profit making or not-for-profit, manufacturing or service based. Throughout this chapter you are encouraged to understand the term 'customer' in this wider context, and not just as someone who interacts with a profit-centred business. Most people think of the term 'customer' in the context of a profit-making facility. Whilst it is true that the marketing concept has been more widely adopted and practised in the profit-making sectors of the economy, the fundamental principles of marketing are equally applicable in the not-for-profit sectors; a fact that is often overlooked. Marketing can be used by public sector organisations such as museums, libraries, universities and sports centres.

▶▶ A historical perspective

The concept of marketing is neither complicated nor original. Quotes such as 'the customer comes first', 'the customer is king' or 'the customer is always right' have been used in commerce since trade began. A more formalised adaptation of this business-oriented approach has now developed into a management discipline and overall business philosophy which, taken as a whole, is now called 'marketing'. Marketing is based on the premise that the customer is the most important person to the organisation. Marketing is principally concerned with exchange or trade. Trade in its most basic form has existed ever since people were able to produce a surplus. Historically, this surplus was agricultural produce that was often traded for manufactured goods such as textiles or earthenware. Exchange brought into existence places that facilitated trade, such as village fairs and local markets. The emergence of trade allowed people to specialise in producing particular goods and services that could be exchanged in markets for other goods they needed.

▶▶ The modern era

The first half of the twentieth century saw the emergence of Germany and the United States as competing industrial powers. Although Britain faced strong competition from economically emerging nations in areas such as textiles, coal and steel, the British economy continued along a path of industrial expansion in the period up to the First World War. Incomes generated in other countries resulted in a worldwide increase in total effective demand for goods and services. The total value of UK trade increased even though its share of international trade started to decline.

To better understand the notion of marketing orientation and putting customers first, we start by examining its historical development as it took place in the UK. We must also examine the different philosophical views that pertained in relation to business at different periods of time.

▶ Adam Smith

Perhaps the most enduring of quotations that emphasises marketing orientation comes from Adam Smith at the time of the Industrial Revolution when he wrote 'Wealth of Nations' (Smith, 1776):

> Consumption is the sole end and purpose of all production and the interests of the producer ought to be attended to only as far as it may be necessary for promoting that of the consumer.

However, in the same quotation, he went on to point out that producers do not take this logic seriously:

> The maxim is so perfectly self-evident that it would be absurd to attempt to prove it. But in the mercantile system, the interest of the consumer is almost constantly sacrificed to that of producers who seem to consider production, and not consumption, as the ultimate end and object of all industry and commerce.

This far-reaching quotation was cited at the time of the Industrial Revolution. It is also true that the notion of marketing orientation and putting customers first has, in some organisations, only been taken up relatively recently, as we go on to explain.

▌▌▌ Vignette 1.1

J osiah Wedgwood (1730–95) understood the market for good quality, competitively priced earthenware and enabled ordinary people to enjoy style and quality.

Josiah Wedgwood (1730–95) was an English potter whose works are among the finest examples of ceramic art. Wedgwood was born in Burslem, Staffordshire, on 12 July, 1730, into a family with a long tradition as potters. At the age of nine, after the death of his father, he worked in his family's pottery. In 1759 he set up his own pottery works in Burslem. There he produced highly durable cream-coloured earthenware that so pleased Queen Charlotte that in 1762 she appointed him royal supplier of dinnerware. From the public sale of Queen's Ware, as it came to be known, Wedgwood was able, in 1768, to build a village near Stoke-on-Trent, which he named Etruria, and a second factory equipped with tools and ovens of his own design. At first only ornamental pottery was made in Etruria, but by 1773 Wedgwood had concentrated all his production facilities there. During his long career, Wedgwood developed revolutionary ceramic materials, notably basalt and jasperware. In 1754 Wedgwood began to experiment with coloured creamware. He established his own factory, but often worked with others who did transfer printing (introduced by the Worcester Porcelain Company in the 1750s). He also produced red stoneware; basaltware, an unglazed black stoneware; and jasperware, made of white stoneware clay that had been coloured by the addition of metal oxides. Jasperware was usually ornamented with white relief portraits or Greek classical scenes. Wedgwood's greatest contribution to European ceramics, however, was his fine pearlware, an extremely pale creamware with a bluish tint to its glaze. Wedgwood's basalt, a hard, black, stone-like material known also as Egyptian ware or basaltware, was used for vases, candlesticks and realistic busts of historical figures. Jasperware, his most successful innovation, was a durable unglazed ware, most characteristically blue, with fine white cameo figures inspired by the ancient Roman Portland Vase. Many of the finest designs were the work of the British artist John Flaxman. Wedgwood's wares appealed particularly to the rising European bourgeois class and porcelain and decorated and glazed earth-

enware factories suffered severely from competition from him. The surviving factories switched to the manufacture of creamware (called on the Continent *faience fine*
or *faience anglaise*) to try to imitate and compete with Wedgwood. Even the great
factories at Sèvres, France and at Meissen, Germany found their trade affected.
Jasperware was imitated in biscuit porcelain at Sèvres, and Meissen produced a glazed
version, which they even called *Wedgwoodarbeit*.

▶▶ Different types of business orientation

Marketing maturity is a gradual developmental process. By evolving
through lower stages of development, enlightened firms appreciate that
the satisfaction of consumers' needs and wants is the rationale for everything a company does. Such companies have progressed to a marketing
orientation. Of all the stakeholders in a business, the customer is the
most important, for it is by the satisfaction of customer needs, and the
profit that should result from doing this, that all other stakeholder needs
are satisfied.

To summarise, and to give an idea of what is now universally recognised within business, it can be said that there are three basic types of
business orientation:

▶ production orientation
▶ sales orientation
▶ marketing orientation.

Each of these is now briefly explained.

▶ Production orientation

In the nineteenth and early twentieth centuries, the primary purpose of
all business and industrial activity was thought to be production. Manufacturers were in a 'supplier's market' and faced with a virtually insa-
tiable demand for anything that could be produced. Henry Ford made
his famous statement to the media in 1913 when he produced his first
production line Model 'T' Ford:

You can have any colour you like, as long as it is black.

This was certainly a production-orientated statement and during this
period firms concentrated on improving production efficiency in an

attempt to bring down costs. In America, in the economic recession of the 1920s and 30s, simply to produce was no longer good enough and firms had to begin to focus their attention on the changing needs of the marketplace. This ultimately led to the idea of marketing orientation and it was America, in the 1930s, that saw the origin of this philosophy.

▶ Sales orientation

Gradually, business people began to appreciate that, in a highly competitive environment, it was simply not enough to produce goods as efficiently as possible. The sales department was thought to hold the key to a firm's prosperity and survival, and sales volume became the success criterion. In a sales-oriented firm, selling is a major management function, and is often given equal status with that of production and finance. Here the emphasis is on 'pushing' a company's products or services to often unwilling customers.

Why do you feel it took until the twentieth century to formally recognise marketing orientation, even though it was first informally recognised and practised by some entrepreneurs at the time of the Industrial Revolution?

This is probably more useful as a topic for debate. The answer lies in the fact that theory in marketing, and indeed most other business disciplines, is established by observing the phenomenon (as a kind of case study or series of case studies) and then establishing that a trend exists. Once this becomes an established tendency (through statistical or behavioural observation), then it becomes a theory. In the case of the recognition of marketing orientation, as we shall see, it was not until the twentieth century that the trends referred to here became known as 'marketing orientation'. In the physical sciences it is perhaps easier to establish theories, because most of the experiments are laboratory based and observation and statistical testing prove or disprove a theory. In the behavioural sciences (such as marketing), theory rests upon observing the phenomenon as it happens and then recording what happened. Only when sufficient experience has been gained and trends established can it be called a theory. Even then such theories are often not based upon hard evidence. This is why many physical scientists tend to have disdain for the behavioural sciences, because of their imprecision, and indeed the behavioural sciences are sometimes collectively referred to as 'soft sciences'.

▶ Marketing orientation

Under the marketing concept, it is the customer who becomes the centre of business attention. Firms now see the identification and satisfaction of customers' needs and wants, rather than production or sales, as the key to prosperity, growth and survival. In a marketing-oriented organisation, the whole firm appreciates the central importance of the customer and realises that without satisfied customers there will be no business.

The Chartered Institute of Marketing defines marketing in its constitution (2003):

> Marketing is the management process responsible for identifying, anticipating and satisfying customer requirements profitably.

An alternative definition is put forward in the American Marketing Association's constitution (2003):

> Marketing is the process of planning and executing the conception, pricing, promotion and distribution of ideas, goods and services to create exchanges that satisfy individual and organisational objectives.

The Chartered Institute of Marketing definition more succinctly sums up the overall aim of marketing, but the American Marketing Association's definition is more precise as it identifies the tools through which marketing realises its objectives. Borden (1964) first published a paper called the 'The Concept of the Marketing Mix'. Hence these tools became known collectively as the 'marketing mix' which essentially means manipulating the 'four Ps' (a term coined by E. Jerome McCarthy and which includes price, product, place and promotion – see Kotler, 1997, p. 92) in their most effective way. This theme is expanded in later chapters.

▌▌▌ Vignette 1.2

Henry Ford pioneers the mass production and mass marketing of motor cars.

Pioneering automotive engineer Henry Ford held many patents on automotive mechanisms. He is best remembered, however, for helping to devise the factory assembly approach to production that revolutionised the auto industry by greatly reducing the time required to assemble a car. Born in Wayne County, Michigan, Ford showed an early interest in mechanics, constructing his first steam engine at the age of 15. In 1893 he built his first internal combustion engine, a small one-cylinder petrol model, and in 1896 he built his first car. In June 1903 Ford helped to establish the Ford Motor Company. He served as president of the company from 1906 to 1919 and from 1943 to 1945. In addition to obtaining numerous patents on auto mechanisms, Ford served as a vice president of the Society of Automotive Engineers when it was founded in 1905 to standardise US automotive parts. In 1905, when there were 50 start-up companies a year trying to get into the auto business, his backers at the new Ford Motor Company were insisting that the best way to max-imise profits was to build a car for the rich. But Ford was from modest, agrarian Michigan roots. And he thought that the people who made the cars ought to be able to afford one themselves so that they too could go for a drive on a Sunday after-noon. In typical fashion, instead of listening to his backers, Ford eventually bought them out. And that proved to be only the first clever move in a plan that would make him the father of twentieth-century American industry. When the black Model T was introduced to the market in 1908, it was hailed as America's Everyman car. Ford instituted industrial mass production, but what really mattered to him was mass consumption and mass marketing of his products. He calculated that if he paid his factory workers a real living wage and produced more cars in less time for less money, many people would buy them, including his workers. Almost half a century before Ray Kroc sold a single McDonald's hamburger, Ford invented the dealer-fran-chise system to sell and service cars. In the same way that all politics is local, he knew that business had to be local. Ford's 'road men' became a familiar part of the American landscape. By 1912 there were 7000 Ford dealers across the country. In much the same fashion, he worked on making sure that an automotive infrastruc-ture developed along with the cars. Just like horses, cars had to be fed, so Ford argued for petrol stations everywhere possible. And, as his 'tin Lizzies' bounced over the tracks of the horse age, he campaigned for better roads, which eventually led to an interstate-highway system that is still the envy of the world.

▶▶ Modern marketing developments

The notion of 'relationship marketing' was first introduced into the aca-demic marketing literature by researchers, such as Berry (1983), who were involved in examining customer care issues. The discipline of mar-keting as a business subject in its own right had been developed from the experience of firms and university business school researchers involved in consumer markets and based largely in America. These ideas seemed to work well in the consumer markets of developed economies throughout the world, especially in the USA but also, to some extent, in Europe, where the concept arrived from America and was applied by firms as an overriding business philosophy much later than in the USA. American colleges were teaching marketing at their business schools and firms were applying these concepts back in the 1950s. In

Europe this did not really happen until the late 1960s and 70s. Consumer marketing firms were the first to embrace the new thinking, with industrial firms adopting the ideas much later.

Today the essence and the focus of modern marketing have changed. The basic definition of marketing, as a business process concerned with satisfying customers' needs and wants more effectively and efficiently than the competition, remains valid. This basic marketing concept is as applicable today as it was back in the 1950s when marketing ideas were first developed. However, the methods, techniques and processes used to achieve marketing objectives within many organisations have changed quite dramatically if you compare the methods and general philosophy employed by firms today with those used in an earlier era. If you read a basic marketing textbook or article from the 1970s or even from the 80s and one from the present time, you will notice topics in the more recent publications which were not even discussed in earlier versions. Subjects such as 'internal marketing', 'relationship marketing', and 'customer relationship management' (CRM) in particular, are all fairly recent areas to be examined and discussed within the marketing literature.

The direction of modern marketing today is concerned with the establishment and maintenance of longer term relationships with customers. This 'longer term' perspective, some would even suggest a 'lifetime' or 'lifelong' view, of customer 'value' and the buyer–supplier relationship is often referred to as 'relationship marketing'. Relationship marketing has evolved out of the more 'transaction'-based form of marketing used by the majority of commercial firms up to the beginning of the 1980s, where marketing firms tended to take a more short-term view of customers as the next 'transaction' ahead. Not only has the more conventional 'transactional' marketing evolved into relationship marketing but also relationship marketing itself has become incorporated into a more integrated model. In fact, relationship marketing was the precursor of what today is called customer relationship management or CRM for short. It would be true to say that relationship marketing is an intrinsic part of the CRM paradigm or model. Basically, the direction of marketing has altered from the shorter term view of customers as the next 'transaction' to seeing customers as a long-term source of income. There are situations where the firm wants to sell a product or service only once and does not expect or even want to see the customer more than once. However, in many marketing relationships firms do want repeat business and attempt to retain their customers.

How would you respond if somebody asked you to defend marketing on the basis that it was no more than a fancy word for selling?

This should be relatively easy to do in terms of explaining sales orientation and marketing orientation. Although this is discussed later in the text, when we look at marketing in more detail, it could also be argued that selling is really part of marketing. Marketing includes selling, together with considerations of advertising, pricing, the product or service, distribution channels and logistics, a study of customers and the segments into which they fall, marketing research to discover customers' needs, and more besides.

▶ The development of relationship marketing

Relationship marketing is a business idea that has emerged from a growing body of literature expressing lack of faith in the more conventional 'transactional' marketing approach. Something more was required. This dissatisfaction applied to all areas of marketing but especially business-to-business and services marketing where the limitations of the more conventional marketing approach were first identified. As far back as 1954, the management 'guru' Peter Drucker said:

> There is only one valid definition of business: to create customers. It is the customer who determines what the business is. (Drucker, 1954, p. 1)

Customers are paramount to any business and the general object of relationship marketing is the acquisition, satisfaction and retention of customers so that firms can stay in business. It had been accepted for some time in industrial markets that relationships between buyer and seller firms needed a more long-term 'interaction approach' rather than the short termism of the next transaction. It was also generally accepted that many of the relationships formed between members of the marketing 'team' and members of the buying firm's 'team' were largely informal and often left to chance, even though they were very important in the marketing process. This new way of looking at things based around the 'interaction approach' eventually evolved into the 'relationship marketing' paradigm. This paradigm has now been accepted by marketing organisations operating in all market sectors and not just industrial sectors. As we have said, with the addition of advances in IT, this concept has now evolved further into a full system of CRM and is still developing.

Discussing relationship marketing, Gronroos (1990) proposed a marketing strategy continuum, ranging from 'transaction marketing', which was regarded as more appropriate to business-to-consumer marketing particularly in the field of fast-moving consumer goods (FMCG), through to relationship marketing. This approach was seen as more suitable for business-to-business marketing and services marketing. Copulsky and Wolf (1990) used the term 'relationship marketing' to identify a type of database marketing. In their model, marketing firms select suitable customer targets for the promotion of products and services using a database marketing approach. This use of a customer database is very similar to its use in the modern CRM model. For example, in marketing communications under the CRM approach, a commercial message sent to customers may well be 'tailor made' to match their interests or requirements. The response may be assessed and used to produce various measures including the projected lifetime value of the customer, another key CRM concept. McKenna (1991) linked relationship marketing to the organisational structure of a business. According to McKenna the entire business needed to be organised to produce a relationship marketing approach rather than it being merely a business process.

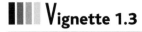 ## Vignette 1.3

U K private pension industry mis-sold financial products to an unsuspecting public.

Unless you work in the financial services industry or you are fairly knowledgeable about financial matters, things like pension funds and investment funds probably leave you cold. All you probably want to know, along with a lot of other people, is that your retirement will be taken care of financially and your mortgage will be paid off in full before you retire. The last thing you want to happen is to reach the age of 65 years, or whatever age you have planned to retire, only to find your pension is nowhere near large enough for you to enjoy your retirement in the way you had hoped. You do not want to find that you have got to use your retirement 'lump sum' or annuity to pay off a residual amount on your mortgage because your insurance endowment policy failed to grow to the amount expected and promised by the insurance company who sold it to you. However, these things happened to a large number of people in the 1990s. Many people were persuaded by the promises made by insurance companies and pension companies to take out inappropriate financial products which would significantly affect their future financial health in a big way. This was a classic case of selling orientation. So-called 'financial consultants' or 'experts' used technical language to confuse the ordinary man in the street into buying financial products, usually endowment polices, that were totally unsuitable to the client's needs. All these consultants were really interested in were the short-term commissions they would earn on the policies rather than the long-term financial health of the clients they were selling to. This fiasco led to a big overhaul of the financial services industry with a range of professional qualifications being introduced for people selling financial products to the public. Many of the pension and insurance firms were faced with large bills, running into millions of pounds for compensation for people who had been mis-sold financial products.

◗ CRM systems need to be integrated

CRM systems should enable marketing organisations to provide total customer care, from initial acquisition of the customer right the way through to product delivery and aftercare services. CRM is a totally comprehensive approach which provides 'seamless' integration of every aspect of business that relates to the customer whether this be marketing, sales, customer service or field support – through the integration of people, process and technology. It does this by using the power of Internet technology. The object of CRM is to create a long-term, mutually beneficial relationship with customers. The modern CRM concept requires a fully integrated system, which starts with the acquisition of the customer, through constant development of the customer, managing the relationship, customer care and retention of the customer. CRM, when used by companies effectively turns the marketing firm into a 'learning organisation'. The marketing firm tries to learn as much as possible about its customers in order to provide them with superior service. This means firms can offer their customers the products and services they want in order to satisfy their requirements. This, in turn, helps the firm to develop and cement long-term relationships with its customers, which is really what customer relationship management is all about. The marketing firm requires information from a variety of sources in order for it to carry out this task. The use of computer 'database' technology enables the firm to store, update and profile customer details and likely requirements. Products, services and marketing communications can be designed for specific customers and targeted to them more accurately.

SELF-CHECK

In terms of long-term business planning, do you feel the initial driving force behind planning is:

- *production*
- *finance*
- *sales,* or
- *marketing*

when a company is:

- *Production oriented*
- *Sales oriented,* or
- *Marketing oriented?*

The obvious answer might be: production, sales and marketing in that order. In the case of production orientation this is clearly the case, because production produces what it wants to produce and demand for products tends to outstrip their supply. In the case of sales orientation it is not sales that are the driving force, because sales tactics are merely the tools that are used to move products that have not been automatically taken up by the marketplace. Thus, production is still the driving force in a sales-oriented organisation. In the case of a marketing-oriented company, customers' needs are the starting point for business planning. These are revealed through marketing research and other means. It is marketing that ultimately interprets these requirements into physical products as well as appropriate messages that are designed to appeal to customers' needs.

▶▶ Summary

We have described how marketing has come to occupy the important place it holds in business today. It is really only since the end of the Second World War that marketing has developed in the UK as a formal business concept with a codified philosophy and set of techniques. It has also been demonstrated that marketing is now central to planning in businesses that operate in a competitive environment. The marketing-oriented firm achieves its business objectives by identifying and anticipating the changing needs and wants of specifically defined target markets. The subject of targeting is addressed in Chapter 3. The techniques used for identifying customer requirements, in the subject of marketing research, are discussed in Chapter 6. Business planning, therefore, starts with customers, and it is the responsibility of marketing to assemble these requirements through the marketing plan into the corporate business plan. As a consequence, it is from customers' needs, and subsequent marketing planning to meet these needs, that other functions in a business operation take their respective leads.

FURTHER READING

Armstrong G. and Kotler P. (2000) *Marketing: An Introduction* (5th edn), Chapter 1, 'Understanding Marketing and the Marketing Management Process', Prentice Hall, Englewood Cliffs, NJ.

Blythe J. (2001) *Essentials of Marketing*, Chapter 1, 'What do Marketers Do?', Pearson Education, London.

Cateora P.R. and Ghauri P.N. (2000) *International Marketing: European Edition*, Chapter 1, 'The Scope and Challenge of International Marketing', McGraw-Hill, Maidenhead.

Cowell D. (1984) *The Marketing of Services*, Butterworth Heinemann, Oxford.

Davies M. (1998) *Understanding Marketing*, Chapter 1, 'Introduction to Marketing', Prentice Hall, London.

Ivanovic A. and Collins P.H. (1989) *Dictionary of Marketing*, Peter Collins, Teddington.

Keegan W.J. and Green M.S. (2000) *Global Marketing* (2nd edn), Chapter 1, 'Introduction to Global Marketing', Prentice Hall, London.

Lancaster G. and Massingham L. (1999) *Essentials of Marketing* (3rd edn), McGraw-Hill, Maidenhead.

Lancaster G.A. and Reynolds P.L. (1999) *Introduction to Marketing: A Step-by-Step Guide to All The Tools of Marketing*, Chapter 1, 'Marketing Defined ', Kogan Page, London.

Piercy N. (1992) *Market-led Strategic Change*, Butterworth Heinemann, Oxford.

Plamer A. (2000) *Principles of Marketing*, Chapter 1, 'What is Marketing?', OUP, Oxford.

▶▶ References

Berry L.L. (1983) 'Relationship Marketing' in Berry L.L. et al. (eds) *Emerging Perspectives on Services Marketing*, American Marketing Association, Chicago, pp. 25–8.

Borden Neil H. (1964) 'The Concept of the Marketing Mix', *Journal of Advertising Research*, **4** (June): 2–7.

Copulsky J.R. and Wolf M.J. (1990) 'Relationship Marketing: Positioning for the Future', *Journal of Business Strategy*, July–August, pp. 16–20.

Drucker P. [1954](1986) *The Principles of Management*, HarperCollins, New York, p. 1.

Gronroos C. (1990) 'Relationship Approach to Marketing In Service Contexts: The Marketing and Organisational Behaviour Interface', *Journal of Business Research*, 20 January, pp. 3–11.

Kotler P. (1997) *Marketing Management, Analysis, Planning, Implementation and Control* (9th edn), Prentice Hall, Englewood Cliffs, NJ, p. 92.

McKenna R. (1991) *Relationship Marketing*, Century Business, London.

Smith A. (1776) 'An Enquiry into the Nature and Causes of the Wealth of Nations'.

2

Marketing and the Organisation's Micro- and Macroenvironments

▶▶ The microenvironment

The microenvironment denotes those elements over which a firm has control or which it can influence in order to gain information that will help it in its marketing operations. In other words, these are elements that can be manipulated, or used to obtain information to provide greater satisfaction to the company's customers. The objective of marketing philosophy as discussed in Chapter 1 is to make profits through satisfying customers. This is accomplished through the manipulation of the variables over which a company has control, in such a way as to optimise this objective. The variables are what are termed 'the marketing mix' which is a combination of all the 'ingredients' in a 'recipe' that is designed to prove most attractive to customers. In this case, the ingredients are individual elements that marketing can manipulate into the most appropriate mix. E.J. McCarthy (see Kotler, 1997) further described the variables the company can control in order to reach its target market as the 'four Ps'. Each of these is discussed in detail in later chapters, but a brief discussion follows on each of these elements of the marketing mix, together with an explanation of how they fit into the overall idea of marketing.

▶ The four Ps and the marketing mix

The four Ps stand for:

1. Product
2. Price

3. Place
4. Promotion.

Product and price are clear, but place and promotion need more explanation.

Place, it is felt, might be better termed 'placement' because it comprises two distinct elements. The first element is channels of distribution, that is, the outlets and methods through which a company's goods or services are sold. A channel can be a certain type of retail outlet or it can be salespeople selling a company's industrial products through, say, a channel that comprises buyers in the chemical industry. The other part of place refers to logistics that relate to the physical warehousing and transportation of goods from the manufacturer to the end customer. 'Placement' might be a better description as it refers to the placing of goods or services from the supplier to the customer. In fact, place has its own individual 'mix', termed the 'distribution mix'.

Promotion also has its individual mix, called the 'promotional mix'. This promotional mix comprises advertising, sales promotion, selling and public relations. 'Promotion' is a slight misnomer, because in advertising circles the term promotion usually means 'sales promotion'. Some writers separate 'selling' from promotion and call it 'people' as it is too important an element of marketing to be grouped together with promotion, although in reality it is still promotion (through word of mouth). This fifth 'P' (people) represents those who contact customers on a regular basis with the objective of ultimately gaining orders and these people comprise the sales force and other marketing personnel. We can see that selling is a component part of overall marketing. There are two more Ps for service marketing (process and physical evidence) and these are dealt with in Chapter 17.

 Consider the distinction between the idea of the marketing mix and McCarthy's four Ps. Are they the same, or do you feel that there is a distinction?

In marketing literature the terms are quite often used interchangeably, but the reality is that McCarthy's four Ps are very specific in that they are the tools that can be used by marketing people to target customers (see Figure 2.2 for a fuller explanation). The marketing mix, on the other hand, is wider than this and includes customers, their individual and group buying behaviour and the market segments into which they fall. It also includes appropriate strategies for targeting these groups of customers. Again, this is explained more fully in the next section.

❯ Models of marketing

Figure 2.1 sums up what is meant by marketing at a simple level. It is one of the earliest models to attempt to explain what is meant by marketing.

In Figure 2.1 we see information coming from customers to a supplying company. This information is noted and goods or services are supplied to customers in line with customer needs. The information flow represents an exchange of ideas whilst the operation flow represents an exchange of understandings.

Figure 2.2 is a more precise diagram of what is meant by marketing and one which we can understand from what has already been said.

This more detailed model better explains what we understand about marketing. The bottom line represents elements of the marketing mix over which a company has control. These elements are manipulated to best suit customers' needs and tastes and represent an operational flow where things have to be done in order to arrive at the optimum marketing mix. There are submixes within individual elements of the marketing mix. This bottom line also equates to the earlier notion of the four Ps, or rather the five Ps, as personal selling has been separated from promotion and becomes part of 'people'.

The top line represents an information flow from the market to the firm. Data is collected through investigating the marketplace on an informal and formal basis. A whole range of techniques is available for this process which are collectively termed 'marketing research'. A more advanced strategic model that incorporates marketing research is embodied in a marketing information system (MkIS) that is dealt with in Chapter 5. In addition, data is collected from customers in relation to their likely future purchases and this is known as 'sales forecasting'. A range of techniques is available for sales forecasting, which lies at the very heart of marketing and business planning, and this is also covered in Chapter 5.

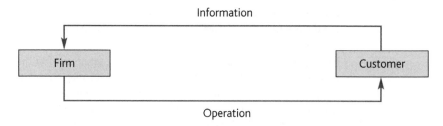

Figure 2.1 Simple diagrammatic representation of marketing

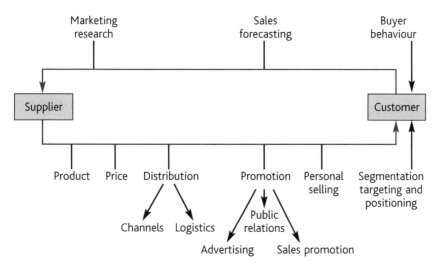

Figure 2.2 Model of the process of marketing

We can now see how marketing orientation works. Customers are the starting point and sales forecasting and marketing research determine their likely requirements and tastes. This information is processed internally within the organisation and products and promotional messages are devised to suit customers' needs, to allay their purchasing fears and to reinforce their expectations. Goods and services are supplied as and when required, in the quantities needed and when they are requested – neither later nor earlier. This latter point is reinforced, as modern marketing dictates that customers demand goods on a timely basis, and this is the basis of the concept of 'just-in-time' manufacturing which we discuss in more detail in Chapter 10.

Customers are segmented (divided) according to their various needs and requirements in order that different messages can be relayed and product modifications made to suit the specific desires of small groups of customers. Segmentation, along with the strategic implications of targeting and positioning, forms the basis of the next chapter. Customers behave in a certain way towards purchasing products and services. Such behaviour is influenced by family, work colleagues, members of societies and even clubs to which individual buyers belong, plus many other competing influences. This is termed 'buyer behaviour' and is supported by a range of techniques which are discussed under the headings 'Models of consumer behaviour' and 'Organisational buying behaviour' in Chapter 4.

Returning to the notion of the marketing mix, this relates to those elements over which the company has control in reaching its customer base and includes E.J. McCarthy's four Ps as well as segmentation, targeting and positioning.

Non-marketing people frequently allege: 'Marketing is merely an elegant term for selling.' Refute this allegation.

This is relatively easy. You simply explain that selling is but one element in the marketing mix, whereas marketing is much broader. As you proceed through the text you will discover that marketing pervades a modern organisation, and lasting customer satisfaction should be the driving force for all businesses.

▶ The place of marketing alongside other elements of business

Marketing is one function within business. Arguably it is the most critical as it interprets customers' needs and requirements into products and services and repeat business, without which a business cannot continue. A modern view of marketing puts customers at the centre and marketing as the interpretative function surrounding the customer, with other major functions of business around as shown in Figure 2.3. The idea is that all functions of business should be geared towards customer satisfaction and this has led to the notion of 'customer care' which is discussed later.

Traditional organisation charts put marketing alongside other major functions and Figure 2.4 illustrates this relationship. This organisation chart represents the ideal 'textbook' structure. In practice, companies tend to evolve and develop in a more haphazard manner, so organisation

Figure 2.3 Marketing in the modern organisation

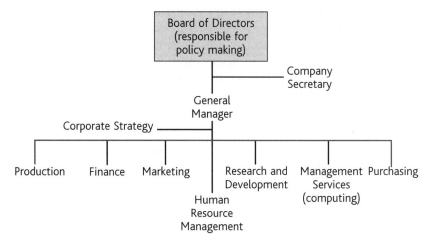

Figure 2.4 A traditional organisation chart

charts can be found that possess little relationship to the ideal structure. As a company grows structures sometimes evolve through the forceful personality of a head of department whose department has assumed a position of power within an organisation, when there is no justification for this. For example, the material control department might report directly to the managing director rather than being a subfunction within purchasing. Another common example, is where a sales director can be found in the line alongside a marketing director. In such a situation, it might be a powerful sales director in a sales-driven organisation who has not assumed responsibility for marketing, but who is too powerful to put into a subordinate position under marketing. With this background in mind, the organisation chart shown in Figure 2.4 relates more to an 'ideal' structure.

In this organisation chart we can see the place of marketing alongside other major functions of line management.

At the top, a board of directors is responsible for giving the organisation its strategic direction. Members of the board are not necessarily full-time employees. In many large companies, board members come from outside the organisation and the expertise they lend to the board can vary. These directors may be strategy experts, financial experts, people who lend distinction to an organisation (for example possess a title) or who are on the board of directors of other companies and can bring a cross-fertilisation of ideas, financial links and possible inter-firm dealings.

The general manager translates policy into tactics and is responsible for day-to-day operations. Normally, the general manager is a member of the board and in such cases the title would then be managing director.

The company secretary is responsible for legal and administrative matters as well as serving as secretary to the board of directors. This person ensures that board meetings take place at intervals stipulated in the company's articles of association, and that policies that are decided are implemented. For this reason, the role of company secretary is a lateral relationship and not in the line of command. This also applies to corporate strategy, whose function may be carried out by general management, but is often a separate function. This relatively small function's role it is to ensure that subdivisions in the organisation have a plan (for example a marketing plan) and that each of these plans fits into the overall corporate plan without there being any mismatches (for example marketing might plan to market more than the firm can produce). The subject of marketing planning is dealt with in Chapter 15.

Major line functions are responsible for translating strategy into tactics in terms of the organisation's everyday operations and this includes such tactical issues as manufacturing, training and recruitment, design and selling. As discussed in Chapter 1, marketing is a modern function that takes in the function of selling (although in practice the two functions are often separated). In many companies, heads of these line functions are sometimes members of the board of directors in which case they would then have 'director' behind their title (for example marketing director, financial director). In such cases their responsibilities would cover both strategic matters (as a member of the board of directors) and tactical issues (being a functional head of department).

In the organisation chart shown in Figure 2.4, apart from the general manager, which do you feel is the most important function in a business concern?

This should have opened up a useful debate to which there is no precise answer as it all depends upon the individual circumstances of the company. However, it can be said that in retailing organisations, the role of the purchasing department is of paramount importance, because it is mark-up on goods purchased and then sold that determines the prosperity of the company. In fast-moving consumer goods (FMCG) manufacture, branding of products is often very important and here marketing might be the most important function. In engineered products, when delivery and quality is important, the prime function might be production. In a financial services company it might be finance. There is no one correct or incorrect answer as it is a matter of emphasis.

◗◗ The proximate macroenvironment

The term macroenvironment denotes all forces and agencies external to the marketing firm itself. Some of these will be closer to the operation of the firm than others, for example a firm's suppliers, agents, distributors and other distributive intermediaries and competing firms. These closer external constituents are collectively referred to as the firm's 'proximate macroenvironment' to distinguish them from wider external forces found, for example, in the legal, cultural, economic and technological subenvironments.

The proximate macroenvironment consists of people, organisations and forces within the firm's immediate external environment. Of particular importance are the subenvironments of suppliers, distributive intermediaries and competitors. These can each have a significant effect upon the marketing firm.

◗ The supplier environment

This consists of other businesses that provide the marketing firm with raw materials, product constituents, and services or, in the case of retailing firms, possibly the finished goods themselves. Both retailers and manufacturers depend on many suppliers. The buyer/supplier relationship is one of mutual economic interdependence, both parties relying on the other for their commercial well being. Although both parties seek stability and security from their relationship, factors in the supplier environment are subject to change, such as industrial disputes which can affect delivery of materials to the buying company, or a sudden increase in raw material prices which forces suppliers to raise their prices. Whatever the product or service being purchased by the marketing firm, unexpected developments in the supplier environment can have an immediate and serious effect on a firm's commercial operations. Because of this, marketing management, through the marketing intelligence component of its marketing information system should continually monitor potential changes in the supplier environment and have contingency plans ready to deal with adverse developments.

▌▌▌ Vignette 2.1

Steel suppliers are producing too much steel worldwide, which is depressing prices, and leading to calls for protectionist economic polices.

Steel producers worldwide are producing too much steel, roughly one third more than the global market can absorb. This is having a damaging effect on the steel industry where margins have been cut right down as excess supply drives down prices. Cheap steel is good for manufacturers who have never had it so good in terms of being in a buyers' market. Many manufacturing firms in Western economies, including the USA, are turning to cheaper imports from the developing world, putting enormous pressure on domestic steel producers to compete by cutting their profit margins to the bone. The USA is trying to persuade the biggest steel producing nations of the world to cut back on production in order to avoid a financial crisis in the industry. US representatives will be talking to government ministers in Russia, Ukraine, South America, Tokyo, China and the EU. In the last year, demand for steel has fallen due to the worldwide economic downturn resulting in the lowest prices for 20 years. The US Government is considering USA import restrictions on cheap imported steel and other steel producing countries, such as those in the EU, are worried that with some of the USA market closed the cheap steel will find its way into their markets, making their supply and demand imbalances even worse. Many countries feel that America should put its own house in order first and reduce its own steel production. Steel production is still fairly labour intensive and cutting back production leads to unemployment – something no government wants. Steel is also a strategic industry and countries need to retain a certain capability in production in case overseas supplies are disrupted or in case of war when steel is needed for armaments. Nonetheless, says the USA, if steel production worldwide is not brought more in line with demand everyone in the industry will suffer.

▶ The distributive environment

Much reliance is placed on marketing intermediaries such as wholesalers, factors, agents and distributors to ensure that products reach the final consumer. It may appear that conventional methods of distribution in any particular industry are relatively static. This is because changes in the distributive environment occur slowly. Companies sometimes fail to appreciate the commercial significance of cumulative change. Existing channels may decline in popularity over time, while new channels may be developing unnoticed by the marketing firm. Nowhere has this creeping change been more apparent over recent years than in the retailing of FMCG. In the 1960s well over half of all FMCG retail trade was accounted for in the independent sector plus a further large proportion to cooperative societies. Nowadays, the sector represented by the larger food multiples has well in excess of this combined proportion. This theme is expanded in Chapter 9.

▶ The competitive environment

Management must be alert to potential threats of other companies marketing similar and substitute products whether they are of domestic or foreign origin. In some industries there may be many numerous manufacturers worldwide posing a potential competitive threat. In other industries, there may be only a few. Whatever the type, size and composition of the industry in question, it is essential that marketing management has a comprehensive understanding of competitive forces. Companies need to establish exactly who their competitors are and the benefits they offer to the market. This knowledge means that they will be able to compete more effectively.

For an organisation of your choice, cite three examples of individual firms or organisations that fall under each of the subdivisions of the proximate marketing environment.

This should be a matter of thinking around local, national or international organisations, about which you have read, or with which you are familiar. The list can be endless.

▶▶ The wider macroenvironment

Changes in the wider macroenvironment may not be as close to a company's day-to-day operations, but they are equally important. The main factors making up these wider macroenvironmental forces fall into four groups:

1. Political and legal factors
2. Economic factors
3. Social and cultural factors
4. Technological factors.

(These are referred to as 'PEST' factors in a marketing analytical context although some texts refer to it as 'STEP'). A PEST analysis means listing all possible points that may affect the organisation under review under each of the PEST headings. PEST is sometimes expanded to include 'legal' factors separately (making the acronym SLEPT). Sometimes 'environmental' factors are separated as well (making the acronym PESTLE). More recently 'ecological' factors have been separated (making the acronym STEEPLE). However, for our purposes the original PEST factors provide a convenient means of analysis. The ability of companies to understand and react to environmental forces is of vital importance to marketing success. In fact an individual organisation's new technology may be the external environmental force of technology that is affecting other organisations! Carl and Valarie Zeithaml (1984) give examples of environmental management strategies that firms can use to influence the largely uncontrollable environment.

▶ The political and legal environment

Domestic political considerations are of prime concern, but firms involved in international operations are faced with additional dimensions. Many firms export and may have joint ventures or subsidiary companies abroad. In many countries, the domestic political and economic situation might be less stable than in the UK.

▍▍▍ Vignette 2.2

European Aeronautic Defence and Space Company affected by international political instability.

The international political environment became very unstable and unpredictable in the latter part of 2001. Much of that instability was caused by the appalling events in New York and Washington DC on 11 September of that year. The war against terrorism that was pursued in Afghanistan has resulted in many countries experiencing indigenous instability and political unrest amongst their populations. Problems in the Middle East with the Israeli and Palestinian conflict continuing to explode across the world's news stage are another considerable source of worry for the whole world. Countries such as Indonesia and Pakistan have seen riots in the streets and the Establishment of these countries is trying to contain political unrest. The war in Iraq in 2003 was the most recent manifestation of such instability. Many industries all over the world have been affected by these events. The world economy is heading towards a recession and many people are postponing unnecessary purchases and feel in no mood to go on holiday or go out to shows and restaurants. The tourism industry has been badly affected but perhaps the worst hit have been the world airlines and those firms involved in aircraft production. The European Aeronautic Defence and Space Company make the European Airbus. Because of the international situation more airlines are attempting to postpone their orders for the Airbus. Many airlines placed orders for the airbus prior to the 11 September tragedy, but now the demand for air travel has fallen off significantly with many of the smaller airlines facing the possibility of bankruptcy. A further tragedy in Queens, New York on Monday 12 November, when an Airbus crashed just after taking off from Kennedy Airport, has exacerbated the situation. The political situation can change in a very short time. People are now afraid to fly to certain parts of the world because of political unrest and the possibility of further terrorist acts.

Marketing firms operating in such environments have to monitor the local political situation very carefully. Many legal, economic and social developments in our society are a result of political decisions, for example privatisation of state industries and the control of inflation. Whatever the industry, changes in the political and legal environments at both the domestic and international levels can affect a company and need to be fully appreciated.

▶ The economic environment

Economic factors are of concern as they are likely to influence, among other things, demand, costs, prices and profits. These factors are largely outside the control of individual firms, but their effects on individual enterprises can be profound. Political and economic forces are strongly related. A much quoted example is the 'oil crisis' caused by the Middle East war in 1973 which produced economic shock waves throughout the Western world, resulting in dramatically increased crude oil prices. This in turn increased energy costs as well as the cost of many oil-based raw materials, such as plastics and synthetic fibres. This contributed significantly to a world economic recession, and it serves to demonstrate how dramatic economic change can upset traditional structures and balances in the world business environment. These economic factors are largely outside the control of the individual firm, but their effects on individual enterprises can be profound. One of the weaknesses of economics as a social science is the relatively poor predictability of economic variables. Not even the experts, such as Sylvia Nasar (1988) in the USA, have produced anything like accurate long-range economic forecasts for economic conditions throughout the 1990s. Changes in world economic forces can be highly significant to marketing firms, particularly those engaged in international marketing. However, an understanding of economic changes and forces in the domestic economy is also important as these forces have most immediate impact. One such factor is a high level of unemployment, which decreases effective demand for many luxury consumer goods, adversely affecting demand for industrial machinery required to produce such goods. Other domestic economic variables are the rate of inflation and the level of domestic interest rates, which affect the potential return from new investments and can inhibit the adoption and diffusion of new technologies. In addition to these more indirect factors, competitive firms can also pose a threat to the marketing company. Economic changes pose opportunities and threats and, by understanding and carefully monitoring the economic environment, firms should be in a position to guard against potential threats and capitalise on opportunities.

▍▍▍ Vignette 2.3

UK retail firms nervously watch the economic environment as unemployment shows signs of rising.

The level of consumer spending in 2001 pleasantly surprised the UK retailing sector. Some economic commentators were then predicting a slowdown in spending as consumers were worried about losing their jobs as the world slid slowly into a recession. However both spending and employment had been holding up well and supporting the rest of the economy. Unfortunately as of mid November 2001 things looked as if they were about to change for the worse. The number of people out of work and claiming unemployment benefit in the UK rose in November 2001 for the first time in a year. Economic forecasters were worried that the once buoyant labour market conditions were coming to an end. High levels of employment have been instrumental in supporting consumer confidence in the UK. It has been the high level of consumer spending, related to consumer confidence that has 'propped' up the economy and stopped it falling into recession. With all Western economies showing signs of economic slowdown, particularly the USA economy which drives the rest of the world, it was contended that this would put further pressure on the Bank of England to cut interest rates further to stimulate the economy. Slowly falling unemployment was one of the major strengths of the UK economy during 2001 and this allowed the economy to keep growing where other Western economies had been slowing down. Job security affected consumer confidence in a positive way and helped maintain high levels of spending in the retail sector. If people are worried about their jobs they are much more likely to 'batten down the hatches' and forego postponable and unnecessary spending. The situation has remained relatively stable until summer 2003. Retailers now watch with bated breath as the situation unfolds. They are particularly concerned for the all-important Christmas period when much of their profits for the year are made.

▶ The sociocultural environment

This is the most difficult element of the macroenvironment to evaluate. It relates to changing tastes, purchasing behaviour and changing priorities. The type of goods and services demanded by consumers is a function of social conditioning and attitudes and beliefs. Core cultural values are those firmly established within a society and are difficult to change. They are perpetuated through family, religion, education and the institutions of society. They act as relatively fixed parameters within which marketing firms must operate. Secondary cultural values tend to be less strong and are more likely to undergo change. Generally, social change is preceded by changes over time in a society's secondary cultural values, for example the change in social attitude towards credit. As recently as the 1960s, personal credit, or hire purchase, was looked upon unfavourably and people having such arrangements tended not to discuss it openly. Today, offering instant credit is an integral part of marketing, with most people regularly using credit cards and store accounts. For many people it is often the availability and terms of credit offered that are major factors in deciding to purchase a particular product.

Marketing firms have had to respond to changes in attitude towards health, for example in the food industry people now question the desirability of including artificial preservatives, colourings and other chemicals in food. The decline in the popularity of smoking is a classic example of how changes in social attitudes have posed a significant threat to an industry, forcing tobacco manufacturers to diversify out of tobacco products and into new areas of growth.

Changes in attitudes towards working women have led to an increase in demand for convenience foods, 'one-stop' shopping and the widespread adoption of time-saving devices such as microwave cookers. Marketing firms have reacted to these changes. In addition, there have been changes in moral attitudes from the individualism of the 'permissive society' of the 1960s and early 1970s. The present emphasis is on health, economic security and more stable relationships. These contribute to a dynamically changing sociocultural environment that must be considered by companies planning for the future.

▶ The technological environment

Technology is a major macroenvironmental variable that has influenced the development of many products we now take for granted such as television, video and home computers. Marketing firms play a part in technological progress thus also playing a part in innovating new developments and new applications.

One example of how technological change has affected marketing activity is in the development of electronic point of sale (EPOS) data capture at retail levels. The laser checkout reads a bar code and then stores information that is used to analyse sales and re-order stock as well as giving customers a printed readout of what they have purchased and the price charged. Manufacturers of FMCG, particularly packaged grocery products, have had to respond to technological innovations by incorporating bar codes on their product labels or packaging. Thus, a change in the technological environment has affected the products and services that firms produce and the way in which they carry out business operations.

Conduct a PEST analysis for an organisation of your choice.

The answer to this depends, of course, upon the organisation you have chosen. As an approximate guide, you should have been able to cite around 10 or more separate factors under each of the four headings.

▶▶ Other macroenvironmental factors

Macroenvironmental factors discussed so far are not an exhaustive list, but merely demonstrate principal areas of environmental change. Other subenvironments may be important to marketing management, for example in some countries the religious environment may pose an important source of opportunities and threats. In the UK, demographic changes are considered important by a number of firms.

The UK population has been relatively stable at approximately 59 million for many years, but the birth rate is falling, while people are living longer. Firms that produce goods and services directed at those with small children (for example Mothercare) have seen their traditional markets remain static. Some have diversified by offering products targeted at older age groups. A larger older sector of the population offers

SELF-CHECK

Distinguish between the proximate macro-environment and the wider macro-environment.

This should have been easy. The former falls under the headings of:

■ the supplier environment
■ the distributive environment

■ the competitive environment

The latter encompasses:

■ Political
■ Economic
■ Sociocultural
■ Technological

opportunities for firms to produce goods and services to satisfy their needs. The over-55 group is now the modern marketer's major opportunity. In advanced economies like the UK and USA it is this age group that has the largest disposable income, and products and services such as holidays and pension-related financial services are being specifically targeted towards this sector.

▶▶ Summary

We have examined the company's microenvironment and investigated variables over which it has control through the marketing mix. This led to a description of marketing and its various subdivisions, including information from the marketplace in terms of forecasting and marketing research. Marketing was then examined alongside other business functions. The company's proximate macroenvironment was examined under supplier, distributive and competitive subenvironments and finally the wider macroenvironment was examined under the headings: political and legal, economic, sociocultural and technological factors.

The chapter can be summarised by looking what has been covered in terms of a number of layers in the environment, from customers to marketing and resources of the company, to the organisation's proximate macroenvironment and finally to its wider macroenvironment. This is illustrated in Figure 2.5.

The outer layer consists of the wider macroenvironmental PEST factors.

The next layer is the proximate macroenvironment described earlier. This includes the organisation's 'publics' – a public relations term dealt with in detail in a Chapter 13. It means any group of individuals who are affected by or are in touch with the company in any context (for example companies that supply finance or people who live near the company's manufacturing plant).

The next layer is the organisation's strategic marketing planning and control system and the details of this are dealt with in Chapter 15.

Tactics that deliver strategy are the four Ps and these are shown in the next layer.

The final inner circle is the most important, being customers from whence all planning should start. Being a 'customer led' organisation is at the very centre of marketing orientation.

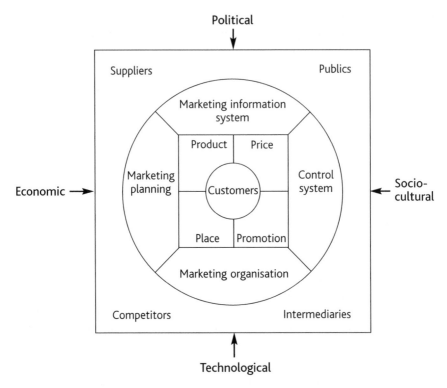

Figure 2.5 An organisation's various environments

FURTHER READING

Adcock D. (2000) *Marketing Strategies for Competitive Advantage*, Chapter 3, 'Analysing External Markets and Internal Assets for Strategic Decisions', John Wiley & Sons, Chichester.

Armstrong G. and Kotler P. (2000) *Marketing: An Introduction*, (5th edn), Chapter 3, 'The Global Marketing Environment', Prentice Hall, Englewood Cliffs, NJ.

Blythe, J. (2001) *Essentials of Marketing*, Chapter 2, 'The Marketing Environment', Pearson Education, London.

Davies M. (1998) *Understanding Marketing*, Chapter 2, 'Marketing Planning, the Environment and Competitive Strategy', Prentice Hall, London.

Kotler P., Bowen J. and Makens J. (1996) *Marketing for Hospitality and Tourism*, Chapter 5, 'The Marketing Environment', Prentice Hall, Englewood Cliffs, NJ.

Lancaster G.A. and Massingham L.C. (1999) *Essentials of Marketing: Text and Cases* (3rd edn), Chapter 2, 'The Marketing Environment', McGraw-Hill, Maidenhead.

Lancaster G.A. and Reynolds P.L. (1999) *Introduction to Marketing: A Step-by-Step Guide to All The Tools of Marketing*, Chapter 1, 'Marketing Defined', Kogan Page, London.

Nickels W. and Burk-Wood M. (1997) *Marketing, Relationships, Quality, Value*, Chapter 3, 'Environmental Analysis, Ethics and Social Responsibility', Worth Publishers, New York.

Plamer A. (2000) *Principles of Marketing*, Chapter 2, 'The Marketing Environment', OUP, Oxford.

Soloman M. and Stuart E. (1997) *Marketing, Real People, Real Choices*, Chapter 3, 'Decision-making in the New Era of Marketing: Enriching the Marketing Environment', Prentice Hall, Englewood Cliffs, NJ.

▶ References

Kotler P. (1997) *Marketing Management, Analysis, Planning, Implementation and Control* (9th edn), Prentice Hall, Englewood Cliffs, NJ, p. 92.

Nasar S. (1988) 'Preparing for a New Economy,' *Fortune*, 26 September, p. 86.

Zeithaml C.P. and Zeithaml V.A. (1984) 'Environmental Management: Revisiting a Marketing Perspective', *Journal of Marketing*, Spring, pp. 46–53.

3 CUSTOMERS AND MARKETING

▶▶ Segmentation defined

The marketing concept places customer needs at the centre of the organisation's decision making. It has been explained that the need to adopt this approach stems from a number of factors, including increased competition, better-informed and better-educated customers and, most importantly, changing patterns of demand that have given rise to the need to segment markets. This change stems from the fact that higher standards of living and a trend towards individualism have meant that consumers are now more able to exercise their choice in the marketplace.

Market segmentation can be defined as the process of breaking down the total market for a product or service into distinct subgroups or segments where each segment may conceivably represent a separate target market to be reached with a distinctive marketing mix. Segmentation and the subsequent strategies of targeting and positioning start by recognising that increasingly, within the total demand/market for a product, specific tastes, needs and demand may differ. It breaks down the total market for a product or service into individual clusters of customers, or segments. Customers who share similar demand preferences are grouped together in each segment.

Effective segmentation is achieved when customers sharing similar patterns of demand are grouped together and where each group or segment differs in their pattern of demand from other segments in the market. In most markets, for either consumer or industrial goods, some kind of segmentation can be accomplished on this basis.

Activity

In order that you can more fully appreciate the idea of segmentation, think of the following products and decide if segmentation is possible:
- **Dishwasher detergent**
- **Washing powder**
- **Chocolates**
- **Motor cars**

For dishwasher detergent, if we are considering this only for household use, the answer is 'no' in that separate groups of purchasers are not identified. However, if one is considering dishwasher detergent for households and for industrial use then the answer must be 'yes', because for canteen or restaurant use it will be packed in larger sizes and probably in more utilitarian packaging.

Washing powder is generally a product that has not been segmentable, but more recently different formulations of washing powder have been introduced – for severe stains, coloured clothes, white clothes, woollens, and so on. However the best selling and highly promoted brands tend not to segment and are anxious to promote a uniform image to sustain their market share.

Chocolates are certainly segmentable in terms of groups of people to whom they are meant to appeal and attempts are made to give a 'personality' to specific brands.

Motor cars are obviously segmentable into, for example, sports cars, estate cars, saloon cars, together with different versions under each of these categories in terms of engine size and tuning. In fact, manufacturers now make a virtue of the fact that of the many vehicles produced only a few need be the same.

▶▶ Targeted marketing efforts

Most companies realise that they cannot effectively serve all the segments in a market, and must instead target their marketing efforts. For example, in developing a new car, the manufacturer will have to make a decision on many issues, such as should it be a two-, four-, or five-seater model, with a 1000, 2000 or 3000cc engine? Should it have leather, fabric or plastic seats? The overriding factor when deciding these issues is customer demand. Some customers (segments) may want a five-seater 2000cc model with leather upholstery, while others may prefer a four-seater with a 1000cc engine and fabric seats. One solution would be to compromise and produce a four-seater 1500cc model with leather seats and fabric trim. Clearly, such a model would go some way to meeting the requirements of both groups of buyers, but there is a danger that because the needs of neither market segment are precisely met, most of the potential customers will purchase from other suppliers who do cater for their specific requirements. Ironically, one of the biggest post-war car failures was the much heralded and much hyped American Ford Edsel car. This is the car that was said to have been produced following extensive marketing research, the results of which were aggregated, and the end product was a car that satisfied the true needs of very few buyers, making it the most spectacular flop in modern motoring history. Ironically, it is now much sought after as a collectors' car.

Target marketing is thus defined as the identification of the market segments that are the most likely purchasers of a company's products. This idea of how companies target their marketing efforts was put forward by Abell (1979) when he suggested targeting strategies based upon customer group concentrations or customer need concentrations, or a combination of each.

 Vignette 3.1

Kwik Save targets the economically minded shopper.

Most people shop for grocery products. However not everyone is looking for the same thing when shopping. Some people look for a high level of in-store customer service. Others look for good product range or good quality produce. Some people want quality at any price and have the money to pay for it. Another segment is prepared to forgo many of these facets of grocery shopping as long as they can purchase their grocery items at a bargain, or at least highly competitive, price. This 'economic' shopper segment of the market is the one that Kwik Save targets and which forms the bulk of their customers. Kwik Save is a very successful grocery retail chain that has gained a reputation for extremely keen prices, excellent sales promotions and discounted items. The firm advertises widely in all the major media including nation-wide television, commercial radio and newspapers. The company's communications are effective, compelling and to the point. The essence of the message is always the same – cheap prices. Kwik Save is a 'limited line' discount store and its customers are those who are looking for value for money. Kwik Save does not offer the same extensive range of products as ASDA, Tesco or J. Sainsbury and does not have the same ambience in its stores. Many of the stores are somewhat utilitarian on the inside with little in the way of 'frills'. The store shelving is again very basic and some of the items are simply displayed in their packing cases with a hole cut out of the side for the customer to access the goods. There is sometimes a queue at the tills because the firm economises on till staff to save money. In fact the company economises on all aspects of its business and passes the savings on to its customers. People shopping at Kwik Save know this and that is why they are prepared to put up with a lower standard store and limited lines of merchandise compared with the leading grocery multiples. However, this is what the customers visiting Kwik Save want. The store understands its markets and gives customers what they want.

Specifically, the advantages of target marketing are:

1. Marketing opportunities and unfilled 'gaps' in a market may be more accurately appraised and identified. Such gaps can be real (for example sweet, strong, harsh or mild) or they can be illusory in terms of the way people want to view the product (for example happy, aloof, silly or moody). In the case of the former, product attributes can fulfil these criteria whereas for the latter these attributes might well have to be implanted in the minds of customers through an appropriate advertising message.
2. Market and product appeals through manipulation of the marketing mix can be more delicately tuned to the needs of the potential customer.
3. Marketing effort can be concentrated on the market segment(s) that offer the greatest potential for the company to achieve its goals – be they goals to maximise profit potential or to secure the best long-term position for the product or any other appropriate goal.

◗◗ Effective segmentation

Theoretically, the base(s) used for segmentation should lead to segments that are:

1. *Measurable/identifiable:* here, the base(s) used should lead to ease of identification in terms of who is in each segment. It should also be capable of measurement in terms of the potential customers in each segment.
2. *Accessible:* here, the base(s) used should ideally lead to the company being able to reach selected market targets with its individual marketing efforts.
3. *Meaningful:* the base(s) used must lead to segments that have different preferences or needs and show clear variations in market behaviour and response to individually designed marketing mixes.
4. *Substantial:* the base(s) used should lead to segments that are sufficiently large to be economically and practically worthwhile serving as discrete market targets with a distinctive marketing mix.

The third criterion is particularly important for effective segmentation, as it is an essential prerequisite when attempting to identify and select market targets.

In segmentation, targeting and positioning, a company must identify distinct subsets of customers in the total market for a product where any subset might eventually be selected as a market target, and for which a distinctive marketing mix will be developed. The following represents the sequential steps in conducting a segmentation, targeting and positioning exercise:

1. Select base(s) for segmentation and identify appropriate market segments
2. Evaluate and appraise the market segments resulting from step one
3. Select an overall market targeting strategy
4. Select specific target segments
5. Develop a product positioning strategy for each target segment
6. Develop an appropriate marketing mix for each chosen target segment in order to support the product positioning strategy.

▶▶ Segmentation bases in consumer product markets

Geographic segmentation consists of dividing a country into regions that normally represent an individual sales person's territory. In bigger companies, these larger regions are sometimes broken down into areas with an individual regional manager controlling salespeople in distinct areas. In international marketing, different countries may be deemed to constitute different market segments.

Demographic segmentation consists of a wide variety of bases for subdividing markets:

▶ *Age* is a good segmentation variable for items like clothes where the fashion-conscious young are more susceptible to regular changes in style, and older segments are perhaps more concerned with factors like quality and comfort.
▶ *Sex* is a strong segment in terms of goods that are specifically targeted towards males or females and again an obvious example is clothing. Fashion can be a powerful element when purchasing, and a large industry surrounds this principle.
▶ *Income* as a segmentation base is less popular in the United Kingdom than the USA. This is probably due to our conservative nature and matters like income tend to be regarded as a private matter. It would

be difficult and embarrassing asking this question as part of a marketing research survey. In the UK we tend to use the next variable, 'social class', as a segmentation variable and from this a person's income can be deduced.

▶ *Social class* is probably the single most used variable for research purposes, and the National Readership Survey divides everybody in the UK into the categories shown in Table 3.1.

▶ *Education* is often related to social class, because generally the better educated tend to attain better jobs. It is acknowledged that a person's media habits are related to education. Accordingly, newspapers design to aim their news and newspaper content towards the upper or lower ends of the social spectrum, and encourage advertisers to target their advertising appropriately, depending upon whether an advertiser's product has an up-market or down-market appeal. In fact they publicise their readership profile by the percentage of ABC1 and so on groups that actually read their newspapers or magazines – information which is ascertained through independent auditors. This is done principally to alert advertising agencies that place their clients' advertising according to the social classes targeted by their products.

▶ *Nationality* or ethnic background now constitutes a growing and distinctive segment for potential target marketing. Food, clothing and hair care are obvious examples of products that fit into this variable.

▶ *Political* is perhaps a less obvious segmentation base. An individual's political leanings might well influence the way he or she behaves in terms of purchases made. Such purchases are of course reflected in the types of newspaper and other media that is read, and this, in turn, contains advertising which is aimed at people who read such media, so political leanings might be more significant than it initially seems.

Table 3.1 Social class and grade structure in the UK

A	Upper middle class (higher managerial, administrative or professional) comprising about 3% of the population
B	Middle class (intermediate managerial, administrative or professional) comprise approximately 10% of the population
C1	Lower middle class (supervisory, clerical, junior administrative or professional) containing around 25% of the population
C2	Skilled working class (skilled manual workers) who comprise around 30% of the population
D	Working class (semi- and unskilled manual workers) or around 27% of the population
E	Lowest levels of subsistence (state pensioners with no other income, widows, casual and lowest grade earners) who form the remaining 5%, or thereabouts, of the population

▶ *Family size* will have an effect on the amount or size of purchases, so this is a meaningful segmentation variable.

▶ *Family life cycle* follows on from the above and tends to determine the purchase of many consumer durable products. This is based on the notion that consumers pass through a series of quite distinct phases in their lives, each phase giving rise to different purchasing patterns and needs. For example, an unmarried person living at home will probably have very different purchasing patterns from someone of the same age whom has left home and is recently married. Wells and Gubar (1996) have put forward what is now an internationally recognised classification system in relation to life cycle as shown in Table 3.2.

▶ *Sagacity* is a refinement of the family life cycle grouping system, attributing different behavioural patterns and aspirations to people as they proceed through life. Four main stages of life cycle are defined as:

  ▶ *Dependent:* (mainly under 24 living at home)
  ▶ *Pre-family:* (under 35s who have established their own household, but without children)
  ▶ *Family:* (couples under 65 with one or more children in the household)
  ▶ *Late:* (adults whose children have left home or who are over 35 and childless).

  Income groups are then defined as being in categories: 'better off' and 'worse off'. Occupation groups are defined as white (collar) – the A, B and C1 social groups – and blue (collar) – the C2, D and E social groups. The system works as shown in Figure 3.1.

Table 3.2 Family life cycle segmentation base

Bachelor stage	young single people not living with parents (which gave rise to the category of 'YUPPIES' or 'young, urban, professionals')
Newly marrieds	no children (sometimes referred to as 'DINKIES' meaning 'double income – no kids')
Full nest I	with the youngest child being under six years of age
Full nest II	where the youngest child is six or over
Full nest III	an older married couple with dependent children living at home
Empty nest I	with no children living at home, but the family head is in work (sometimes referred to as 'WOOPIES' meaning 'well off older persons')
Empty nest II	where the family head is retired
Solitary survivor in work	
Solitary survivor retired	

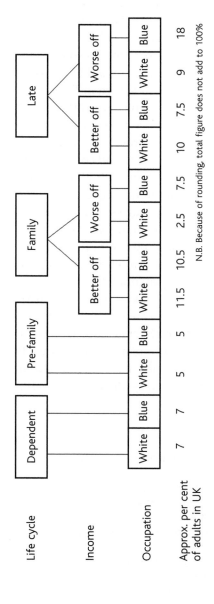

Figure 3.1 Sagacity life cycle groupings
Source: Research Services Limited

▶ *Type of neighbourhood and dwelling (ACORN)* uses as its underlying philosophy the fact that the type of dwelling and area a person lives in is a good predictor of likely purchasing behaviour, including the types of products and brands that might be purchased. This classification analyses homes, rather than individuals, as a basis for segmentation. It is termed the ACORN system (A Classification of Residential Neighbourhoods). The source of this is the 10-yearly population census, the last one being in 2001. This system was developed by Richard Webber for Consolidated Analysis Centres Incorporated (CACI). It breaks down the census of population into various categories of homes as shown in Table 3.3.

These ACORN classifications are further subdivided into yet smaller groupings. For instance, Group C that refers to 'Older housing of intermediate status', is broken down into:

C8   Mixed owner-occupied and council estates
C9   Small town centres and flats above shops
C10   Villages with non-farm employment
C11   Older private, housing skilled workers.

▶ *Mosaic system* is an extension of the ACORN system except that it is based on individual postal codes (or zip codes). Each post code in the UK consists of up to seven letters and figures. An individual post code represents approximately ten dwellings and each of these groups of dwellings is given an individual Mosaic categorisation, of which there are 58 categories. The idea of 'mosaic' comes from the notion that if a different colour was ascribed to each category and superimposed on a map of the UK then the resulting pattern would resemble a mosaic. The full Mosaic listing is not reproduced here, but by way of illustration some of them are described below:

		Per cent of population
M1	High status retirement areas with many single pensioners	1.0
M15	Lower income older terraced housing	1.5
M25	Smart inner city flats, company lets, very few children	1.5
M33	Council estates, often Scottish flats, with worst overcrowding	1.3
M46	Post 1981 housing in areas of highest income and status	0.2
M50	Newly built private estates, factory workers, young families	3.3
M57	Hamlets and scattered farms	0.7

Table 3.3 ACORN classification system

Acorn group	Type of dwelling	Approx. % UK population
A	Agricultural areas	3
B	Modern family housing, higher incomes	18
C	Older housing of intermediate status	17
D	Poor quality older terraced housing	4
E	Better-off council estates	13
F	Less well-off council estates	9
G	Poorest council estates	7
H	Multi-racial areas	4
I	High status non-family areas	4
J	Affluent suburban housing	16
K	Better-off retirement areas	4
U	Unclassified	1

Source: CACI

Altogether, the demographic bases described constitute the most popular bases for segmentation in consumer product markets, since they are often associated with differences in consumer demand and as such they are meaningful to advertisers. For instance, occupation and social class are linked because of the way that occupation is used to define social class. It is, therefore, relatively easy to reach different social classes through their different media and shopping habits, although boundaries between the purchasing power of different classes become blurred when, for example, skilled manual workers are able to earn higher incomes than their counterparts in lower or intermediate management.

Direct or behavioural segmentation takes purchasing behaviour as the starting point for segmentation. Bases include:

▶ *Usage status* when distinctions may be made between say 'light', 'medium' and 'heavy' users of a product.
▶ *Brand loyalty status* where customers can be divided into a number of groups according to their loyalty, or their propensity to repurchase a brand. Status categories are:
  ▶ *Hard core loyals* purchasing the same brand every time
  ▶ *Soft core loyals* with divided loyalties between two or more brands, purchasing these on a random basis
  ▶ *Shifting loyals* sometimes called 'brand switchers', purchasing one brand, staying with it for a period, and then purchasing another

brand and staying with it for a certain period. They might then return to the original brand

- ▶ *Switchers* show no particular preference or loyalty to a particular brand, and their purchasing pattern cannot be clearly determined.
- ▶ *Benefits sought* is a base that determines the principal expectation(s) a purchaser is seeking from the product. For instance, in the case of motor oil purchasers might be looking for cheapness, a well-known brand, its viscosity or its engine protection reputation.
- ▶ *Occasions for purchase* for instance can relate to the purchase of holidays.

Lifestyle or psychographic segmentation is based on the idea that individuals have characteristic patterns of living that may be reflected in the products and brands they purchase. The advertising agency, Young & Rubicam, has developed a classification called 'Four Cs' where C stands for consumers. These categories are:

- ▶ *Mainstreamers* or the largest group who do not want to 'stand out from the crowd'. They are the largest segment (over 40 per cent of the population) and tend to purchase branded products over supermarket brands.
- ▶ *Reformers* are people who are creative and caring, many doing charitable work. They largely purchase supermarket brands over branded products.
- ▶ *Aspirers* are usually younger people who are ambitious and keen to 'get on' at all costs. Their purchases tend to reflect the latest models and designs.
- ▶ *Succeeders* are those who have 'made it' and do not see the need for status symbols sought by aspirers. They like to be in control of what they are doing and this includes purchases where they have clear ideas of what they feel is a good product and what is of less use.

Consider the following products and services. Suggest some of the more obvious segmentation bases in respect of each of these.

- Insurance services
- Holidays
- Coffee
- Frozen foods

Insurance services are segmented in numerous ways and are then tailor-made to suit these specific segments. Examples are car insurance, health insurance, property insurance, pension plans and domestic appliance extended warranty insurance.

Holidays, for example, can be segmented on the basis of activity holidays, sightseeing holidays, exotic destination holidays, beach holidays and historic venue holidays.

Coffee can be segmented on the basis of taste, ease of preparation (ground coffee or instant coffee) or occasions for use (for example some are more appropriate for evening drinking, others more suitable for breakfast drinking).

Frozen foods can be, for instance, ready meals for convenience eating, exotic foods, standard frozen vegetables, chips, ice cream or frozen desserts. All of these products are designed to suit different eating occasions like 'a quick and easy meal', 'special occasion', and so on.

▶▶ Segmentation bases in organisational/industrial markets

Segmenting an industrial market introduces additional bases, uses similar bases and also precludes some of the ones more frequently used for consumer product markets. The most frequently encountered bases in this context are:

- *Type of application/end use:* for example adhesives for home, office and industrial use.
- *Geographical:* for example Scotland, Wales, northwest, northeast, southeast, or by country/region, for example USA, Pacific Rim, Middle East.
- *Benefits sought:* closely related to above, but more concerned with what the product does for the purchaser, for example detergents for general cleaning or detergents that are used in a production process.
- *Type of customer:* for example banks or insurance companies or people who purchase for public authorities.
- *Product/technology:* for example fibres for the carpet industry or the clothing industry.
- *Customer size:* for example large customers may receive different treatment to small customers. This segmentation variable is called 'key account selling' where the sales manager might deal personally with major accounts.
- *Usage rate:* for example light users or heavy users; regular or sporadic users.
- *Loyalty of customer:* for example regular purchasers (be they for large

or small purchases) and sporadic purchasers. Treatment given to loyal customers might differ to that accorded to occasional customers.

▷ *Purchasing procedures:* for example centralised versus decentralised purchasing (that can affect the buyer/seller relationship), the extent to which purchasing is carried out by tightly defined, or more flexible, specifications that allow the seller more latitude in making suggestions, the extent to which purchasing is by tender (that is, by some kind of closed bidding system) or by open negotiation.

▷ *Situational factors* consider the tactical role of purchasing circumstances. In some situations it needs a more detailed knowledge of customers and in others the buyer/seller relationship is kept only to commercial issues.

▷ *Personal characteristics* relate to the people who make purchasing decisions.

▊▊▊ Vignette 3.2

Airtours changes its name and re-segments its markets.

Airtours, the travel group, has expanded and diversified so much over recent years that a large part of its business has little to do with what the name suggests, that is, air travel and packaged tours. Airtours owns car hire and cruise holiday companies and so the name is becoming increasingly inappropriate. The company already has a Web-based online booking service branded as MyTravel, which seems a more suitable name for the group's business operations. MyTravel is to be applied to all of the group's 700 or so high street travel shops, including those at present branded as Travelworld, Holiday World and Going Places. The retail side is to be divided into three segments, MyTravel Megastores which are mainly large out of town operations, MyTravel which will be substantial stores, although not megastores, located in the major towns and cities and MyTravel Local which will service the retail travel needs of the small towns. The Airtours brand will be kept for some existing operations related to airline travel. The company is hoping that the new brand name will have the effect of integrating all of the travel services provided under a single umbrella corporate brand name. Airtours is facing problems because of the reduction in holiday travel as a result of the 11 September, 2001 tragedy in America. The firm has also been affected by the war in Iraq. To manage risk the firm has refinanced with its banks and reduced capacity.

As in consumer markets, industrial, or more correctly organisational market segmentation (which is dealt with in detail in the next chapter) may be on an indirect (associative) or a direct (behavioural) basis. Many bases may be used in conjunction with each other to obtain successively smaller subsegments of the market. The essential criteria for consumer

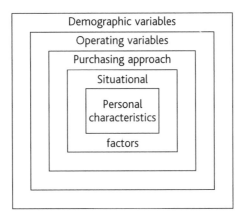

Figure 3.2 A nested approach to segmentation in industrial markets

market segmentation (identifiable, accessible, substantial and meaningful) are applicable to bases for industrial market segmentation.

A 'nested' approach to segmentation was suggested by Shapiro and Bonoma (1984) on a hierarchy ranging from the broad to the specific (Figure 3.2).

At the centre we have people who make buying decisions and their personalities must be considered. 'Situational factors' looks at the tactical role of the purchasing situation which demands customer knowledge. 'Purchasing approach' examines customer-purchasing practices (for example who makes buying decisions, considered in detail in Chapter 4 under 'The decision-making unit'). 'Operating variables' allows more exact pinpointing of potential and existing customers within the final category, 'demographic variables' which is a broad description of the segments related to customer needs and patterns of usage.

Consider the following industrial products or services and suggest likely segmentation bases:

- valves
- banking services
- artificial fibres
- adhesives
- paints

In the case of valves the most obvious base is by end use – for example for use in the water, oil and gas industries

Banking services can be based upon the requirement that is needed – an overdraft for working capital, a bank loan for a more permanent requirement, a source of investment

Artificial fibres are an example of end use segmentation – fibres for spinning into carpet yarn or perhaps clothing yarn

Adhesives can be for use, say, in an office or for industrial applications

Paints can be for exterior or interior use, different types of finishes and, of course, different types of colours

▶▶ Effective segmentation

Once market segments have been identified, a marketer's task is to assess these various market segments. This appraisal should related to sales and profit potential, or in the case of non-profit organisations, an ability to add to organisational aims. This means that each segment should be viewed in terms of its overall size, projected rate of growth, actual and potential competition, nature of competitive strategies and customer needs. Companies that decide to follow a concentrated or differentiated targeting strategy must then decide which of the market segments it wishes to serve. A decision to select specific target markets must be based on factors such as company resources, competition, potential of the segment and company objectives.

Characteristics that can make a market segment attractive are:

1. It has sufficient current profit and sales potential to meet the organisation's aims and objectives.
2. Competition in the segment is not too intense.
3. There is good potential for future growth.
4. The segment has some previously unidentified requirements that the company has recognised and is in a position to serve particularly well.

▶▶ Product positioning

The company has to develop a product positioning strategy for each segment it chooses to serve. This is to ensure that its products occupy a planned place in chosen target markets, pertinent to competition in the marketplace. The notion of product/brand positioning is applicable to both industrial and consumer markets, and the key aspects of this approach are based on certain suppositions:

1. All products and brands have both objective attributes (for example sweet/sour; dark/light; fast/slow) and subjective attributes (for example modern/unfashionable; happy/sad; youthful/elderly).

2. Buyers may think about one or more of these attributes when considering a product and/or brand to purchase.

3. Potential customers have their own thoughts about how the various competing products or brands rate for each of these particular attributes. In other words, the positioning of the brand along the parameters of these attributes (for example 'entertaining' on the one hand to 'mundane' on the other) takes place in the mind of a customer.

▌▌▌ Vignette 3.3

A dams Childrenswear Limited, children's clothing specialists, move upmarket in search of higher margins.

Adams, the 0 to 10 years children's clothing retail group, has repositioned itself over recent years. The quality of its products was often regarded as being at the cheaper end of the market along with Woolworth's Ladybird brand. At the top end of the high street providers came Marks & Spencer plc, which still has pole position in the quality stakes. There are of course many smaller specialist stores that supply good quality 'designer' type children's clothing for those families fortunate enough to have the income to buy them. However, in the regular high street stores Marks & Spencer set the standard for quality with Boots and British Home Stores just behind them. There are greater profit margins on higher quality products and consumers in these segments are generally more affluent and hence less price sensitive. Adams has successfully repositioned its stores in the minds of consumers to be on a par with Marks & Spencer in terms of quality but offering better value for money. Many people who traditionally would have shopped for their children's clothing at Marks & Spencer are going to Adams' stores and liking what they see in terms of comparable quality with a cheaper price tag. Adams' clothes can be found in over 400 stores within the UK, Eire, Middle East, Malta, and Cyprus.

The next step is to decide which attributes will best appeal to the company's target market. The marketer can then establish the most advantageous position for the company within a particular segment of the market.

The final step in this appraisal of segmentation, targeting and positioning is to develop appropriate marketing mixes. This involves the creation of marketing programmes that will support a chosen positional strategy in selected target markets. The company must therefore determine the 'four Ps' of its marketing mix, that is, what price, product, distribution (place) and promotional strategies will be necessary to achieve the desired position in the market.

There are four acknowledged strategic options for target marketing:

1. *Undifferentiated marketing* where there is one single marketing mix for every potential customer in the market.
2. *Differentiated marketing* where there are many marketing mixes for different segments of the market.
3. *Concentrated marketing* that has a single marketing mix for a segment of the total market.
4. *Custom marketing* that attempts to satisfy each individual customer's requirements with a separate marketing mix.

For the following product categories, determine which of the four strategic options quoted best fits each of the categories listed:

■ **a meal out**
■ **mining machinery**
■ **washing powder**
■ **chocolates**

■ *A meal out:* custom marketing
■ *Mining machinery:* concentrated marketing
■ *Washing powder:* undifferentiated marketing
■ *Chocolates:* differentiated marketing

In terms of the tactics involved in targeting, what must a company do in order to target its marketing efforts towards a specific group of customers?

A company should devise a different marketing mix for different segments of the market. Essentially this means manipulating the marketing mix to suit individually chosen market segments and the process of this manipulation is called 'market targeting'.

Consider the so-called 'silent revolution' referred to in Chapter 1 and consider the situation pre-Second World War when wealth was polarised into a minority who possessed most of the wealth and the majority who possessed very little. Now look at the percentage distribution of population amongst the social grades in Table 3.1. It can be that these percentages relate more to a normal distribution curve than was the situation between the wars. In terms of marketing, what is the implication of this observation?

The implication is that this more even distribution amongst the social classes and thus of wealth has meant that consumers are able to afford more in terms of personal possessions. Goods classed as luxury goods between the wars are now classed as utility goods and are needed in order to partake in a 'modern' lifestyle. Thus, individuals need a larger and more complicated bundle of possessions. A good example of a service that was a luxury possession between the wars is a telephone. Now it is a utility product essential for domestic and social purposes for the majority of the population, and trends suggest that mobile telephones are undergoing a similar transition. In addition, goods are now expected to last for a shorter period of time, as with clothes, where fashion rather than functionality is more important. In addition, people now have more comprehensive wardrobes to suit different social and work occasions.

▶▶ Summary

We now appreciate how marketing works. Having defined the purpose of segmentation we have looked at the obvious and the less obvious bases for segmentation in both consumer and industrial markets. We have also ascertained that used well, the techniques and concepts described can contribute significantly to overall company marketing success. Market segmentation, targeting and positioning decisions are thus more strategic than tactical.

Segmentation variables should be examined in detail, especially new segments. These should be authenticated in terms of viability and potential profit.

Targeting investigates specific segments in terms of how they should be approached.

Positioning relates to how products are perceived in the minds of consumers and a suitable marketing mix should then be designed.

FURTHER READING

Adcock D. (2000) *Marketing Strategies for Competitive Advantage*, Chapter 6, 'Segmentation as a Strategic Tool', John Wiley & Sons, Chichester.

Armstrong G. and Kotler P. (2000) *Marketing: An Introduction* (5th edn), Chapter 6, 'Market Segmentation, Targeting and Positioning for Competitive Advantage', Prentice Hall, Englewood Cliffs, NJ.

Blythe J. (2001) *Essentials of Marketing* (2nd edn), Chapter 4, 'Segmentation, Targeting and Positioning', Pearson Education, London.

Davies M. (1998) *Understanding Marketing*, Chapter 4, 'Targeting, Segmentation and Positioning', Prentice Hall, London.

Kotler P., Bowen J. and Makens J. (1996) *Marketing for Hospitality and Tourism*, Chapter 9, 'Market Segmentation, Targeting and Positioning', Prentice Hall, Englewood Cliffs, NJ.

Lancaster G.A. and Reynolds P.L. (1999) *Introduction to Marketing: A Step-by-Step Guide to All The Tools of Marketing*, Chapter 2, 'Segmentation, Target Marketing and Positioning', Kogan Page, London.

Nickels W. and Burk-Wood M. (1997) *Marketing, Relationships, Quality, Value*, Chapter 8, 'Market Segmentation, Targeting and Positioning', Worth Publishers, New York.

Plamer A. (2000) *Principles of Marketing*, Chapter 3, 'Segmentation and Targeting', OUP, Oxford.

▶▶ References

Abell D.F. (1979) 'Strategic Windows', *Journal of Marketing*, July, pp. 21–6.

Shapiro B.P. and Bonoma T.V. (1984) 'How to Segment Industrial Markets', *Harvard Business Review*, May–June, pp. 104–10.

BUYER BEHAVIOUR

▶▶ Importance of understanding customer motives

Marketing's task is to identify consumer needs and wants, and develop products and services that satisfy them. To be successful, it is not enough simply to discover what customers require, but to find out why it is required. Only by gaining a deep and comprehensive understanding of buyer behaviour can marketing's goals be realised. This understanding works to the advantage of both parties allowing the marketer to become better equipped to satisfy consumer needs efficiently and establish a loyal group of customers with positive attitudes towards the company's products.

Consumer behaviour can be defined as:

> The acts of individuals directly involved in obtaining and using economic goods and services, including the decision processes that precede and determine these acts.

Buyer behaviour is a system in which the individual consumer is the core, surrounded by an immediate and a wider environment that influences his or her goals that are satisfied by passing through a number of problem-solving stages leading to purchase decisions. The study and practice of marketing draws on many sources that contribute theory, information, inspiration and advice. In the past, the main input to the theory of consumer behaviour has come from psychology. More recently, the interdisciplinary importance of consumer behaviour has increased so that sociology, anthropology, economics and mathematics contribute to its science.

▶▶ Social and cultural influences

Culture is 'learned' behaviour that has been passed down over time, reinforced in our daily lives through the family unit and through educational and religious institutions. Cultural influences are powerful and a company cannot expect to develop products and market them successfully if it does not understand the culture in which a market operates.

Culture, although powerful, is not fixed. Changes in culture tend to be slow and are not fully assimilated until a generation or more has passed. An example is the custom of marriage that has been openly challenged in the UK over the past thirty years. When couples first began to set up home together and raise families outside marriage, society, for the most part, adopted an attitude of condemnation, whereas today there is a more relaxed attitude to those who choose to ignore the convention.

The twentieth century witnessed significant cultural changes, for example, changing attitudes towards work and pleasure. It is no longer accepted that work should be difficult or injurious to mind or body and many employers make great efforts to ensure that the workplace is as pleasant an environment as possible, realising that this increases productivity. Employees now more frequently regard work as a means to earn the money to spend on goods or services that give them pleasure, and not just to pay for the necessities of life. The shortened working week, paid holidays and labour-saving devices in the home have all led to increased leisure time that influences how, when and what the consumer buys. Another major cultural change in the twentieth century has been the changing role of women in society. Increased independence and economic power have not only changed the lives of women, but have also influenced society's and women's own perception of their socioeconomic role.

In most Western societies, when considering culture, we must also consider subcultures. Immigrant communities have become large enough in many countries to form a significant proportion of the population of that country, and marketers must consider them because of their interactive influence on society and because they often constitute individual market segments for certain products. Subcultures also exist within the same groups sharing common nationality. Their bases may be geographical, religious or linguistic differences and marketers must recognise these differences and regard them as providing opportunities rather than problems.

Why do you feel modern marketing practice increasingly needs to take buyer behaviour motives into consideration when devising new or modified products and services?

It would be easy to repeat what has already been said so far in this chapter and this would be acceptable. However, the question asks for *modern* marketing practice and here lies the clue. The world is becoming increasingly cosmopolitan with the movements of groups of people from one country to another and an assimilation of their subculture into that of the new country. There has also been a move towards more cosmopolitan tastes through travel and foreign holidays. We have looked at segmentation bases in the previous chapter and from this you will have seen that many sophisticated subsegments are now possible. More precise targeting of marketing efforts is necessary to reach these subsegments and this has led to the growth of more direct methods of marketing. It is, therefore, essential that marketers understand the buying motives of such subgroups when manipulating their marketing mixes through promotional appeals, new product designs and other strategies in order to more precisely target such subgroups.

▶▶ Specific social influences

▶ Social class

This is the most prominent social influence. Traditionally, one of the chief determinants of social class was income. However, pay structures have changed such that C2, D and E categories have moved towards levels previously enjoyed by A, B and C1 categories. Classification of consumers on the basis of 'lifestyle' is now more meaningful. Income aside, social class is an indicator of lifestyle and its existence exerts a strong influence on individual consumers and their behaviour. Evidence suggests that whatever income level a consumer reaches, basic attitudes and preferences do not change much. As consumers, we usually identify with a particular class or group, but often it is not social class that is revealing, but that which the consumer aspires to. Income and/or education allows people to 'cross' social class barriers and adopt lifestyles that are different from those of their parents. They tend to absorb the influences of the group to which they aspire and gradually reject the lifestyles of their parents and relations. Occupation is thus a strong determinant in an individual's behavioural patterns, including buyer behaviour.

Marketers should make decisions on the basis of information revealed by objectively designed research, without preconceptions or associations with inferiority or superiority in 'lower' or 'higher' social groupings. This is the only way that changes in behaviour can be identified.

What are the implications of the last statement that encourage marketers to make decisions based on information from research rather than preconceptions related to individuals belonging to higher and lower social groups?

In the past people were less mobile in the physical sense, were more likely to stay in the locality in which they were born, and would probably take up similar occupations to those of their parents. The family unit was relatively stable and divorce was a rare occurrence. Thus, one could, in those days, make generalisations about social class being relatively 'permanent' from one generation to the next.

However, there is now an expectation that young, better-educated people will move to different parts of the country or the world. Higher education is now more widely available to the broader spectrum of social groups, and young people are able to attain qualifications and expertise their parents could only dream about. As they become better qualified, so the positions they can attain are different to those of their parents. Such positions usually entail greater mobility. The family group bonding has become eroded and family meetings between children and parents take place only at holiday periods because of distances involved in travelling. The probability is that children have taken on different social attitudes from those of their parents. Indeed, many such parent/offspring meetings are sometimes stressful, because parents cannot appreciate that their children have 'changed so much'.

▶ Reference groups

This means groups of people whose standards of conduct mould an individual's dispositions, beliefs and values. This group can be small or large. Reference groups range from the immediate family to a place of work. They can also be found in a person's social life. An individual is unlikely to deviate too far from the behavioural norms laid down by the members of a club or hobby group. Reference group theory does not state that individualism cannot exist within a group, but it suggests that even rigid independent thinkers will at least be aware of what is considered 'normal' within a group.

In a small group like the family, advice and opinions of those who are regarded as knowledgeable will be highly regarded. Such people are termed 'opinion leaders'. Extraneous group influences might also be at work in opinion forming, where the ideas of opinion leaders outside the immediate group are taken up by 'opinion followers'. For some products a deliberate direct plea is made to 'snob appeal' by using the strategy of making a company's products acceptable to opinion leaders, or famous personalities (who are paid for their endorsement), in the hope that other sectors of the population will follow them.

The family is perhaps the strongest reference group for most people because of its intimacy and permanence. Strong associations mean that individuals within this group will influence each other.

The family life cycle traditionally contains six stages, although more subdivisions are sometimes quoted:

1. *Unmarried* where financial commitments and family responsibilities tend to be low, with disposable income being high. These younger unmarried consumers tend to be more leisure-oriented and more fashion conscious. This segment comprises a very important market for many new and innovative products.
2. *Young newly married couples – no children* focuses its expenditure on items considered necessary for setting up home.
3. *Young married couples with children* where expenditure is child-oriented, and there is little surplus cash for luxury items. Although they are receptive to new product ideas, this group sees economy as being the overriding factor when making purchases.
4. *Older married couples still with children at home* where disposable income will probably have increased, often with both parents working and children being relatively independent. In some cases, children may be working and parents are able to engage increasingly in leisure activities often in the form of more than the 'standard' annual holiday. Consumer durables, including major items of furniture, are often replaced at this stage. Such purchases are often made with different motivations to the original motivations of strict functionality and economy that was necessary at an earlier life-cycle stage.
5. *Older married couples with no children living in the home* where disposable income can be quite high. However, tastes are likely to be firmly rooted reflected in unchanging purchasing patterns. Marketers will have difficulty attempting to change predispositions, so the best policy will be through attempts to refine and add value rather than to introduce new concepts and ideas.
6. *Older retired couples and single people* when most consumer durables have been purchased with only occasional replacements being needed. Purchasing is low and patterns of purchasing are conservative and predictable. This group of consumers is increasing rapidly.

Such people tend to be less reliant solely on the 'state pension', which is boosted for many by occupational pensions from former employers. This allows this group to lead more active lives and the tourist industry now actively targets this market segment.

In the past the tendency was for clearer demarcations of purchasing responsibility in terms of which partner was responsible for which purchases. Nowadays, this distinction is far less clear as family roles have tended to merge in terms of women taking on traditionally viewed male roles and vice versa. Marketers should, therefore, engage in research before determining who to target with marketing efforts.

Do you feel that social class or family life cycle is the best base for segmentation?

The two are interlinked, because one can belong to a particular social class, yet be in any of the family life cycle stages that have been mentioned. This means that marketing appeals can be made to particular classes within each of the stages that have been cited.

▶ Individual buyer behaviour

As well as being influenced by the outside environment, people also have their own individual beliefs. It is important that we know what these are in order that we can better understand how individuals respond to marketing efforts. Individuals are different in terms of how they look, their education, their feelings and their responses to marketing efforts. Some behave predictably and others less predictably according to personality. Individual consumers absorb information and develop attitudes and perceptions. In marketing terms, this affects an individual's needs as well as determining how to satisfy them. The task of marketing is to identify patterns of behaviour that are predictable under given conditions and which will increase the marketer's ability to satisfy customer needs, which is at the very heart of marketing. To more fully understand this concept we concentrate on five psychological concepts that are recognised as being important when attempting to understand buyer behaviour:

1. Personality and self-concept
2. Motivation
3. Perception
4. Attitudes
5. Learning.

Personality and self-concept

This means how we think other people see us and how we see ourselves. As individuals we might wish to create a picture of ourselves that is acceptable to our reference group. This is communicated to the outside world by our individual behaviour. Marketers are interested in this behaviour as it relates to our purchase and consumption of goods. The sum of this behaviour is an individual self-statement and is a non-verbal form of communication. This self-image is expressed in a way that relates to our inner selves and this promotes acceptance within a group. Direct advertising appeals to self-image are now being made through behavioural segmentation bases defined earlier.

'Self' is influenced by social interaction and people make purchases that are consistent with their self-concept in order to protect and enhance it. The constant process of re-evaluating and modifying the self-concept results from a changing environment and changing personal situations.

Personality is the principal component of self-concept. It has a strong effect on buyer behaviour. Many purchase decisions are likely to reflect personality, and marketers must consider this when making marketing appeals. Psychological theory suggests that we are born with instinctive desires that cannot be satisfied in a socially acceptable manner and are thus repressed. The task of marketing is to appeal to inner needs, whilst, at the same time, providing products that enable them to be satisfied in a socially acceptable way.

Motivation

An early thinker in a motivation context was the psychologist Sigmund Freud (1856–1939). His theories have been criticised, but they are of fundamental value. He was responsible for identifying three levels of consciousness:

▶ The conscious that includes all sensations and experiences of which we are aware
▶ The preconscious that includes memories and thoughts which we have stored from our experiences and we can bring to mind when we wish
▶ The unconscious that is the major driving force behind our behaviour including our wishes and desires of which we are not always aware.

Within these levels of consciousness are mental forces at work attempting to reconcile our instincts with the social world in which we live, and these are not always in accord, so we experience emotional difficulties. Freud's term for these is:

▶ The 'Id' which is the reservoir for all our physiological and sensual instincts. It is selfish and seeks instant gratification regardless of social consequences
▶ The 'superego' which develops as we grow and learn from family, friends, teachers and other influences. It functions as our internal representation of the values and morals of society in which we have grown up. It is a potent force and comes into conflict with the demands made by our id for the gratification of what might be anti-social desires
▶ The 'ego' which attempts to resolve the conflict between the id and the superego and tries to redirect our id impulses into socially and morally acceptable modes of expression.

Marketers are interested in motivation when it relates to purchasing behaviour. This behaviour relates to the motive for wishing to possess the goods or services in question, and it has been termed 'goal-related behaviour'. For a motive to exist there must be a corresponding need. Motives like hunger, thirst, warmth and shelter are physiological. Others, like approval, success and prestige are psychological. Motives like staying alive are instinctive whilst motives like cleanliness, tidiness and proficiency are motives that are learned during life. We can also discern between rational and emotional motives. Most purchasing decisions are a composite of such motives and quite often a deciding factor might be price which is of course more of an economic restriction than a motive. It can, therefore, be seen that a number of motives might be at play when making a purchasing decision, some stronger than others and the final decision might be a compromise solution.

In 1954 the psychologist Abraham Maslow put forward his classic 'hierarchy of needs' as shown in Figure 4.1. This hierarchy is now central to much thinking in buyer behaviour.

Physiological needs are concerned with self-preservation and these are the basic needs of life involving those elements required to sustain and advance the human race. Safety needs relate to protection against danger and deprivation. Once more basic needs have been satisfied, behaviour is influenced by the need for belonging, association and acceptance by others. In many texts the next two needs are put together, but here we have separated respect and self esteem in terms of confidence, competence and knowledge and have then placed achievement in terms of qualifications and recognition above this. The final need is what

Figure 4.1 Hierarchy of needs
Source: Maslow (1954)

Maslow termed 'self-actualisation' which means self-fulfilment in terms of becoming all that one is capable of being and one has reached the pinnacle of personal potential.

Vignette 4.1

United States consumers become more concerned with safety needs rather than 'self-actualising'.

Since the tragedy of 11 September, 2001, many consumers in the USA have stopped 'self-actualising' and spending for pleasure and have instead started to save their money for an uncertain future. What money they are spending is often on products and services to do with satisfying safety needs. For example, because of fears of further terrorist attacks, sales of gas masks, protective clothing and shelters have risen dramatically. Evidence suggests that many areas of the US economy were beginning to slow during the latter part of 2001. This was particularly evident in high technology sectors where growth slowed considerably and share prices plummeted, sometimes dragging down the rest of the stock market with them. However retail sales seemed to be strong as consumers cheered themselves up by shopping. The USA is after all a consumer society, the biggest in the world. The US economy was slowing, President Bush expressed concern for jobs and Allen Greenspan, head of the USA Federal Reserve, cut interest rates to try and increase business confidence and get businesses investing and consumers spending. Large tax rebates also put more money in people's pockets and thus pumped spending power into the economy. However this was before the September 2001 atrocities in New York and Washington DC. In September 2001 retail sales within the USA fell at the greatest rate since 1992,

prompting economic commentators to say with some confidence that the US economy was officially in a recession. Amongst those sectors hardest hit were clothing
stores (5.9% down), restaurants and bars (5.1% down) and car dealers (4.6% down).
Now the war in Iraq is over people are showing signs of a more positive attitude.
However, worries about further attacks on the US are likely to depress confidence for
some time. People do not feel like going out a celebrating at a Broadway show or an
expensive restaurant or even spending money on expensive goods, when they are
worried about the future. Because more people are staying at home many are spending more on home improvement products such as fitted kitchens. They are also
spending more on health care, insurance and household security.

When more basic needs like hunger and thirst have been satisfied,
individuals move to satisfy the higher order needs towards the apex of
the pyramid and look increasingly for satisfactions that will increase
status and social acceptability. When the apex of the pyramid has been
reached and other satisfactions have been achieved, the prime motivation is then one of acquiring products and accomplishing activities that
allow self-expression. This can be in the form of hobbies, particularly
collecting, which may have been desired for a long time, but have been
neglected until lower order needs have been satisfied. It is not possible
to formulate marketing strategies on the hierarchy theory on its own.
Its value is that it suggests that marketers should understand and direct
effort at specific needs of customers as suggested by the hierarchy.

**Think of one product or service that falls into each of the six
sections of the pyramid in Figure 4.1.**

The answer to this will differ between different individuals according
to their particular circumstances and backgrounds. Lower order needs
are easiest, but higher order needs differ according to the background
of individuals and their aspirations. Higher order needs tend to be fulfilled as individuals become older and approach the retirement period
of life, and they realise that although they may not have attained all
their aspirations, they have done so as far as possible. It is at this stage
that people start looking for self-actualisation in terms of hobbies and
recreations that had not previously been possible owing to the pressures of working life.

Maslow was not the only theorist to focus on human needs as the
motivating force behind human behaviour. McGregor (1960) argued that
two sets of theories motivate people and these he labelled Theory X and
Theory Y. Such motivations apply principally to the place of work, but

the workplace is where attitudes and opinions are accumulated, so its relevance to marketing is indirect. Under Theory X certain assumptions are made:

▶ people have an inherent dislike for work and will avoid it if possible
▶ because of this, they must be coerced, controlled, directed and threatened with punishment in order to complete their work satisfactorily
▶ people like to be directed and do not crave responsibility. They have little ambition and want security.

Under Theory Y he makes an alternative set of assumptions:

▶ people are not naturally passive or resistant to organisational needs. They have become so as the result of experience in organisations
▶ motivation and the capacity to develop and assume responsibility are all present and it is management's responsibility to develop these characteristics
▶ it is management's responsibility to organise production towards economic ends, but it is their task to arrange conditions and methods of operation so people can achieve their own goals best by directing their own efforts towards organisational objectives
▶ if the right conditions prevail, individuals will not only accept responsibility, but will actively seek it
▶ most people in an organisation are capable of imagination, ingenuity and creativity in problem solving
▶ industrialisation has meant that such capabilities are under-utilised.

There are two ways in which human behaviour can be interpreted, depending upon whether the observer assumes Theory X or Theory Y. What McGregor argued was that management by control (Theory X) was based on an inaccurate set of negative assumptions and that organisations would work more effectively if 'management by objectives' (MBO) or Theory Y, was applied.

Herzberg (1959) contributed to motivation through his 'Motivation-hygiene' theory. He believed that performance is at its pinnacle when people are satisfied with their jobs as long as necessary resources are provided to carry out this work effectively. Satisfaction with work and personal happiness do not necessarily work in harmony, but when they do and when people are stretched to the limits of their ability there may be a feeling of 'self-actualisation' (see Figure 4.1). This feeling might be more evident in recreational or home situations, and less common in the workplace because of conditions and deadlines imposed in an occupational situation. According to Herzberg 'self actualisation' depends on what he terms 'motivators' and these he distinguishes from another set of factors termed 'hygiene factors'. Motivators can positively contribute to satisfaction at work, whereas hygiene factors cannot promote satisfaction, but they can prevent dissatisfaction. He uses a medical analogy to describe hygiene factors and cited the case of unhygienic conditions as being a source of infection that may make a person unhealthy. In an organisation, *hygiene factors* are:

▶ financial reward
▶ supervision
▶ working conditions
▶ company policy
▶ status and relationships with colleagues.

Similarly, in an organisation *motivators* are:

▶ recognition for achievement
▶ opportunities for advancement
▶ responsibility
▶ the job itself.

It can be seen that *motivating factors* are those that are part of the job, whereas *hygiene factors* are more concerned with the job environment.

Under 'motivation' we have discussed theories put forward by Freud, Maslow, McGregor and Herzberg. What do you feel is the practical value of these theories to marketers?

At this stage there might be a temptation to say: 'Very little'. Some might see relevance in Maslow's hierarchy of needs, but might view the rest as being irrelevant. Others might see an indirect bearing in the theories of others in terms of discussing motivation in a less direct sense, in the knowledge that how we are motivated might reflect the way we purchase. However, the point is that in order for marketing to develop as a science it must have theories. Theories are a way in which thinkers can communicate with each other in concise terms, and these theories have central relevance to the subject of motivation. As marketers we are interested in motivation from a purchasing behavioural point of view so their relevance is justified because as marketers our knowledge would be incomplete without an understanding of the basic building blocks behind motivation.

Perception

Unlike motivation that requires a reaction to a stimulus, perception relates to the meaning that is assigned to that stimulus. As marketers we are interested in how buyers perceive and react to products in relation to matters like quality, aesthetics, price and image, since products exist not only in practical terms, but also in how they are perceived by consumers in relation to need satisfaction. This perception by buyers is affected by the nature of the product itself, the circumstances of the individual buyer, and by the buyer's unique situation in terms of how ready they are to make a purchase and whether they need it at a particular point in time. It is, or course, necessary that the product or service (that is, the stimulus) receives the attention of the potential buyer. Buyers have numerous stimuli competing for their attention, so marketers must make their stimuli as interesting and attractive as possible as potential buyers act only on information that is retained, and this is the foundation of how the product or service is communicated, together with the choice of media. There is of course no certainty that perception of a product or service will be as the marketer expected, even though the marketer has successfully alerted the consumer to a particular offering through successful manipulation of the marketing mix. Consumers can be influenced by many illogical motives as well as practical ones presented to them by the marketer. These might be favourable or unfavourable preconceptions from personal experience, from peer group or family advice, or from other psychological motives, all combining to alter and shape the final perception and indeed the ultimate buying decision.

Attitudes

Our strongest attitudes are implanted in our formative years and these come largely from the influence of close family group and other social interactions. More refined attitudes develop later. In marketing terms, the sum total of our attitudes can be regarded as a set of cognitions a potential buyer has in relation to a potential purchase or a purchasing environment. This is why certain stores or companies go out of their way to engender favourable attitudes and it is why manufacturers seek to induce loyalty towards their particular brands or products. Once this attitude has been established in the mind of the consumer, it might be difficult to alter. Even a minor dissatisfaction can cause a fundamental shift in disposition. This process can work for and against a manufacturer or retail establishment and one method of attempting to change attitude is through promotional appeals and a programme of public relations. These subjects are dealt with in later chapters.

Learning

Experience precedes learning and this can alter perceptions and attitudes. It also intensifies a shift in behaviour, so when a buyer perceives that certain products are more favourable than others within his or her reference group repeat purchases are made to promote this acceptability. Every time a satisfactory purchase is made, the consumer is less likely to depart from this purchasing behaviour. A result is *brand loyalty*, and the ultimate success of marketing is in terms of customers making repeat purchases or becoming 'brand loyal'.

In the context of marketing, learning is a result of information received through advertising or other publicity or through some reference group or other. To have an effect on motives or attitudes, marketing effort should associate the product with positive drives and reinforcing messages.

A fundamental aim of marketers is to bring about satisfaction for customers, and this is the basis of the concept of marketing. Having looked at some of the issues that make up consumer behaviour, we can look at the consumer's central goal. Because consumers are continually occupied in a quest for satisfaction, competitive offerings will always have potential appeal. Firms must seek continuous improvement to products or services and the levels of support they provide. This is a matter of balancing costs and potential profit with customer demands, as 'total satisfaction', can be an unrealistically expensive goal.

▶▶ Models of consumer behaviour

Now we have examined psychological factors that influence consumer behaviour we are in a position to examine consumer behaviour by presenting a series of models that endeavour to explain the purchase decision process in relation to appropriate variables.

▶ The buyer/decision process

Different buying tasks present different levels of complexity to the purchaser. The 'AIDA' model presented in Figure 4.2 considers the steps leading to a purchase in the form of a sequential problem-solving process.

Strong first proposed this classical model in 1925 and it is still useful today because it is easy to apply as it describes the activities involved in the buyer decision process. Products and services vary in the complexity of decision making involved in their acquisition. The purchase of a new shower unit, for instance, is more complicated than purchasing a tube of shower gel.

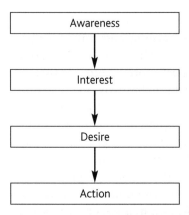

Figure 4.2 AIDA model of buying behaviour

Robinson et al. in 1967 put forward a model that viewed purchasing as a problem. This is shown in Figure 4.3 and it describes the activities involved in the purchasing process.

An individual needs a particular product. Information is sought from a variety of sources including family and friends ('word of mouth') from advertising, from catalogues, from visits to retail establishments and from many other sources. The more complex the product, the greater will be this information search. The task of marketing is to ensure that the company's products receive high exposure during this *information search* period and that the best points of the product are

Figure 4.3 The buyer/decision model

emphasised during the *evaluation of alternatives* phase. This will put the company's product in the best light prior to the *purchase decision*, because even at that stage the consumer is still susceptible to further influences in relation to making the correct choice. Marketers must be aware of *post-purchase behaviour* as this can affect repeat business and as much importance should be attached to after-sales service as to the initial sale. This reduces the degree of dissatisfaction (or dissonance) in the case of genuine complaints. For sales of major items like new motor cars most companies follow up a sale by some form of communication by letter or telephone with their customers. This builds confidence in the mind of the customer in having made the 'correct' purchasing decision. The terminology that is attached to this kind of after-sales follow-up is 'customer care'.

Knowledge of how the buyer/decision process works is critical to the success of marketing strategy. For simple products, marketing's task is to direct the purchasing routine in favour of the company's products, perhaps through a mass advertising campaign. For more complicated purchases, it is important that customers are helped in their problem-solving process and that reassurance is provided to show that their choice was a wise one.

Of the two models that have been put forward in relation to the buyer/decision process which do you feel is most useful as a tool of marketing?

The AIDA model is perhaps more of a tool for marketers in that they must ensure that their products or services display the characteristics of creating attention, generating interest, forming a desire to possess and bringing about action through purchasing. The other model is less useful in that it merely describes the consumer decision-making process from problem recognition (that the product or service is needed) to post-purchase behaviour (how they feel after the purchase has been made).

▶ The adoption process

The buyer/decision model (Figure 4.3) was not specifically designed for new products and its substance was concerned with search and problem solving. The model shown in Figure 4.4 relates to new products. It begins with awareness. Marketers must first create awareness and then assist customers through subsequent stages of the process. Consumers cannot begin to consider a new product or service as a solution to need-related

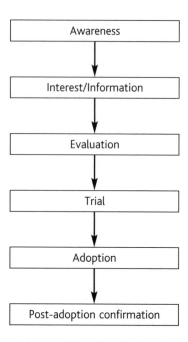

Figure 4.4 The adoption process

problems without this awareness. Successful innovative products should attempt to be problem solving as far as the customer is concerned.

Awareness can come about as a result of the marketing effort of the company or simply by 'word of mouth' communication. If the product has potential *interest* and appeal, potential purchasers will seek further *information*. Consumers then *evaluate* the new product against existing products and make an initial adoption by obtaining a *trial* sample, which might be a free sample or a *trial* purchase. The *adoption* stage is when a decision is made whether to use the product (in the case of a fast-moving consumer good on a repeat purchase basis). *Post-adoption confirmation* is when the product has been adopted and the consumer seeks reassurance about the wisdom of the purchase. After a major purchase, dissonance (termed cognitive dissonance) is present in the sign of unease that what was thought to be value for money at the time of purchase may not, after all, turn out to be good value. Such dissonance should be countered by the provision of some kind of follow-up – either written or by telephone.

A more detailed model is suggested in Figure 4.5 that develops the adoption process. A series of inputs feed into the knowledge base. The 'self' input includes psychological notions of perception, attitudes, motivation and learning. Similar to other inputs, they set the scene for

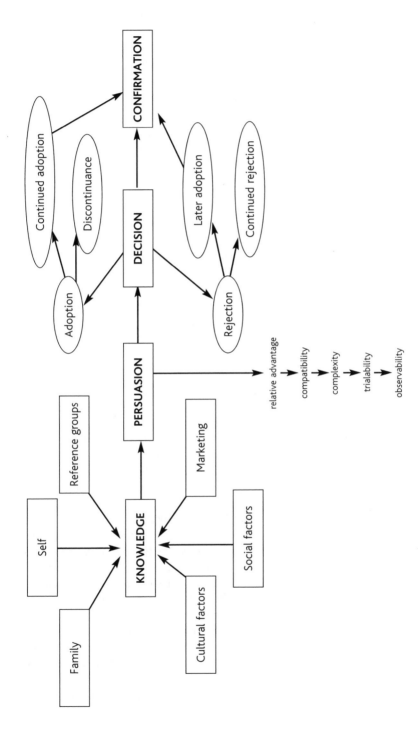

Figure 4.5 New product purchasing decision process

knowledge to be interpreted into a favourable situation of awareness. Figure 4.5 also shows that persuasion governs the rate of adoption that is affected by relative advantage, compatibility, complexity, trial opportunity and observability. The model allows for review after the decision stage, and here consumers can be sensitive to the influence of external information sources from promotional appeals and from such influences as reference groups.

It can be seen that many inputs contribute to knowledge, ranging from personal factors to company marketing activity. Persuasion is important and a number of factors which are functions of the product itself can lead to a decision about whether or not to purchase the new product or service. The decision means adoption or rejection. If it is adoption, then good experience can lead to its continued adoption, but if experience of the product or service is bad it will be discontinued. Conversely, rejection might be the decision and this might be followed by continued rejection or later adoption, perhaps in the latter case through hearing good experience of reference group members who have purchased. Continued adoption and later adoption need confirmation in order to continue the repeat purchase pattern.

What is meant by each of the terms that are cited under 'Persuasion' in Figure 4.5?

- 'Relative advantage' means how much better the service or product is over other offerings in the marketplace.
- 'Compatibility' is the degree to which the product or service conforms to the buyer's purchasing needs.
- 'Complexity' is a function of the product or service in that, for instance, a new brand of toothpaste is less complex than an innovative type of food processor.
- 'Trialability' is a function of the product or service and it simply relates to how easy it is to try it out at as small a cost as possible. For instance, a new brand of toothpaste might be given free as a trial sample or at a bargain 'introductory offer' price. A camcorder might be supplied as a demonstration model for a short period on loan. A new car can be demonstrated on a test drive, but it is quite often some time after the purchase has been made that real opinions about the newly purchased car are formed.
- 'Observability' is also a function of products in particular, because, like motor cars, they can be observed in use. However, a service like an insurance policy is a more abstract concept, so it rates low on this factor, as it relies upon description and other evidence for its sale.

Diffusion of innovations is a process that is examined in detail in Chapter 7 under Product diffusion and adoption. It is, however, important that we look at innovator categories as far as purchasing behaviour is concerned because consumers, as individuals, can be more, or less, receptive to new product or service ideas.

The process of the diffusion of innovations proposes that certain groups of consumers will take on new ideas more quickly than other groups and they tend to influence later consumer groups. These groups have particular common features.

1. *Innovators* are the first small segment to take on new product ideas and they are likely to be younger people, from well-educated, relatively affluent backgrounds, having a high social status. They are likely to be unprejudiced, discerning people whose understanding of the new product has been more objectively established than just through salespeople or company promotional material.
2. *Early adopters* possess some of the characteristics of innovators, but they are more likely to be part of 'local' systems, acting as opinion leaders within their specific group.
3. *Early majority* adopters tend to be above average in terms of social class and rely upon company promotional efforts for data. Opinion leaders of the early adopter category tend to be their biggest inspiration.
4. *Late majority* adopters tend to adopt because earlier groups have generally accepted it.
5. *Laggards* make up the final group. They are more careful, older and of a lower socioeconomic standing.

Adopter categories tend to differ depending on the new product or service being marketed.

Vignette 4.2

Bioforce AG of Roggwill, Switzerland market saw palmetto complex to men who are worried about enlarged prostate and prostate cancer.

Many men of a certain age suffer prostate gland problems. The symptoms are discomfort and problems with urinating. Sometimes the condition can become more serious and turn into prostate cancer, a major cause of death in males. Most men are unaware of the problem but their behaviour usually changes when they are made aware of the facts. A good case if ever there was one for medical education of the general public. There are drugs available for the treatment of prostate problems, most notably the drug Finasteride, but these drugs can have unpleasant side effects such as sexual dysfunction in males. Evidence suggests that men in general are terribly ignorant of potential prostate dangers and many do not even know where the prostate gland is located in the body or indeed what function the gland has. In fact 1 in 13 men develop prostate cancer and it is the second biggest cancer killer next to lung cancer. As men live longer prostate cancer is more likely to increase as its incidence is higher in those men over 50 years of age. In fact the incidence of prostate cancer is likely to grow by more than 50% over the next 20 years, according to experts. Generally men seem to be bad at looking after their own health and only do something about it when things start to go wrong. However prevention is always better than cure. There have been attempts by governments throughout the world to raise awareness of prostate problems. One natural remedy for prostate problems is an extract of the plant saw palmetto that is marketed by Bioforce of Switzerland. Saw palmetto has long been used in Europe to treat enlarged prostate or benign prostatic hyperplasia (BPH). American use lags far behind Europe, in part because Americans are not aware of the extensive European research on the herb. American physicians generally do not prescribe any drug other than Finasteride (Proscar®), Terazosin HCl (Hytrin®), or Doxazosin mesylate (Cardura®) for BPH. But unlike these drugs, particularly Proscar®, saw palmetto usually works quickly and is a totally natural remedy for which you do not need a doctor's prescription. With the saw palmetto extract most men achieve some relief of symptoms within the first 30 days. Saw palmetto is, according to industry sources, one species with several different names, including Serenoa repens, Serenoa serrulata, and Sabal. The industry is attempting to standardise on the name Serenoa repens, which is the way most research identifies it. Florida is the biggest producer of saw palmetto. Small patches can be found from the southeast coastline of South Carolina and southeastern Georgia to southern Mississippi. But it does not grow naturally in Texas, Mexico, or the Caribbean. It grows in every Florida county, but much of its production centres in south Florida. Bioforce markets the extract at all major herbalists, with 50 ml costing between £6 and £7. The extract is taken in water each day. The product is set to become increasingly popular as more and more men start to try to prevent the onset of prostate related problems.

❭ Hierarchy of effects

Lavidge and Steiner (1961) produced a 'hierarchy of effects' model of purchasing behaviour in 1961. The model starts at the *awareness* stage, although there is a stage prior to this which is when the potential purchaser is completely unaware of the product or service offering and it is through marketing communication that such awareness is made known. (See Figure 4.6.)

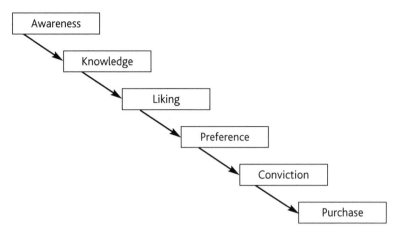

Figure 4.6 The innovation/adoption model

	Consider the models of purchasing behaviour that have been discussed. Now consider three phases of purchasing as being: the pre-transaction phase, the transaction phase and the post-transaction phase. Which component parts of each model fall under each of these purchasing phases?

	Pre-transaction	*Transaction*	*Post-transaction*
Figure 4.2	awareness, interest, desire	action	
Figure 4.3	problem recognition, information search	evaluation of alternatives, purchase decision	post-purchase behaviour
Figure 4.4	awareness, interest, information	evaluation, adoption, trial	post-adoption confirmation
Figure 4.5	knowledge	persuasion, decision	confirmation
Figure 4.6	awareness, knowledge	liking, preference, conviction, purchase	

▶▶ Organisational buying behaviour

The term 'organisational buying' reflects purchasing in three different buying situations as shown in Figure 4.7.

Industrial buying and organisation buying are used interchangeably in the literature, but as we see, industrial buying is really a subset of

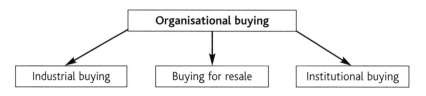

Figure 4.7 Elements of organisational buying

organisational buying. The process of organisational buying behaviour differs from consumer buying in that psychological and emotional considerations attached to the latter should not apply here. However, organisational buyers are human, so clearly some 'emotion' might be involved, but generally it can be said that commercial considerations are of prime significance when arriving at purchasing decisions.

 Think of three purchasing situations involved in each of the three subheadings of organisational buying.

- *Industrial buying:* purchasing man-made fibres for a spinning plant; purchasing a new lathe for the factory's machine shop; purchasing silicon chips for incorporation in the motherboard of a computer.
- *Buying for resale:* purchasing fruit and vegetables for a supermarket chain; purchasing fashion clothing for next season; a wholesaler purchasing fancy glassware from an overseas factory for stockholding with a view to promoting it for onward sale to domestic retail outlets.
- *Institutional buying:* purchasing uniforms for the fire service; purchasing medical equipment for a hospital; purchasing stationery materials for a local government department.

The chief similarity between consumer and organisational purchasing is that they both represent a need-satisfying process. This need reflects itself in buying behaviour, and this is why it is important that marketers understand purchasing motives to effectively target marketing efforts in a way that satisfies these needs.

 In each of the subdivisions that comprise organisational buying, what do you feel will be the principal criterion when making purchasing decisions?

This is a difficult one, but it should make you think about the constraints under which purchasing in each of the three situations described operates. It depends, of course, upon individual buying situations in terms of the importance that is attached to each and it also depends upon the type of purchase being made, so what follows is a generalisation.

In 'industrial buying' the principal criterion will be to keep production satisfied in terms of raw materials and components in order that they can complete work for the company's customers.

In 'buying for resale' the principal criterion will be to purchase at a 'keen' price in order to apply a reasonable mark-up and keep the company profitable.

In institutional buying the main criterion will be in terms of budget constraints. Typically, the public, through revenue that is raised through taxes and levies, indirectly funds institutional buying. Spending should, therefore, be kept within the predetermined spending limits that have been agreed as part of the funding process.

It can be seen that organisational purchasers have to work within stricter purchasing constraints as they have the commercial and budgetary interests of their respective organisations to serve. They also have logistical elements like delivery schedules to maintain. There is little opportunity for 'impulse' purchasing in which everyday consumers can indulge. As purchasing professionals they normally have a great deal of technical and commercial knowledge about their prospective purchases.

▶ Models of organisational buying

In Figure 4.8 we propose a model of the organisational purchasing decision process. It is, perhaps, more precise in its application than models that were suggested for consumer buying behaviour as items for organisational purchase require a more businesslike description through a formal specification at the 'need description' and 'product specification' stages. Likely suppliers tend to be more rigorously vetted prior to a first order being placed, and it is not uncommon for purchasing and other executives to visit the supplying company beforehand, in order to ascertain whether or not the supplying company measures up to quality, financial and other reliability criteria. The purchase routine specification will instruct the supplying company in relation to quantities to be deliv-

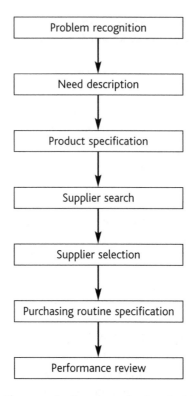

Figure 4.8 The organisational purchasing decision process

ered at specific dates through a delivery schedule if the entire order is not all needed at once.

Having said that organisational purchasing is more 'scientific' than consumer goods purchasing, individual organisational purchasers are of course subjected to the marketing actions and efforts of their current and potential suppliers. Reference groups also exist within organisational situations, and there can be influences from outside the purchasing department. It should also be recognised that individual buyers have discrete psychological attributes that can also influence decision making.

Figure 4.9 shows a more refined model that was developed by Wind in 1978.

He contended that it is critical for marketers to locate powerful buyers, because they tend to have more direct say in purchasing decisions at the negotiation stage. This does not necessarily mean those who are most important within the organisation at which the marketing approach is being directed. Buyers of relatively low status may be able

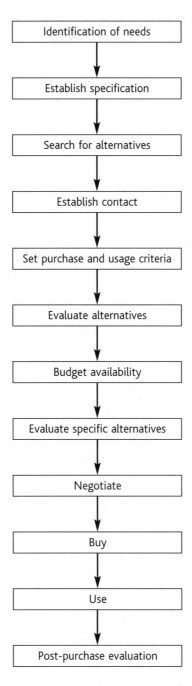

Figure 4.9 Wind's organisational purchasing model

to impede a purchase for a variety of reasons. Five power bases have been identified in this respect:

1. *Reward* Ability to provide monetary, social, political, or psychological rewards to others for compliance.
2. *Coercive* Ability to withhold monetary payments or other punishments for non-compliance.
3. *Attraction* Ability to elicit compliance from others because they like you.
4. *Expert* Ability to elicit compliance because of actual or reputed technical expertise.
5. *Status* Compliance from the ability derived from a legitimate position of power in a company.

❱ Organisational and consumer purchasing compared

How do purchasers in organisational buying situations differ from consumer buyers in their purchasing decision-making processes?

- Rationality of purchasing motives
- Derived demand especially in industrial buying situations, where demand is dependent upon purchases further down the supply chain and this creates demand further up the chain
- Small numbers of individual buyers
- Large number of influences on individual buyers
- Often multi-person purchasing decision-making unit
- Suppliers are sometimes in active competition with each other
- Industrial customers may have more power
- Many products are pre-specified by the buyer's organisation
- Commercial relationships between buyers and sellers is often long term
- Unequal purchasing power of customers
- Distribution is more direct
- Higher value of purchases
- There is sometimes a geographical concentration of purchasers
- Company policies, for instance in relation to suppliers being 'listed' for a particular quality standard, may act as a constraint on the buyer
- Possible 'reciprocal' purchasing arrangements, in that certain markets may be closed off because of a mutual trading agreement
- A sale is often preceded by lengthy negotiation
- Relationships between buyers and sellers tend to be more long term, rather than depending on a single commercial transaction

▶ The structured nature of organisational purchasing

Each time a consumer makes a purchase from a retailer, a derived demand is created for a series of materials and components that make up the final product. Added to this is an elaborate chain of supply from companies who buy and sell ancillary products like packaging materials, machinery and maintenance equipment. In order that companies can control this flow of goods and services, they must organise purchasing activities so they have:

1.   A constant supply of goods and services of the requisite quality as and when required
2.   A system which monitors supplier performance in terms of the above
3.   A system of review of existing suppliers and potential suppliers.

The larger the organisation, the more structured methods of buying should be. There should be an established procedure for each of the steps outlined in Figure 4.8. Purchasing tends to be more critical in flow-production situations than in jobbing manufacture. Even a minor delivery or quality problem could cause substantial losses in terms of lost production and loss of customer goodwill. Organisational purchasers tend to be more demanding than consumer purchasers because of the implications just outlined, so the notion of 'customer care' has profound significance in modern marketing.

▌▌▌ Vignette 4.3

Many firms are today outsourcing their security needs to specialist providers – Rentokil Initial lead the field in providing these services within the UK.

The general trend in relation to organisational buying of security services within the UK is towards outsourcing to specialist providers. This not only leaves firms to specialise in what they know best, for example manufacturing, retailing or even the provision of education in universities, but is also often a more cost-effective strategy. Rentokil Initial has capitalised on this growing trend and has diversified from the core businesses of the two merged organisations – Rentokil (pest control) and Initial (cleaning services to industry) – into a range of additional services, including security. Rentokil Initial employs some 96,000 people and operates in over 40 countries including the major economies in Europe, North America, Asia Pacific and Africa. The firm is committed to improving the environment and protecting health and property. Rentokil Initial's success is derived from the motivation of its staff at all levels to provide its customers with the Rentokil Initial quality of service. This quality has led to the names Rentokil and Initial becoming major international brands. Rentokil Initial today is a major provider of hygiene services, pest control services, security services, tropical plants, parcels delivery, conferencing, and facilities management. It is a global business services company. Electonic Security Systems offers the complete, professional security solution to clients looking for total peace of mind in terms of personal safety and protection of property and contents. The extensive range of services the firm provides encompasses every security requirement needed to safeguard businesses today. Manned guarding includes static guards, mobile patrols and officers specialising in airport, special event and exhibition security as well as keyholding for commercial, industrial and retail premises. Electronic Security provides state-of-the-art intruder detection, CCTV systems to monitor human activity or production processes, access systems and fire detection and suppression systems. Separately, Electronic Security Systems provides a total design–install–maintain facility to meet the demands of any size or complexity of security system encompassing management systems, microphone detection, taut wire detection and microwave fencing. With years of experience of operating in almost every market across both the public and private sectors, Electronic Security Services has a proven track record for delivering a quality service.

▶ Organisational buying situations

Three types of organisational buying situation have been identified, together with the problems surrounding each, as shown in Figure 4.10.

From the viewpoint of suppliers' marketing departments, each purchasing situation suggests a different marketing mix. This is in order to fit the particular circumstances, depending upon whether the company is an 'in' supplier currently supplying, or an 'out' supplier seeking to become an 'in' supplier.

What do you feel are the principal characteristics of organisational demand?

- Demand is derived from the demand for other products further down the distribution chain
- Price tends to be relatively stable
- Demand tends to fluctuate as it is often linked to external economic circumstances and there is sometimes evidence of stocking up on the part of purchasers

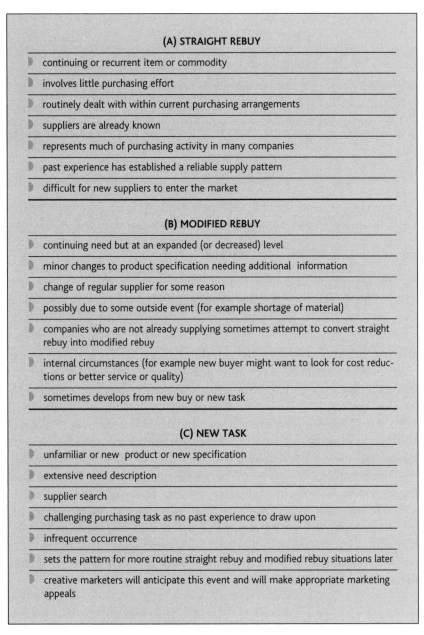

(A) STRAIGHT REBUY

- continuing or recurrent item or commodity
- involves little purchasing effort
- routinely dealt with within current purchasing arrangements
- suppliers are already known
- represents much of purchasing activity in many companies
- past experience has established a reliable supply pattern
- difficult for new suppliers to enter the market

(B) MODIFIED REBUY

- continuing need but at an expanded (or decreased) level
- minor changes to product specification needing additional information
- change of regular supplier for some reason
- possibly due to some outside event (for example shortage of material)
- companies who are not already supplying sometimes attempt to convert straight rebuy into modified rebuy
- internal circumstances (for example new buyer might want to look for cost reductions or better service or quality)
- sometimes develops from new buy or new task

(C) NEW TASK

- unfamiliar or new product or new specification
- extensive need description
- supplier search
- challenging purchasing task as no past experience to draw upon
- infrequent occurrence
- sets the pattern for more routine straight rebuy and modified rebuy situations later
- creative marketers will anticipate this event and will make appropriate marketing appeals

Figure 4.10 Organisational buying situations

▶ The decision-making unit (DMU)

The scope and role of organisational buyers vary widely according to the type of service or commodity being purchased and whether pur-

Gatekeepers	control the flow of information to and from the people who buy (for example a buyer's secretary or an assistant buyer).
Users	are individuals who work with, or use the product. Depending upon how purchasing decisions are made, they are sometimes involved in product specification.
Deciders	are people who make the buying decision. In many cases this is the buyer, but on some occasions it can be the specifier or, in a tightly budgeted situation, the accountant.
Buyers	have authority to sign orders and make the purchase. They may also help shape the specification, but their principal role is in supplier negotiation and selection.
Influencers	can affect the buying decision in different ways (for example technical people may have helped in a major or minor way to develop the product specification).

Figure 4.11 The decision-making unit (DMU) or buying centre
Source: Webster and Wind (1972)

chasing is a centralised or decentralised function. Large retail chains now tend to centralise their purchasing in order to employ specialist buyers who can negotiate keen terms and conditions. Some companies employ buyers who have only superficial knowledge of the products offered and handle only the commercial aspects of the sale. Whatever the buying structure, organisational salespersons know that the buyer is not always the final decision maker.

The predominant difference between consumer and organisational buying is that organisational buying involves group decision making. In 1972 Webster and Wind proposed that there were distinct roles in the purchasing process, sometimes taken up by different individuals, and sometimes by the same individuals combining some of these roles as shown in Figure 4.11. They termed this idea the 'buying centre' or the 'decision-making unit (DMU)'.

 Apart from using sales representatives, what means do organisational marketers have for targeting the DMU?

- Direct mail
- Press advertising
- Sales literature
- Editorial publicity
- Exhibitions

- Seminars and demonstrations
- Public relations
- Sponsored films
- House magazines
- Posters
- Radio and TV (although these might be relatively expensive)

▶ Future developments in organisational purchasing

Manufacturing companies (especially those operating flow-line production) now hold less stocks of components and raw materials. In some manufacturing situations, stockholding is theoretically non-existent. This is termed *just-in-time* management, or *lean manufacturing*. It requires delivery of goods exactly when required with zero defects. Should defects occur, a company's production is quickly stopped, so reliability of supply is of prime importance. In such situations, relationships tend to be long term and it is just as common for buyers to visit sellers (termed *reverse marketing*) as it is for sellers to visit buyers (*traditional marketing*). The term used to describe these long-term relationships is *relationship marketing*.

It is important to recognise that just as consumer goods' buyers are responsive to the actions of sellers, industrial buyers are individuals who possess personalities. The personal impression that the buyer or member of the DMU has of a company's image, as well as the personal accord that the salesperson can achieve, can influence purchasing decisions. This human factor also extends to the individual relationships that the buyer might have with colleagues within the selling organisation. As we move towards long-term relationships, this trend will increase and the notion of *customer care* will become increasingly important. Companies also have 'personalities' which are an amalgam of attitudes and policies reflected in the way outside people view the organisation.

reference group is a group of people whose standards of behaviour influence a person's attitudes, opinions and values. In general, people will tend to imitate and seek advice from those closest to them. Reference groups can be quite small, for instance, the family group. The frame of reference can also be large, for instance, a person involved in a certain occupation is likely to behave in the manner expected and accepted by his or her immediate colleagues and the wider occupational group. Reference groups are also found in a person's social life.

▶▶ Summary

Although we have identified factors that are common to consumer and organisational buying behaviour, it is emphasised that the two groups of buyers are approached differently. Requirements of consumers are established and marketing response is communicated mainly through mass media and direct-response marketing methods like 'individualised personal mailings' from a mailing list. In organisational markets, buyers and sellers also communicate through the mass media, but to a lesser extent as they also rely on personal interaction. Organisational buyers tend to work to obtain satisfaction for the company's commercial needs. Much consumer behaviour has a psychological foundation. Although organisational purchasers have an explicit rationale for their actions, this does not imply that they are impervious to psychological influences. Nowhere is this more important than in a market where products or services on offer are broadly similar. It is here that organisational marketers should attempt to modify their marketing programmes to serve specific needs and requirements.

FURTHER READING

Armstrong G. and Kotler P. (2000) *Marketing: An Introduction* (5th edn), Chapter 5, 'Consumer and Business Buyer Behaviour', Prentice Hall, Englewood Cliffs, NJ.

Blythe J. (2001) *Essentials of Marketing*, Chapter 3, 'Consumer and Buyer Behaviour', Pearson Education, London.

Cateora P.R. and Ghauri P.N. (2000) *International Marketing: European Edition*, Chapter 7, 'Business Customs and Practice in International Marketing', McGraw Hill, Maidenhead.

Davies M. (1998) *Understanding Marketing*, Chapter 5, 'Consumer and Organisational Buying Behaviour', Prentice Hall, London.

Keegan W.J. and Green M.S. (2000) *Global Marketing* (2nd edn), Chapter 4, 'Social and Cultural Environments', Prentice Hall, London.

Lancaster G.A. and Reynolds P.L. (1999) *Introduction to Marketing: A Step-by-Step Guide to All The Tools of Marketing*, Chapter 3, 'Consumer and Organisational Buyer Behaviour', Kogan Page, London.

Plamer A. (2000) *Principles of Marketing*, Chapter 7, 'Buyer Behaviour', OUP, Oxford.

◗◗ References

Herzberg F., Mausner B. and Snyderman B.B. (1959) *The Motivation to Work* (2nd edn), John Wiley & Sons, New York.

Lavidge R.J. and Steiner G.A. (1961) 'A Model for Predictive Measurements of Advertising Effectiveness', *Journal of Marketing*, October.

McGregor D.M. (1960) *The Human Side of Enterprise*, McGraw-Hill, New York.

Maslow A.H. (1954) *Motivation and Personality*, Harper & Row, New York, pp. 80–106.

Robinson P.J., Faris C.W. and Wind Y. (1967) *Industrial Buying and Creative Marketing*, Allyn & Bacon, Boston, MA, p. 14.

Strong E.K. (1925) *The Psychology of Selling*, McGraw Hill, New York, p. 9.

Webster F.E. (Jr) and Wind Y. (1972) *Organisational Buying Behaviour*, Prentice Hall, Englewood Cliffs, NJ, p. 2.

Wind Y. (1978) 'The Boundaries of Buying Decision Centres', *Journal of Purchasing and Materials Management*, **14** (Summer).

5 MARKETING INFORMATION SYSTEMS AND FORECASTING

▶▶ Introduction

Information is of strategic value to the marketer as well as contributing to tactical and routine operational decision making. Knowing what kind of information to obtain and how to make effective use of it are key skills of strategic marketing management. The possession and use of information gives the firm an opportunity to gain competitive advantage over other suppliers. Armies win wars, not just because of superior military power, but because they have effective intelligence-gathering procedures. Likewise, firms are waging a commercial war in a free-market, competitive economy. They too will have a better chance of 'winning' if they have superior intelligence to their competitors.

In a proactive marketing organisation the acquisition and management of information cannot be left to chance; it is far too important for that. All aspects of information, including its collection, storage, processing, retrieval and use, must be managed. The marketing-oriented firm needs some form of process to carry out this activity – a system devoted to managing the entire information needs of the organisation. Such a system is the subject of the first part of this chapter and is referred to as a 'marketing information system' (MkIS). Marketing research is part of an integrated marketing information system. Marketing research is introduced in this chapter, but a more comprehensive treatment is given in Chapter 6.

Marketing is the management process that anticipates and delivers customer value more effectively than the competition and, in a profit-making organisation, does so at an acceptable level of profit. Note the word 'anticipates'. Many markets are dynamic rather than static. The only thing certain about the future is that it will be different from today. Marketing management needs to anticipate and stay ahead of these changes. Much marketing decision making at a strategic level requires some form of prediction or forecast of likely future conditions across a variety of areas. It is true to say of any information system or decision support system, that the end product is usually a decision about the future made in the present often based largely on information about the past. This process by its very nature involves forecasting. Hence, the second part of this chapter is devoted to the important marketing area of forecasting. It should be noted that forecasting is used in a wide range of areas. For example, in logistics the forecasting of production materials or component parts is very important. In production, error processes in production can be predicted and monitored.

▶▶ Marketing information systems

A marketing information system (MkIS) is a systematic process for the management of marketing information. The term 'system' conjures up visions of complex computer networks, especially to those managing smaller enterprises. They feel it might be too sophisticated for their business and must require technical skill to design and implement. In fact, this is not true. Every firm must organise the collection, storage and distribution of information to its managers in order to function effectively. As we now explain, such a system can be purely manual. Companies of all sizes carry out information audits to design systems that will meet their information needs and give them a competitive edge. Kotler (1997) defined a marketing information system:

> A marketing information system (MkIS) consists of people, equipment and procedures to gather, sort, analyse, evaluate and distribute needed, timely and accurate information to marketing decision makers. (p. 109)

Whilst it is true that in many companies a MkIS is operated as part of a computer system, if computing capability is unavailable the design and implementation of an MkIS is still possible and there is no reason why it cannot be based entirely on a manual system of reference cards and files. Such a system will lack ease of storage and retrieval, but a manual system is better than having no system at all and leaving the management of information to chance. To manage a business well is to manage its future and this means managing information from a diverse set of sources which is collected, stored, analysed and distributed effectively at the right time, to people who need it to make marketing decisions.

'To manage a business well is to manage its future and to manage its future is to manage information'. To what extent do you think the above statement is true and why? Use examples to illustrate the points made.

The first thing to discuss is what you think management is all about. There are a number of ways of looking at the role of management within the organisation. Getting things done and using other people to do it, is a view of management that is often expressed. Making decisions about the future in the present, using information obtained from the past and the present, is another interesting 'definition'. The next thing is to examine the concept of strategy. Strategy is long term in nature and is concerned with the broad general direction of the organisation in the future, often over a five to ten year time horizon or even longer.

Of course, day-to-day operational activities and operations need to be managed effectively. This process is usually carried out by 'middle' managers. Senior managers should concern themselves with matters that affect the future direction and performance of the organisation. Long-term strategic decisions are not made on a 'whim', far from it, they should be made on the basis of information. A good example here is the US software giant Microsoft. Microsoft has come to an arrangement with the University of Cambridge to set up a software development 'campus' along the same lines as the Microsoft complex near Seattle in the USA. The objective of the firm is not simply to develop the latest version of Windows or whatever, but to develop computing concepts for the next decade which most people would not even be able to understand at present. Microsoft are thus thinking strategically and have based their investment decision on the best information available.

Many small firms could increase their marketing capability if they were to make full use of the information at their disposal. Such a system need not cost a lot. As we discuss later, much valuable information is generated every day in the course of a firm carrying out its business activities and more information can be collected externally with little cost and effort and without the necessity of employing marketing research procedures. Marketing research can also be carried out by smaller firms with a limited budget. Few small firms make the best use of marketing information so that those that do can gain a significant competitive advantage.

▐▐▐ Vignette 5.1

CACI Limited offer InSite, the geographical information system for marketing professionals.

CACI Limited, based in London and Edinburgh, is an international leader in micromarketing, direct marketing and information systems development. Founded in 1975 in the UK, CACI Limited employs over 300 staff in four offices and has an annual turnover in excess of £31 million. It is a wholly owned subsidiary of CACI International Inc., famous for its ACORN (A Classification of Residential Neighbourhoods) geodemographic targeting system. CACI Marketing Systems provides the best and most current data, demographics, desktop software, segmentation, online reports, mapping and marketing analysis to many industries, non-profits and government agencies. The company has developed a new software product for the marketing profession which is basically a 'geographic information system' called InSite. InSite is a business tool designed for professionals who make decisions involving local market planning, customer or product segmentation, or the geographic distribution of services or resources. As you can imagine, such a tool will have a wide application within the marketing profession. InSite is used extensively by retail, leisure and financial organisations. It is adapted to the needs of each industry by using data sets and application modules that are appropriate for site location, network planning, customer profiling, media planning and other marketing and planning tasks. CACI's consultants use the InSite software every working day to provide a range of analysis based on geodemographic, marketing and lifestyle data unparalleled by any other organisation in the UK. This practical understanding of the use of geographic information systems is reflected in the attention paid to applications, implementation and support.

▶▶ Components of the MkIS

Kotler (1997) suggests that an MkIS should be made up of four separate but interrelated parts. Three of these component parts or 'subsystems' collect and produce information. The fourth subsystem takes information provided from the other three parts, processes and models it and carries out other procedures on the data that add value to it and enhance its value to marketing decision makers. When most people think of marketing information they think of marketing research. Formally produced marketing research information is valuable. However, marketing research is not the only form or source of marketing information. The modern firm needs to gather information from whatever sources it can and process and make effective use of it. The MkIS will ideally carry out all of these information functions in a systematic and planned manner. The concept of an integrated marketing information system is shown in Figure 5.1.

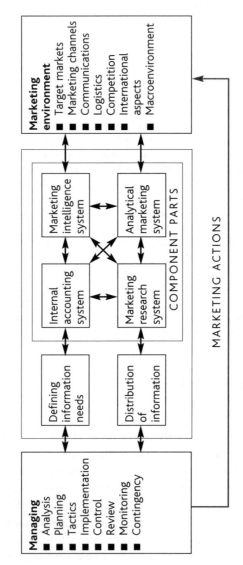

Figure 5.1 A marketing information system

▶ Internal accounting system

Firms generate data as part of the general process of carrying out business. The generation, recording, storage and retrieval of data is referred to as the 'internal accounting system' of the firm. The term evokes thoughts of financial and cost accounting information. Actually it refers to all information received and generated by the firm. Perhaps a better name for this system would be the 'internal documentary system' of the firm as this describes it more accurately. Firms tend to use standard commercial forms and documents that are universally recognised and understood by people in other businesses. Such standard business forms and documents are available from business stationers and the firm then has its name and logo printed on the form. These internally generated documents are usually in the form of multi-copies. A copy is sent to the customer and other copies are stored in various parts of the documentary system of the firm such as the accounts department and the sales office. In larger companies accounts have to be audited under the Companies Act and management is required to store copies of all incoming and internally generated commercial forms and documents for a period of six years.

Internally generated and data inwardly received comes in many forms. For example purchase orders are received by the firm from customers. Delivery notes are generated by a firm and signed by the customer on delivery. The time between the dates on the two documents gives the total order processing time. This can be monitored to make sure predetermined service delivery levels are being adhered to. When defective goods are returned to the marketing firm for whatever reason, a goods return slip is usually generated. Again, this document can be used to monitor quality performance of either internally manufactured goods or goods bought in from other suppliers. The total number of goods returned or total number of complaints about goods as a percentage of goods sold provides a measure of performance. Sales force expenses as a percentage of sales, number of telephone enquiries converted into sales, orders for particular products that might indicate seasonal or cyclical demand are all illustrations of the kind of data that is included under this heading. The uses to which internally generated and internally received data can be put for marketing planning, monitoring and control purposes are numerous. A few examples are mentioned above and more are given in the next section when we discuss collecting data internally for sales forecasting purposes.

The important thing for the management of marketing firms to realise is that information is available and can be retrieved from within the 'internal accounting' system of the firm with a little effort and at little cost. Many firms have a wide variety of valuable marketing information that is under-utilised. It is not enough simply to know that such data exists; for it to be of practical value as a planning, monitoring and control resource, management needs to know how to use it effectively. The value of any data set can be significantly enhanced by applying certain analytical techniques and procedures. This is discussed in more detail later.

▶ The marketing intelligence system

We saw in the previous section that firms produce a wealth of information internally through the process of managing and administering their business. Apart from the official purposes for which such information was generated, for example sending out invoices, auditing and so on, it often remains a neglected marketing resource. There are other information sources that are often under-utilised by marketing management. The type of information we refer to is not formally collected marketing research information, but that which is collected in an ad hoc manner. The system that attempts to collect, collate and manage this source of 'loosely' collected information is referred to as the 'marketing intelligence system'. Kotler (1997) defines the marketing intelligence system as follows:

> A Marketing Intelligence System is a set of procedures and sources used by managers to obtain their everyday information about pertinent developments in the marketing environment. (p. 112)

In the course of carrying out business for the firm, members of staff come across potentially valuable and interesting information. In many firms such information is thought to be of little consequence. Often the people who might have access to such information may be of a lower working status within the firm. They do not think that what they have to say would be of interest to management. Unfortunately, management is often to blame because of their condescending attitude.

Members of the sales force confer with customers on a daily basis. It is their business to keep informed of what is 'going on' in terms of developments in the market, competitors' products, prices and concessions in terms of customers and future customers and their future purchasing plans. Salespeople attend conferences and courses. They staff

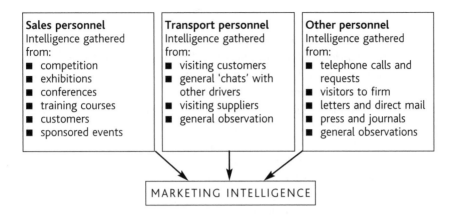

Sales personnel Intelligence gathered from:	Transport personnel Intelligence gathered from:	Other personnel Intelligence gathered from:
■ competition ■ exhibitions ■ conferences ■ training courses ■ customers ■ sponsored events	■ visiting customers ■ general 'chats' with other drivers ■ visiting suppliers ■ general observation	■ telephone calls and requests ■ visitors to firm ■ letters and direct mail ■ press and journals ■ general observations

MARKETING INTELLIGENCE

Figure 5.2 The marketing intelligence system as
a subsystem of the overall MkIS

stands at trade shows and exhibitions, attend sponsored events and assist with hospitality. It is their business to network effectively with other salespeople within the industry and attempt to keep abreast of changes and capitalise on opportunities that present themselves. Salespeople possess a wealth of marketing intelligence gathered during the course of their job, but not many firms make full use of this potentially valuable and important source of commercial intelligence. The use of sales personnel to collect and supply marketing intelligence is but one example of the type of information that can make up the firm's marketing intelligence system. Delivery drivers, receptionists, maintenance engineers and many others come into contact with suppliers and customers during the course of their work and all have the potential to contribute to the marketing intelligence part of the firm's MkIS.

Figure 5.2 shows the component parts of a company's marketing intelligence system.

▶ The marketing research system

Marketing research is discussed separately and in more depth in Chapter 6 and only a summary of the subject is presented here. This is the final input to the marketing information system, the other component part, as we see in the next section, produces output. The marketing research system makes use of both secondary data (data already in existence) and primary data (data collected for a specific piece of research for the first time).

Secondary data

Secondary data can come from many sources. For example, college and university libraries contain much secondary data in the form of past business dissertations. Secondary data includes a range of official governmental sources collected under the direction of the Central Statistical Office. This data is collected on a regular basis to assist various governmental departments and agencies make better and more effective decisions on matters concerning social and economic policy. Such data is not collected to help marketing researchers directly. Some of the surveys commissioned by the Central Statistical Office are very costly. The Census of Populations surveys every household in the country every ten years, the last one being in 2001, with inter-census samples between the main census. The Census of Production surveys every firm over a certain size in the country on an annual basis. Such information can be purchased from The Stationary Office quite economically and much is available free of charge in the larger public libraries. Secondary data comes in the form of 'multi-user reports' such as Keynote or Mintel publications. These publications usually cover one industry in the case of Keynote, or four or five product areas as with Mintel. Mintel also provide in-depth special reports on particular industries.

Academic books and journals are another source of secondary material. Most major newspapers are kept in libraries on microfiche or compact disc and many have good sections on markets and general business and economic topics. Company reports and abstracted company data are kept on Extel and McCarthy systems usually on compact disc for use with a computerised retrieval system.

Primary data

Primary data collection takes four forms:

(i) *Interviews* – usually qualitative and exploratory in nature. Depth interviews, where respondents are interviewed 'in depth' individually, and group discussions, where 8 to 12 people are interviewed in a group setting, are common in this type of data collection. Depth interviews and group discussions can be totally exploratory and unstructured; semi-structured in as far as the interviewer (or moderator in group discussions) has at least some idea of the question areas to be covered in the interview session; or structured. Structured interviews are not meant to be formal 'question and answer sessions' and they still retain the flexibility common to qualitative research approaches, however, they are conducted by means of an interview schedule and devices like attitudinal rating cards or the use of projective techniques such as sentence completion tests are administered during the interview. Depth interviews and group discussions are often used at the start of the research process in an 'exploratory' context. Results are not intended to be conclusive; indeed depth interviews and group discussions are usually conducted with small samples of respondents and results are from too small a sample to have statistical validity. Interviews like these are often used to 'get a feel' for the research situation. The techniques are versatile and can be used during, or even after, the main research has been conducted, sometimes to go back and qualify or clarify certain points. Such techniques are discussed in more detail in the next chapter.

(ii) *Observation* – can include human observation and the use of devices such as cameras, tape recorders and so on. Some marketing research firms specialise in 'audit' type research and these are forms of observational techniques. The retail audit is a research process that monitors sales and other related information, such as price, of a wide range of products within stores. Manufacturers of such products pay the auditing company to 'track' the sales of their own products and collect information on competitors' products. The consumer panel is similar to the retail audit except that brand purchase is monitored or 'audited' in people's homes. For both retail audits and consumer panels, use is made of modern information technology in the form of bar-code readers and computer modems, to both record and transmit information to the research company.

Observation can involve devices observing things, such as a video camera observing traffic passing a potential retail site or an electrode on the road counting traffic to ascertain the price that can be charged for poster site rentals. It can involve devices observing people using cameras and tape recorders or even turnstiles monitoring or counting people as they move around a store. It can involve people observing things, such as a quality control inspector observing a production process. It can involve people observing people such as an undercover store detective. The same principle is used in marketing research in the form of 'mystery shoppers' who visit stores in the guise of ordinary shoppers to check out prices, service and so on. Observation is a particularly important marketing research technique and is often used in conjunction with other methods. It is valuable in research situations when it is difficult to ask questions, for example when researching the behaviour of small children or animals, such as cats and dogs, in order to develop a new baby food or pet food.

(iii) *Surveys* – usually involve a questionnaire to collect the information. These come in many different forms and can be administered in different ways. Many questionnaires are sent by post for self-completion. Sometimes interviewers call on households or hold interviews in the street or shopping mall (sometimes termed 'mall intercepts'). Questionnaires are sent by post, fax and, increasingly, by Internet. Questionnaires are used to collect more quantitative information than information obtained from depth interviews or observational methods. This data is coded and processed using a data analysis package. Whatever the purpose of the research survey and the nature of the organisation conducting the research, the principles of survey and questionnaire design are the same. These are explained in more depth in the next chapter.

(iv) *Experimentation* – can be used in a 'laboratory' or a field setting. In a 'laboratory setting' experiments are easier for the researcher to control, for example under artificially controlled conditions the researcher can take into account outside influences that might affect experimental results. A 'blind' paired comparison test into the texture or taste of competing food products, such as canned ham, is an example. Factors that might influence consumer preferences, such as knowing the brand name or the price or having seen advertising, can be eliminated from the experiment or statistically accounted for in the test results. When we say 'laboratory' we do not mean it in the same way as physicists mean laboratory, although some marketing experiments involving recall or measurement of certain physical parameters such as blood pressure or heart rate may well be conducted in such a place. These 'lab' experiments in marketing are often carried out in market halls or other venues in the centre of towns and are often referred to as 'hall tests'.

The problem with laboratory type experiments is that although they are easier to design, set up and conduct than field experiments, results from such tests may have little validity in the 'real' world. Laboratory experiments, by their nature, are often undertaken in heavily controlled artificial environments. What a person remembers about an advertisement they have been shown under controlled conditions may not necessarily be the same as what they are able to recall in a busy high street on the way from work. Because of this, laboratory experiments are said to have high levels of 'internal validity' but low levels of 'external validity'.

As the name suggests, field experiments are undertaken in the real world, rather than in a controlled artificial laboratory environment. The best example of a field experiment is a 'test market'.

Here, a certain area of the country is chosen for the test. This area has to be representative of the wider market for it to have validity, or at least any differences must be taken into account statistically. Television areas are often chosen because there is a great deal of demographic and other secondary data already available to the researcher by TV region. A control area is also chosen as a 'benchmark' so the researcher can see what is happening in the overall market that is unconnected to the test variables. New products, new packs, promotions, advertising and other marketing 'tools' can be tested in a limited 'test market' environment so that problems can be identified and put right prior to going national with a product launch or advertising campaign. Because test market operations take place in a 'real world' setting they are difficult to control. The dynamic and often chaotic nature of the real world makes it difficult to measure test results and separate them from what is happening irrespective of the test, although proper use of a control group can reduce this problem. Because of these problems field experiments are said to have a high degree of external validity, but a low level of internal validity.

▶ The analytical marketing system

This subsystem of the MkIS does not produce new data. Rather it takes data from the other three component parts of the system as data input to enhance its value. Users of the system are able to do this by applying what are termed 'management science' techniques to the data, thereby transforming it into a form that makes it more easily understood and valuable to marketing decision makers. The ultimate goal is to prepare a marketing plan which is part of the overall corporate plan and these issues are dealt with in Chapter 15.

Management science or operational research is a detailed subject, but the following headings are meant to provide a general 'feel' for this subject area:

▶ *Simulation:* Marketers often want to know what likely problems may occur in a given situation without having to experience the situation in 'real life'. It is possible to simulate many marketing situations using statistical or mathematical techniques. For example 'queuing theory' can be used to predict the effects of bottlenecks in the 'flow' of customers within a hypermarket. Markov chains, sometimes referred to as 'brand switching matrices' can be used to simulate competitive response to a price cut or promotion and the effects on relative brand shares using probability to predict brand-switching behaviour.

▶ *Optimisation:* Linear programming can be used to calculate optimum levels of output, marketing mix elements, and so on. Marginal analysis, making use of differential and integral calculus, can assist management in making similar decisions, particularly the optimisation of the overall marketing mix.

▶ *Forecasting:* This is covered in more depth later in this chapter, so only a brief mention of techniques is given. Information collected from formal marketing research and marketing intelligence gathering of internally generated information can be used as input data in a variety of forecasting models. Data collected over a period of time can be extrapolated into the future by using time series techniques. The use of such techniques allows the manager to model seasonality and cyclical effects. Trend fitting, using a mathematical function of known 'curves' can also be used to forecast sales and model likely future product life cycles. Linear and multiple regression are more sophisticated forecasting techniques that make use of 'econometrics'.

▶ *Hypothesis testing:* In many marketing situations, particularly marketing experiments, managers have certain hypotheses or strong ideas that they want to test scientifically. Methods such as chi square and analysis of variance allow scientific testing of relative differences in the effectiveness of marketing variables.

The techniques discussed are just some of those available to marketing scientists to enable them to enhance the value of marketing information. They convey the general principles of what goes on within the analytical marketing system. A diagrammatic representation of such a system is shown in Figure 5.3.

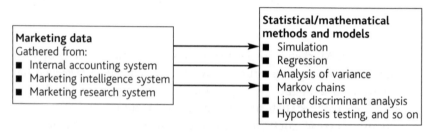

Figure 5.3 Analytical marketing system

Can salespeople provide management with useful marketing intelligence?

Salespeople basically work for the firm in order to sell and their primary skill is applying sales techniques. Often the remuneration package offered to the sales force by management is loaded towards earned commission. If salespersons do not sell they do not earn commission. Salespeople on such terms tend to be more concerned with selling and have little time for anything else, and this tends to concentrate their minds.

Hence it is not that salespeople are incapable of providing useful marketing intelligence, but rather a question of whether they have the time to do so. If they are expected to adopt this expanded role and provide management with such intelligence then they must be given time to do so. The pressure to sell must, to a certain extent, be lessened. Providing such intelligence must be built in to their remuneration package.

Salespeople are 'in the front line'. They come into contact with customers and salespeople from competing firms. They are active performers in the marketplace. They have the opportunity to collect much valuable marketing intelligence and they must be given the encouragement, time and financial incentive to do so.

▶▶ Designing, implementing and controlling the MkIS

▶ Design

An MkIS is intended to aid marketing decision making and, to ensure that the system meets the needs of users, attention must be paid to its design. Organisations differ in their information requirements and ways of doing things. The MkIS must be designed to fit the way marketing personnel go about their daily activities. Access and use of the system must be as easy and natural to potential users as the use of a telephone.

The first step in the design process is to conduct an analysis of how people do their jobs and how they pass on the results of their work in the form of information. This process is called a 'systems analysis'. After this, an 'information audit' is required to find out what information each member of the marketing team requires in order to carry out their job effectively. When these exercises have been carried out and results analysed, management will be in a better position to design an effective system.

▶ Implementation

New ideas, new procedures and even new managers are often met with a certain amount of suspicion and scepticism. Before a new system is implemented, staff should have the nature and the purpose of the new system explained to them. It should be emphasised that the system will improve job efficiency, increase staff productivity and make working life better. Some will have fears about the impact of the new system on job security. It should be fully explained that the system is there for the benefit of all and is not intended to replace anybody. Staff training should take place before the system comes into use. Clearly, some staff will cope and some will not, and this will undoubtedly foment distrust and resistance towards the new system. The new system should have the support of top management, otherwise it will be regarded as the latest management fad, not to be taken seriously. There will probably be initial teething problems, so patience will be required.

▶ Control

As mentioned earlier, there is a tendency to regard any new system with a degree of suspicion. It means yet more demands on time, more bureaucracy and form filling. Many feel that if they let the new system die a natural death people will forget it and things will revert back to normal. For the new system to survive, someone must be given authority and responsibility for its up-keep and management. A manager should be responsible for the MkIS to ensure that proper procedures are followed and that correct information is produced and distributed. This manager should be stationed at an 'information centre' that acts as the hub for the whole system. This can be an office or simply a desk within an office. The important thing is that the management and up-keep of the system is not left to chance, but that there is someone with responsibility and authority to keep the system working.

▶▶ Cost/benefit aspects of MkIS

The MkIS should have been designed to produce information that is relevant, pertinent and useful to users of the system in terms of assisting them in improving their marketing decision-making. In fact, the rationale for a firm adopting a formally designed MkIS is that the system helps members of the marketing team make better decisions and to make them faster. Management do not want to go to the expense and trouble of designing and implementing an MkIS to simply make the firm look as if it is up to date in adopting the latest marketing ideas. Such a system is only needed if it directly or indirectly generates a financial return.

Information, like any other product has a marginal cost and a marginal value. Theoretically, the marketing firm should continue to collect and store information up to the point where the marginal cost of information equals marginal value. We say 'theoretically' because in reality it would be difficult to calculate the cost and revenue functions of marketing information, and certainly difficult to work out the marginal value of an additional piece of information. Working out the marginal cost of collecting, processing and storing an additional piece of information would be less difficult. The principle of applying marginal analysis to marketing information is shown in Figure 5.4.

Looking at Figure 5.4(a) it can be seen that the firm is collecting $X1$ amount of information and the marginal cost, $C1$, of collecting this amount of information is greater than the marginal value, $V1$. Hence the firm is experiencing negative net value at the margin. The value of an additional piece of information is less than the cost of providing it. In Figure 5.4(b) we see the opposite situation. The firm is collecting $X2$ amount of information. At this level, the marginal cost is $C2$, which is

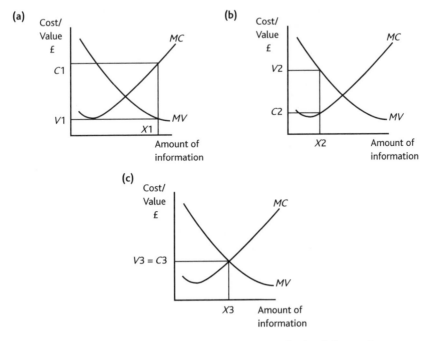

Figure 5.4 Applying marginal analysis to marketing information

well below the marginal value $V2$, so it would pay the firm to go on collecting information as they are experiencing positive returns from its collection, albeit at a diminishing rate. In the final diagram, Figure 5.4(c) it can be seen that at the information level $X3$ the marginal cost $C3$ is just equal to the marginal value $V3$. At this point the value of collecting marketing information is maximised, and hence this is the optimal level of data from a cost/value point of view.

Explain the terms 'information audit' and 'systems analysis' in the context of planning an MkIS.

An MkIS is not intended to produce information for its own sake. It is not simply information that marketing staff would like to have, but it is pertinent information. In designing the system, attention should be paid to establishing the type and amount of information users of the system require in order to perform their marketing functions as efficiently as possible. A survey could be carried out with questionnaires being sent to each staff member asking about their information needs. This might be followed up by individual interviews or group sessions. This process audits what information is being used at the present time and identifies how information acquisition, storage and dissemination amongst staff might be improved. This is what is meant by the 'information audit'.

The administrative systems of marketing departments vary among different organisations. There will be similarities, but generally the way a marketing department arranges and carries out various tasks is likely to differ from firm to firm and will be influenced by many factors including:

The type of industry the firm is in, the size of the firm, whether it markets products or services or both, whether it is involved internationally, whether it is involved in the marketing of consumer goods and/or services or whether it is involved in industrial or business-to-business marketing activities.

Because the process of marketing differs to some extent between organisations, it stands to reason that the kind of marketing information system required by firms will also differ. In order that management can design an effective MkIS it will have to be done on an individual basis. There are general principles that must be followed. To do this management will have to have a good understanding of marketing processes and procedures used by staff within the firm. The MkIS can then be designed to reflect the way marketing operations and procedures are undertaken within the firm. It is this process that is referred to as 'systems analysis'.

▶▶ Forecasting

Managerial decision making involves forecasting future conditions and these tend to be long term and strategic in nature rather than operational. Forecasting information helps management to make operational decisions that take up a lot of time. It is frequently said that forecasting is the key to success, and poor forecasting can lead to high inventories and associated costs that use up working capital, or result in underproduction and unrealised market potential.

Forecasting is important in most areas of the firm, but forecasting of sales is particularly important since predicted sales are the base on which all company plans are built. There are several methods available to the forecaster: subjective or objective methods or a combination of the two (for example Bayesian forecasting).

Do you agree with the idea that producing accurate sales forecasts is essential in a well-structured marketing organisation?

Marketing management requires sales forecasting information in order to plan and make informed and effective decisions about the future. Much of a manager's time is concerned with making decisions in the present to do with the future with little to guide him or her except what has happened in the past. Hence in most decision making we are forced to 'take a position' on likely future events. We use forecasts every day, but whether we call them 'forecasts' is another matter.

Marketing or sales managers, out of practical necessity, also have to predict future conditions especially, in their cases, the position regarding future sales. They need accurate sales forecasts to make a wide variety of decisions for different points in time. For example, in marketing short-term sales forecasts are required for products in order to plan total promotional effort and sales strategies. Such forecasts define the primary targets that the selling operation must achieve and provide the generating force behind the managerial process of objective setting, planning, organising and coordinating. The sales budget and individual salesperson quotas are derived from short-term forecasts that serve as immediate planning tools in the setting of short-term objectives and in scheduling resources within the marketing department. Short-term sales forecasting has been used here by way of illustration. Management also requires forecasting information to make medium- and long-term decisions.

▶ Forecasting terminology

In many texts the term 'forecast' refers to objective, quantitative techniques and 'predict' denotes subjective estimates. In this chapter the terms 'subjective' and 'objective' forecast are used.

The development of a forecasting system requires a considerable amount of data to be collected and analysed for usefulness and validity. The company's ability to acquire relevant data influences which of the wide choice of forecasting techniques should be used, and a forecast will only be as good as the data used in its compilation.

▶ Data collection

There are two main categories of existing data:

1. *Internal data* generated within the company, for example previous company plans, sales statistics and other internal records.
2. *Secondary data* from external sources, for example government and trade statistics and published marketing research surveys.

Most forecasting situations use both sources. Data can also be generated expressly for the forecasting task using marketing research, for example a sample survey. This is an expensive way of collecting data and existing data should be examined first as this may be sufficient.

▶ Internal data sources

Internal documentation and records are valuable sources of information, especially in the case of immediate and short-term forecasting. There are questions that can only be answered by a close examination of a company's own data which is routinely collected, recorded and stored.

The most useful and economic source of internal data is 'desk research' that should form the starting point for data collection in any forecasting exercise. The accuracy of such data should be validated, but sometimes it is difficult for the forecaster to obtain information due to inflexibility of the system or lack of cooperation from departmental staff. To succeed in obtaining appropriate internal data the forecaster must know the firm and its staff well and must have authority from top management to encourage full cooperation.

The forecaster should take a systems analysis approach, looking carefully at what records are kept and how data is obtained, altered, processed and circulated throughout the firm and record every document, as well as noting the type of document, the function it serves, its origin and destination. Most company systems start with an inquiry from a customer and end with a customer invoice. A picture must be built up of the overall system from members of staff to the total departmental system and ultimately the company as a whole. 'Unofficial' records kept by members of staff for their own use are often very useful to a forecaster and these might only come to light after a careful search.

▶ Data from the sales department

The sales department is where the company and customers interact and it provides a great deal of information:

1. *Sales volume by product and by product group:* These combine to give total sales volume, but also show each product or product group in the overall mix in terms of its contribution to total volume.
2. *Sales volume by area:* Either salespersons' territories, standard media areas as used by the Joint Industry Committee for Television Advertising Research (JICTAR) or other geographical areas.
3. *Sales volumes by market segment:* Segmentation may be regional or, in industrial markets, by type of industry. This will show which segments are likely to remain static, which are declining and which show growth possibilities. Where the company deals with a small number of large companies, segmentation may be by customer, and changes in demand from any of these may be important when forecasting sales and material requirements.
4. *Sales volume by type of channel of distribution:* In a firm that has a multi-channel distribution policy, the effectiveness and profitability of each channel can be calculated. It also allows for trends in patterns of distribution to be identified and used when forecasting future channel requirements. Channel information by geographical area may show a difference in the profitability between various types of channel in different parts of the country, allowing for profitable geographical channel differentiation. A more realistic forecast can be developed from information gathered by type of retail outlet, agents, wholesalers, distributors and factors, revealing promising channel opportunities and resulting in more effective channel management.
5. *Sales volume over time:* This reveals actual sales and units sold and allows for seasonal variations, inflation and price adjustments.

6. *Pricing information:* The effects of price increases and decreases can be established through historical information, giving an opportunity to forecast effects of future changes.
7. *Communication mix information:* The effects of previous advertising campaigns, sponsorship, direct mail programmes or exhibitions can be evaluated, as can the effects of various levels of expenditure in marketing communications, giving a guide to future effectiveness.
8. *Sales promotional data:* This allows assessment of past promotional campaigns in terms of their individual effects on sales.
9. *Sales representatives' records and reports:* Customer files kept by sales representatives contain detailed information on live customers such as company information, likely future requirements and so on. Reports made to the sales office contain much information that is useful to a forecaster.
10. *Enquiries received and quotations sent:* Written and verbal enquiries from customers leading to a detailed quotation being submitted provide information that is useful to the forecaster. This is especially so if patterns can be established in percentages of enquiries that are followed by orders and the time that elapses between quotation and order. Numbers of quotations converted into orders indicates the firm's market share.

▶ Data from other departments

Accounts department

Accurate cost data is available from the management accountant, and previous management reports are a useful source of information on such matters as:

- Number of new customers in a given period
- Number of withdrawals
- Number of items sold by product in volume and monetary terms
- Total sales by salesperson, area, division and so on.

Production capacity can be forecast using information on staff that is given in management accounting reports, including absenteeism. Historical information can be obtained from past budgets with variance analysis showing budgeted figures against actual figures. Information such as orders received, despatched and on hand should be accessible in the accounts department.

Purchasing department
Useful information to be gathered here includes previous purchase orders, material lists, requisitions, material status schedule reports, information on suppliers and stock control data relating to reorder levels, buffer and safety stock levels, economic order quantities and stockturn of inventory.

Despatch department
Here the forecaster can find chronological information on what goods were despatched and by which method of transport, including copies of advice notes and other delivery documents.

Production department
Works orders, material lists, design information, order completion dates and much other information can be obtained from this source.

Departmental plans
Activity and changes in company policy or methods of operation already planned could have significant bearing on a forecast. For example, plans to expand the sales department or increase promotional activity will affect a sales forecast.

In addition to these sources of information, departments such as personnel and research and development can provide useful information; the choice of sources will depend on the type of forecast required.

▶▶ Forecasting methods I: subjective methods

These are *qualitative* techniques relying on human judgement rather than numerical computation. They are sometimes known as *intuitive* or *judgmental techniques* using experience and judgement.

▶ Executive opinion (or jury) method and sales force composite method

The sales or marketing manager makes an informed subjective forecast that is then discussed with executives from production, finance and other departments, who deliver a 'verdict' on the forecast. Thus the forecast is based on the collective experience of the group. The sales force composite method is also included here and this is when the sales manager does a similar exercise in consultation with individual members of the sales team.

Advantages

▶ The sales forecast is put together by people with many years' experience in a particular industry.

▶ The final forecast is based on the collective experience of a group, rather than the opinion of a single executive.

▶ As the forecast is based on a consensus opinion, variations in individual subjective estimates are eliminated.

▶ Because of the status of the contributing panel, figures are viewed as having a high source credibility by people using the information.

Disadvantages

▶ Possible production of a pessimistic forecast by sales personnel when sales quotas or targets are linked to payments of bonus or commission in order to boost earnings.

▶ Forecasts based on guesswork because of salespeople not having enough time to devote to producing them. The salesperson's expanded role leaves little time for forecasting activity, especially when a large number of product forecasts are required on a regular basis.

▌▌▌ Vignette 5.2

Top qualitative forecasting team predicted 'official' economic recession in the USA.

Qualitative forecasting techniques are used not only in industry but also by official government departments and committees involved in the forecasting of macroeconomic conditions. The USA demonstrated evidence of economic slow down throughout 2001 and many were fearful of a recession. However, consumer spending continued to support the economy even though the high technology sector seemed to fall from grace on the nation's NASDAQ and Dow Jones stock market indices. The business-cycle dating committee of the National Bureau of Economic Research (NBER) is a qualitative forecasting panel made up of academic economists. During the latter part of 2001 the committee had been weighing the possibility of officially declaring that the US had entered its first recession for a decade. NBER is the non-partisan body that traditionally sets official US recession dates. The six members of the business-cycle dating committee are chairman Robert Hall of Stanford University; Martin Feldstein, former Reagan economic adviser, Harvard University professor and president of the NBER; Jeffrey Frankel, also of Harvard; Ben Bernanke of Princeton University; Robert Gordon of Northwestern University; and Victor Zarnowitz, professor emeritus of the University of Chicago and a member of the Conference Board, a New York business research group. The panel makes use of secondary data sources, which may be survey and other quantitative data. However the dating and timing of an official recession by the panel is based upon a qualitative consensus of all the members present after having considered the available evidence and using their own considerable experience in macroeconomic matters. In November 2001 the panel finally came to a decision that the USA entered a formal recession in May 2001.

▶ Customer-use projections

Survey techniques such as market research surveys or simply conversations between sales representatives and existing and potential customers, can make clear purchase intentions of customers and/or users. Test marketing, in a small representative area, is also used to produce forecasts and is similar to surveys. This method uses survey techniques to ascertain purchase intentions of customers and/or users. Such surveys range from a sales representative talking to existing and potential customers and reporting back to head office, to more formal market research surveys. In consumer markets, where the population is often large, a sample survey is usually undertaken. Such a survey can be at two levels: the customer's intention to buy; or the distributive intermediary's intention to stock and promote the product(s). In industrial markets, where the number of customers may be relatively few, sampling may not be necessary. This method is seldom used on its own, but more often in conjunction with other forecasting methods. Test marketing is also used to produce forecasts and is similar to surveys. A small representative area is used and the results form the basis of a forecast. Pat Seelig (1989) proposes using simulated test marketing that is, a test market in a laboratory.

Advantages
- ▶ Prospective purchasers provide information on what, and how much, they are likely to buy in the future.
- ▶ Information is elicited with the use of proven marketing research methodology such as sample surveys, projective techniques and questionnaires.
- ▶ Production of sales forecasts can be subcontracted to professional market research agencies, particularly useful when time is short.

Disadvantages
- ▶ Sample surveys are expensive and time-consuming, and not suited to producing forecasts on a regular basis.
- ▶ There may be variance between what respondents say they are going to purchase and their actual purchases.

▶ There is a limit to how often the same people (for example a company's purchasing manager) can be approached.

It appears from evidence that the jury of executive opinion and sales force composite methods have greater application than customer-use projections, particularly in industrial markets where a close relationship exists between suppliers and customers.

▶▶ Forecasting methods II: objective methods

Objective methods of forecasting are 'statistical' or 'mathematical' in nature. Historical data is analysed to identify a pattern or relationship between variables and this pattern is extended or extrapolated into the future to make a forecast. Objective methods can be classified by considering the underlying models involved. They fall into two categories: 'time series models' and 'causal models'.

▶ Time series models

Time series analysis uses the historical series of one variable to develop a model for predicting future values. The forecasting situation is treated like a 'black box', with no attempt made to discover other factors that might affect its behaviour. According to Ledbetter and Cox (1977) time series methods are used extensively in industry for many applications including short-term sales forecasting and stack control procedures involving forecasting the demand for components and other stock items. As Reynolds and Greatorex (1988) state, because time series models treat the variable to be forecast as a function of time, they are useful when other conditions are expected to remain constant, most likely true of the short-term rather than the long-term future. Such methods are particularly suited to short-term, operational, routine forecasting, usually up to six months or one year ahead of current time.

Time series methods are not very useful when there is no discernible pattern of demand. Their purpose is to identify patterns in historical data, model these and extrapolate them into the future. Such methods are unlikely to be successful in forecasting future demand when the historical time series is erratic. Because it is assumed that future demand is a function of time, causal factors cannot be taken into consideration. For example, such models would not be able to incorporate the impact of changes in management policy.

▶ Causal models

Causal models exploit the relationship between the time series of the variable being examined and one or more other time series. If other variables are found to correlate with the variable of interest, a causal model can be constructed incorporating coefficients that give relative strengths of the various causal factors. For example, the sales of a product may be related to its price, advertising expenditure and the price of competitors' products. If the forecaster can estimate the relationship between sales and independent variables, then the forecast values of independent variables can be used to predict future values of the dependent variable (in this case sales).

Such techniques are epitomised by two simpler models, 'moving averages' and 'exponential smoothing' that are now discussed. Other, more sophisticated, time series models include 'decomposition models' and 'auto-regressive moving averages' (Box-Jenkins) techniques.

 **Vignette 5.3**

BFS Inc. of Massachusetts, USA, market 'Forecast Pro' the professional quantitative forecasting package for industry.

Many firms avoid using sophisticated quantitative forecasting procedures because they require a particular statistical skill, which the management of many firms do not possess. Small firms in particular lack the necessary expertise and time to carry out quantitative forecasting procedures. Now there is a piece of software on the market to enable any manager with reasonable quantitative skills, but not necessarily expertise in forecasting, to produce professional quantitative forecasts. Forecast Pro is the leading forecasting software for professionals in sales, marketing, finance and manufacturing. Forecast Pro uses proven statistical forecasting methods, coupled with a powerful expert system, to bring users unsurpassed forecasting accuracy with the minimum of technical fuss. Whether the user is forecasting sales, revenues, demand for service or any other important variable, Forecast Pro will make the task work easier, quicker and more accurate. Many software experts agree that Forecast Pro is an impressive piece of software. For example *PC Magazine* said that 'Forecast Pro is an effective tool that will save you time, improve the accuracy of your forecasts, and educate you on the nature of times series data. Forecast pro is a winning package'. It would seem that many agree that Forecast Pro, marketed by Business Forecast Systems (BFS) of Belmont, Massachusetts, USA, strikes a good balance between ease of use features that a novice forecaster needs and the power and flexibility that an experienced forecaster requires.

▶ Example of objective methods (moving averages)

Coverage of the technical aspects of exponential smoothing and causal techniques are covered in more specialist texts on forecasting. What we have provided is an example of one of the more simple objective techniques, moving averages. This is to illustrate what we mean by 'objective methods of forecasting'.

Simple moving average (time series)
The simple moving or 'rolling' average is a useful and uncomplicated method of forecasting the average expected value of a time series. The process uses the average individual forecasts (F) and demand values (X) over the past n time periods.

   A suffix notation is used, which may seem complicated, but is quite simple: the present is referred to as time t and one period into the future by $t + 1$, one period into the past by $t - 1$, two periods by $t - 2$, and so on. This is best appreciated with reference to a time diagram:

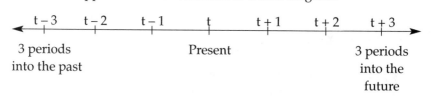

The simple moving average process is defined by the equation:

$$F_{t+1} = F_t + \frac{1}{n}(X_t - X_{t-n})$$

where F_{t+1} is the forecast for one period ahead, F_t is the forecast made last time period for the present period, n is the number of time periods, X_t is the actual demand at present time, and X_{t-n} is the actual demand for period $t - n$.

Weighted average
The simple moving average has the disadvantage that all data in the average is given equal weighting, that is:

$$\frac{1}{n}$$

More recent data may be more important than older data, particularly if the underlying pattern of the data has been changing, and, therefore, should be given a greater weight. To overcome this problem and increase the sensitivity of the moving average, it is possible to use weighted averages, with the sum of the weights equal to unity, in order to produce a true average. In decimal form a weighted moving average can be expressed as:

$$F_{t+1} = 0.4X_t + 0.3X_{t-1} + 0.2X_{t-2} + 0.1X_{t-3}$$

(Notation as defined for the simple moving average).
Problems common to all moving average procedures remain, the major ones being:

1. No forecast can be made until n time periods have passed, because it is necessary to have values available for the previous $n - 1$ periods.
2. The sensitivity or speed of response of moving average procedures is inversely proportional to the number of periods n included in the average. To change the sensitivity, it is necessary to change the value of n which creates problems of continuity and additional work.

The methods of simple and weighted moving averages discussed so far are only suitable for reasonably constant (stationary) data; they are unable to deal with a significant trend. An example of a 'stationary time series' is shown in Figure 5.5. It can be seen from the graph that over a period of nine months the time series fluctuates randomly about a mean value of 200 units that is not increasing or decreasing significantly over time.

In the time series shown in Figure 5.6, the underlying mean value of the series is not stationary. If a 'line of best fit' is drawn through all of the points, it can be seen that while the actual values are fluctuating randomly, the underlying mean value is following a rising linear trend.

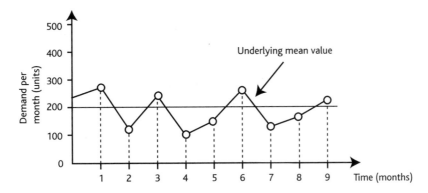

Figure 5.5 Example of a stationary time series

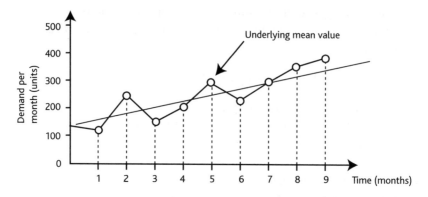

Figure 5.6 Example of a time series with a linear underlying trend

Double (linear) moving average

A method of moving averages designed for a reasonably stationary time series cannot accommodate a series with a linear trend. In such situations forecasts tend to lag behind the actual time series, resulting in systematic errors. To counter such error factors, the method of *double (or linear) moving averages* has been developed. This method calculates a second (or double) moving average that is a moving average of the first one. The basis of the principle is that a single moving average MA'_t will lag behind the actual trend series X_t and the second moving average MA''_t will lag behind MA'_t by approximately the same amount. The difference between the two moving averages is added to the single moving average MA'_t, to give the level (a_t). The difference between MA'_t and MA''_t can then be added to the level (a_t) to produce a one- or *m*-period-ahead forecast.

The double moving average procedure can be summarised as follows:

1. The use of a simple moving average at time *t* (denoted as MA'_t)
2. An adjustment, which is the difference between the simple and the double averages at time *t* $(MA'_t - MA''_t)$
3. An adjustment for trend from period *t* to period *t* + 1 (or period *t* + *m*, if the forecast is for *m* periods ahead).

The updating equations for the double moving average are as follows:
Single moving average

$$MA'_t = \frac{X_t + X_{t-1} + X_{t-2} + \ldots + X_{t-N+1}}{N}$$

Double moving average

$$MA_t'' = \frac{MA_t' + MA_{t-1}' + MA_{t-2}' + ... + MA_{t-N+1}'}{N}$$

Level component

$$a_t = MA_t' + (MA_t' - MA_t'') = 2MA_t' - MA_t''$$

Trend component

$$b_t = \frac{2}{N-1}(MA_t' - MA_t'')$$

Forecast

$$F_t + M = a_t + b_t M$$

The general principle of the double moving average is shown diagrammatically in Figure 5.7.

Although the double moving average has the advantage of being able to handle data with a trend, it has the disadvantage of requiring extra data. N data points are required to update each MA_t' and MA_t'', that is, $2N$ or twice the number required for the simple moving average must be stored. Clearly, the necessity for substantial data storage makes the double moving average less attractive in practice than other techniques that provide similar results from less data. This is particularly so if short-term forecasts are required on a routine basis (for example weekly) for a large number of items.

This discussion of sales forecasting is not an exhaustive treatment of the subject, but it gives an understanding of the main methods and techniques. More advanced techniques such as Bayesian forecasting, expo-

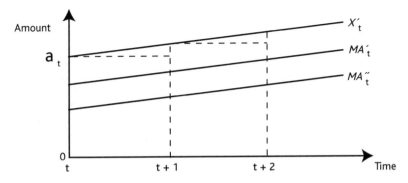

Figure 5.7 Diagrammatic representation of the principle of the double moving average

nential smoothing, multiple regression and other 'econometric' techniques are beyond the scope of this text and a more robust treatment is given in advanced specialist texts on forecasting.

Give a formal definition of a marketing information system.
A marketing information system consists of people, equipment and procedures to gather, sort, analyse, evaluate and distribute needed, timely and accurate information to marketing decision makers.

Why do firms need a formal marketing information system?
Information is the 'lifeblood' of successful marketing. Marketing, probably more than any other area of business with the possible exception of accounting and finance, depends on pertinent, up to date information in order to make effective decisions. Management of a marketing oriented firm cannot leave collection, storage, analysis and dissemination of vital information to chance. A formal system is needed to capitalise on information from a many sources, not just marketing research. Such a system goes by the name of a 'marketing information system'.

'To manage a business well is to manage its future and to manage the future is to manage information.' Do you agree or disagree with this statement?
The general business environment is dynamic and constantly in a state of change. Political, economic, social, technological and demographic factors are constantly changing. In order to keep abreast of these changes and continue to offer value to customers and shareholders a company must anticipate change and use the firm's resources to produce products and services that will be regarded as valuable in an ever-changing marketplace.

'It is not a question of whether or not marketing management will make sales forecasts in order to make decisions, merely how they will be produced.' Is this statement true?
Managers have to make decisions. The present is already with us and whilst there are some operational decisions that need to be taken now, most management decisions concern the future. This is as true of marketing as it is of any other form of management. Marketing is concerned with future demand, and this means being concerned with sales. Some form of 'position' on the level and nature of future sales must be taken. Whether marketing chooses to produce forecasts formally or informally, or use qualitative or quantitative techniques is a matter of choice. What is certain is that sales forecasts of some sort form the centre of decision making in sales and marketing.

What are the main drawbacks in using a survey of buyers' intentions to produce medium-term sales forecasts?
Intuitively, contacting a selection of customers and asking them what their purchasing plans are regarding product requirements seems sensible. The information comes not from people who are once removed, but directly from purchasers. One of the main problems is that people do not necessarily do what they say they intend to do. Business people are generally enthusiastic about their business and looking forward to future growth. They often tend to look on the optimistic side. When asked about medium-term investment and purchasing plans their reply is often based on an optimistic picture of future conditions. Consequently, what they say they are going to do and what actually happens are often different.

▶▶ Summary

This chapter has dealt with marketing information systems and some of the simpler techniques of sales forecasting. The general theme has been that in a purposeful, proactive marketing organisation the acquisition and management of information cannot be left to chance. What is required is a formal system devoted to the information needs of the organisation, that is, a marketing information system. We have examined the concept of such a system and how it can be effectively designed, established, monitored, controlled and managed. Marketing research forms part of the system, but this is part of a much wider collection of sources. We have examined these sources and the type of information available. Forecasting is the logical starting point for business planning, so if the forecast is incorrect then strategic and tactical plans will be affected. The most important link is with Chapter 15 which deals specifically with planning and control. Forecasting impinges on other areas like marketing research (Chapter 6). Indeed, marketing research provides a range of forecasting techniques such as qualitative depth interviews and group discussions. Sales forecasting is linked to marketing information systems. An information system or decision support system contributes to decisions about the future, usually made in the present and often based on information collected about the past and for this reason sales forecasting is an important function of a firm's marketing information system.

FURTHER READING

Armstrong G. and Kotler P. (2000) *Marketing: An Introduction* (5th edn), Chapter 4, 'Marketing Research and Information Systems', Prentice Hall, Englewood Cliffs, NJ.

Blythe J. (2001) *Essentials of Marketing*, Chapter 4, 'Sales Forecasting in – Segmentation, Targeting and Positioning', Pearson Education, London.

Blythe J. (2001) *Essentials of Marketing*, Chapter 5, 'Market Research,' Pearson Education, London.

Bolt G.J. (1981) *Market and Sales Forecasting: A Total Approach*, Kogan-Page, London.

Chisnall P.M. (1992) *Marketing Research* (4th edn), McGraw-Hill, Maidenhead.

Crimp M. (1992) *The Marketing Research Process*, Prentice Hall, Maidenhead.

Davies M. (1998) *Understanding Marketing*, Chapter 3, 'Marketing Research', Prentice Hall, London.

Keegan W.J. and Green M.S. (2000) *Global Marketing* (2nd edn), Chapter 6, 'Global Information Systems and Market Research', Prentice Hall, London.

Lancaster G.A. and Lomas R.A. (1985) *Forecasting for Sales and Materials Management*, Macmillan – now Palgrave Macmillan, Basingstoke.

Lancaster G.A. and Reynolds P.L. (1999) *Introduction to Marketing: A Step-by-Step Guide to All The Tools of Marketing*, Chapter 4, 'Marketing Information Systems', Kogan Page, London.

Lancaster G.A. and Reynolds P.L. (1999) *Introduction to Marketing: A Step-by-Step Guide to All The Tools of Marketing*, Chapter 5, 'Sales Forecasting', Kogan Page, London.

Makridakis S. and Wheelwright S.C. (1978) *Forecasting Methods for Management*, Wiley, New York.

Plamer A. (2000) *Principles of Marketing*, Chapter 6, 'Market Research', OUP, Oxford.

Plamer A. (2000) *Principles of Marketing*, Chapter 18, 'Sales Forecasting in Selling and Sales Management', OUP, Oxford.

▶▶ References

Kotler P. (1997) *Marketing Management, Analysis, Planning, Implementation and Control*, Prentice Hall, Englewood Cliffs, NJ, Chapter 4, pp. 108–45.

Ledbetter W.N. and Cox J.F. (1977) 'Operations Research in Production Management and Investigation of Past and Present Utilisation' *Production & Inventory Management*, **18**(84): 84–92.

Reynolds P.L. and Greatorex M. (1988) 'Monitoring Short Term Sales Forecasts'. Paper presented to the Marketing Education Group (MEG). Conference, July (see conference proceedings), pp. 578–86.

Seelig P. (1989) 'All over the Map', *Sales and Marketing Management*, March, pp. 58–64.

6 MARKETING RESEARCH

▶▶ Introduction

Marketing orientation, whether product or service based, profit or non-profit based, is the identification and satisfaction of customer needs and wants in a more effective and efficient way than that of the competition. The marketing concept rests on market focus, customer orientation and coordinated marketing effort. In a profit-making business a firm attempts to achieve this level of customer satisfaction as a way of staying ahead of the competition and making a profit. In a not-for-profit organisation, management substitutes profit for some other criterion like maximum social benefits, and so on. A political party for example would be likely to substitute maximising votes for financial profit. A university might substitute 'research excellence' or 'providing maximum opportunity' for profit. In order for organisations to be able to arrange resources in a way that enables them to produce what is termed 'bundles of satisfaction' that satisfy the genuine desires of specifically defined target markets better than the competition, they need to know what the market regards as valuable. The concept of value is a subjective issue and lies within the mind of the individual customer. In a broad sense marketing management needs to understand the 'minds' of its target markets, their attitudes and value systems. It needs a formalised, managerial approach to this task. This is the role of marketing research.

Without the information that marketing research provides, management cannot apply the marketing concept as an overriding business philosophy. This chapter complements Chapter 5, Marketing Information Systems and Forecasting, and it will be seen how the subjects are closely related.

Philip Kotler (1997) defines marketing research as:

the systematic design, collection, analysis, and reporting of data and findings relevant to a specific marketing situation facing the company. (p. 114)

The result is the improvement in marketing decision-making. Marketing research is a 'scientific' approach to building value in the eyes of the company's target market. The aim of marketing research is to find, in a systematic way, reliable, unbiased answers to questions about the market for goods or services and to look at people's ideas and intentions on many issues. Marketing research is concerned with the process of collecting, analysing and interpreting facts to establish what it is that people want and why they want it.

Marketing research is employed in the planning, evaluation and control of marketing tactics and strategy, but it is also used in helping to make policy decisions in the non-commercial public sector. Research must be carefully planned with a disciplined and systematic approach, and a series of steps should be taken in the development, planning and execution of research.

▥ Vignette 6.1

George Gallup, of Gallup poll fame, is 'father' of the modern marketing research industry.

Information is necessary for any marketing firm. George Gallup is often regarded as the 'father' of the modern marketing research industry because he pioneered the collection and analysis of social science data for use by commercial firms. Gallup understood the sort of information firms required, how to get it, what to do with it and how to turn the findings of his research into commercially valuable recommendations for future marketing plans. George Gallup was born in Iowa, USA in 1901 and studied journalism at the University of Iowa. He was interested in finding out why people read particular publications and how satisfied they were with the content and presentation of commercial publications such as newspapers and magazines. He began to try and measure these things whilst still a student. His doctoral work was in psychology and was entitled 'An Objective Method for Determining Reader Interest in the Content of a Newspaper'. Gallup used scientific methodology drawn from the universities for social science research. Much of this methodology was developed at such institutions as the London School of Economics and Political Science and at Harvard University in Cambridge, Massachusetts. Gallup used sample surveys with scientifically constructed sampling techniques. His work at the University of Iowa started a career that would last the rest of his life. Raymond Rubicam, another pioneer working in the advertising field, and who created the advertising firm Young & Rubicam, offered Gallup a job. Gallup employed his newly developed techniques to research advertising effectiveness. This work was extended to other areas of the marketing mix and the Gallup organisation provided a fully developed marketing research service. George Gallup was very interested in politics and created the Gallup poll to carry out scientific political surveys into voters' intentions. It is for this side of his work that he is perhaps best remembered. George Gallup did a great service to the marketing industry and many of his techniques are still used today in commercial marketing research. He fully deserves the accolade 'father of the modern marketing research industry' because he developed much of what is still used today by marketing research companies.

▶▶ Marketing research and marketing information systems

Formal marketing research provides a large proportion of the information requirements of the firm, but not the total requirements. There are other sources of marketing information apart from formal marketing research. The information requirements of the modern marketing firm should be managed in a systematic way. What is needed is a formal system that can assist in the collection, storage, retrieval and analysis of various forms of marketing information, not simply information collected using formal marketing research. Such a system is the marketing information (MkIS) that was the subject of Chapter 5. The concept of the MkIS and the role of formal marketing research is shown in Figure 6.1 and this provides an additional view to those provided in the previous chapter.

It can be seen that the MkIS is made up of four main component parts. Three of these collect information in its 'raw' form. These are the 'internal data', 'intelligence data' and 'marketing research data' components. The information from these three is fed as 'input data' to the fourth component, described as 'models and statistics'. This component adds value to data produced from the other three components by alter-

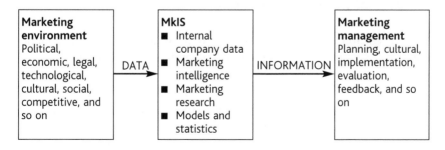

Figure 6.1 A marketing information system (MkIS)

ing it or modelling it in some way. Using the data in a sales forecasting model would be a good example. Basically the 'models and statistics' part of the system employs operational research methods and other management science techniques to data derived from the other three component parts and, in so doing, makes the information more useable and valuable to marketing management.

Explain the role of marketing research within the context of a firm's overall marketing information system (MkIS).

To manage a business well means managing its future and to manage its future requires effective management of information. In this sense, information is viewed as the 'lifeblood' of successful marketing operations. Formal marketing research is an important source of specific forms of marketing information. Marketing research is so important to the customer-oriented organisation that it is often referred to as the 'eyes and ears' of marketing. However, although formal marketing research is of paramount importance to the marketing-oriented firm it does not provide all the modern firm's information requirements. Information can be derived from other sources that have little to do with the collection of data through formal marketing research. For example, data generated internally as part of the firm's administration system may provide a rich source of information highly relevant to marketing management. Data collected 'informally' from company employees, particularly salespeople, van drivers, van sales and service engineers constitutes a valuable source of marketing intelligence. The use of operational research techniques can enhance the value of information obtained from other sources. Formal marketing research provides a valuable source of marketing information. Along with information from other sources it represents input data for the overall marketing information system.

▶▶ Types of marketing research

Market research activities can be classified by their purpose or general objective. For example, some market research exercises are intended to produce results that are purely exploratory in nature. Such research is usually carried out at the beginning of the overall research project. Other research may produce data that is descriptive or predictive or conclusive. These general classifications of marketing research are now examined in more detail.

▶ Exploratory research

As the name suggests exploratory research is usually undertaken at the initial stages of the research process. Exploratory research is basically 'let us have a look' activity. It is not designed to enable the researcher to draw firm conclusions but rather to enable him or her to establish the general parameters of the research situation. The use of secondary data, that is, data that is already in existence usually in printed form or on some kind of computerised data retrieval system, is an important part of the exploratory process. In terms of primary data collection, that is, data collected for the first time specifically for a particular research exercise, qualitative research methods are more often employed than quantitative methods. Depth interview and group discussions allow researchers to explore respondents' opinions and attitudes on key issues. Both of these interviewing techniques employ relatively small samples and thus by their very nature can only hope to provide general exploratory information. Nonetheless information gained from qualitative exploratory research enables the market researcher to plan a more effective research programme than would be the case if this stage were missing. Exploratory research lays down foundations enabling the rest of the research exercise to be built more soundly.

 Vignette 6.2

The UK-based Association for Qualitative Research (AQR) seeks to take the industry forward by being a catalyst for change.

Qualitative research is an important tool in the marketing researchers' armoury. It enables them to investigate people's motivations, attitudes and behaviour and is often used in the exploratory stage of the research process. However, it is a versatile tool and can also be used in the main body of the research project, often as the main research tool. As part of the marketing research industry, qualitative research is represented by its own professional body, The Association for Qualitative Research (AQR), the leading authority on qualitative issues within the UK and internationally. Founded in the early 1980s, AQR is a recognised and respected professional body in the area of marketing services. The AQR has over 1000 members who are directly involved in qualitative research. Many of them are researchers, including academic researchers, but also clients of research services and planners. The AQR seeks to develop the profession and take the industry forward by being a catalyst for change. It provides a forum in which qualitative research issues can be examined, discussed and developed. The organisation has an educational programme and new skills and techniques are developed and disseminated into the profession through this programme, often on an international basis. Members become part of a wide business network and are kept informed about developments throughout the industry. The AQR is an open association and seeks membership from all those involved in qualitative research. It aims to promote quality research throughout the industry, to maintain professional standards in qualitative research, innovate new thinking and processes and provide a vehicle through which members can interact and develop their professional skills.

▶ Descriptive research

As the name suggests, descriptive research is intended to describe certain things that marketing management is likely to be interested in such as market conditions, customer feelings or opinions towards a company, purchasing behaviour and so forth. Such research is not intended to allow the researcher to establish causal relationships between marketing variables and sales or consumer behaviour, or to enable predictions of likely future conditions. Descriptive research tells the researcher 'what is', and just like exploratory research, usually forms part of an ongoing research programme. Once the researcher has established the present state of affairs in terms of market size, main segments, main competitors and so on, he or she may proceed to types of research of a more predictive and/or conclusive nature. Descriptive research usually makes use of descriptive statistics to help the user understand the structure of data and any significant patterns that may be found in the data. All measures of central tendency such as the mean, median and mode are used with measures of dispersion such as variance and standard deviation. Descriptive research result are often presented using pictorial methods like graphs, 'pie charts', histograms and so on.

▶ Predictive research

The objective of predictive research is to enable the marketing researcher to predict matters like future market conditions in terms of market growth or decline, increased competition, greater import penetration, future price levels or changes in consumer taste. A number of marketing research techniques can be used to generate such information. When using qualitative research such as depth interviews or group discussions, the researcher can interview individual salespeople or 'experts' in the industry. Group interviews may be held in order to arrive at a consensus as to what might happen within a certain market or industry. Opinions can be elicited from respondents for various time periods into the future. Similarly, questionnaire surveys can be used to elicit information. For example the whole sales force might be surveyed to ask their opinion concerning future sales or market conditions. A survey of buyers' intentions is a popular method of obtaining sales forecasting information. Formal statistical and mathematical techniques developed for forecasting exercises can be used. Secondary data obtained from existing printed or stored sources, as well as survey information from qualitative interviews, can provide the forecaster with valuable input data that can be used in formal forecasting models such as exponential smoothing or regression.

▶ Conclusive research

When using conclusive research the researcher is usually trying to establish causal relationships between marketing variables such as price, advertising or packaging and some other variable such as sales or patterns of consumption. In doing so it is necessary to use a formal experimental design to test a specific hypothesis. For example, the marketing manager might need to establish which set of merchandising materials, price promotion and shelf configurations is most effective in achieving sales within a multiple grocery store chain. Assuming there were four different versions of each of the marketing variables, for example four merchandising 'sets', four price promotions that could be used in store and four different shelf configurations, then the researcher would want to know which permutation of these marketing variables was most effective. The researcher might set up an experiment where each permutation of experimental treatments was randomly allocated to retail stores. Differences between stores could be accounted for in the experiment. The experiment should be allowed to run until sufficient data had been generated. The results would then be analysed and used to see if the hypothesis that one set of experimental treatments is more effective in generating sales than the others was true or false. Statistically designed experimental methods such as Analysis of Variance (ANOVA) might be used. In particular, as the researcher is attempting to test for interaction between marketing variables, something called a 'Factorial' ANOVA design would be most likely to be used.

Experimental exercises that enable the researcher to establish causation in tests have a number of things in common. The researcher starts with the marketing variables to be tested, known as the 'independent variables'. These variables are applied to a given situation and certain effects are monitored. These effects are usually sales, but might be something else such as behavioural changes of some kind, for example store loyalty. These effects are regarded as 'dependent variables' because they are dependent on the marketing variables discussed earlier. Experiments are set up with the purpose of trying to establish scientifically, using statistical tests, whether the effects seen in the dependent variables are attributable to changes in the independent variables, that is marketing variables, and if so, the nature and strength of these effects. The marketing researcher wants to know whether experimental effects caused by independent variables acting upon dependent variables are in any way commercially exploitable.

▶▶ Stages in the research process

Marketing research is a planned formal approach to the collection of marketing information and follows a number of logical steps:

1. *Problem definition* – leads to a preliminary statement of research objectives to provide information that is needed in the following areas:
    ▶ Motivations, values, beliefs, feelings, opinions
    ▶ Evaluations, attitudes, intentions
    ▶ Knowledge, facts, behaviour, actions
    ▶ Demographic, socioeconomic (on or from people, stores, companies, brands, products).
    This information is required for:
    ▶ Exploration, description, prediction or evaluation
    and it comes from:
    ▶ Secondary data sources, internal and external to a company
    ▶ Primary data sources (that is, from fieldwork).
2. *Review of secondary data sources*
    ▶ Company records, reports, previous research
    ▶ Trade associations, government agencies, research organisations
    ▶ Advertising/market research agencies
    ▶ Books, periodicals, theses, statistics, conference proceedings, and so on.
3. *Select approach for collection of new/primary information*
    ▶ Experimentation
    ▶ Observation
    ▶ Surveys – mail, telephone, personal
    ▶ Motivational research techniques – depth interviews, group interviews, projective techniques.

4. *Determine details of research design* – methods, sample design.
5. *Data collection.*
6. *Analysis and interpretation of data.*
7. *Evaluation of results and recommendations.*

◗◗ Tools of marketing research

◗ Motivational research techniques

The aim is to uncover underlying motives, desires and emotions of consumers that influence their behaviour. Such techniques penetrate the subconscious and there are two approaches: the *psychosociological approach* that relies on group behaviour of consumers and the impact of culture and environment on their opinions and reactions; and the *psychoanalytic approach* that relies on information drawn from individual respondents in depth interviews and projective tests. Freudian interpretations dominate such analysis.

Techniques used include:

1. *Depth interviewing* involving interview and observational methods. Topics for discussion are chosen by an interviewer and indirect questioning leads the respondent to free expression of motives, attitudes, opinions, experiences and habits in relation to advertisements, products, brands, services, and so on. Depth interviewing is based on the psychoanalytical principle of 'free association' interviewing. The depth interview is not intended to be a simple formal question and answer session using a structured questionnaire, as such an exercise would simply involve administering a questionnaire by personal interview. A depth interview in this context is intended to be something more subtle and sophisticated. Depth interviews fall under the heading of qualitative research, and they are concerned with collecting information on beliefs, attitudes and opinions rather than more quantitative information that might more readily lend itself to statistical analysis. Depth interviews usually involve small samples and they are expensive and time consuming. Although interviews may only take an hour or so to conduct, research will take longer than this in terms of preparation, making appointments, listening to tapes and making transcripts and analysing information.
2. *Focus groups* are where the interviewer stimulates and moderates group discussion. In this method freedom of expression and interac-

tion between individuals is encouraged. This is also known as *group discussions* or *group interviewing*.

3. *Sensitivity panels* are a form of group discussion or focus group where respondents are trained to take part in such groups and members of the group are used periodically for different research subjects such as different products or packages, advertisements and so on.

How, if at all, does the information gained by the market researcher from a depth interview differ from that of a group discussion?

If the information gained from these two methods were the same there would be little point in using two different approaches. As the name suggests, it is claimed that the individual 'depth interview' allows the researcher deeper access to respondents' feelings and thoughts. Topics of a personal nature, such as personal hygiene or borrowing can only be discussed in any depth in a one-to-one situation.

A group discussion allows the researcher to take advantage of 'group synergy' or 'group dynamics'. Whilst a group discussion may not enter the depths of exploration that is often experienced in a depth interview scenario, group discussion interviews often explore topics in substantially more breadth than can be achieved within a depth interview setting. Group dynamics often produce a 'snowball effect' where topics are discussed and certain hitherto unknown aspects of the topic are identified and discussed by the group. In a sense a group seems to take on a life of its own, with the conversation taking routes completely unexpected by the researcher at the start of the exercise. This process can lead to a frustrating dead end, but often it can produce qualitative research information of significant value.

▶ Surveys (using questionnaires)

This is the most commonly used method of data collection using mail, telephone or personal interview. Questionnaires can be self-administered or used in an interview situation, depending on:

▶ Cost
▶ Timing
▶ Type of information needed
▶ Amount of information needed
▶ Ease of questioning
▶ Accuracy required.

The practicability of any survey by questionnaire is best checked by a pilot survey. To check the questionnaire:

1. Use a non-probability 'purposeful' sample, as it is not intended to use the 'results' in the final data set. At this stage we are only testing the design of the questionnaire, whether it is of a suitable length, sequencing of questions, whether the questions are easily understood and so on.
2. Pilot testing should involve well-trained and experienced staff because it is important to get the questionnaire right as the success of the survey depends on it. It is possible that three or four versions of the questionnaire will need to be tested before it is right. The last pre-test should use the final approved questionnaire.

▶ Questionnaire design

Information collected must be accurate, so design of a questionnaire is of great importance. The questionnaire should consist of questions that have the same meaning, a single meaning and the intended meaning to everyone. Questions should be numbered and have instructions to the investigator concerning the conduct of the interview. Answer codes should be near to the right-hand side, and lines drawn at suitable intervals to bring clarity to the design.

The types of question most commonly used are as follows.

1. *Open-ended questions* give the informant a hint of what answer might be expected. A question that begins 'What do you think of...?' will bring forth large amounts of data that cannot always be satisfactorily summarised, but this type of question is useful in the pilot stage to show the range of likely answers.
2. *Unaided recall questions* do not mention the nature of the answer material and avoid asking leading questions like: 'How did you travel to the station to catch this train?'
3. *Dichotomous questions* offer two choices of answer, usually 'yes' and 'no'.
4. *Multiple-choice questions* ('cafeteria' questions) offer a graduated range of possible answers, listed in order from one extreme to the other.
5. *Thermometer questions* ask informants to rate their feelings on a numerical scale, for example 0–10. This type of question seeks to

minimise the disadvantage of discreet classification in the multi-choice question.

6. *Checklists* are a standard way of prompting the memory of respondents without them being biased by the interviewer. However, brand leaders may be selected more frequently because of the weight of advertising.

Rules for question design

1. Use simple words that are familiar to everyone (that is, 'shop' not 'outlet', 'shopkeeper' not 'retailer').
2. Keep questions short.
3. Avoid asking double-barrelled questions (for example 'Have you a radio and television set?').
4. Do not ask leading questions (for example 'Do you buy instant coffee because it is the quickest way to make coffee?').
5. Do not mention brand names (for example 'Do you consider Hitachi to be the best audio equipment?').
6. Do not ask questions that might offend (for example 'Do you work or are you a housewife?').
7. Avoid using catch phrases.
8. Avoid words that are not precise in their meanings (for example 'Does this product last a reasonable length of time?').
9. Direct questions will not always elicit the expected response as perhaps not all possible answers have been foreseen (for example the question 'Are you married?' does not cover the possibilities of divorce, separation, and so on).
10. Questions concerning prestige goods may not be answered truthfully. Rewording can avoid this (for example 'Have you a television capable of receiving teletext transmissions?' might be better asked by 'How many hours per week do you watch television?', followed by 'Do you watch teletext transmissions, that is, Ceefax or Oracle?').
11. Only questions that respondents can answer from knowledge or experience should be asked.
12. Questions should not depend on the respondent's memory.
13. Questions should only allow one thought to be created in a respondent's mind to avoid confusion and inappropriate answers. This particularly applies to questions beginning with 'Why ...?'.
14. Avoid questions or words with an emotional bias (for example use Conservative/Labour, and not Tory/Socialist).

The first questions asked should gain the interest of the informant, and should be easy to answer in a factual way. More difficult questions should come later, with those of greatest importance being about a third of the way through. Transition from question to question should be smooth and logical. Details of the respondent (age, address, full name, occupation and so on) should appear at the end. The questionnaire must have a title and contain cross-references to others if needed. Standard information required includes the respondent's name, home address, sex, age (within a group), income group and occupation, the interviewing district identification, the place and date of the interview and the interviewer's name.

Answers should be recorded in one of the following ways:

▶ Writing a number
▶ Putting a cross or a tick in a box
▶ Underlining correct answers
▶ Crossing out incorrect answers
▶ Writing in a predetermined symbol
▶ Ringing a number or letter.

Open-ended questions should be followed by enough space to allow for answers to be recorded verbatim.

There are a number of basic questions that should be asked:

1. Is each question clearly worded?
2. Does it break any of the basic rules of question design?
3. Is each question concerned with one factor only?
4. Are questions ones that will elicit the answers necessary to solve the research problem?
5. Is each question unambiguous and will both investigator and informants have similar understandings of the question?
6. Are all possible answers allowed for?
7. Are recording arrangements foolproof?
8. Will answers to each question be in a form in which they can be cross-tabulated against other data on the same or other questionnaires?
9. Will answers be in a form that will allow at least some to be checked against established data?

▶ Marketing experiments

An experiment is a way of gathering primary data from which the researcher is able to establish causation of effect amongst the variables being experimentally tested. It can be carried out in an artificial 'laboratory' type setting or as a field experiment, the best example of which is a *test market*. Here, researchers choose a representative geographical area or one where they can statistically adjust data to make it representative of a wider market area such as the UK as a whole. The test market is like a model of the total market. Test markets can be expensive, but being a field experiment they have the advantage of realism or 'external validity' over laboratory experiments. 'Simulated test markets' can reduce costs as they are not full test markets and involve surveying a small sample of consumers and showing them pictures or samples of products and ascertaining their preference as if they were really 'shopping'.

Other techniques include *extended user tests, blind* and *simple placement tests*. In addition, there are the techniques used in pre- and post-testing of advertising themes and copy. Marketing experiments are one of the four main classes of research methods whereby marketing researchers collect primary information, that is information collected for the first time specifically for a particular research exercise. Three other classes of techniques are:

▶ *Interviews,* such as depth interviews and group discussions or focus groups
▶ *Observation* such as retail audits and consumer panels
▶ *Surveys* such as a postal questionnaire or telephone survey.

▌▌▌▌ Vignette 6.3

A.C. Nielsen the global marketing research firm offers simulated test marketing services to clients with their own BASES system.

A.C. Nielsen is a global marketing research agency, which offers specialist professional services in retail measurement and consumer panels. These are the services the firm is most well known for but they offer a range of other customised research services including decision support, merchandising, modelling and analytics, media and entertainment research and test marketing services. Their services are offered globally but particularly in the Americas, Europe, the Asia Pacific region and a number of emerging markets. Nielsen has developed a simulated test marketing system called BASES. The system is for use with new products and is designed to take the risk out of a launch or re-launch. The system covers most of the stages in the new product development process (see Chapter 7, under the heading 'The process of new product development') from concept development and testing through to commercialisation and launch of the product. It does not cover the initial idea generation process. BASES uses information to simulate likely product life cycle behaviour and forecasts sales information to enable the calculation of break even points and future profit streams. The information from the BASES system allows clients to optimise the allocation of their marketing resources and maximise the success of their product launch. Nielsen claims that their system allows researchers to understand the dynamics and nature of consumer behaviour and response in each country where the model is used. The model is adapted for the market conditions of individual countries and so far Nielsen has applied the BASES model successfully in nearly 50 countries. Firms can use the model in a number of different ways. The information from the model helps clients when introducing new products or services, adding products to existing lines, relaunching established brands and identifying product concepts with the best potential.

▶ Observational techniques

Sometimes it is only possible to collect the data required by observation. It may be humans observing humans; humans observing things, for example cars; or electromechanical devices such as cameras or tape recorders and so on observing things or people. Retail audits and consumer panels are also classified as observational techniques. Retail audits are conducted by specialist firms like A. C. Nielsen. They conduct product audits in retail stores every month. Product managers buy this retail sales data and other supporting information on a continuous month by month basis. Other related information on competitors' products is also available. The consumer panel is a home audit where a wide range of households are monitored as to purchasing habits. Respondents are of different socioeconomic groups, family size and stage in the family life cycle. They record their purchases using a special bar-code reader and send the data to Nielsen 'down the telephone line' using a coupler. Observational techniques are a useful source of primary data and the method is often used in conjunction with other methods.

▶▶ Main research areas

▶ Product research

This involves all aspects of design, development and testing of new products, as well as improvement and modification of existing products. Activities include:

▶ Comparative testing against competitive products
▶ Test marketing
▶ Concept testing
▶ Idea generation and screening
▶ Product elimination/simplification
▶ Brand positioning.

❯ Pricing research

Techniques such as the *buy–response model* can be used to:

▶ assist in establishing a more market-oriented pricing strategy
▶ see what kinds of price consumers associate with different product variations (for example packaging)
▶ establish market segments in relation to price.

❯ Distribution research

This is concerned with two separate but interrelated facets – channels of distribution and physical distribution. In terms of channels, marketers continually attempt to create competitive advantage by selecting innovative, creative and more effective channels. Channels evolve over time and new channel formats develop, for example the Internet holds out much promise as a shopping medium particularly for financial services such as insurance, mortgages and personal banking. Other forms of 'non-shop shopping' have grown in popularity like the use of mail order tied in with the growth of direct mail as a communication medium. Television shopping is now increasing in popularity in the UK. Television shopping is available on terrestrial television channels as well as on satellite and cable television. Other retail formats have become increasingly important like huge out-of-town shopping complexes. Marketing research has an important role to play in evaluating the efficiency of existing channels and forecasting likely future retail developments both in terms of actual channel formats likely to be used in the future and technology used in such channels.

Techniques like *retail audits* can monitor the effectiveness of different types of distribution channel and detect regional variations. They can identify which channels are in decline. They can tell which channels are likely to experience future development and a growth in popularity. For example shopping areas within petrol stations have grown considerably over the past ten years in terms of turnover and the range of products on offer. Qualitative research such as depth interviews and group discussions as well as larger scale sample surveys using questionnaires, can be used in appraising existing channel efficiency and in predicting likely future developments.

New developments in physical distribution can be monitored and even predicted using marketing research techniques. Many new developments originate overseas necessitating an international dimension, for example the concept of 'just-in-time' delivery originated in Japan. Materials handling and vehicle technology are continuously developing with implications for logistics. Computer technology has now made available 'tracking systems' so customers can establish exactly where their order or delivery is in the order processing cycle and even establish exactly where a particular consignment is anywhere in the world.

▶ Marketing communications research

This is concerned with the appraisal and evaluation of each element of the marketing communications mix including advertising research, evaluation of below-the-line sales promotions, sponsorship evaluation and evaluation of direct mail, trade journals, exhibitions, personal selling, corporate communications, telephone marketing, communication on the Internet and much more. Research is needed at various points in the communications process. In the first instance a firm will need to research the characteristics of customers or potential customers for their product or service. These customers may form distinct market segments. In terms of marketing communications planning these represent 'target audiences' for future campaigns. Once target audiences have been defined it is necessary to establish the most effective media to use to send marketing messages. What television programmes are they most likely to watch? What newspapers, magazines, journals or commercial radio programmes will be most effective in getting the necessary message across? Marketing communications involves business-to-business as well as communication with householders. Many consumer goods are also sold through marketing intermediaries such as wholesalers.

In business-to-business (B2B) communications personal selling is important. In many industrial firms up to 90 per cent of the marketing budget is spent on personal selling. Trade exhibitions, direct mail, sponsorship, transport livery, corporate work-wear, telephone marketing and trade journals are important business-to-business marketing communication tools, although some are used in both B2B and consumer marketing communications, for example telephone marketing, exhibitions and sponsorship.

Once target audiences have been identified and appropriate communications media have been established, further research is needed at a pre-campaign level to put communications messages together. A one-way model of marketing communications is shown below in Figure 6.2 to explain this point.

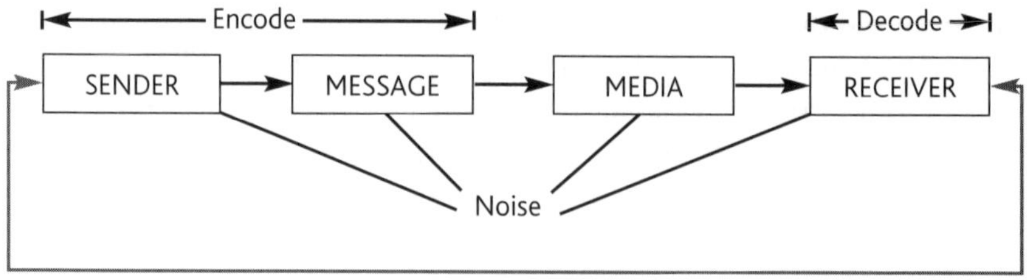

Figure 6.2 A sample one-way model of marketing communications

Figure 6.2 illustrates the process whereby the marketing firm (the sender) develops a message that is sent using a particular medium to the receiver (the target audience). The effectiveness of communication is then evaluated through a feedback loop, and future messages can be adapted accordingly. Marketing research has an important part to play at every stage of the communications process, identifying the target audiences, selecting the most effective communication media, developing the message and evaluating how well the message was communicated to the target audience and with what effect.

SELF-CHECK

Why is marketing research so critical to the effective practice of modern marketing?
Marketing is the process of establishing what individuals, who collectively constitute a market, regard as valuable. Value is a subjective concept especially for more sophisticated consumer products. In order to organise the resources of an organisation to create value, marketing management needs to understand the value system of individuals and organisations (who are themselves a collection of individuals). Marketing research, as part of an integrated marketing information system, helps provide the information management needs to carry out the marketing task effectively.

What is the role of exploratory research within the overall marketing research process?
A sound house is built on good foundations. Likewise, when a painter and decorator decorates a room a large part of the job is preparation, making sure that all woodwork is sanded and smooth and that all the defects have been filled in on the walls. In the same way, good quality marketing research is based on careful preparation. It needs to be built on sound 'foundations' if it is to have any true validity. Exploratory research, as the name suggests, enables the researcher to establish the general parameters of the research situation, thereby putting him or her in a much better position to design an effective research project.

Is the use of a census better than a sample when carrying out survey work?
Not necessarily. Some form of error can occur in all forms of survey work. If you carry out a census, it is true that every single member of a defined population will have been surveyed, thereby leaving no possible chance of errors entering results due to sampling. However, sampling error is but one source of error that researchers have to deal with. In fact, in many survey situations the error attributable to non-sampling error is greater than that commonly attributable to sampling error in situations where a sample rather than a census has been used. Sampling error is cased by a sample result being differ-

ent from true population values. Non-sampling error is error caused by everything else. If a sample is carefully chosen, the results are likely to reflect the true population parameters within an acceptable and calculable degree of error. Size is not so important, although all other things being equal, it is better to have a larger rather than a smaller sample. It is how the sample is selected that is important. Sampling gives an acceptable degree of accuracy if properly carried out, and money saved by using a sample instead of a census can be spent reducing the risk of non-sampling error.

▶▶ Summary

Marketing is the business process whereby business firms strive to create 'bundles of values' in the form of products and services that customers will willingly buy. In the value creation process, marketing firms attempt to at least meet, but preferably exceed, customer expectations. To remain competitive marketing firms have to create customer value more effectively and efficiently than competitors. Firms that are market-driven and customer-focused in this way are said to be 'marketing oriented' firms. However 'value' is somewhat subjective being perceived in the minds of individuals and groups of people and changes all the time. For example, what we regard as fashionable today in terms of clothing or popular music might not be thought so next year. What is now regarded as unimportant may be important in a decade. 'Green' and environmental issues were not matters that concerned people fifteen years ago, whereas in the twenty-first century most people express some concern about them. Concern is now reflected in a wide range of products that are 'environmentally friendly', 'ethical' or 'healthy'. In order to keep up with the changing tastes and value systems of customers, the activities of the competition and changes in the external business environment, marketing firms need information. Long-term marketing strategy and marketing plans at tactical and operational levels need information. Information is the lifeblood of a marketing oriented firm. Without the right kind of information, effective marketing is not possible. Market research provides marketing firms with a wide range of useful information. However, marketing research on its own is insufficient, as it must form an intrinsic part of the wider marketing information system.

FURTHER READING

Armstrong G. and Kotler P. (2000) *Marketing: An Introduction* (5th edn), Chapter 4, 'Marketing Research and Information Systems', Prentice Hall, Englewood Cliffs, NJ.

Blythe J. (2001) *Essentials of Marketing*, Chapter 5, 'Market Research', Pearson Education, London.

Chisnall P.M. (1992) *Marketing Research* (4th edn), McGraw-Hill, Maidenhead.

Crimp M. (1992) *The Marketing Research Process*, Prentice Hall, Harlow, Essex.

Davies M. (1998) *Understanding Marketing*, Chapter 3, 'Marketing Research', Prentice Hall, London.

Keegan W.J. and Green M.S. (2000) *Global Marketing* (2nd edn), Chapter 6, 'Global Information Systems and Market Research', Prentice Hall, London.

Lancaster G.A. and Reynolds P.L. (1999) *Introduction to Marketing: A Step-by-Step Guide to All The Tools of Marketing*, Chapter 4, 'Marketing Information Systems', Kogan Page, London.

Plamer A. (2000) *Principles of Marketing*, Chapter 6, 'Marketing Research', OUP, Oxford.

▶▶ References

Kotler P. (1997) *Marketing Management, Analysis, Planning, Implementation and Control*, Prentice Hall, Englewood Cliffs, NJ, Chapter 4, p. 114.

7 PRODUCTS AND SERVICES

▶▶ Introduction

For a marketing plan to be successful it is essential that all elements of the marketing mix support each other. Marketing mixes change between products, services and market situations and this is what makes marketing dynamic; it is the skill of marketing in manipulating the marketing mix that makes a product or service a success or a failure. However, the product or service is important in this calculation for this is the tangible element that will appeal to customers and it is upon this that customer purchases and repeat purchases are based. This is what must provide the end satisfaction, for after all, this is the practical application of the marketing concept. A study of products and services is concerned with design, appearance, how long it will last and how it is perceived by both customers and non-customers.

▶▶ Defining the product

People purchase what is termed a 'bundle of satisfactions'. This includes the physical product or a less tangible service offering. If asked to state what they have purchased most customers will simply mention the product or service in its simplest terms. However, there is much more to a purchase than simply this.

What other satisfactions do you feel customers purchase as part of this 'bundle of satisfactions' that make up what is called the 'augmented product'?

Additional factors such as image, shape and design, performance and value make up this extra 'bundle of satisfac-

> tions'. Added to this are such factors as price and value for money. Purchasers do not readily acknowledge these additional factors.

The task of marketing is to take a more expansive view of what constitutes an augmented product or service and then combine the marketing mix in such a way as to present consumers with the 'bundle of satisfactions' that marketing research has identified as being most pertinent to their requirements.

The augmented product concept is sometimes called the 'extended product', and this definition includes the total marketing effort. Thus a view of the product or service is broader than the mere object or service offering; it is a 'bundle of satisfactions' that gives fulfilment.

 It is easy to envisage a product but services are also discussed. Give three illustrations of service offerings.

- Insurance
- A holiday
- An educational course

▶▶ Categories of products

Given this background, we are now able to present a formal categorisation system for products and services. Such a categorisation is needed so marketing planners can more easily formulate and design their strategies and tactics.

Industrial goods are separated from consumer goods as the first part of this categorisation.

▶ Industrial goods

Industrial goods conjure up images of components and raw materials, but not all industrial goods are tangible. Many additional items and services are important to ensure the smooth running of a factory.

 Name three examples of goods or services that are industrial goods, but not required in the manufacturing process.

- Machinery repair services for the production line
- Computing equipment
- Fork lift trucks

A classification exists to describe categories of industrial goods and services:

▶ *Installations* include plant and machinery required for a company's manufacturing processes. These are critical purchases and can involve complex purchasing decision-making processes with price not necessarily being the deciding factor.

▶ *Accessories* are also capital items but less critical and depreciated over a shorter period of time. They include items like office machinery and materials handling equipment.

▶ *Raw materials* are the most obvious of industrial goods and this is a major task in a purchasing department. Here, buyers specifically look for keen prices coupled with quality and reliability of delivery.

▶ *Component parts and materials* are items that are required in the production process, but are not part of the finished product. They include items like packaging, greases and oils.

▶ *Supplies* include items like cleaning and maintenance materials and stationery. Buying tends to be a more routine process and it is often a matter of reordering, with price being the major criterion, consistent with a standard specification of quality.

This classification is linked to organisational buying behaviour where the fact that buyers deal with larger sums of money and larger quantities makes it a far more professional and organised process than for consumer goods purchasing.

▶ Consumer goods

These are types of products and services with which we are personally familiar. Unlike industrial products, irrational and emotional motives are connected with their purchase and many manufacturers base their marketing efforts on such criteria. As with industrial goods, they lend themselves to a number of subcategories:

▶ *Convenience goods* are everyday necessities which are purchased on a regular basis and whose purchase takes little effort on the part of the buyer. Advertising plays an important role in terms of attempting to persuade the consumer to take a particular brand and such techniques are explained in Chapter 12. Staple convenience goods are products that are purchased for daily consumption and where it is more difficult to differentiate one product from another so little pre-planning goes into their purchase. Many such products like milk and newspapers are delivered to the door.

- *Shopping goods* is the term used to describe durable products and their purchase tends to be at infrequent intervals. More planning goes into their purchase on the part of buyers and buyer behaviour is more complex as illustrated in Chapter 4. The purchasing cycle is also much longer and more complex models of buyer behaviour apply. Further classifications relate to 'homogeneous shopping goods' that are standard items like toasters and kettles and 'heterogeneous shopping goods' that are non-standard and where personal choice plays a more important role.

- *Speciality goods* are major purchases that are made at infrequent intervals after much probing of the market has been undertaken. More purchasing motivations are involved in the final decision and often the final purchase is a compromise decision between a number of purchasing criteria. Examples of such purchases are motor cars and major items of expensive clothing.

- *Unsought goods* are ones that the purchaser has not actively considered buying. Techniques used in their marketing are sometimes dubious and this has led to criticism of marketing. Consumers usually have to be persuaded that they need such products, as it would never occur to them to go out and actively purchase. Insurance typifies such a service, particularly life assurance, where the potential customer does not necessarily see an immediate need for this service. Methods of selling such goods and services tend to be through more directly targeted approaches like direct mail, telephone selling and door-to-door methods.

Consider the subcategories under each of the consumer goods divisions. Give an example of one product or service under each heading.

- Convenience goods – toothpaste
- Shopping goods – electric razor
- Speciality goods – dining room table and chairs
- Unsought goods – home insulation

▶▶ Product management

▶ Organisational considerations

Larger organisations, especially those that produce consumer durables and FMCG, often have a 'product management' system for managing single products or a line of similar products. In FMCG companies it is usually the brand manager's responsibility to manage the image and marketing (but not the selling) of a single product line. This person will act as a liaison between the advertising agency and the company and is responsible for the image of the product and will commission marketing research when it is needed.

This kind of system has been criticised on the grounds that product managers have to rely upon others, especially the sales force, to carry out their ideas. This has the potential for conflict, particularly on the part of the field sales force who have to be sold the promotional idea with which they may, or may not, agree.

Where a system of product management is in operation, the typical organisation of the marketing function is that the marketing manager is in overall control and is directly under the managing director. Beneath the marketing manager is the overall product manager and under the product manager come individual brand managers. Alongside the product manager, under the marketing manager, is the sales manager, and under the sales manager is the sales team organised by geographical or functional splits as described in Chapter 11.

▶ Strategic considerations

A number of routes are open to product managers when devising strategies for product portfolios. Igor Ansoff first introduced his idea of a simple matrix in 1957, shown in Figure 7.1.

Each of the decisions is looked at under their respective headings:

▶ *1/1 decision* takers are true innovators, but their strategy is risky in terms of expenditure costs and the high failure rate of new products. This strategy is referred to as 'diversification'.

Figure 7.1 Ansoff matrix

▷ *1/2 decisions* (new products into existing markets) comprise producers who like to stay ahead of competitors or are able to provide a sustainable advantage that makes their product unique in the minds of consumers. This is a strategy of 'product development'.

▷ *2/1 decisions* (existing products into new markets) relate to manufacturers who seek to expand their total sales volume by moving into an entirely new (to them) market. An example might be an industrial adhesives manufacturer who decides to target the office stationery market by modifying an existing range of industrial adhesives. This strategy is known as 'market development'.

▷ *2/2 decisions* are taken by cautious manufacturers. There is a possibility of such manufacturers being left exposed if their particular market hits a recession. This is a strategy of 'market penetration'.

▶▶ New products

The product or service is the principal component of marketing as it provides revenue without which commercial activity could not take place. Before we describe a formal development routine suggested for new products we list the types of new product categorisation used in marketing:

▷ *Innovative products* are completely new to the marketplace

▷ *Replacement products* might include well-known items, but with a new design and functions

▷ *Imitative products* are common once an innovative product has become successfully established. They are colloquially termed 'me too' products

▷ *Relaunched products* occur when an original product has gone into decline, but the company anticipates sufficient potential sale if the image of the product or its position is altered through manipulating the marketing mix.

 Give an example of a product or service under each of the new product categories cited above.

- *Innovative products* – the electronic wristwatch that acts as a personal organiser by downloading information from a computer screen
- *Replacement products* – a new model of motor car
- *Imitative products* – later personal computers that came out following their introduction by well-known personal computing manufacturers
- *Relaunched products* – personal clothing products

▶ Organisation for new product development

How new product development is managed is critical in terms of potential success or failure. There are a number of different organisational alternatives:

▶ *New product managers* are given the sole task of developing new products. Sometimes this task is part of the duty of a product manager or brand manager.
▶ *New product committees* receive new product ideas from marketing or research and development or from any other source within the organisation and assess their viability in terms of potential success.
▶ *New product departments* exist in large innovative companies and their work cuts across a number of departments. When a new product idea looks to be viable a 'product (or project) champion' is appointed to see development through from its design and development to final launch.
▶ *New product venture teams* comprise people from different parts of the organisation who are brought together on an ad hoc basis so different views can be incorporated in new product decision making. Their task is to develop products within predetermined budgets and time constraints.

▦ Vignette 7.1

Dyson discovers a way of getting 45 per cent more suction than a Dual Cyclone and removing more dust, by dividing the air into 8 smaller cyclones, hence the name Root 8Cyclone™

James Dyson is a man who likes to make things work better. With his research team he has developed products that have achieved sales of over £3 billion worldwide. James Dyson's first product, the Sea Truck, was launched in 1970 while he was studying at the Royal College of Art. A few years later came the award-winning Ballbarrow. Then there was the Wheelboat and the Trolleyball. Even the integral hose, seen on most upright vacuum cleaners, is a Dyson invention. In 1978, James Dyson noticed how the air filter in the Ballbarrow spray-finishing room was constantly clogging with powder particles (just like a vacuum cleaner bag clogs with dust). So he designed and built an industrial cyclone tower, which removed the powder particles by exerting centrifugal forces greater than 100,000 times those of gravity. James Dyson set to work and five years and 5127 prototypes later, the world's first bagless vacuum cleaner from Dyson arrived. The Dual Cyclone™ system was the first breakthrough in technology since the invention of the vacuum cleaner in 1901. The traditional bag had been replaced by two cyclone chambers, which cannot clog with dust. After the

Dyson's outer cyclone has spun out the larger dust and dirt particles, the inner cyclone accelerates the air still further to remove the minute health-threatening particles. As a result the Dyson Dual Cyclone™ became the fastest selling vacuum cleaner ever to be made in the UK. The company then set to work to develop an entirely new type of cyclone system. They discovered that a smaller diameter cyclone gives greater centrifugal force. So they developed a way of getting 45 per cent more suction than a Dual Cyclone and removing more dust, by dividing the air into 8 smaller cyclones, hence the name Root 8Cyclone™.

▶ The process of new product development

The process of new product development goes through a logical series of steps from inception of an idea to its final launch:

- ▶ *Idea generation* comes from a variety of sources. In innovative companies, ideas tend to be research driven. The notion of marketing orientation states that we should look to our customers first (through marketing research) before embarking upon new product development. However, in the case of companies producing 'breakthrough' products this might be difficult as customers will not necessarily be able to envisage what they require. As we discuss later, ideas are not simply generated and made into products that are marketed. Marketing research comes into the equation, but more through procedures such as product testing as explained in Chapter 6. A culture should exist within the organisation that encourages new product ideas that can come from areas other than simply research and development. The sales force should be a regular source of new product ideas, and such data can be gathered from the company's marketing information system as explained in Chapter 5. Brainstorming is a good method of producing new product ideas as long as it is chaired competently, but regular meetings of planning committees should have this as an agenda priority. Venture teams can then be set up to progress likely ideas.

▌▌▌ Vignette 7.2

R ed Bull the 'energy drink' originated as an idea in Thailand called *Krating Daeng*.

Red Bull is an energy drink that dominates the market. Dietrich Mateschitz who lives in Austria developed it. Mr Mateschitz had spent a number of years working with top consumer marketing companies such as Unilever and Procter & Gamble, so he knew quite a lot about consumer behaviour and how to market FMCG successfully. He was also something of an entrepreneur and was on the lookout for a business opportunity which would enable him to start his own successful business. He was on holiday in Thailand when he came across concentrated syrup called *Krating Daeng*, which translated into English means 'Red Bull'. This syrup was very popular and a very good pick-me-up. It was just the sort of product that would be popular in the West with a little alteration and good marketing. After carrying out some research Mr Mateschitz adapted the formula for Western tastes whilst still retaining the power and effect of the original formulation. There were some ingredients, colours and preservatives that had to be eliminated from the original product to make it acceptable to Western markets. The drink was carbonated, and different names were tried. Research looked at different flavours and colours and even different product concepts were examined before Mateschitz finally came up with what is now Red Bull. The product is premium priced, about £1.10 for a small can in UK shops, and is the envy of the industry. The firm is considering a brand extension to Red Bull. Many people mix it with alcohol. A logical extension would be to market the product as a ready-mixed alcoholic drink along the lines of Smirnoff Ice or Bacardi Breezer.

▶ *Screening* is the first stage of sifting viable ideas from less viable ones and issues at this stage relate to potential demand, the company's capability in terms of development and production and profit potential. This is an important stage at which 'Go' or 'Drop' decisions are made. This screening process should have due regard to whether or not the new product will fit into the range of products that the company produces and markets.

▶ *Business analysis* is where the new product idea's financial viability is appraised. By now only 'serious' contenders will remain and a critical stage has been reached. Such analysis needs to take into consideration total costs rather than simply development and production costs.

▶ *Product development* is the point at which the company has committed itself and this is when costs start to increase sharply. Prototypes are developed and can be assessed by marketing research through product appraisal tests. It is here that product refinement and modification will be possible through feedback from marketing research. It might also be the point at which the product is abandoned if expectations do not match reality, rather than risk a 'high exposure' failure in the marketplace.

▶ *Test marketing* is the penultimate stage. This might be appropriate for an FMCG product when it can be tested in test towns or television test areas before going 'national', but this is not always appropriate for more durable products. Here, product placement tests with members of the public are probably more appropriate. The problem

Ideas or concepts

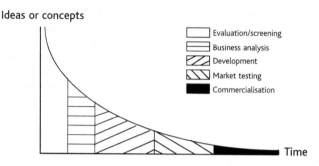

Figure 7.2 Decay curve of new product ideas

with full-scale test marketing is that it allows competitors to see what you are doing, so this disadvantage must be weighed against the advantages of simulating a national launch before full-scale commitment. This is why product testing, rather than high profile test marketing, is better in confidentiality terms.

▶ *Commercialisation* is where the product is launched on the market. All filters have taken place, but even at this stage success is not guaranteed. However, there is a greater likelihood of success if the procedures just described have been undertaken.

American consultants, Booz Allen Hamilton, first put forward the idea of the decay curve of new product ideas as illustrated in Figure 7.2.

In the original research it was discovered that it took 58 new product ideas to produce one potentially successful product. However, even during the 'commercialisation' stage there was still a 50/50 chance that the product would not be successful. Later research suggested that it took considerably fewer new product ideas to produce a successful product. However, this might well have been a function of less 'outrageous' ideas being suggested at evaluation and screening stages.

▶ Factors for successful innovation

International management consultants, McKinsey & Co, conducted research in 1980 that investigated a number of large multinational organisations. The research examined factors deemed to be essential in their successful operation and eight factors were highlighted:

▶ a bias towards action
▶ simple line and team staff organisation

- continued contact with customers
- productivity improvement via people
- operational autonomy and the encouragement of entrepreneurship
- simultaneous loose and tight controls
- stress on one key business value
- an emphasis on sticking to what they know best.

This research has stood the test of time and is still cited as being the critical success formula for successful international enterprise.

▶▶ Product mix and product line

The terms 'product mix' and 'product line' are used in product management in addition to the terms 'depth' and 'width' of the product mix (or product assortment). This latter description means all of the product lines and items that a company offers for sale. Basically, the product line is a group of closely related product items. The width of the product mix denotes the number of product lines carried. The depth of the product mix denotes the range of items within each product line and is calculated by dividing the total number of items carried by the number of product lines. There is another term – 'consistency' – and this relates to the closeness of items in the range in terms of product and marketing characteristics.

Think of an example of a group of product lines. Suggest the mix and depth and width of a separate line of products within the total portfolio of products.

A clothing manufacturer has four separate product lines that comprise men's casual clothing, men's formal clothing, ladies' casual clothing and ladies' formal clothing.

In the ladies' casual clothing product line there are eight separate styles of garment which represent the width of the product mix. There are also ten different sizes within each of these eight separate styles and this represents the depth of the product mix.

By attempting this kind of analysis, product management can look more objectively at its overall product mix and decide whether or not certain lines should be lengthened, shortened or deleted.

▶▶ Product life cycle

Various stages are proposed showing that a product passes through a number of stages in its life from the time it is conceived (the development phase) to the time it is deleted during the decline stage. Marketing people find it is a useful planning tool (Levitt, T. 1982).

The problem with the theory is that it is totally 'believable' and some product managers expect that every product should fit this neat curve. Marketing academics have criticised the concept because when a product is launched it is often killed off prematurely because sales suggest that it has gone into a quick decline. The reality might be that what has happened is probably only a slight dip in the growth curve of the product.

Figure 7.3 shows the curve of product life cycle. On this diagram is superimposed the revenue curve which shows the product recovering its costs of development and launch and then moving into profitability. Naturally, products behave differently, but as a tool of planning the theory has much to commend it.

The shape of the curve can alter and this is useful in illustrating the effect of different marketing conditions. A number of different patterns are shown in Figure 7.4. The first shape represents a 'fad' product which comes quickly into the market and is never seen again. The second shape represents a 'fashion' product whose sales might go in cycles. The third shape represents a product that passes through a number of phases, but where the product manager does not allow the product to become 'stale' after it has entered maturity. This is done by introducing sequential modifications, building on the success of the original product.

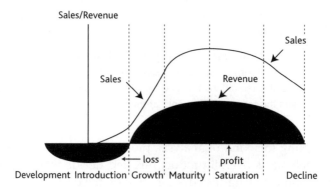

Figure 7.3 The product life cycle

Figure 7.4 Different shapes of the product life cycle

The concepts outlined in Figure 7.4 can be used, as planning tools and curves can be hypothesised that can fit any marketing situation.

Consider a new 'pop' record which has entered the charts. Suggest a product life cycle curve that might equate to the life of this record.

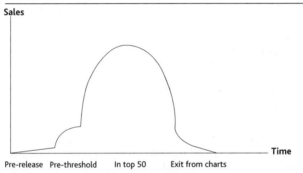

During pre-release the record is sent free to people who might play (and thus promote) the record – namely radio and club disc jockeys. Pre-threshold is when it is first played and small numbers of people start to purchase. It starts its commercial life once it enters the 'top 50' and takes off. It then exits from the charts and sales decline.

The product life cycle is influenced by the nature of the product, changes in the competitive environment and changes on the part of consumers who might display different preferences as the product moves through its life cycle. The shape of the curve, from a manufacturer's viewpoint can also be altered as a result of competitive actions. The product life cycle can be applied to the industry as a whole (which will include a summation of all manufacturers' sales who are marketing that particular product) or it can apply to the sales of a specific product for an individual company.

The time span of the product life cycle can range from a fashion season to many years. In this latter case the maturity and saturation stages will be considerably lengthened.

It is acknowledged that different categories of life cycle exist. We are using soap and shoes as illustrations, so the curve is applicable within one of the following groups:

▷ *product category life cycles* describe a generic product like soap or shoes. Life cycles tend to be long or infinite
▷ *product form life cycles* describe types of product like perfumed soap or plastic shoes. Here, the life cycle is shorter
▷ *brand life cycles* describe various manufacturers' brands of perfumed soap or plastic shoes. This might, in the case of plastic shoes, be linked to a single fashion season with a new brand coming out shortly afterwards, so this kind of life cycle is the shortest of all.

 Vignette 7.3

I'd love a Babycham – the happiest drink in the world has gone back to its roots.

In the 1950s Francis Showering saw the need for an alcoholic drink for women. The product he came up with, made from pears, was called Babycham. The drink embodied the femininity and the style desired by women at the time. Babycham was the first alcoholic drink brand to be advertised on television. In 2003 the Bristol-based product will be 50 years old and is still one of the most distinctive and unique brands in the market sector. The brand is drunk by over 4 million consumers and has been tried by 73 per cent of all UK women. Francis Showering came from a family of cider makers in Somerset going back 200 years. Francis joined the family business of Showerings Limited in 1932 and started to look for new lines to expand the business. He started experimenting by fermenting fruit juices and produced a prize-winning cider. Eventually, with the help of a local research station he produced a clear, sparkling drink made from pear juice. The drink was bottled in large and 'baby' bottles and launched in the Bristol area. During the late 1980s Babycham decided to change its image. Management changed the shape and size of the bottle and got rid of the traditional deer character from its label and advertising. The firm thought Babycham was coming to the end of its product life cycle and decided to 're-vamp' the product to attract a younger and more 'trendy' customer segment. Advertising showed 'funky' men drinking Babycham in discotheques. However the product has now gone full circle and the old bottle, label and 'deer' character are back. The brand has again been relaunched using the deer to take it back to its roots. The design of the Babycham packs focuses on the celebration image of the brand with the use of foil and stars on the label and a return to the old style bottle.

▶ Strategies suggested by each life cycle stage

Successful use of the product life cycle concept is the ability to identify passage from one stage to another. This requires that the company makes use of marketing research and marketing intelligence. The product life cycle can thus be used strategically and suggest an anticipated course of product development for which strategies can be planned ensuring the company's long-term growth in the marketplace. Marketing actions are now suggested appropriate to each of these separate stages. Many policies referred to are explained in greater detail in Chapter 15.

▶ *Development* is the pre-launch phase and during this period confidentiality will have to be maintained in order to keep information away from competitors. It is no secret that in many larger organisations the research and development function is housed entirely separately from the main production unit. As the research and development process progresses from experimentation to the tangible product, in a marketing oriented organisation, the involvement of marketing research tends to increase. This is not to say that marketing research should not be involved at the earlier stages. For instance, focus groups/group discussions would be appropriate in terms of testing out the concept on groups of the general public at an early stage in the process before too much has been committed in terms of research and development expenditure.

▶ *Introduction* is the launch period and the product slowly gains acceptance. There are few (often zero) competitors at this stage, but this is where a number of new products fail. Figure 7.2 indicates that even after a new product idea has gone through its various filter stages there is still an even chance that it might fail. The product is seen to be innovative at this stage and potential buyers should be informed as to what it will do, so advertising tends to be informative. Buyers tend to be 'innovators' as explained later. The product is new and can normally sustain a high initial price (known as skimming and explained in Chapter 8) as there are few or no competitors. Indeed, the product will probably have been expensive to produce and the marketing costs of creating awareness prior to and during its launch might have been high, so this is an opportunity to recoup as many costs as the market will sustain. Distribution is not widespread and is often exclusive within a particular geographical location. Even now, the product may not be totally appropriate in the marketplace in terms of its performance or design features, so product modifications tend to be more frequent.

▶ *Growth* is the period during which competitors start to appear with similar offerings. Indeed, they might well have been conducting parallel research and development, but have been slower in launching their innovative products. Even now the product is still exposed to failure, perhaps through competitive activity as competitors have been able to learn from your mistakes during launch. They will know your price and might undercut, and will know the perceived weaknesses of your product, so they can emphasise the strength of theirs. Although being in the market first is a good policy, it is also a high-risk policy, and unless the company is large enough to sustain a costly failure at this stage, or has other products to fall back upon, then such a policy is very high risk. This growth phase is sometimes termed 'exponential' and it is during this period that sales begin to take off. If the company is small it might be acquired by a larger company. Such acquisitions are normally done on a mutually advantageous basis, but they can be aggressive if the company that has developed the new product is a public limited company and a larger company seeks acquisition through direct offers to shareholders. During this phase, promotion tends to change from one of creating awareness to one of attempting to create an identifiable brand. Promotional expenditure is probably still relatively high. Distribution is also important during this phase. There are two parallel forces at work here. The first is in terms of powerful retail buyers attempting to rationalise the total number of lines they sell. The second is in terms of manufacturers attempting to secure as many distribution outlets as possible, as the product has now lost its innovative appeal. In distribution terms they move from exclusive, then to selective and finally to intensive distribution. The philosophy of the latter is that maximum exposure at the point of sale is probably as important as brand awareness and these issues are detailed in Chapter 9.

▶ *Maturity and saturation* are dealt with together, because the 'maturity' phase is the phase where product sales level off to a gradual peak over a longer period (sometimes years or decades) and the 'saturation' phase is from its peak, gradually downwards to the phase where sales start to decelerate towards the 'decline' phase. Many marketing authors miss out the 'saturation' phase altogether and class all of this phase as 'maturity'. During this phase sales slow down and repeat purchases are prevalent. There are attempts to 'differentiate' products through the addition of 'features'. Price competition is at its maximum as other manufacturers enter the market. These manufacturers come in with 'me too' products which have not had to sustain heavy costs of research and development and promotional costs associated with their launch. Although their brands might not carry the same weight as well-established brands, price is the main competitive weapon and price 'wars' between established brands and newer competitors are commonplace. By now, the 'mystique' surrounding the product has dissipated and consumers feel confident in purchasing a product that bears a relatively unknown brand label. There is an increasing trend among retailers to trim their inventories, so unless the product can offer a sustainable product, brand or price advantage then there will be reluctance to stock. As market growth has ceased, marketing management must attempt to at least retain market share in the face of increased competition and it is at this stage that a number of manufacturers withdraw from the marketplace. If the brand is a sustainable brand name then advertising will be necessary to keep this in the mind of consumers and to keep them loyal to the brand. Promotion to the trade is important as manufacturers wish to retain their distribution outlets. Joint manufacturer/trade promotions are developed with costs being shared on an equitable basis. There is generally a move away from what is termed a 'pull' strategy of promotion towards a 'push' strategy as discussed in Chapter 12.

▶ *Decline* is signalled by a steady and sustained fall in sales after the 'saturation' phase. Marketing research should have told the company that this was due to happen in order that there should be concentration on developing new product lines. However, company management quite often refuses to accept that its products are about to enter the decline phase and stay with them in the hope that the inevitable might not happen. This decline might be the result of a change in customer preferences, but more likely it is because of new products or processes supplanting the existing one. In the UK, examples of industries that have entered such decline are coal and textiles. The phase is characterised by competitive intensity and price-cutting and sales falling continuously during this period. Many producers decide to abandon the marketplace, or are forced to abandon because of financial difficulties. Thus, the decision to abandon the market is critical and, as can be seen from Figure 7.3, this should theoretically happen when the product moves from a positive to a negative revenue situation. However, some manufacturers stay in business during the decline phase. It is only in a few cases that a product will decline completely and never appear again. There will usually be a residual or continued demand, but at far less volume than before. A good example is solid fuel that has largely been supplanted by gas and electricity and, to a lesser extent, oil for home heating purposes. However, there is still demand for solid fuel and as most of the solid fuel processors have now departed from the marketplace there is a vibrant market left for those who have remained.

Consider the product life cycle concept. Try to cite a well-known product item that fits each of the stages within each stage of this life cycle.

- *Introduction* – CD ROMs for personal computers
- *Growth* – personal computers for home use
- *Maturity* – refrigerators
- *Saturation* – traditional ovens
- *Decline* – black and white television

▶▶ Product diffusion and adoption

Everett Rogers' (1962) 'diffusion processes' relates to the speed and extent of take-up of new products and considers the people who are the ultimate target of marketing efforts, rather than the marketplace itself which is the function of the notion of the product life cycle. The diagram that forms the model for the diffusion curve is very much like the model for the product life cycle, and indeed there are similarities. Diffusion theory infers that consumers do not fall into the same category for all purchases, and it describes consumer behaviour in relation to individual needs and preferences (see Figure 7.5).

Figure 7.5 represents the rate at which the product is purchased for the first time by individuals who are categorised into adopter categories, depending upon when in the cycle of time the purchase was made for the

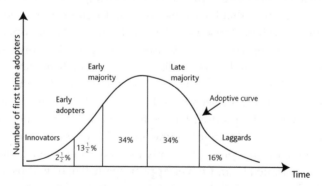

Figure 7.5 The product adoption process/diffusion of innovations
Source: Based on Rogers (1962)

first time. The descriptions that follow are generalisations of each of these adopter categories, but it does not follow that this is always the case – for example 'innovators' for a new type of computer software might well tend to be people mainly from C2 skilled working class backgrounds.

◗ *Innovators* tend to be opinion leaders who are first to purchase and these are basically the same purchasers as those who purchase at the introduction phase of the product life cycle. They are likely to be younger and better educated from reasonably affluent high social status family backgrounds. Their knowledge of the product comes more from their own feelings than from the efforts of marketing people. They represent the first 2.5 per cent of the entire market – which is two standard deviations to the left of the mean.
◗ *Early adopters* possess similar characteristics to innovators, but they are slightly more cautious and less gregarious. They tend to belong more to 'local' groups, but as opinion leaders they are influential. These comprise 13.5 per cent of the market.
◗ *Early majority* purchasers tend to rate slightly above average in terms of social class and now that the product has become more established, they rely principally on marketing information before making their purchase. This group represents 34 per cent of the market.
◗ *Late majority* purchasers tend to be more cautious, but are prone to social pressures to adopt the product for the first time. This group comprises 34 per cent of the total market.
◗ *Laggards* are the final 16 per cent category and they make up the cautious group. They tend to be older and more conservative, generally coming from a lower socioeconomic class.

Diffusion is closely related to the adoption process of individual customers and it has been found that five facets of products lead to a more rapid and wider adoption:

◗ *Relative advantage* in terms of the greater the perceived advantage of the new product to customers the faster it will diffuse.
◗ *Compatibility* relates to the greater the extent to which the new product is compatible with existing products, the faster it will diffuse.
◗ *Complexity* is a disadvantage, because the more complex the new product, the more difficult it will be to understand in the marketplace and the diffusion rate might be slower.
◗ *Divisibility* means the greater the ability of the new product to be used or tried on a limited scale before full commitment on the part of the purchaser, the faster it will diffuse.

▷ *Communicability* means an ability of the new product to be demonstrated or communicated by early purchasers to later potential purchasers, thus hastening the rate of diffusion.

Think of a relatively new product, but one that has diffused up to say 'late majority' first time users. Then think of some people you know who have purchased this product. Then think of some people who have not yet purchased and include those who will probably never purchase the product. In which innovator category do you feel those who have purchased fell when they made their first time purchase, and into which category will those fall who have yet to make a purchase? Is there anything about their behaviour and background that equate to the points mentioned against innovator categories that have been listed?

This is a question for which no answer can be provided, because it depends on the individuals chosen. However, you might be surprised at the conformity between the people you have chosen and the descriptions that have been ascribed to each of the innovator categories.

Reflect on material that was covered in Chapter 4 on buyer behaviour. The adoption process is closely allied to the process cited in Figure 7.5 and it links in neatly in terms of the decision-making processes that take place prior to making the purchase of a new innovatory product or service.

Consider the adoption process. What is this, and how is it related to the diffusion of innovations?

The adoption process can be described as:

Awareness → Interest → Evaluation → Trial → Adoption → Post-adoption confirmation

It is related to the diffusion of innovations, in that this is typically the process purchasers go through before making a major new product purchasing decision, only more so in this case as they have never tried the product before.

Although Figure 7.5 adds up to 100 per cent this is not to say that everybody will ultimately purchase the product or service. If we consider home telephones, it could be said that the country has reached saturation in terms of new subscribers. However, some people do not subscribe because they like privacy or have some other personal reasons for not wanting a telephone, so the market for home telephones will never be 100 per cent of all households. These non-purchasing categories are termed 'non-adopters'.

▶▶ Portfolio models

Alan Zakon suggested the first portfolio analysis in the late 1960s when he was working as a consultant with the Mead Paper Corporation in the USA. He proposed a matrix as shown in Figure 7.6.

Savings account	Sweepstake
Bond	Mortgage

Figure 7.6 Zakon's matrix

The formula was simple. 'Savings account' meant no cash flow but growth; 'sweepstake' meant speculative products; 'bonds' were some cash flow and some growth and 'mortgage' meant large cash flow but no growth. Products or strategic business units (SBUs), were simply assessed on a qualitative basis and then placed in an appropriate box. What the matrix did to was to allow management to look objectively at SBUs in terms of their current situation and make decisions as to their future.

Since this first model, which is more for historical interest than practical application, many models have been developed, the most important and well known of which are now described and evaluated.

▶ Boston Consulting Group (BCG) matrix

The BCG matrix (sometimes called the 'Boston box') has been very successful with much to commend it. It had backing in terms of research, which came principally from the Profit Impact of Marketing Strategy (PIMS) study, which incorporated 57 large companies and 620 subsidiary companies in its database in 1974. By linking market share with profitability, the PIMS study was found to correlate closely with the notion of the BCG matrix. It was popular in that it was simple, and by concentrating on the criteria of market growth and market share it was a tool to which users could relate. The BCG matrix is described in Figure 7.7.

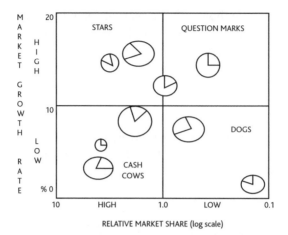

Figure 7.7 BCG matrix
Source: Long Range Planning, February 1977

Each of the circles represents the size of the overall market and the segment taken out of that circle represents the company's share of that total market. Each quadrant is explained:

▸ *Stars* are SBUs with a high market share in a high growth industry and have a good earning potential. However, at what is possibly an early stage in its life cycle, the product is probably costly to maintain because of having to engage in aggressive marketing effort and this might mean high advertising expenses.

▸ *Cash cows* have a high market share but have probably matured in a slow, or zero, growth market. Typically, they are well established with loyal customers and product development costs are relatively low as initial research and development expenditure has been recovered. These are profitable 'safe' products and a strong company has many in its portfolio. Generally, stars move into this position when the market has stabilised.

▸ *Question marks* are sometimes termed 'problem children' or 'wildcats'. Here, market growth prospects are favourable, but they have a relatively low market share, so the SBU has only a weak foothold in an expanding, but probably highly competitive, marketplace. If the SBU is to become a star, then substantial marketing or research and development expenditure might be needed.

▸ *Dogs* are sometimes called 'pets' in this respect, and this is an SBU characterised by low market share and low growth. These are SBUs for potential liquidation, but as 'pet' implies they are probably still there for nostalgic reasons on the part of management. Indeed, when companies are in financial difficulties and the creditors take charge the first thing that is done is to prune dogs from the portfolio. In some circumstances the retention of dogs might be necessary so the company can provide a comprehensive portfolio of products it offers as part of its overall product mix.

In practice companies tend to have a balanced portfolio, but those with a preponderance of 'dogs' are clearly in difficulty. Stronger companies will have a preponderant mixture of 'stars' and 'cash cows'. It does not follow that SBUs progress around each of the boxes in a sequential manner. However, the matrix is dynamic and will change over time as market conditions get better or worse and indeed as products move through their product life cycle stages. Marketing management must attempt to ensure that 'star' and 'cash cow' SBUs remain in their respective positions for as long as possible, as these are the ones that provide most of the company's profits and such SBUs are the company's insurance for the future. Clearly 'question marks' must be looked at in terms of pushing them into the 'star' category through marketing actions. 'Dogs' need careful evaluation to see whether any pruning of the range is needed.

If you work in a company, or if you are closely associated with one, try to put each of that company's products or services into their respective quadrants on a BCG matrix.

This is an activity for which no answer can be given because it will depend upon the company and its portfolio of products. Surprisingly perhaps, few companies attempt to analyse their SBUs in this manner.

▶ The McKinsey/General Electric (GE) business screen

This matrix was developed by consultants, McKinsey & Co, working with General Electric (USA). This was an attempt to try to overcome difficulties encountered when attempting to apply the BCG matrix by using a broader range of company and market factors when assessing the position of SBUs.

The technique uses market attractiveness and business position as its two criteria. Different weights are attached along each axis along the parameters of 'low', 'medium' and 'high'. For the 'market attractiveness' axis, measurements like market growth rate, market size, difficulty of entering the market, numbers of competitors, profit margins and technological requirements are taken into consideration. For the 'business posi-

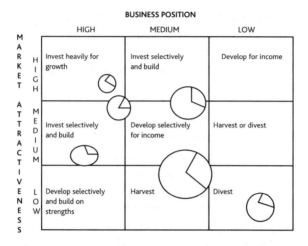

Figure 7.8 General Electric (GE) matrix

tion' axis, this considers matters like size of the SBU, strength of its position compared to that of the competition, capabilities of the organisation in relation to production and research and development and the strength that is displayed within the management of the SBU. The matrix uses nine boxes and is described in Figure 7.8.

As with the BCG matrix, circles represent the size of the overall market and the segments within each of the circles represent that SBU's share of the total market.

As with the activity on the BCG matrix, try to put each of the company's products or services into their respective positions on the GE matrix.

Again, no answer can be given, but you might find that this is an easier matrix to visualise and apply. It is also more plausible in that a nine box matrix gives a greater degree of precision.

▶ Porter's generic strategies and the industry/market evolution model

In 1979 Michael Porter identified three generic strategies for achieving success in a competitive market:

▶ *Overall cost leadership* means producing a standard product at low cost or engaging in heavy advertising in order to undercut competition.
▶ *Differentiation* is selling at a higher price than average something that

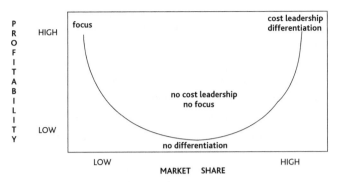

Figure 7.9 Porter's generic strategies
Source: Based on Porter (1980)

consumers will then see as having some unique feature of quality, image or design.

▶ *Focus* concentrates on a specialist product range or a unique segment of the market or a combination of them both.

Figure 7.9 illustrates the profitability implications of these strategies. It can be seen that financial success does not necessarily mean a company has to have a high market share to be successful. Companies can have a small market share and still be profitable (upper left) through specialised product offerings. The upper right sector is also profitable because products can be differentiated or can have a large market as a result of economies of scale that can be reflected in appropriately lower prices to customers. Companies that are 'stuck in the middle' have problems as a result of low profits and a modest share of the market.

Think of a range of products with which you are familiar, for example, compact hi-fi systems. Perhaps you might visit your local electronic store to remind yourself of manufacturers who produce this equipment if names do not spring to mind. With this list of manufacturers in mind, try to put them on the scale as shown in Figure 7.9.

This will be a subjective listing, but in the case of the hi-fi example this is a product that is in the maturity phase of its life cycle, so names will come quickly to mind (that is, heavily branded popular products that are competitively priced) in the top right hand corner and the specialist producers (that is, those with unique product features or high quality images) in the top left hand corner. A few will probably be 'stuck in the middle' which, in the case of the competitive hi-fi market, is not a place in which they will be able to remain for very long.

In 1985 Porter developed a model which furthered this earlier research. His model was based on three broad stages in the evolution of an industry/market:

▷ *Emerging industry* – portrayed by hesitancy on the part of buyers over likely performance of products, their functioning, and possibility of obsolescence as manufacturers leapfrog each other in terms of technological improvements at the early stage of the life of the industry and products being produced.
▷ *Transition to maturity* – distinguished by reduced profits throughout the industry and a general slowing down in growth. Customers become more confident with purchases as they are more familiar with the range of products and manufacturers. The industry settles down in terms of technological breakthrough and most product offerings are similar. Emphasis moves away from product features towards non-product features like branding and advertising.
▷ *Decline* is where substitute products begin to make inroads into the marketplace, customers need change because of social or demographic reasons. The product is basically becoming 'stale' and other products begin to supplant it.

Each of these stages was then looked at in terms of whether the company was a leader or a follower in the particular industry, and the resultant matrix suggesting strategies for each sector is illustrated in Figure 7.10.

'Emerging industries' should be developed to counteract rivalry between competitors, with the possibility of substitute products being developed to put the producer in a powerful bargaining position. 'Transition to maturity' means developing new markets and focusing upon

		GROWTH (emerging industry)	MATURITY (transition to maturity)	DECLINE
STRATEGIC POSITION	LEADER	Keep ahead of the field	Cost leadership Raise barriers to entry Deter competitors	Redefine scope Divest peripheral activities Encourage departures
	FOLLOWER	Imitation at lower cost Joint ventures	Differentiation Focus	Differentiation New opportunities

Figure 7.10 Strategic position in industry life cycle
Source: Porter (1985)

specific market segments as well as attempting to become more efficient. A 'decline strategy' suggests either divesting the product or profitably supplying residual demand.

▶ Shell directional policy matrix

This matrix was suggested by Shell Chemicals in 1975 and it covers the organisation's competitive capabilities against prospects for profitability. There is a suggested strategy for each box in the matrix illustrated in Figure 7.11.

Whatever strategy is selected, it should be 'resilient' and viable in a diverse range of potential futures. It is important, therefore, that each strategy is evaluated against future contingencies. In the matrix, both axes look at criteria for market growth, market quality, the industry situation, plus environmental considerations. Sector profitability, however, specifically looks at these from an overall industry viewpoint, whereas company competitive capability looks at each from a more specific company-based point of view related to market position, product research and development and productive capability. On each factor, a product (or SBU) is given from one to five stars. For example, the factor of 'market quality' might be estimated on the basis of past profit stability in that sector. This evaluation is then converted into a quantified rating (although such a rating has been qualitatively assessed). A similar procedure is undertaken for each of the other three factors, so the overall score on sector profitability is then a total of the ratings on all factors.

PROSPECTS FOR SECTOR PROFITABILITY

		Unattractive	Average	Attractive
COMPANY COMPETITIVE CAPABILITY	Weak	Disinvest	Phased withdrawal	Double or quit
	Average	Phased withdrawal	Custodial	Try harder
	Strong	Cash generation	Growth	Leader

Figure 7.11 Shell directional policy matrix
Source: Based on Shell Chemicals UK (1975)

▶ Arthur D. Little industry maturity/competitive position matrix

The consultants Arthur D. Little developed this matrix which looks at 'stage of industry maturity' alongside 'company's competitive position'. The 'stage of industry maturity' axis is, or course, similar to the various stages in the product life cycle concept. The resultant matrix is illustrated in Figure 7.12.

STAGE OF INDUSTRY MATURITY

COMPANY'S COMPETITIVE POSITION		Embryonic	Growth	Maturity	Ageing
	Dominant				
	Strong				
	Favourable				
	Tentative				
	Weak				

Figure 7.12 A. D. Little competitive position/industry maturity matrix

Factors used to assess the stage the SBU or products are in relate to the rate of market growth, future potential in the industry, product or line of products, number and relative efficiency in marketing related to competitors, purchasing patterns by consumers, ease of competitive entry and complexity/simplicity of technology.

▶ Barksdale and Harris portfolio analysis/product life cycle matrix

Many textbooks do not quote this matrix, but it is felt that it is good in successfully combining the product life cycle concept with ideas from the BCG matrix. A common criticism of the BCG matrix is that new products and declining products are ignored. The Barksdale and Harris model overcomes this problem (Figure 7.13).

The assumptions are that products have a finite span of life, that cash generated and profit margins are positively related to share of market, that costs of production are related to volume and unit costs decrease as volume increases. Each of the categories is now explained.

- *Infants* appear in the pioneering stage and are products that carry risk. Their profits will be small or negative as they consume a lot of promotional costs informing customers of their function and existence.
- *Problem children* are the same as for the BCG matrix with a low market share but high growth, so they are costly to maintain.

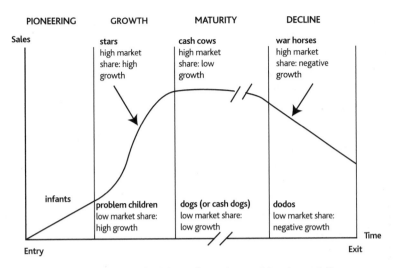

Figure 7.13 Barksdale and Harris combined portfolio

▶ *Stars* are the products to nurture, but are probably high cost in marketing terms. Although they have a high market share and high growth rate, marketing expenditure in the form of informative promotion in a relatively new market will be high.

▶ *Cash cows* as with the BCG matrix are steady income earners with a high market share in a low growth mature market.

▶ *Dogs* are sometimes called 'cash dogs' as they are placed in a low (or even zero or marginally negative) growth sector of a saturated market. However, even though their market share is low they might make a marginal amount of money for the company – hence 'cash dogs'.

▶ *Warhorses* are sustainable SBUs in that they are in a declining market, but possess a high share of that declining market. They have probably been cash cows, but the market trend has worked against them. They should receive the attention of management in terms of sustaining them as long as possible in this declining market, but little should be spent on promotion. Once the time is right they should be withdrawn from the market before they become 'stale' as this could adversely affect the image of the company.

▶ *Dodos* have a low share in a market that is in decline, with little opportunity for cash generation. The only way they could be made profitable might be if many competitors exit from the market and they are turned into 'warhorses'.

Figure 7.14 details the characteristics of each of these groups.

RELATIVE MARKET SHARE

		high		low
MARKET GROWTH	**low**	**Cash cows** Positive cash flow	**Infants** Negative cash flow	**Dogs** Negative cash flow
	medium	**Stars** Modest positive or negative cash		**Problem children** Large negative cash flow
	negative	**Warhorses** Positive cash flow		**Dodos** Negative cash flow

Figure 7.14 Characteristics of product categories in
Barksdale and Harris combined portfolio

**List a typical household product in each of the stages
represented in the Barksdale and Harris portfolio.**

- Infants – waste disposal units
- Stars and problem children (where they are depends on the company) – automatic washing machines
- Cash cows and dogs (again, where they are depends upon the marketing efforts of the particular company) – refrigerators
- Warhorses and dodos (similar again, in terms of how the company markets the product) – black and white television

◗◗ Packaging

Packaging is often classed as part of promotion, and reference is made to it again in Chapter 12. However, packaging is the 'end' part of the product, as the external appearance and finish of a product will have an influence on its ultimate acceptability. Packaging has a number of functions to perform:

- To protect and preserve its contents
- To help in the distribution of goods being transferred from where they were made to the ultimate customer, via a number of logistics intermediaries
- Selling in terms of promotional appeal as far as design and information conveyed on the pack is concerned
- For convenience of users and as an aid to storage of contents

▷ To conform to statutory and voluntary regulations in providing a list of contents or weight.

Packaging is an important aid to selling and many products that cannot be differentiated on product features can be differentiated through packaging and branding. As well as appealing to customers, packaging must appeal to retailers. This includes 'outers' (bulk packaging that bundles together a number of individual products) as well as packages in which goods are packed. Well-packaged products can be an inducement for distributive intermediaries to display and promote a specific brand as opposed to brands of other manufacturers.

SELF-CHECK

In relation to each of the quadrants in Ansoff's matrix, what strategy is suggested by each of the following:

- New products into new markets?
- New products into existing markets?
- Existing products into new markets?
- Existing products into existing markets?

The answers are: Diversification; Product development; Market development and Market penetration

What alternatives exist for the management of new product development?
New product managers; New product committees; New product departments (sometimes appointing a product/project champion); New product venture teams

What are the logical steps in the process of new product development?
Idea generation; Screening; Business analysis; Product development; Test marketing; Commercialisation

List all the stages in the product life cycle
Development; Introduction; Growth; Maturity and Saturation; Decline

List the categories in the 'diffusion of innovation' process

Innovators; Early adopters; Early majority; Late majority; Laggards

List the quadrants in the BCG matrix
Stars; Question marks (or problem children or wildcats); Cash cows; Dogs

The GE matrix has as its measurements 'high', 'medium' and 'low'. What are the two axes on the matrix?
Market attractiveness; Business position

In the Shell directional policy matrix measurements are: 'unattractive' 'average' and 'attractive' & 'weak', 'average' and 'strong'. What axes do each relate to?
'Prospects for sector profitability' and 'Company competitive capability' in that order.

What categories of products are referred to in the Barksdale and Harris combined portfolio?
Infants; Stars; Problem children; Cash cows; Dogs (or cash dogs); Warhorses; Dodos

What are the functions of packaging?
Protection; an aid to distribution; promotional appeal; storage of contents; to display statutory regulations.

▶▶ Summary

This is an important chapter, for without a product or service a company could not function, as it is the rationale for all trade and commerce. The chapter has traced the product or service from categorisations under each of the headings of industrial goods and consumer goods and examined product management issues. New products were examined in terms of categories of new products and suggestions made for new product organisation. The process of new product development was examined and factors for successful innovation discussed after which product mix and product line was explained. The product life cycle was covered including strategies for each stage of the product life cycle. Product diffusion and adoption were examined in terms of innovator categories. An examination was made of portfolio models from the first one to the BCG, GE and Shell matrices plus the work of Porter. The Barksdale and Harris combined portfolio was examined in terms of the relationship between the BCG matrix and the product life cycle. Finally, packaging was considered in the context of the product.

FURTHER READING

Armstrong G. and Kotler P. (2000) *Marketing: An Introduction* (5th edn), Chapter 7, 'Product and Service Strategy' and Chapter 8, 'New-Product Development and Product Life Cycle Strategies', Prentice Hall, Englewood Cliffs, NJ.

Blythe J. (2001) *Essentials of Marketing*, Chapter 6, 'Products, Branding and Packages', Pearson Education, London.

Davies M. (1998) *Understanding Marketing*, Chapter 6, 'Managing the Product in the Marketing Mix', Prentice Hall, London.

Keegan W.J. and Green M.S. (2000) *Global Marketing* (2nd edn), Chapter 11, 'Product and Branding Decisions', Prentice Hall, London.

Lancaster G.A. and Reynolds P.L. (1999) *Introduction to Marketing: A Step-by-Step Guide to All The Tools of Marketing*, Chapter 10, 'Product and Portfolio Analysis', Kogan Page, London.

Morse S. (1994) *Successful Product Management*, Kogan Page, London.

Plamer A. (2000) *Principles of Marketing*, Chapter 9, 'The Product' and Chapter 10, 'Innovation and New Product Development', OUP, Oxford.

Urban G.L. and Hauser J.R. (1993) *Design and Marketing of New Products*, Prentice Hall, Englewood Cliffs, NJ.

▶▶ References

Ansoff, Igor H. (1957) 'Strategies for Diversification', *Harvard Business Review*, September–October, pp. 113–24.

Booz, Allen & Hamilton (1982) *New Product Management for the 1980s*, Booz, Allen & Hamilton Inc, New York.

Levitt T. (1982) *Differentiation of Anything: the Marketing Imagination*, Collier Macmillan, London, pp. 72–93.

Porter M.E. (1979) 'How Competitive Forces Shape Strategy', *Harvard Business Review*, **57**(2): 137–45.

Porter M.E. (1985) *Competitive Advantage: Creating and Sustaining Superior Performance*, Free Press, New York.

Rogers E. (1962) *Diffusion of Innovations*, Free Press, New York, p. 162.

Shell Chemicals UK (1975) The Directional Policy Matrix: A New Aid to Corporate Planning, November.

8 PRICE

▶▶ The importance of pricing

Price is the means whereby an organisation covers costs of research, manufacturing, marketing and other activities. In a profit-making organisation the surplus is profit. Price is also important in not-for-profit organisations. Here, the organisation must ensure that any costs incurred from the sale or dispensation of services must be within the constraints of an agreed budget. Organisational goals and objectives are determined through market conditions, so price is a function of such conditions. Organisational objectives are sometimes compromised by a realisation that certain levels of profit cannot be achieved.

As an element of the marketing mix price is, of course, the source of revenue for the organisation, whereas other elements incur costs. Its importance varies according to market conditions and the type of product or service being marketed, but only in rare circumstances is price the only criterion when purchases are made. Other elements like the brand name, service and warranty considerations, the sales routine and sales promotion all play their part, but the final consideration usually rests upon price, so its importance cannot be underestimated. As price directly determines the amount of profit (or loss) an organisation makes it is important that it is approached in a scientific manner. Organisations should consider pricing in conjunction with marketing objectives and these should be quantified in terms of reaching organisational goals, which is the subject of marketing planning in Chapter 15. So price is the means through which marketing objectives are reached.

Price levels in the economy affect our individual standards

of living as well as the functioning of the economy as a whole. In a market-driven economy the goal must, therefore, be to provide the products and services that we need, but at good value for money, which will be reflected in the prices charged. Competition between providers of goods and services will tend to drive prices down as purchasers look for value, and this principle is at the very centre of marketing.

▶▶ Pricing perspectives

Pricing theory distinguishes three separate approaches. As these have been documented by marketing theorists marketing propositions tend to be cited as being the most sensible ones. However, marketing theories were the last to be developed, so is not surprising that these are more sustainable than the other approaches in a modern commercial environment. Each of these approaches is dealt with later in the chapter, but the general philosophy pertaining to each is dealt with now:

▶ *The economist's approach* This approach contends that price is the means through which supply and demand is brought into equilibrium. The mechanism operates along a range of markets from perfect competition, through imperfect competition to monopoly. The assumption is that profit will be maximised and the only input to purchasing decisions is the relationship between demand and price.

▶ *The accountant's approach* Here, the thrust is upon recovering costs in order to make profits. This is often expressed as a required rate of return. The accountant's approach emphasises the importance of identifying and classifying different costs. The disadvantage with this approach is the tendency to ignore volume of demand and prevailing market conditions.

▶ *The marketer's approach* The marketer's approach emphasises the effect of price on the organisation's competitive market position. This includes factors like levels of sales, market share and levels of profit. Value is emphasised as well as price, and the notion is to set prices at 'what the market will bear'.

These approaches have been briefly explained to provide an understanding of the various views at this stage. Each philosophy is later expanded and elucidated.

▚ Vignette 8.1

Solving London's traffic problems using the price mechanism.

Most major cities in the world have some form of traffic congestion problem. Solving them has always been problematic because there are always so many vested interests to take into consideration. Motorists have certain freedoms and should be free to enjoy their motoring. However many that need to get into cities to work often cannot do so because of the congestion. Shopkeepers and others with business interests welcome people into the city because it bring business and prosperity. On the other hand too much congestion puts a lot of people off visiting cities. Public transport is an option but many people think of public transport as dirty and unreliable. The current mayor of London, Ken Livingstone has come up with a price solution to reduce the demand for people using their own vehicles to access London. Motorists who drive into London will have to pay a tax of £5 or risk a heavy fine. The idea behind the scheme is to price congestion 'out of the market'. If motorists have to pay £5 a day to get into the heart of London they may think twice about it and use public transport instead. It is hoped that the tax will encourage motorists to leave their cars parked at locations on the outskirts of London and use public transport to get into the centre of the city. The London scheme is expected to raise £200 million in revenue which will be ring-fenced for expenditure on the city's public transport system. Basically it is hoped the scheme will dramatically reduce congestion in the city, as much as 15 per cent in the first year, and increase the use of buses, trains and especially the London Underground. Many people are against the scheme. London's ring road does not have the capacity to take the added traffic, which is likely to flood out into residential streets just outside the charge zone as people search for a cheap place to park. Some say it is possible that traffic congestion may even increase as a result of the charge. This happened in Nottingham a few years ago when a scheme to reduce congestion in the inner city resulted in total chaos and had to be abandoned. However others feel that unless we introduce a pricing system we will never be able to control congestion in the UK. The London scheme is seen as a pilot scheme, which if successful will be introduced to other UK towns such as Birmingham and Manchester.

▶▶ Pricing decisions

Price plays an important part in the buyer/seller relationship. As we edge towards the era of 'relationship marketing' that was introduced at the end of Chapter 4, and is examined in more detail later in the text, the significance of price can be reduced, as factors such as quality and reliability of delivery are emphasised as being of equal or even greater importance. A trust develops between sellers and buyers, who mutually agree that prices will be set at a 'fair' level. There is a notion of 'open accounting' that is practised between some firms where price bargaining does not enter into the negotiation equation. Here, long-term suppliers typically provide component parts to a main manufacturer, and show how the final price is computed, including elements like materials, labour and expenses plus the margin for profit. These suppliers also have access to their customers' price calculations including the final make-up. This process is termed 'supply chain integration' (SCI). An acceptable price is agreed between both parties based upon relative profit margins. However, open accounting is perhaps an idealistic situation that is appropriate for component manufacturers supplying large manufacturing plants, but not for the large range of products on the market. In general commercial practice, buyers will view price as a cost that is paid in return for satisfaction, and the seller sees price as a means of cost recovery and profit.

The principal inputs to pricing decisions are customers, competitors, costs and company considerations.

Under each of these four Cs – customers, competitors, costs and company considerations – what do you feel are appropriate criteria that should be examined under each C in terms of pricing considerations?

- *Customers* – what they will be willing to pay that will relate to price levels in the marketplace; the effect of price on long-term relationships; loyalty to a particular product (brand loyalty in the case of FMCG)
- *Competitors* – nature and extent of competition; their numbers; how many or few for the type of market being supplied; how aggressive they are in terms of marketing activity including price; prices they charge
- *Costs* – materials; labour; overheads; considerations as to whether in a highly competitive market goods may be produced on a marginal cost basis, that is, overheads have been recovered on other product manufacture, so the only costs in the equation are direct costs of materials, expenses, labour and a margin for profit
- *Company* – objectives in terms of growth, whether it wishes to be a market leader or a market follower; company image; resources of the company

In addition to these four C factors, there are a number of macro considerations that will affect price including legislation (corporation tax and VAT); tariffs and duty where appropriate; effect of Government on pricing, (for example if the company becomes a powerful player in the industry, perhaps through merger or take-over, any suspicion of prices that are, or might become, too high would probably attract the attention of the Monopolies and Mergers Commission or action might be taken under the Restrictive Trade Practices Act).

▶▶ Concepts of pricing

Economics is the starting point from which understanding pricing commences. Economic theory looks at ideas of utility and value in relation to price. Utility means the aspect of a product or service that makes it capable of satisfying a want or need. Value is the term used to quantify utility, and price is the monetary unit that this value represents.

Accounting provides a more pragmatic approach which contends that costs, competition and demand are the prime factors that relate to pricing decisions, but price should always recover a company's fixed costs (for example rent, rates, heating) and variable costs (direct materials, labour and expenses) plus a margin for profit.

The view of marketing holds that 'prices shall be set at what the market will bear'. In reality this is not as stark as it seems, as factors like competition, costs, long-term goodwill towards customers and even potential for Government intervention have to be considered. Indeed, in the interests perhaps of gaining entry to a market, or maintaining a product line in times of intense competition, there might be situations when the company markets its products anticipating losses in the short term.

Three views have been cited from the theoretical to the logical to the realistic and each is now examined in detail.

▶ The economist's approach

This commences with the notion of supply and demand and this is expressed as demand and supply schedules or curves as shown in Figure 8.1.

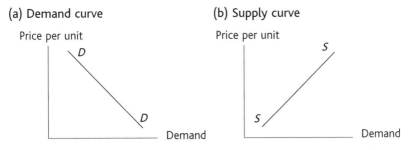

Figure 8.1 Supply and demand curves

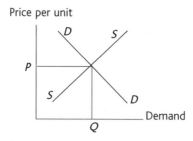

Figure 8.2 The law of supply and demand

In Figure 8.1(a) it can be seen that the lower the price, the greater is the amount demanded and conversely, the greater the price the lower the amount demanded. Conversely, in Figure 8.1(b) the lower the price, the less the amount suppliers will be willing to produce and the higher the price, the more suppliers will be prepared to supply.

In Figure 8.2 we superimpose one over the other, and where the two curves intersect is the market price. So at price P, quantity Q will be demanded.

Elasticity and inelasticity of demand are terms used by economists to describe how price changes affect levels of demand. The term 'elasticity' is described as 'responsiveness'. Inelastic demand is less sensitive to price changes and elastic demand is very responsive to price changes. The concepts are shown in Figure 8.3.

In Figure 8.3(a) we see that a large reduction in price from P to $P1$ will hardly affect the demand which only moves from Q to $Q1$ and this is known as 'inelasticity of demand'. Indeed, when the demand curve is vertical this is known as 'infinite inelasticity'. In Figure 8.3(b) a small reduction in price from P to $P1$ will have a big effect on demand that moves from Q to $Q1$.

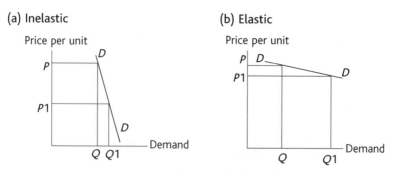

Figure 8.3 Inelastic and elastic demand

Think of a product that has inelastic demand and a product that has elastic demand.

Salt or soap for inelastic demand and colour televisions or hi-fi units for elastic demand.

Thus it can be seen that the incline of the demand curve, or the elasticity of demand for the product, will very much affect pricing decisions. However, in practice, measures of total elasticity or inelasticity of demand are unrealistic. Even when demand is elastic, there is usually some point on the demand curve where a further price reduction would make little or no difference to demand. Determining the exact position of this point is important in demand analysis, as it would make little sense to reduce the price if this would not result in an increase in sales sufficient to offset the price reduction.

Companies market their products in market situations that range from 'perfect competition' to 'monopoly', each representing an extreme on the continuum. Perfect competition is a market in which there are a large number of fully informed buyers and sellers of similar products, and where there are no obstacles to exit or entry on the part of companies. Monopoly is where there is a single producer of a product for which there are no substitutes.

A theory developed by economists that has relevance to marketers is the notion of 'oligopoly' that falls between the extremes of monopoly and perfect competition, towards the monopoly end of the scale. This concept has particular relevance for marketers of FMCG. Here we find a market dominated by a few sellers where each company must ascertain the effects of its policies on the behaviour of its rivals.

The theory maintains that these few sellers are interdependent and the goods they produce are basically similar (or homogeneous). Companies competing in this situation are sensitive to price changes between the various players, because since goods are similar customers will tend to purchase at the lowest price, so if one company lowers prices then the remaining players have to do the same in order to market their products. Therefore price, as an instrument of competition, tends to be less effective than competition that is based upon non-price factors such as branding through advertising and sales promotional activities. Manufacturers produce below their maximum and the price of entry to the system can be prohibitively high, either because of the amount of promotion required to establish a foothold or because of the costs of setting up manufacturing activities in terms of investment in plant and machinery and research and development costs. Therefore, perfect competition is typified by a preponderance of small companies with each player striving to perform at a personal best, whereas in oligopoly the actions of each player very much depend on the actions of other players.

 **Activity**

Although views put forward by economists tend to be theoretical, and are sometimes difficult to envisage in reality, they are useful for marketers to relate to in terms of marketing behaviour. With this background in mind, think of an example of an industry or service provision that more or less equates to perfect competition, oligopoly and monopoly.

- Perfect competition – the restaurant trade
- Oligopoly – motor cars
- Monopoly – the coal industry

Figure 8.4 explains the theory of oligopoly.

At price P the law of demand states that quantity Q will be demanded. If the price is then reduced to $P1$, then $Q1$ will be demanded, so Q–$Q1$ will be the additional amount demanded. However, in a situation of oligopoly where price as an instrument of competition is less effective, then the demand curve will kink to $D1$ and the dark area covered by Q–$Q2$ will be the additional amount demanded. A price reduction in these circumstances is less effective as customers will have been 'pre-sold' their existing products through non-price factors such as advertising and branding, and this is termed 'non-price competition'.

We have put the economist's view of pricing, but the view is devoid of sociological and psychological influences that might influence purchasing decisions. However, it is an essential starting point when

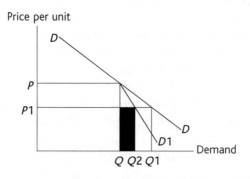

Figure 8.4 Oligopoly

attempting to understand the market. The next approach to pricing is the accountant's approach.

▶ The Accountant's approach

The philosophy underlying the accountant's approach to pricing is to achieve a targeted rate of return on investment from a given level of sales. Once total costs have been determined, the company decides on the percentage of profit it requires. To accomplish this objective consistently the company must be a market leader; otherwise fluctuations in demand will affect the value of profits. In such a situation, companies have a clear idea of the volume of surplus they seek to achieve and can then estimate the profit margins needed to realise this. This approach is termed 'cost plus' pricing.

This, however, is a rather mechanistic approach not usually used in practice, although mark-up pricing which simply adds a fixed percentage to the cost of goods and services, is still used in the more traditional sectors of the retail trade. The reality is that overall profit margin is normally the result of several pricing strategies applied to a variety of products in response to changes in the marketplace. Therefore, the percentage of 'plus' that is applied in respect of each contract or product line is a function of market conditions and individual customers. This means that it is more a decision for marketing than for finance. However, the target rate of return that is expected, should equate to the overall percentage that has been agreed with finance. If certain contracts are agreed with customers at less than this target rate of return, then this shortfall should be made up on other contracts that should be priced at more than this target rate of return. This technique is more flexible than simple cost plus pricing in that it allows marketing more flexibility when dealing with customers and the technique is termed 'target pricing'.

Under what circumstances can you envisage cost plus or target pricing as being particularly appropriate?

In a manufacturing situation where the company has to make and perhaps install something that is unique and purpose designed. Such a product might be the design, manufacture and commissioning of an oil refinery. Here the client is probably asking for tenders from a number of companies so the company must estimate the likely costs of such a project and then add a margin on top of this for profit, knowing that other bidders will be in a similar situation.

The accountant has to control the flow of cash in an organisation and there is normally a need to recoup high costs of development as early as possible in the life cycle of a product. However, it is through finance that a balance is kept between many other demands on the company's limited resources. This means that a fine balancing act has to be performed when attempting to meet the conflicting demands and requirements of, for instance, production, research and development, training and marketing. It can be seen that the accountant's view of pricing is more governed by the internal workings of the company than with the vagaries of the marketplace.

In any manufacturing concern, there are fixed costs like depreciation and maintenance of plant and equipment, rent and rates for factory buildings and the costs of a minimum labour force that the company has to pay regardless of levels of output. Variable costs also have to be added and these are a function of the level of output that includes direct labour, materials and energy costs. Total costs are the sum of fixed and variable costs. This is shown in Figure 8.5 which explains the concept of break-even analysis.

From the figure it can be seen that variable costs increase in direct proportion to the volume produced or sold, and the sum of these is total cost. The break-even quantity (BEQ) occurs when a certain number of units sold at a given price generates sufficient revenue to exactly equal total costs. Total revenue is the amount of money that the company receives and this will increase with output. Therefore, the gap between total revenue and total costs prior to the break-even point will represent a loss to the company and the gap between these after break-even will represent profit. Figure 8.5 then represents a straight 'cost plus' approach to pricing that assumes a balanced fixed and variable cost element and an unchanging profit margin. In reality it is not as

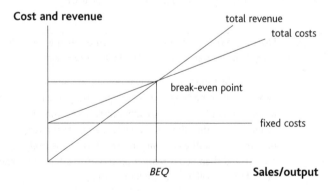

Figure 8.5 Break-even analysis

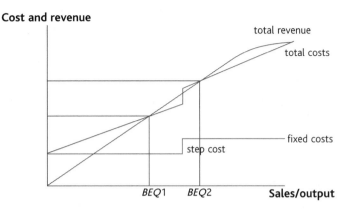

Cost and revenue

Figure 8.6 Break-even analysis showing step cost and
revenue reduction with increased sales

simple as this, as there are elements of extra costs and reduced revenues that must be considered. As output and sales increase to a certain level there will be additional costs like commissioning a new production line which will incur a 'step cost'. As sales grow there will be a tendency to trim profit margins in order to attract more customers. This is explained in Figure 8.6.

In this figure *BEQ*1 represents the normal break-even concept as shown in Figure 8.5 and after this point total revenue exceeds total costs. Between *BEQ*1 and *BEQ*2 there is a step cost that is a reflection of another production unit being established to cope with increased output. At this point, total costs exceed total revenue for a short period. At *BEQ*2 the second break-even occurs and once again total revenue exceeds total cost. However, shortly after this, total revenue begins to tail off as a result of price reductions that have to be made in order to sustain increasing levels of sales, and ultimately this moves to a point where total revenue and total costs are again equal. What Figure 8.6 infers is that demand must be taken into consideration when deciding the amount of 'plus' in cost-plus pricing decisions.

Demand oriented pricing might be viewed as being preferable to cost-based pricing, but we should be aware of practical limitations when it is related to break-even analysis. It assumes that costs are static, whereas they can vary considerably (both up and down). Revenue is over-simplified as market conditions can change rapidly, and even if they return to the condition on which the analysis was originally based, actual revenue may not be as predicted. With these provisos taken into account, break-even analysis related to demand can be an effective price computational technique, especially if costs and demand levels are stable, even if only in the short term. It should, however, be appreciated that accurate demand estimation is difficult to achieve despite an organisation's best efforts in attempting to provide accurate forecasting.

Now we have considered economists' and accountants' relatively disciplined views of pricing, we are in a position to look at marketing's approach. It should be emphasised that these views are theoretical constructs, and the purpose of theory is to enable the world of reality to be viewed in a more ordered and disciplined manner.

▶ The marketing approach

The pricing techniques we have examined pay less attention to demand than they do to cost. Marketing techniques place more emphasis on the combined elements of the marketing mix as well as aspects of consumer behaviour in relation to the way price is perceived.

Improvement or maintenance of market share is a common pricing objective and this is market-based. When a market is expanding, prices charged by a company may not encourage a corresponding improvement in market share. A downwards price adjustment might increase sales in an expanding market to a level where the return on investment increases in monetary terms, although the percentage return on each unit sold might have fallen. Market share is a key to profitability and this is an indicator of an organisation's general health. Price levels and profit margins carry much of the responsibility in a marketing mix designed to maintain or improve market share.

Smaller firms generally have little influence over the level of prices in a market and organise their businesses so that costs are at a level that allows them to fall in line with the prices charged by market leaders and price leaders. This is termed 'going rate' pricing. Prices tend to be market led with little scope for any deviation from the established price structures. As long as returns are considered to be adequate, there is justification for keeping things as they are by conforming to price levels that have been established by the leaders. It should, however, be noted that price leadership does not equate to total authority in the marketplace. Many price leaders are not necessarily market leaders. Non-price competition can improve a company's market share through manipulation of the marketing mix, so the group with the final influence in price setting is indirectly end consumers who react to a company's manipulation of its marketing mix through their individual purchasing actions.

If a company desires rapid growth in sales, then, if clear product superiority cannot be sustained, price is the component of the marketing mix that must be manipulated. In such circumstances, the firm must appreciate the competitive conditions in which it is operating and a price cutting action should always be made with caution. This caution is not only in terms of competitors' reactions, but a sudden price reduction might also affect the balance of other elements in the marketing mix.

In relation to the last statement, give an example of a product where a substantial price reduction might adversely affect its position in the marketplace.

In the case of a strongly branded line of perfumes.

Profit maximisation is a natural policy for any business to pursue. However, market conditions can make it impossible to maximise profits on all products, in all markets, at the same time. For this reason, companies employ pricing techniques that can promote sales, but reduce profits on certain products in the short term. The overall objective is to maximise profits on all goods that are to be sold over a period of time. The company's product mix should, therefore, be considered as a complete entity, rather than as a range of products whose profits have to be maximised individually. This idea might run counter to the product/brand manager system that was put forward in Chapter 7 and which looked at product issues, with the premise that each product or brand manager was in control of a specific SBU whose objective was to maximise profits. However, a more global view, like the one expressed here, sometimes has to be taken by the marketing manager or director which might mean that certain product lines be held back in the interests of maximising overall profitability of the company.

 Vignette 8.2

Priceline.com® offers big savings for customers by allowing them to name their own price!

Priceline.com® was set up in 1998 and since then has been a truly successful 'dotcom' company. Since the firm opened for business they have sold over 7.5 million airline tickets at discounted rates, 2.5 million hotel room nights and 2.5.million rental car days. A lot of Internet companies have turned out to be more 'hype' than reality but Priceline.com® is different. The firm is successful because it delivers real, measurable savings to its customers, which they can see for themselves, are genuine. Since starting out the firm have saved their customers millions of pounds. The firm's 'Name Your Own Price™' service operates with some of the top companies in the business, for example Delta Airlines. The firm's brand-name partners are willing to give the firm's customers significant discounts because they are prepared to be flexible. The firm's brand-name partners will allow the customer to name their own price and will shield the name of the brand from the customer until the price offered is accepted. Only then will the customer know the name of the airline that has accepted their offer. The same principle works for hire cars and hotel rooms. For example, here is how the process works for car hire. Instead of spending hours calling around or surfing the Web for the best rental rates, you can use Priceline.com® to Name Your Own Price®. It only takes a few minutes to complete a rental car request. You pick the location, car type, dates and times, and then Name Your Own Price®. Priceline.com® then take your request to their participating rental car companies for the location you select. If a car rental company accepts your request, they will immediately book the car you requested at the price you want to pay. With Priceline.com®, you'll always rent from one of the top five brand-name rental car companies: Alamo, Avis, Budget, Hertz or National. And you always get unlimited mileage. If the firm finds a rental car company willing to accept your request, you'll only be charged a small processing fee to cover the costs involved in finding you a rental car. Currently, Priceline.com® offers rentals at most US airports (rentals must be picked-up and dropped-off at the same location). The firm is adding new locations every week. More than 100,000 rental cars go unused every day. That's lost revenue for the national brand-name rental car companies, and a great opportunity for Priceline.com® customers. Even when rental car companies have cars sitting on their lots unused, they worry about discounting too much – even though they may want to. Priceline.com® offers these companies a method to heavily discount their rates and provide Priceline.com® customers with great savings in return for some unique tradeoffs. Because Priceline.com® is a buying service and not a shopping service, all rentals are sold on an 'all sales final' basis. Once your request is accepted, your reservation will be non-cancellable and non-refundable.

Break-even analysis has already demonstrated that to ensure profitability, prices must ultimately exceed costs. It is logical then to consider cost as the first step when planning price levels. However, market based pricing strategy should begin with the consumer and then work back towards the company. Pricing decisions must be consumer-oriented for it is customers who ultimately decide whether the product is purchased or not.

When making market based pricing decisions, a number of sequential steps should be taken:

- *Customer or market identification* is to focus the marketing decision-maker's mind on the market from the beginning. It prevents price from being perceived separately from other marketing mix elements.
- *Demand estimation* or more correctly, sales forecasting, is a skilled process that should provide the company with a series of potential demand levels at different selling prices. The potential sales volume will directly affect costs, and the price necessary for profit maximisa-

tion can then be calculated. The price a company is able to charge will vary according to market conditions and chosen market segments in addition to less tangible criteria such as the value customers place on a given product.

▶ *Assessing competitive reactions* assumes great importance when products are easily inaugurated and markets are easy to enter. Even when a company's products or services can be differentiated in some way, it is often not long before competitive offerings appear. This competition comes from three sources:
1. Direct or 'head-on' competition from similar product offerings
2. Competition from substitute products or services
3. Competition from products that are not directly related, but which compete for the same funding sources or disposable income.

Give an illustration of two products or services that might compete for the same funding.

Expensive perfume manufacturers and jewellery manufacturers might sometimes be in competition, as these items are often purchased as gifts.

▶ *Market share analysis* is to consider production factors against the anticipated share of the market. If a large market share is envisaged, then the price will probably need to be competitive. If production capacity is insufficient to meet the demand that the anticipated market share will produce, then there is little point in setting a low price that will bring in orders that cannot be fulfilled.

We now explain two marketing pricing strategies to which reference is frequently made. These strategies are 'market penetration' and 'market skimming' and they relate principally to new products. Such pricing decisions should be taken at the start of a product's life cycle, for that decision will help determine the volume of sales for that product over its life.

A market penetration strategy relies on economies of large-scale production to allow the product to be introduced to the market at a price low enough to attract a large number of buyers as quickly as possible. This will tend to constrain possible competitors by creating a low price as a barrier to market entry. If product design and manufacture are costly to set up and operate and are also conducted on a large scale, then this too will deter competitors. The aim is to attain a high, or even total, initial market share and keep this share high during the later stages of the product's life cycle.

Figure 8.7 explains this idea, and it can be seen that the product is introduced at an attractively low 'penetration' price at the beginning of its life cycle. As a result, demand for the product is high at the early stages, whereas the product life cycle concept suggests a slowly rising trend at the beginning which only begins to rise substantially during the growth phase. This policy is suitable for products that have high demand elasticity and where reductions in unit costs can be attained through large-scale operations. Here, a large volume of sales is essential from the outset to keep production levels high, as high production is a function of the manufacturing process.

 Name a type or class of product where a penetration pricing strategy tends to be used.

New mass-produced models of motor cars.

A market skimming policy infers that a company will initially charge the highest price that the market will bear, and promotional effort is initially directed towards a small percentage of the potential market. These customers are likely to be innovators who will purchase during the introduction stage of the product's life cycle, followed closely by early adopters who are also more receptive to new concepts and products. Their income levels and generally higher social status make them less sensitive to high initial prices.

To be able to reach a wider group of customers once innovators and early adopters have purchased, the company reduces its prices progressively thus skimming the most advantageous prices from each successive adopter group. Price reductions are successively brought in as sales slow at each phase, until the product has reached all the target market.

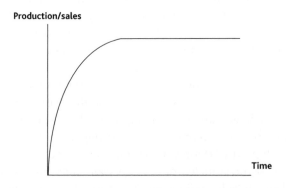

Figure 8.7 Penetration pricing

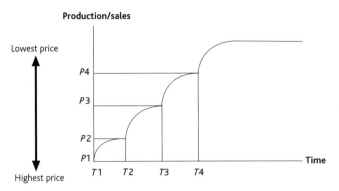

Figure 8.8 Market skimming

Figure 8.8 illustrates market skimming and here it can be seen that individual 'skims' have been taken at certain times.

In Figure 8.8 the new product is introduced at time $T1$ at a high initial price $P1$. The product is meant to appeal to the AB social grades at this stage. They make their first purchases and the market then begins to tail off, so prices are reduced to $P2$ which brings in C1 social classes at time $T2$. The same thing happens again at time $T3$ when C2 social classes are brought in by bringing down the price to $P3$. The final skim is price $P4$ at time $T4$ which brings in the DE social grades and this is when the product has left growth and reached its maturity phase.

The above explanation was illustrative, as the timing of skims does not always relate to social class demand. 'Innovator' categories for, say, a new software product might well be 'technically minded people', perhaps mainly in the C2 or C1 social classes, whereas 'innovator' categories for an expensive new brand of perfume might well be 'A' and 'B' social grades. In some cases the new innovation is introduced as a refined 'de-luxe' model, with simpler versions appearing later at reduced prices.

 | **Think of a product or service that has used market skimming as its pricing policy.**

Personal computers have already been mentioned and this is an obvious example. However, products such as micowave cookers and pocket calculators have gone through this process and currently we are witnessing digital cameras doing the same.

To be successful, a skimming strategy must relate to a product or service that is distinctive enough to exclude competitors who might be encouraged to enter the market in the early stages as a result of the high prices being attained. Other elements of the marketing mix must assist this skimming strategy by advancing a good quality, distinctive image.

A skimming strategy is particularly relevant for new products because at the earlier phases of the product's life cycle, competition is minimal and the uniqueness of the new product can create opportunities for non-price competition. In addition, the market can be effectively segmented or 'cherry picked' because of innovators who will be willing to purchase regardless of the initial high price. At a more practical level, high initial prices can lead to quicker recovery of research and development plus production set-up costs, and they can keep demand within the capacity of production whilst production levels are building up.

We have examined three approaches to pricing and it has been demonstrated that it is the marketplace rather than the company that exerts the greatest influence in price determination. Marketing may be faced with a general level of demand for a given product or product type, but inside this level of demand there are opportunities for tactics to be developed which centre principally on customers. It is upon such tactics that the next section focuses.

▐▌▌ Vignette 8.3

Tesco plc, the UK multiple grocery chain, loses its battle with Levi Strauss to sell cut-price jeans in its stores.

- -

Tesco, the UK mutiple grocery chain has lost its battle with the number one branded jeans company Levi Strauss to sell heavily discounted Levi branded jeans in its stores within the UK. The European Union's highest court upheld the right of Levi Strauss to protect the brand image of its world famous jeans and to chose to distribute and price its products in any way it sees as being in its customers' best interests. Levi Strauss Inc. welcomed the news and maintained that they had the right to decide the way in which the company distributed their own products and to decide how best to serve their customers. Levi Strauss's management thought that selling their jeans alongside groceries undermined the exclusive image of the Levi brand which the company had painstakingly and expensively nurtured and built up over many years. Levi, like many other manufacturers, prices its products to wholesalers differently in different countries. The wholesale prices of Levi jeans in the USA for example is significantly cheaper than the wholesale price in Europe. Many people who go to the USA on holiday are sometimes surprised at the comparatively low price of many American branded products, including well known brands of clothing. However Levi Strauss never intended the jeans sold to wholesalers in the USA to be sold to large retailers within the UK. The firms sell wholesale to European intermediaries and they are expected to supply the needs of European retailers including Tesco. Tesco has been fighting to import the jeans from countries with lower wholesale prices than those available through official European stockists and then to sell them in the UK at a discount to Levi's own official stockists. Levi Strauss was not particularly happy about this plan as you can imagine. Tesco started the legal battle four years ago when it began sourcing Levi jeans in the USA and selling them at nearly half the price offered elsewhere in UK high street stores. Levi Strauss said that they were pleased that the court established that Tesco was acting illegally by importing Levi jeans from lower cost, non- EU countries and selling them in Europe, undermining the official pricing policy of their own outlets, without the consent of the company.

▶▶ Tactical pricing issues

Some consumer-goods purchasers attach great importance to prestige when making purchases. This element is rarely admitted and is seldom consciously acknowledged, for the buyer does not always realise that it forms part of the purchasing decision. It does, however, allow for psychological pricing techniques to be applied. In such cases, the customer sees value in the exclusivity that can be achieved through high prices, so the image projected as a result of the purchase might enhance that person's lifestyle. When we consider prestige pricing this produces a demand curve as shown in Figure 8.9.

It can be seen that price reductions below a certain level can decrease demand since the product loses its exclusive image if price becomes too low and this produces what is termed inverse demand.

For certain products there are psychological price bands within which price reductions have little effect. If, however, the price is reduced so it falls into the next psychological price bracket, then demand will increase, resulting in a step-like demand curve. This thinking is also at the basis of what is termed 'odd/even pricing'. Prices like £9.99 are applied which means one penny change out of £10.00 and it somehow

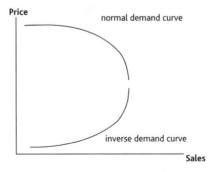

Figure 8.9 Prestige pricing

looks a lot less expensive than £10.00 because this is a sum that is in the next psychological price band. 'Price lining' is a variation of this and is used a lot in the USA by retailers who sell all of their stores' products in a number of distinct price bands like $49.95; $59.95 and $69.95 for such items as trainers.

A company's discount structure is a major factor in pricing decisions and in some industries a 'trade discount' for members operates. These are typically trade professions like building or plumbing. Customers who purchase in large volumes may also expect to pay a lower price than would be the case for smaller purchases. Discounts are sometimes offered to encourage large purchases. Discounts can also be offered to encourage sales of a new product or increase demand for slow-moving products. A rebate policy may also be applied to payment terms to encourage prompt payment, typically less 2½ per cent net monthly account.

In easily segmented markets, companies sometimes charge different prices to different segments for a product that is basically the same and this is referred to as 'price discrimination'. In such cases it often takes only a minor modification to allow a discriminatory price to be charged. Such a discriminatory price can also be based on the individual customer or the location in which the product is being marketed.

Give an illustration of price discrimination.

Reduced rates offered to students on bank charges whilst they are students, in the expectation that they will become permanent customers.

What are the three basic philosophies of pricing?
'Economist'; 'accounting' and 'marketing' approaches

What is the difference between elastic and inelastic demand?
In a situation of elastic demand a small downward or upward movement of price will greatly affect levels of demand, whereas in a situation of inelasticity of demand large price movements have little effect on demand levels.

What are the principal characteristics of oligopoly?
Few sellers of basically similar goods; all produce below their maximum; emphasis on non-

price competition; entry to the marketplace might be artificially high through high costs of seeking to establish a branded product.

What are the principal features of cost-plus pricing?
Fixed costs and variable costs are added, onto which is added a margin for profit.

How does target pricing differ from cost-plus pricing?
The percentage of 'plus' can be manipulated by the marketing department as long as the 'plus' at the end of the period equates to what was agreed at the beginning of the period.

In break-even analysis what is a step cost?
An extra fixed cost at a certain volume of

production that is incurred as a result of a new factory or production line or other capital item being brought into commission to cope with increased demand.

Explain the principal characteristics of penetration pricing.
A low initial price that captures market share very quickly in order to keep out competition and allow the company to produce at high volume from the outset.

What is market skimming?
When a product is introduced, a high initial price is charged to skim off certain segments to which the product will initially appeal. The price is then lowered by successive stages to attract further groups of purchasers.

What is prestige pricing?
Where the customer sees value in exclusivity and is willing to pay a higher price in the interests of 'image'.

Describe price lining.
Normally used in retail outlets where a similar range of merchandise is offered to the public at a limited number of specific prices.

▶▶ Summary

An organisation's willingness to adapt and modify price levels according to the needs of customers and the market conditions which prevail is a pointer to the level of its marketing orientation. Marketing management has, therefore, to devise pricing strategies that are compatible with other elements of the marketing mix.

Knowledge of economic and accounting theory is a precursor to understanding the wider issues involved when making pricing decisions, and to this extent these approaches have been given consideration. Marketing approaches have been discussed, for it is recognised that price embodies more than simply an exchange transaction for a product or service. To this extent, psychological and behavioural implications of price have been investigated as well as the more practical issues of market based pricing theory.

FURTHER READING

Armstrong G. and Kotler P. (2000) *Marketing: An Introduction* (5th edn), Chapter 9, 'Pricing Products: Pricing Considerations and Strategies', Prentice Hall, Englewood Cliffs, NJ.
Blythe J. (2001) *Essentials of Marketing*, Chapter 7, 'Pricing Strategies', Pearson Education, London.
Davies M. (1998) *Understanding Marketing*, Chapter 7, 'Pricing', Prentice Hall, London.
Keegan W.J. and Green M.S. (2000) *Global Marketing* (2nd edn), Chapter 12, 'Pricing Decisions', Prentice Hall, London.
Lancaster G.A. and Reynolds P.L. (1999) *Introduction to Marketing: A Step-by-Step Guide to All The Tools of Marketing*, Chapter 11, 'Price', Kogan Page, London.
Plamer A. (2000) *Principles of Marketing*, Chapter 12, 'Pricing: Underlying Principles' and Chapter 14, 'Pricing: Applications', OUP, Oxford.

9

CHANNELS OF DISTRIBUTION

▶▶ Introduction

Of all the areas in marketing, distribution has only recently commanded the interest of researchers, yet distribution is an intrinsic part of any organisation's marketing mix and has an important strategic role to play. Often strategic and competitive advantage can be gained by using innovative and imaginative channels. For example, the home magazines *Living* and *Family Circle* are distributed almost entirely in supermarkets and what is more important is that, unlike the majority of other magazines on sale in the store, these two are sold on the shop side of the checkout till. Now other publications have copied the example of these two magazines, but for a long time these two publications managed to carve out a strategic competitive advantage simply by choice of distribution channel. When examining the flow of goods and or services through a distribution channel, it is helpful to use the analogy of the system being a pipeline with main pipes, subsidiary branches, free flows and blockages. Marketing communicators in the field of sales promotions talk of consumer promotions as 'out of the pipeline' or 'pull' promotions, whereas promotions aimed at company employees or marketing intermediaries are referred to as 'into the pipeline' or 'push' promotions. In this context they are referring to products or services either being pulled through the distribution pipeline by consumer demand or 'pushed' into the distribution pipeline by salesperson or dealer incentives.

▶▶ Components of distribution

Distribution is made up of two components: 'channels' and

'physical distribution' or 'logistics'. Channels of distribution are covered in this chapter and logistics in Chapter 10. The term 'distribution system' refers to that complex of agents, wholesalers and retailers through which manufacturers move products and services, such as life insurance, to their intended markets. Marketing channels are usually made up of independent firms or entrepreneurs who are in business to make a profit. These are known as 'marketing intermediaries' or 'middlemen'. Distribution channels may also include a combination of owned and independent outlets or franchise arrangements. Along with physical distribution, which is part of the total business logistics function, channels of distribution contribute to what economists refer to as 'time' and 'place' utility. Goods and services may be provided, but to be of economic value they need to be made available for consumption in a certain place, for example a public house in the case of beer, and at a certain time, for example right now. The correct choice of channel can add significant real and perceived value to the product or service offering and is an important area of the marketing mix. In fact the 'P' designating 'place' in McCarthy's 4Ps actually refers to channels of distribution and should perhaps more correctly have been termed 'placement'.

The marketing process of addressing the satisfaction of specific needs and wants is not simply confined to the end users of the product, but must be applied to all intermediaries in the distribution chain.

How would you describe a 'channel of distribution system'? Use examples to illustrate the points made. Remember that the term 'distribution system' refers to a total system that has two separate yet interrelated parts, that is physical distribution (logistics) and channels of distribution.

This activity asks you to consider 'channels of distribution' only. The term 'channel of distribution system' refers to a complex system of agents, factors, wholesalers and retailers through which marketing firms move their products (and services) to their intended markets. Marketing channels, or marketing intermediaries, are usually made up of independent firms who are themselves in business to make a profit and have needs and wants of their own. Distribution arrangements differ in their length and complexity. For example, Avon cosmetics are sold and delivered to customers through direct agents who receive stock direct from the manufacturer. Kleeneze use a network of agents and distributors on a hierarchical 'multi-level marketing' basis. Hallmark Greeting Cards use independent agents to sell stock to wholesalers who split bulk and sell on to small retailers, who in turn sell to the public. Distribution outlets may include a combination of owned and independent outlets or semi-independent outlets like those found under franchising arrangements.

A central tenet of marketing is that organisations need to understand their customers. In situations where a manufacturer delivers goods on site direct to the user the definition of who the customer is straightforward. However, where a sophisticated, multi-layered distribution system is used there can be a hierarchy of customers. Often it is marketing intermediaries who are the immediate customers of the manufacturing firm. Hence, being 'customer focused' applies to immediate customers in what is termed the 'task environment', which includes suppliers as well as marketing channel members.

◗◗ Indirect versus direct systems

The choice of distribution system depends on whether the manufacturer decides to sell directly to customers, employing salespeople, or to use intermediaries such as agents, wholesalers and retailers. Generally speaking, distribution channels in industrial and business-to-business (B2B) markets tend be direct. Many products in industrial markets are buyer specified rather than supplier specified and are often unique 'one-off' products made specifically to a client's own specification, or are standard products that have been adapted in some way to meet specific client needs. In the case of products like machine tools they are often also installed and tested before being handed over to the client. That is not to say that marketing intermediaries are never used in B2B markets as items like electrical equipment are often sold to the trade through wholesalers known as 'factors', rather than being supplied direct from the manufacturer. The three most common channel configurations are illustrated in Figure 9.1.

Direct distribution is less common in consumer markets, particularly for FMCGs such as packaged groceries. There has, however, been a move towards direct distribution within the consumer durable and consumer services sectors. For example, firms such as Kitchens Direct encourage customers to order fitted kitchens direct from the factory rather than through retailers such as MFI, B&Q or Wickes. Direct distribution has also developed at a remarkable pace within the UK financial services sector. First Direct, now a subsidiary of the Bank of Scotland, led the way by offering consumers low cost insurance by telephone. This use of direct telephone marketing has now spread throughout the financial services sector and it is now possible to order pensions, mortgages and open conventional bank accounts by telephone with the service provider. Direct distribution of goods was pioneered in the UK by companies like Avon Cosmetics and Betterware. The growth in what is termed 'network' marketing or 'multi-level' marketing (MLM) has also accelerated the use of

(a) Selling directly

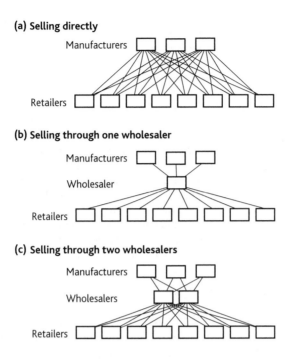

(b) Selling through one wholesaler

(c) Selling through two wholesalers

Figure 9.1 Examples of different channel configurations

direct distribution. The company Kleeneze uses the MLM approach with a team of independent, self employed agents and distributors at various managerial levels within the MLM hierarchy. The decision to use direct or indirect distribution is based on cost factors, including the following:

1. numbers of potential customers in the market
2. how concentrated or dispersed they are
3. how much each will buy in a given period
4. costs associated with the practical side of the distributive operation, including transport, warehousing and stockholding.

 Vignette 9.1

Betterware, the home products group, goes from strength to strength using catalogues and the Internet as distribution channels.

Betterware has a proud history extending back over 70 years to 1928 when two enterprising young East Enders named Clark and Willis thought it would be a good idea to sell the brushes they made from door to door. This popular innovation allowed the Company to grow rapidly and spread well beyond its East End origins. The firm has moved a long way since then and the modern organisation operates from its state-of-the-art international distribution centre near Birmingham and has businesses as far afield as Latin America and Australia. The diversity of products in the Betterware range has increased in a similar manner and the firm's catalogues are now filled with unique and exciting ideas for all around the home. The same attitude to quality and service, which inspired the company's founders, still prevails in the modern organisation. Without this, and an unwavering commitment to innovation throughout the entire business, Betterware would just not be able to compete with traditional retail stores and other direct marketing companies offering similar products, such as the Kleeneze Group. The company offers customers the option of ordering through the more traditional catalogue or online over the Internet. Betterware products are made to a very high standard using materials which give customers the best combination of quality and value for money. Many of the firm's products have been designed and manufactured to their own exacting specification as part of their commitment to quality and innovation. Their aim is to provide product quality not only through the suitability of the materials used but also through attention to detail in the way the products work.

Selling direct through the company's own sales force is viable when there is a large enough potential sales volume. Industrial goods manufacturers tend to use direct selling and direct delivery, although some use wholesalers or factors. Consumer goods manufacturers generally use a network of marketing intermediaries because of the dispersion of retail outlets and large numbers of potential customers. Manufacturers sell to wholesalers who 'break bulk', add a mark-up and sell to retailers. Manufacturers sell direct to large multiples, particularly in the packaged grocery market and these multiples in effect act as their own wholesalers through distribution depots that are dedicated to individual multiple chains. Whatever method is used, the point is that manufacturers rely on these middlemen for ultimate marketing success, as they have responsibility for taking the product to the ultimate consumer.

What do you understand by 'multi-level marketing'? Using examples distinguish between the use of multi-level marketing systems such as those employed by the Kleeneze Group, to direct agent distribution such as that used by Avon Cosmetics Ltd.

Multi-level marketing is a form of distribution that uses a hierarchical 'cascade' of agents and distributors. Some people are suspicious of this form of arrangement as it evokes memories of 'pyramid selling'. This was a 'get rich quick' scheme developed in the 1960s, whereby agents were appointed to sell products to subagents who appointed sub-subagents and sold to them, and so on. At the end of the line, the product was prohibitively expensive as a result of numerous mark-ups, so people at the end of the line (who could least afford it) ended up as losers. This practice is now illegal in the UK. In multi-level marketing an agent is recruited by another practising agent and then sells the product door to door, usually using catalogues posted through the door, followed by an attempt to secure orders. The commissioning agent receives a percentage of sales revenue earned by subagents as well as his or her own retail selling commission. If agents at this second level recruit further agents, the agent at the first level also gets commission from their sales as well. Eventually the idea is that the original agent concentrates on managing a network of agents and successful agents might receive commissions from many subagents at different levels in the multi-level marketing structure. Like many marketing innovations, multi-level marketing originated in the United States where it is a successful and popular system.

Direct marketing uses dedicated agents door to door. This seems similar to multi-level marketing, but direct marketing is a simpler form of distribution. There is no building up a hierarchical team of agents and no cascading downstream of commissions from various levels within the system. Direct marketing systems like that used by Avon Cosmetics only uses the first level.

▶▶ The nature of distribution

Change in channels of distribution is often slow and hardly noticeable. There is now evidence that the rate of change is accelerating as new channels for products and services are being developed all the time. Consider the expansion in the range of goods offered for sale in petrol stations in the UK. There is growth in availability and popularity of television shopping, particularly in the United States where it now forms a major channel for some goods and services. Because of the changing nature of channel formats over time and the introduction of completely new formats, often due to technological developments, marketing management must continually scan the business environment to identify likely changes and developments to stay competitive. Consider the likely impact of shopping on the Internet over the next 25 years as more and more households use the new technology.

The rationale for choosing one channel system over another is its effectiveness in assisting the distribution of products from the producer to the final customer. Marketing management should think of this process in terms of the concept of product 'flows' through the distribution 'pipeline'. As with a water system, products too can face 'blockages' and other problems may hinder the free flow of goods. The idea of 'flow' within channels is illustrated in Figure 9.2.

A firm does not often change its channel policy. Setting up a distribution arrangement, particularly if the arrangement is 'selective' or 'exclusive' rather than 'mass' distribution, requires extensive discussion, negotiation and attention to legal agreements. Because distribution arrangements are relatively long term, they are classed as strategic rather than tactical or operational decisions, for the following reasons:

1. Channel decisions directly affect the rest of the firm's marketing activities. For example, the selection of target markets is affected by, and in turn affects, channel design and choice.
2. Once established, a channel system may be difficult to change, at least in the short term. Because optimal channel arrangements for a given product are likely to change over time, albeit slowly, manufacturers need continually to monitor the distributive environment and reassess their existing channel structure with a view to exploiting and capitalising on any changes.

The word 'channel' is derived from the French word for canal. In marketing terms this can be interpreted as the route taken by products as they flow from their point of production to points of intermediate and final use. Marketing is the primary element in a continuous cycle that starts and finishes with needs and want of consumers. Marketers should identify needs and wants of potential consumers and then organise the organisation's resources to produce goods and services that meet or exceed the desires and expectations of customers. On completion of the manufacturing process, the finished product is moved through an often complex system of marketing intermediaries and finally into the hands

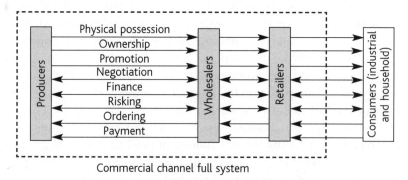

Commercial channel full system

Figure 9.2 The 'flows' in marketing channels

of consumers. Channels of distribution are the means whereby the product can be made available to consumers and this availability provides value in the form of time and place utility.

▶▶ Strategic elements of channel choice

The degree of market exposure sought by a company dictates the formulation of channel policy and how many marketing intermediaries are used. Choice of channel strategy will depend on a number of factors including the nature of the product or service, the technical complexity of the product and its servicing arrangements as well as the desired image the marketing firm wishes to portray in the minds' of consumers. Three distribution strategies can be distinguished:

1. *Intensive distribution* strategy is used by producers of convenience goods and certain common raw materials who aim to stock their products in as many outlets as possible. The dominant factor in the marketing of such products is their place utility. Producers of pens, cigarettes and confectionery try to enlist every possible retail outlet, ranging from multiples to independent corner shops. With such products, every exposure to the customer is an opportunity to buy, and the image of the outlet used is not a significant factor in a customer's impression of the product.
2. *Exclusive distribution* to recognised official distributors can enhance the prestige of a product and develop a high quality brand image. Exclusive distribution is a policy of granting dealers exclusive rights to distribute in a certain geographical area and is often used in conjunction with a policy of exclusive dealing, where the manufacturer requires the dealer not to carry competing lines, as in car dealerships. By granting exclusivity, the manufacturer gains more control over intermediaries regarding price, credit and promotion policies, greater loyalty and a more aggressive sales effort.
3. *Selective distribution* lies between the extremes just described. Instead of spreading its marketing effort over the whole range of possible outlets, the manufacturer concentrates on the most promising of profitable outlets. Selective distribution is also used where facilities, resources or image of the outlet can have a direct impact on customer impressions of the product, as in the case of expensive brands of perfume. Some products may require certain storage and marketing facilities, for example frozen food intermediaries must have adequate deep freeze display facilities.

What kind of distribution strategy might be chosen for a high priced, reasonably prestigious brand of perfume?

Products can be viewed as 'bundles of attributes' in the minds of consumers. Some attributes are real such as colour, weight and taste. Many are implied through packaging, branding, pricing and distribution. Choice of distribution channel can have a significant effect on the perceived quality and value of a brand. There are some perfumes that are so prestigious that they cost hundreds of pounds for a few milligrams. Such products are usually purchased by the very rich and are to be found in exclusive outlets in major cities like Paris, London, Tokyo and New York. This activity asks you to consider an appropriate distribution strategy for a reasonably prestigious brand of perfume. There are many such brands that spring to mind, but perhaps the most universally recognised prestige brand is Chanel No. 5 perfume, which is popular all over the world. Chanel decided to use selective distribution for this particular product. The perfume is highly priced in line with the desired brand image. Much attention is paid to the packaging which includes the container, label and outer packaging. It is advertised in appropriate publications as a luxury, prestige product. The brand is not as expensive as some of the more exclusive Paris perfumes. In fact it is positioned at the top end of the 'popular' perfume market. It will not be seen for sale in limited line discount stores because this would not maintain the correct positioning for the product. It is sold in stores that have a facility for demonstrating and selling cosmetics, ranging from Boots to Harrods.

▶▶ Changing channel systems

Cravens (1988) stated that channels do change and manufacturers often respond too slowly to such evolution. Individual changes may be small when viewed in isolation, but cumulative change can be significant. When planning long-term channel strategy, companies need to monitor such change and attempt to anticipate future macroenvironmental developments. A good example of such change that is now upon us has just been cited in relation to Internet developments. We discussed earlier the growth in the use of direct marketing channels by companies such as First Direct and Kleeneze. A period of approximately ten years, from the mid-1980s to the mid-1990s, saw what could be described as a revolution in the distribution of financial products and services. The next change in distribution channel systems is already taking place. The magnitude of this development is in the way we are likely to order and receive goods and services. The technology driving this change is based on the fibre-optic cable that provides many thousands of communication channels that can be used simultaneously. The UK is currently being 'wired up' with such optical fibre cables being fed into every home, businesses and other establishments such as hospitals and public sector offices.

The World Wide Web (WWW) is a powerful marketing tool and television 'shopping channels' have become popular. Orders will shortly be able to be placed via a television handset and the goods delivered direct to the door. Payment is made by tapping a credit card number into a hand-set, or by ringing a toll-free number to give credit card details. It is estimated that web site technology will be a bigger marketing tool than cable and satellite television. To gain strategic competitive edge firms must embrace change and be a part of that change.

Change has been most noticeable at retail levels where significant changes in practice have occurred over the past thirty years. This period has seen an increasing polarity in the turnover distribution of retail firms. At one end of the spectrum are the very large-scale operators: multiples, discount chains and the cooperative movement. At the other end there are still a large number of small shops, some completely independent and others linked to wholesalers. In the UK during the past 50 years the number of shops has declined, with an increased concentration of market share in the hands of a relatively small number of large multiples. This concentration is particularly marked in the grocery sector with large multiples holding almost 80 per cent market share at the present time. Large multiples have grown at the expense of cooperatives, independents and smaller multiples.

 How do you see the development of 'non-shop' shopping over the next decade?

This is an interesting question and the answer will depend on a number of factors. The first thing to discuss is the nature of shopping itself. People go shopping for a variety of reasons and not simply to obtain a certain product or service. If you take large out-of-town shopping centres, such as Meadowhall in Sheffield or the Metro Centre in Tyneside, shopping is an occasion, an experience, or even a leisure pursuit. The first question to answer then is how popular will non-shop shopping become? Do we really want to buy all our goods and services from the Internet, catalogues or television shopping channels? Is shopping simply another chore to get done in the simplest way possible? Is shopping more than just obtaining goods? People go shopping for a complex array of psychological and sociological reasons and there will always be a need for people to engage in the physical act of shopping.

In this sense the successful development of non-shop alternatives may be more limited than the predictions would suggest. Looking at technological trends it seems that dedicated television shopping channels will grow in popularity over the next decade. Such channels are popular in the United States and are growing in popularity in Europe with the increased adoption of satellite and cable television. Direct distribution systems like multi-level marketing are growing in popularity. The real technological breakthrough is the development of the World Wide Web which is still developing as a distribution channel but has enormous potential for the future.

▶▶ Types and classification of channel

Marketing channels can be characterised according to the number of channel levels. The number of intermediaries involved in the channel operation determines on how many levels it operates. There are four main types of channel level existing in consumer markets as shown in Figure 9.3.

The first three levels are straightforward. The three level channel typically constitutes three intermediaries, a merchant wholesaler or what is termed a 'jobber' who intervenes between the other two, the wholesaler and retailer. Industrial channels are usually more direct, as Figure 9.4 shows.

Many consumer markets are becoming more like those found in industrial markets. The trend in consumer markets seems to be a more direct form of marketing that often removes the need for any kind of 'middleman' and allows the manufacturer or service provider to deal directly with the end users. This trend has been particularly marked in

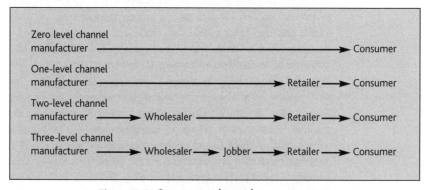

Figure 9.3 Consumer channel arrangements

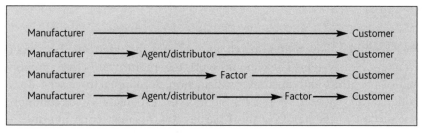

Figure 9.4 Industrial channel arrangements

the financial services industry. In the past if a customer wanted a financial product such as insurance, a mortgage or a personal equity plan he or she would probably have visited a bank manager, an insurance broker or an independent financial adviser. Today, it is common for customers to deal directly with firms offering the financial product, often by telephone or the World Wide Web. There seems to be less of a need for a complex array of intermediaries taking a share of the 'mark-up'. This form of direct distribution has allowed providers of many financial products to improve their profit margins and at the same time reduce the cost of such products to customers and give a more convenient and efficient service.

▶▶ Channel conflict and cooperation

When a firm designs a distribution channel system for their products there are a number of factors to be taken in to consideration. Channel strategy must be derived from overall marketing strategy for, in the long-term, channel arrangements are changed infrequently. This is a compelling reason for marketing to select intermediaries with care, as the decision is likely to have a long-term effect. In planning a distribution system, management attempts to achieve a smooth running system where channel members work together towards the same ends. All members of the channel, at whatever level, should see the relationship as being mutually beneficial. The reality is often quite different as we now examine. Channel members are often independent businesses and sometimes have conflicting goals and aspirations. This can lead to tension, hostility and inefficiency within the channel system, which can be damaging for all parties, not just the original manufacturer.

▶ Conflict

Each member of the marketing channel system should ideally be part of an integrated system. They should work together towards the common end of profit through customer satisfaction. A manufacturer who does not deal directly with customers then places responsibility for commercial success in the hands of third parties (that is, marketing intermediaries). These are usually independent firms with their own sets of aspirations, needs and wants, which are not always the same for every channel member and this can result in channel conflict. The overall channel system should be a set of interlocking and mutually dependent elements and it is in the interests of all channel members for there to be a high degree of cooperation.

Channel conflict is a situation in which one member of a distribution channel system views another as an adversary. As a result such a channel member might act towards the perceived 'enemy' in a hostile way and may even attempt to cause commercial harm. Such actions may upset a finely tuned distribution structure and have adverse consequences for other members of the channel system, many of whom are likely to be independent businesses in their own right. It might also have commercial consequences for the manufacturing firm that is relying on channel cohesion to achieve satisfactory distribution objectives. Conflicts in distribution channels may take different forms, as originally highlighted by Joseph Palamountain (1955):

Horizontal conflict
Horizontal conflict relates to marketing intermediaries who are at the same level in the channel system and of the same type of intermediary, for example two 'cash and carry' wholesalers working in the same town or two retail stores in the same area stocking a similar range of goods. This type of conflict is illustrated in Figure 9.5.

Vertical conflict
Unlike horizontal conflict which takes place amongst marketing intermediaries at the same level in the channel system, vertical conflict

Figure 9.5 Diagrammatic representation of horizontal conflict

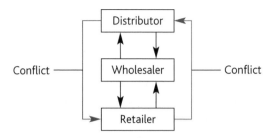

Figure 9.6 Diagrammatic representation of vertical conflict

takes place amongst marketing intermediaries at different levels or layers in the channel system. This type of conflict is potentially more damaging to the manufacturing firm as it can destroy the free flow of goods through the channel pipeline and cause a blockage that may have serious consequences for the commercial interests of the manufacturing firm and other channel members. The principle is illustrated in Figure 9.6.

Intertype conflict

Intertype conflict refers to competition among different types of intermediary at the same level in the channel system. This kind of competition has increased in recent years especially with the growing practice among intermediaries of 'scrambled' merchandising, a practice that involves intermediaries dealing with products that were previously outside their normal product range. Intertype conflict can be seen as a kind of Darwinian evolution taking place among different sorts of channel intermediary at the same level within the channel system, for example cash and carry wholesalers versus conventional wholesalers. Over time the most profitable, efficient and popular type of channel configuration will emerge and dominate until further configurations evolve and compete against the established order and the whole cycle starts again. This third type of channel conflict is illustrated in Figure 9.7.

Figure 9.7 Diagrammatic representation of intertype conflict

▶ Cooperation

Without proper coordination activities within the overall channel system will not operate in an efficient manner thus causing commercial problems to the manufacturer and channel members. Channel members are often independent businesses that have to make a profit to survive and have commercial needs and wants of their own that must be considered. The long-term objective of channel management is to achieve the maximum level of service for final customers in the most efficient manner. At the same time this has to be achieved in such a way that individual channel members, often independent businesses themselves, can obtain commercial returns that are satisfactory to them and adequately compensate them for their contribution to the efficiency of the channel system as a whole.

Once a marketing mix has been established to produce the right kind of goods and services for chosen target markets, a decision must be made as to how and where these products and services can be made available. This should be done in a way that fits in with the rest of the company's marketing strategy and brand image. Lancaster and Massingham (2001) recommend four major steps in the coordination process. The first step is to determine the level of service outputs demanded by the final users of the channel system. The second is to determine which channel members have the capability to perform the necessary tasks. The third step is to determine which strategies should be used to bring about the required results. The fourth step is concerned with possible channel conflict which has already been discussed. Figure 9.8. identifies these four major steps in the coordinative process.

Ideally, channel members should plan their objectives together so they are mutually beneficial, avoid harmful and potentially unprofitable arguments and conflicts, and work together to provide an integrated system. The channel system should aim to add value by way of exploiting a 'synergistic dividend'. Synergism is a phrase used in strategic planning that refers to situations where the sum of all parties acting together produces an effect greater than simply adding up the effects of each individual component part working in isolation. Channel members should attempt to coordinate their objectives, plans and activities with other intermediaries in such a way that the performance of the total distribution system, to which they belong and play an important role, is enhanced. In reality such cooperation is rare, for two main reasons:

1. Channel members are often independent business having to make a profit to survive. They are too busy looking after their own affairs to

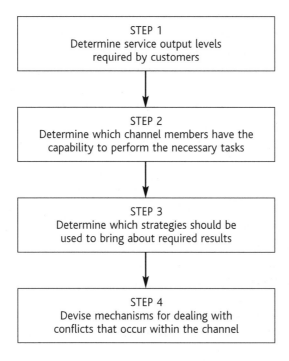

Figure 9.8 Stages in the channel coordination process

pay attention to or even care about what goes on at the other levels of a channel system.

2. Channel members tend only to show interest in and concern for those other channel members that impact directly on their business, for example intermediaries immediately above and below in the channel system from whom they buy and to whom they sell.

The concept of a unified integrated channel system is perhaps more theoretical than a practical reality. Channel members tend not to function as components of a well ordered system but tend to behave as independent businesses with scant regard for other members of the channel system unless they impact directly on their own business affairs. All this makes the management of a channel system a challenge.

◗◗ Changes in the structure of retailing

The dynamic nature of the changing business environment impacts on all marketing intermediaries at every level in the channel system. In

Chapter 2 we examined the subject of marketing and the macroenvironment and saw how changes in the external business environment are largely, but not totally, outside the control of the firm and how they have an impact on marketing policies and practices of the marketing organisation. Factors in the external environment whether political, social, legal or technological all have a consequence for a firm's future marketing actions. These external environmental factors are driven by interrelating forces that bring about change. Sometimes change is quick and dramatic, for example, the unification of Germany after the fall of the Berlin Wall. Usually change takes place at a slower pace, in fact so slow that it is imperceptible and can only be appreciated retrospectively. Nothing illustrates this principle more than the changes that have taken place within the retail environment over the past 30 years.

Vignette 9.2

Tesco.com home shopping service delivers grocery products and a whole range of other products and services to your door.

We hear a lot about the World Wide Web (WWW) and the Internet and how this new information technology is going to change the face of shopping. Whilst it is true that direct marketing in general and Internet-based shopping in particular are becoming increasingly popular, there is little evidence that the more traditional store-based shopping will become a thing of the past. The format of retail stores may change and is indeed changing at this moment. Many people now prefer to shop away from congested town centre locations in purpose built shopping complexes such as Meadowhall near Sheffield or the Trafford Centre near Manchester for example. For a large number of people shopping is more than just a chore. They enjoy browsing and many treat shopping as a leisure activity. Even grocery shopping is a pleasurable experience for a lot of people. There is a certain market segment however who either do not particularly like shopping, particularly for the weekly groceries, or who are too busy to shop in the traditional sense. Tesco.com home shopping is aimed at this particular market segment. Tesco now allows registered shoppers to order all of their grocery requirements online using the Internet and the products are delivered to the customer's home the following day. Payment is made online by credit card or store card. And it is not just grocery products Tesco offer to the home shopper. At the Tesco virtual warehouse there is a variety of goods on offer, including CDs, DVD products, flowers, clothing, toys, Christmas gifts, a toddlers' section, fashion, electrical goods, home living and a comprehensive range of financial and related services, to name but a few. Tesco.com home shopping aims to offer an efficient and reliable service at a competitive price to the discerning home shopper.

▶ The 'wheel-of-retailing'

This concept refers to evolutionary changes in retailing. The wheel appears to be turning with ever increasing speed with each retailing innovation taking less time to achieve maturity. It took around 50 years for department stores to reach maturity, supermarkets took around 25 years and hypermarkets and megastores only 10 years. This concept can be compared to Charles Darwin's theory of evolution which states that a changing environment leads to adaptation and hence evolution. Environmental changes that have occurred which have caused this evolution can be summarised as follows:

▶ Economic factors have compelled retailers to increase their scale of operation to achieve economies of scale both in the size of establishments and buying power. This has resulted in retailing hypermarkets and megastores. Retailing has also become more concentrated with only a small number of retail multiples controlling around 80 per cent of FMCG trade.

▶ Resale Price Maintenance (RPM) was abolished in the 1964 by the Resale Prices Act. The practice of RPM meant that retailers had to sell at manufacturer stipulated prices under the threat of having supplies withheld. Prior to 1964 protection from price competition was afforded to small retailers from growing organisations such as Cohen Stores (later Tesco). Indeed Cohen Stores, it has been contended, deliberately sold at below manufacturers' stipulated prices, with a subsequent cutting off of supplies, for the publicity of 'selling too cheaply'. As a result of the restriction of having to sell at manufacturers' stipulated prices, retailers relied on non-price competition, resulting in the level of personal service in many stores being higher than needed. Customers might have preferred to sacrifice service in the interests of lower prices. With the abolition of RPM and bigger stores going for cut prices as their principal medium of attraction, many smaller shops went out of business along with a number of the wholesalers who supplied such outlets. Multiples expanded into the 'freed-up' market, and used their purchasing economies to compete on price and pass on savings to customers. This led to the self-explanatory phrase, 'Pile it high, and sell it cheap'. Thus, multiples expanded at the expense of independents. At the same time the cooperative movement, although being collectively large enough to take advantage of this environmental change, was too slow to react. This was principally as a result of having too many individual democratically controlled societies (that is, cooperative retail societies owned by members who shopped there) each with their own management structure. There was no centralised control so it was not possible to impose a central policy to take advantage of this environmental opportunity. The irony is that it was cooperative stores that pioneered the notion of self-service during the Second World War to free up labour to help in the war effort, but the movement failed to capitalise on this saving at the end of the war and reverted to personal service.

▷ Selective employment tax (SET) was a tax on selected occupations, introduced in 1966. Retail shop workers were seen as being 'non-productive' so a tax of 7 per cent was imposed on employers with a view to encouraging companies to automate to save labour costs. As labour became more expensive, capital investment became comparatively cheaper and many retailers were attracted to labour-saving checkout systems which gave impetus to the introduction of self-service. These large capital investments meant that operators needed a faster turnover and the consequence was that the shelf life of consumer goods became shorter. Multiple chain retailers of FMCG were able to sell fresher merchandise, which fact they exploited through advertising, so SET indirectly helped them to expand at the expense of independents.

▶ Growth of multiples

As has been discussed, multiples were able to eliminate wholesalers from commercial transactions through central buying directly from manufacturers, in effect acting as their own wholesalers. Bulk purchases have meant advantageous prices from producers, whilst independents have still to purchase through wholesalers, so there are difficulties for small retailers in terms of price competitiveness. Some groups of wholesalers attempted to counteract this growing competition from multiples by setting up their own groupings called 'voluntary groups', and here retailers were invited to affiliate and display the group's logo and accept the 'rules' of operation. Notably, Spar is still a successful voluntary group operator nowadays, but many groups have ceased to trade in the light of competition from the larger multiples.

The 1970s witnessed the introduction of 'economy' lines by multiples. These were 'no frills' products carrying no advertising or promotion and were wrapped in plain factual packaging. This exacerbated the 'pile it high and sell it cheap' image of multiples.

However, during the early 1980s retailing witnessed the introduction of 'own label' products which were brands commissioned by individual multiples from manufacturers, and bearing the chain's own logo. Specifications for such products meant they had to be perceived as being amongst the best of traditional branded lines; not to be associated with economy line products of the 1970s. The first multiple to do this was Sainsbury's, with others quickly following. The outcome has been that power in retailing has passed from manufacturers' brands to retailers' own label brands. The problem for manufacturers was that many have become, in effect, the production 'arm' of multiples with no power in the marketplace in terms of branded products. Many producers resisted this move to 'own label' by refusing to supply. However, such is the purchasing ability of multiples, that very few manufacturers still refuse to supply, with notable exceptions being Kellogg's and Nestlé. These producers make a virtue of not supplying 'own label' by clearly stating in their promotion that they do not manufacture products for anyone else. However, despite these exceptions, in the UK (unlike many other countries) power within retailing has moved from manufacturers to retailers.

▶ 'One-stop' shopping

The motor car is the principal reason why customers now shop less frequently, with a week or longer periods between shopping trips becoming the norm. Shopping is also more of a family occasion, especially amongst the middle classes, so many husbands, along with other family members tend to share in this task. This has accounted for the growth of 'out-of-town' shopping centres where most of a family's needs can be bought within the same complex. Well-known multiples have set up in certain centres with satellite establishments supplying goods they do not market. Such stores tend to be hypermarkets or megastores and the principal reason why this trend might slow is because of planning restrictions and a recognition that these out-of-town centres will lead to a decay of traditional town centres.

As well as increased mobility, most people own freezers which enables them to transport and store large quantities of frozen food. Microwave cooker ownership has increased sales of 'instant' meals, many of which are cooked from frozen.

A final point in the growth of 'one-stop shopping' is the movement of population from urban to suburban centres. Congestion in towns discourages car drivers who prefer to shop in large out-of-town establishments where parking is convenient and normally free.

Activity

Has the concept of 'one-stop shopping' reached its natural limit in terms of development or can it go further? If it has further to go, how do you see its future development?

Over the past 30 years or so we have witnessed the growth of one-stop shopping in hypermarkets. These stores have been concerned mainly with grocery products. Basically you can now go to any of the large multiple retail stores, such as Asda, and carry out a month's total grocery shopping all under one roof. This is a one-stop grocery shop. This idea seems to be developing for shopping as a whole. In the USA we have seen the development of stores such as Sears, where it is possible to buy virtually anything in one store. America has also been at the forefront of shopping mall development where there is a wide range of different shops in an enclosed mall. In the UK we have seen the development of large out of town retail developments like Meadowhall near Sheffield. Despite concerns expressed by town planners about the decimation of conventional town-centre shopping, these shopping 'cathedrals' point the way to future developments. What route such developments will take is difficult to predict, but worldwide retail trends seem to point to a Meadowhall type model.

▶ Scrambled merchandising

The consumption of food products in an advanced society is relatively income inelastic, in that customers do not buy more food when they have more money. They tend to 'trade up' to better quality foods. Multiples have consequently diversified into non-food items to advance their turnover and profits. Many now sell clothing, electrical goods, plants and flowers and have extended their traditional range of food products. A number have, however, become even more diversified (for example gone into publishing). However, recently a number have moved back to their core business of food retailing because of a confusion of image associated with retailing extraneous products.

▶ Franchising

This system of selling and distribution is organised through a contract between a principal seller (franchiser) and distributive outlets (owned by franchisees). It is sometimes referred to as 'business format' franchising.

Such a scheme depends on the franchiser having an idea, a name, a 'secret process' or specialised equipment or goodwill that will be attractive to customers. If this is the case, the franchiser will then grant the franchisee a licence, for some kind of commercial consideration, for the franchisee to exploit that name, idea or product. Such a licence agreement includes rules for operating the business and such matters as:

- a royalty
- an initial fee
- a share of profits
- the obligation to make bulk purchases from the franchiser
- certain rules of hygiene and presentation, possibly involving training.

These, and other considerations, depend on the product or service.

The modern business format franchise was developed in America, although its roots can be traced back to the UK with the 'tied house' arrangement between brewers and their outlets. Franchising has increased in strength in the UK since the early 1960s. It is a contract between a franchiser and each independently owned establishment of the franchisee. The franchiser's brand and reputation are used for marketing a product or service and the support received by the franchisee from the franchiser depends on the initial agreement. The contract is usually written to minimise the risks in opening a business. What attracts new franchisees is that others have successfully followed the 'blueprint'. The franchiser supplies the franchisee with a business package or 'format', a trade name and specific products or services for sale. Examples of such franchise agreements are DynoRod, Little Chef and Mister Minit.

 Vignette 9.3

Subway, the number one USA food franchise becomes the major competitor to typical 'fast food' fare.

Subway is the USA's number one fast-food franchise retail chain. It has built up a reputation for value for money, cleanliness and healthy, low fat food. People are moving over to Subway in the USA in their thousands for their lunch, snacks and even their evening meals. Subway has moved into Europe and is hoping to repeat its commercial success on this side of the Atlantic. There are now advertisements in the British press asking people if they are interested in becoming a Subway franchisee. From its beginnings in Bridgeport, Connecticut in 1965, Subway has grown into a £2.6 billion firm with more than 14,500 franchises in 76 countries. The company has recently won the top spot on the 22nd Annual Franchise 500® listing. It was 1996 when Subway last found itself in the coveted No. 1 position in the listing. At that time, when founder Fred DeLuca was asked to predict the future and try to see where he thought Subway was heading he said that it would see explosive growth.

His prediction seems to be correct. Today the firm is focused on building their customer base further through product improvements and increased store distribution. Subway saw the addition of more than 600 new franchises in 2000, as well as a 16 per cent increase in store sales volume. The company has developed the Subway Select line of gourmet sauces and sandwiches and a low-fat line of sandwiches which are particularly popular with weight conscious customers. The firm has also increased advertising spend, which has made people notice Subway even more. Nobody could have possibly missed, in the USA at least, the prominent Subway advertisement that ran in 2000 featuring Jared Fogle, who lost 245 pounds eating Subway sandwiches. With the popularity of the '7 Under 6' menu (seven sandwiches with 6 grams of fat or less), many see Subway as a fresh and healthy alternative to greasy burgers and the more traditional fast food.

▶ Miscellaneous

There has also been growth in other forms of selling over the past 30 years, including:

- ▶ 'Party Plan' is popular for products like cosmetics, kitchenware, jewellery and linen. A 'party' is organised, usually in the home of the hostess who invites friends, and then receives a 'consideration' in the form of cash or goods based upon what her guests purchase.
- ▶ 'Door-to-door' direct selling is relatively expensive, but wholesaler and retailer margins are eliminated. As long as the salesperson can build up a regular list of clients for relatively frequently purchased items then it can be successful. Avon Cosmetics and Betterware are examples of companies who are successful in this respect.
- ▶ Automatic vending is used for beverages, cigarettes, chocolate, and many other products. Vending machines are placed in convenient locations such as bus stations, colleges, public houses and factories. Vending machines have been used since the 1950s to provide entertainment through juke-boxes and, more recently, arcade games. Cash-dispenser machines are relatively new and, in addition to dispensing cash, they can answer balance enquiries, take requests for statements and chequebooks and accept deposits.
- ▶ Mail order business is through catalogue or non-catalogue sources. The first relies on comprehensive catalogues to obtain sales, sometimes using agents to deal with order collection and administration for a commission. Products can be purchased interest-free and extended credit terms are available. There are some specialist mail order houses that deal with a limited range of lines that are difficult to access in shops (for example clothes for large people). Non-catalogue

mail order depends on press and magazine advertising and is often used to sell a limited range of specialist or unusual products.

▶ Other direct marketing techniques include using direct mail, where a promotional letter and instructions on ordering are sent through the post. Such methods are used by book and record clubs. Television can also be used, with orders being placed by a telephone call to a free number and leaving credit card details on an answering machine. Telephone ordering is sometimes combined with press advertising, especially in colour supplements.

▶ Television shopping via online computer is still at an early stage, but it should become more popular if companies invest enough in its development. This direct form of retailing is economical as orders are often placed directly with the manufacturers.

▶ The World Wide Web (WWW) on the Internet is a medium that encourages customers to search for a seller rather than the other way round. We now speak of the 'virtual value chain' and 'market space' rather than a conventional marketplace. The WWW is still in its infancy as a marketing tool, but it is growing in importance, particularly in the area of marketing communications.

▶▶ World Wide Web and the Internet

The profession of sales and marketing, as with most things in this world, is changing and evolving all the time. The use of the Internet, the rise of e-commerce, the growing importance of direct marketing are some of these changes. Others include the increasing focus in marketing on building relationships with customers, and the emphasis on customer retention over customer acquisition, that is a relationship marketing approach to business. These are only a few of the developments influencing the way firms carry out business today. Firms have to adapt, keep up with new developments and invest in the latest computer software and systems to stay up with, let alone ahead of, the competition.

Business in general and marketing in particular have become more and more affected by, and in many areas dependent upon, computer-based technology. Furthermore, technological progress itself is getting faster in all areas, not just in the world of computers. Technology seems to be moving forwards at an ever increasing rate. Some people have difficulty keeping up. The marketer must also be aware of, and be prepared for, future developments in technology and attempt to forecast what these developments might be. Delphi technological forecasting is one such method that could be employed. The present Internet revolution, which has been accelerating for some years now, with the World Wide Web and the Internet at its very core, has been cited as one of the most important commercial innovations ever to occur in the world of marketing. This development is likely to affect every facet of nearly every organisation's business operations, but especially the marketing function. e-Commerce, which is a generic name for the use of the Internet and World Wide Web in commercial activities, can, if used wisely, help to improve all areas of business. It can be useful in bringing in new customers and communicating to existing customers. It can be instrumental in improving service levels to customers, creating growth potential by expanding communications across geographic boundaries, tracking customers and the progress of their orders, data mining of databases for segmentation and direct marketing, better targeting of marketing communications, reducing distribution costs and speeding up growth.

Some experts regard the Web as the innovation that will totally change the way firms carry out marketing. Many argue that for firms' marketing activities to be successful using the new technology, a totally new model of marketing is required for the Web-based society in which these firms will be conducting commercial activities. In the USA, more than two-thirds of firms are setting up computer-based systems such as intranet and/or extranet (a limited, closed loop Internet) facilities. Some experts are calling the new developments a 'paradigm shift' in marketing thinking and practice. This means that the new technology is not just resulting in marketing firms doing fundamentally the same thing but with more up-to-date technology. It means that firms have to alter the whole way they think about doing marketing, they require a new way of looking at things, or a totally new 'paradigm'. As in many other technological innovations, America seems to be at the vanguard and functioning as a driver or propellant for the dissemination of the new computer-based technology and the new marketing methods that go with it, across the globe. These are tools that have the potential to increase profits by cutting costs, improving productivity, efficiency and communications and reducing paper work. The World Wide Web (WWW) or Internet distribution channel will reach a massive £1 trillion by the year 2004, according to many experts on the subject. Some products and services are ordered and delivered via the Internet, for example MP3 digital music files. Other products and services are merely shopped for and ordered via the Web, for example airline tickets or cameras. The World Wide Web has special qualities, which differentiates it from other forms of business communications. Because the Web is so different from the more traditional media, such as newspapers, posters, television and radio, its use is dramatically changing the way in which some marketing activities are conducted. In fact some marketing activities could not be carried out at all without the use of Web-based technology, for example MP3 digital music services and players.

▶ Challenges to management of Internet marketing

The growing importance of the Internet as a commercial communication tool is excellent for business firms because it provides additional, potentially profitable, commercial opportunities. The Internet offers unique opportunities for marketing firms and their customers to communicate with each other via a mass medium on a new 'mediated' environment. Business firms and customers are now in positions to build relationships with one another effectively and cost efficiently. Both can actually contribute to the relationship in 'real time'. Firms can learn on an individual basis how to satisfy the needs and wants of their customers by using Internet technologies. The new technology also challenges business thinking, because the Internet and its relationship marketing 'business model' may conflict with more traditional marketing methods. Using a hypermedia computer mediated environment (HCME), which is what the Internet and the World Wide Web actually are, is very different from conventional marketing media, such as newspapers and television. Firms will need to redefine their operations in terms of organisational structure, production, marketing, communications, sales, aftersales services, and overall strategic planning processes. Successful Web strategies can only be achieved by embracing the new technology positively and from a complete organisational standpoint. They should be part of overall comprehensive corporate strategies formulated by the top management. Internet marketing strategies should be integrated within the entire organisation and the Internet should not be viewed as simply an additional, tactical marketing and advertising channel.

<table>
<tr><td rowspan="2">SELF-CHECK</td><td>Explain the 'wheel-of-retailing' concept
The wheel-of-retailing concept is similar in many ways to the idea of the product life cycle, but is applied to retail configurations and formats rather than products. Basically the idea is that retail formats evolve and change over time and in this sense have a life cycle.</td><td>Under what conditions might you choose to employ a selective distribution strategy?
There are many possible conditions under which this might be appropriate. A product may require special storage facilities so only distributors with these facilities are used to stock your products. Another might be if a</td></tr>
</table>

product requires a particular skill or expertise to demonstrate and market effectively and staff may require specialised product training. It might be that the distribution channel should reflect the type of brand image that has been built up, so selective distribution might be called for.

Explain the term 'retail concentration'
Retail concentration refers to a measure indicating how many separate retail firms control the retail market. In the packaged grocery market for example, a few of the major players such as Sainsbury's, Tesco and Asda have the bulk of market share.

What do you understand by the term 'non-shop shopping'
Consumers can now purchase many goods and services without actually visiting a shop. Examples of non-shop shopping are ordering goods by mail order, ordering from a satellite television shopping channel and ordering goods via the Internet or World Wide Web.

Are channels of distribution and physical distribution (business logistics) separate, but interrelated, business areas?
Channel management is concerned with the selection and management of marketing intermediaries and final channel selection and management. Physical distribution is concerned with all the processes that get the final product to the point of purchase, involving materials handling, stock control, transport and warehouse location. Both management areas are concerned with providing time and place utility or value for the final customer. It is true that the overall subject of distribution can be divided into two component parts for the purposes of study, but from a management point of view channel decisions and logistics decisions must be made in relation to each other.

▶▶ Summary

The subject of distribution is made up of two separate but interrelated components, channels of distribution and physical distribution management. Physical distribution management, which forms part of the wider subject of 'logistics management' is covered in Chapter 10. In this chapter we have been concerned with channels of distribution that refer to an often complex arrangement of agents, wholesalers and retailers through which marketing firms move products and services to their intended point of purchase. The correct choice of channel is of vital importance to the commercial success of any company. A strategic, competitive advantage can be gained from such choices. When examining the flow of products or services through a distribution channel system it is useful to use an analogy and think of the distribution system as a pipeline. The pipeline has main pipes, subsidiary pipes, free flow and blockages. In consumer markets marketing channels can be made up of a complex array of marketing intermediaries. In some situations direct marketing is used which aims to cut the 'middleman' from the system. In industrial marketing channels direct distribution is more common, especially when products being ordered are 'buyer specified'. Wholesale firms are also used in industrial channels although they are often referred to as 'factors'. Likewise, industrial firms make use of agents and distributors just as in consumer markets. The subject of channels is an important area of marketing and, along with physical distribution, forms a major area of strategic marketing management.

FURTHER READING

Adcock D. (2000) *Marketing Strategies for Competitive Advantage*, Chapter 12, 'Channel Management and Value Added Relations', John Wiley & Sons, Chichester.

Armstrong G. and Kotler P. (2000) *Marketing: An Introduction* (5th edn), Chapter 10, 'Distribution Channels and Logistics Management', Prentice Hall, Englewood Cliffs, NJ.

Blythe J. (2001) *Essentials of Marketing*, Chapter 8, 'Distribution', Pearson Education, London.

Cateora P.R. and Ghauri P.N. (2000) *International Marketing: European Edition*, Chapter 15, 'The International Distribution System', McGraw-Hill, Maidenhead.

Davies M. (1998) *Understanding Marketing*, Chapter 8, 'Distribution', Prentice Hall, London.

Keegan W.J. and Green M.S. (2000) *Global Marketing* (2nd edn), Chapter 13, 'Global Marketing Channels and Physical Distribution', Prentice Hall, London.

Lancaster G.A. and Reynolds P.L. (1999) *Introduction to Marketing: A Step-by-Step Guide to All The Tools of Marketing*, Chapter 12, 'Channels of Distribution', Kogan Page, London.

Plamer A. (2000) *Principles of Marketing*, Chapter 14, 'Channel Intermediaries', OUP, Oxford.

▶▶ References

Cravens D.W. (1988) 'Gaining Strategic Marketing Advantage', *Business Horizons*, September–October, pp. 44–5.

Lancaster G.A. and Massingham L.C. (2001) *Marketing Management*, McGraw-Hill, Maidenhead, p. 451.

Palamountain J. (1955) *The Politics of Distribution*, Harvard University Press, Cambridge, MA.

10

Logistics Management

▶▶ Introduction

As mentioned in the previous chapter, distribution management is divided into two separate but closely interrelated subject areas – channels of distribution and physical distribution management. Having chosen a network of intermediaries who take over management of goods as they move along the channels of distribution, the company has to consider how these goods can be transferred from the manufacturer to the consumer. This activity falls within the scope of physical distribution management (PDM) which is a critical area of overall marketing management owing much to the concept of logistics developed by the military. The term 'physical distribution management' is somewhat outdated and the subject is now referred to as 'total business logistics management'. This technique is concerned with more than delivering finished products to customers. It is a total system that starts with sourcing and finishes with the planning of transport for outward delivery. Logistics management is concerned with the entire process of obtaining materials from suppliers, storing, processing, retrieving, and delivering goods to customers.

▶▶ Scope of logistics management

Logistics covers every stage of the physical distribution process, as follows:

▶ raw materials and component parts being ordered and delivered to the factory
▶ materials handling and storage, stock control

- sales forecasting from which the requirements for individual components parts, transport and storage are derived
- order processing
- purchasing and replenishment of stock
- packing
- delivery
- achievement of set service levels
- warehouse location
- fleet management and scheduling
- management and operation of an information system which keeps records, aids forecasting, scheduling, model building and produces documentation needed for efficient management of the operation.

▌▌▌ Vignette 10.1

The Institute of Logistics and Transport maintains professional standards within the physical distribution industry.

The Institute of Logistics and Transport was formed in June 1999, after the integration of the Institute of Logistics and The Chartered Institute of Transport in the UK. The Institute sees itself as a focus for professional activity and as the guardian of professional quality and competence within the logistics profession. Its aim is to promote awareness of the importance of logistics and transport in the economic and social life of the nation and to develop policy advice to the government and others. The favoured definition of logistics used by the Institute is 'the time related positioning of resource'. The resource can be transport, storage, manufacturing capacity or information. The Institute states that modern business logistics is based on much the same concept as the original military term used to describe the organisation of moving, lodging and supplying troops and equipment. Logistics aims to deliver value to customers. Transport is a major component of the supply chain but not the only component. The Institute views logistics as the process of designing, managing and improving such supply chains, which often includes sourcing, purchasing, manufacturing, storage, materials handling, stock control and transport and distribution. The Institute publishes surveys, guidelines and general titles of interest to members. Some are published in collaboration with people or organisations within industry or the universities. The Institute also offers a range of professional qualifications to its members ranging from GNVQ to a Masters degree.

Marketing has many definitions including the process of getting the right goods to the right place at the right time. This definition sums up the importance of time and place. Products are viewed as a 'bundle of attributes' many of which are implied as they are created by branding, packaging and advertising. The core product is part of the total product offering. In order for the value of goods and services to be fully realised they must be available to customers at the right place and at the right time. What this availability is will depend on the nature of the product or service and the situation or occasion when they are used. For example if you walk into a public house for a drink of beer, you expect beer to be available there and then. A Christmas present only has value on Christmas day. If you order flowers by telephone to send to someone on St. Valentine's Day they are of little use if they are delivered the day after. On the other hand, if you order a new car from a showroom you may be prepared to place an order and wait several weeks to get exactly the car you want in terms of the colour, engine size and trim required. In the case of Valentine's Day flowers or the glass of beer, the time and the place of consumption form an intrinsic part of what the customer perceives to be the 'total product offering'. For other products and services time and place are less important. Business logistics plays a key role in the creation and delivery of the notion of time and place utility.

Do customers take a holistic view of product and service offerings and see them as a total 'bundle of attributes'?

You should start by defining the nature of a product or service. In particular you should examine the concepts of real, tangible product attributes and those that are less tangible and more implied to the customer through the use of marketing. An example here might illustrate the points that you are trying to get across. For example Perrier water is basically water containing a few trace elements and minerals and some natural carbonated gas. However, it is marketed as much more than a bottle of water. The implied attributes include sophistication, style, cleanliness, health and many other positive attributes. The shape and colour of the bottle, the brand name and design of the label, even the place where it is sold, all contribute to the image the consumer has of Perrier. It is viewed holistically as a 'bundle of total product attributes'.

In many industrial markets, factors such as stock availability and reliability of delivery are as, if not more important, than price. The speed at which a firm can process an order and deliver to the required location, at the required time, with the desired level of reliability may well be over the long term the deciding factors in awarding a contract, even if the supplying firm is less competitive on price. Different industrial sectors and segments have distinct service sensitivities. Delivery can provide the marketing firm with a long-term competitive advantage that can be a strategic tool. To be really effective all functions within logistics must be fully integrated, which is what is at the heart of 'Total Business Logistics'. Because the activities making up logistics management are often complex and specialised, they need to be managed by professional staff who can make correct decisions. The main reason for the increasing importance of physical distribution management as a marketing function is the nature of the business environment itself. In the past it was usual for companies to hold large inventories of raw materials and components. Although industries and individual firms differ in their stock-holding policies, nowadays, stock levels are kept as low as functionally possible. Holding stock ties up capital which is 'dead money' and not earning for the company. A more cost-oriented approach by management has had the effect of moving the responsibility for carrying stock onto the supplier and away from the customer. Gilbert and Strebel (1989) pointed out that this has an effect throughout the value chain, with each member exerting demands on the next to provide higher levels of service. Because logistics has such an important long-term strategic dimension within marketing strategy it is necessary for logistics policy to come from senior marketing staff. Logistics decisions should form part of the strategic marketing plan.

Why is it necessary for all the functions making up logistics management to be fully integrated?

Customers do not necessarily differentiate between the various component parts that make up a product or service offering. Research into consumer and organisational buyer behaviour has shown that customers view the product or service offering in its entirety as a bundle of product attributes, some of which are real and tangible and some of which are implied and intangible. The total product or service offering is the result of the imaginative and creative formulation of an appropriate marketing mix. In a sense, the Four Ps are put together in such a way as to create the desired product/service perception in the minds of specifically defined target markets or segments. Logistics falls under the 'Place' heading of the marketing mix and along with channel selection and management produces the time and place utility dimensions of the total product or service offering. The level of customer service that logistics provides is unlikely to be split up into its component parts of materials handling, invoice processing, stock availability or delivery availability. Each of these elements is of little importance to the customer. Most customers, especially in consumer markets, are unaware of the plethora of logistical expertise that brings a product to a point of consumption at the desired time. To have value as a business function, logistics needs to be integrated and part of the marketing programme.

▶▶ History and development of logistics management

In the Second World War, the Korean War and Vietnam War, supplies officers were faced with the task of moving a diversity of materials across seas and continents. Marketing management saw that these skills could be applied to physical distribution management (PDM). Military planners had used the developing science of operations research, sometimes involving sophisticated statistical and mathematical techniques, to work out logistical strategies. Such techniques have since enabled logistics managers to optimise operations in terms of time, materials cost and manpower. It was seen that distribution could be organised in a scientific way and this led to the development of business logistics. During the Second World War the UK had to rely on financial help from the USA to keep going during the war and to help it to reconstruct after the war. During the war, factories were converted to war production from civilian production as was explained in Chapter 1. Operational researchers and production planners realised that production could be made more efficient through scientific organisation. This maximised the use of scarce wartime resources, many of which had to be imported which proved expensive both in terms of money and lives lost protecting British convoys. These scientific techniques were applied to wartime production and greatly reduced costs and increased the effectiveness of the war effort.

Staying with the military analogy, battles and wars have been lost, not because an army could not fight or because of lack of manpower or equipment, but often through lack of ammunition, lack of food and drink or lack of blankets and warm clothing. It is said that armies 'march on their stomachs', meaning that a well-fed army has the strength and endurance to fight. It is often seemingly small things that matter in the success of military campaigns. Successful armies organise themselves to have a wide range of vital supplies in the right place at the right time, and get supplies there more effectively and efficiently than their enemies. They can thus seal a strategic, competitive advantage that may possibly decide or at least influence the outcome of the battle.

As with war, so with business, which is a form of non-violent commercial warfare. Competitive firms are involved in a 'battle for the customer'. A firm's strategic objective is not taking a hill or a town from the enemy, but market share, turnover or profit margins. However, the principles are the same and the commercial battle for business is more likely to be won with the aid of effective logistics back-up.

With sophisticated marketing analysis has come an awareness of the costs of physical distribution. Businesses must provide customer satisfaction to make profits. To achieve this, goods must be in the right place at the right time. A balance must be struck between the costs of physical distribution and customer satisfaction. Greater levels of service usually mean greater costs and achieving the balance is the task of physical distribution management.

PDM has increased in importance as a marketing function because of the increasingly demanding nature of the economic environment. Twenty years ago many companies held large stocks of raw materials and components, but today stocks are generally kept to a minimum with responsibility for carrying stock falling on the supplier. Stocks form part of a company's working capital and this is typically partially financed through a bank overdraft that is a reflection of interest rates. Companies seek to lessen such charges which means less stock-holding, with each marketing channel putting pressure on the next to provide a high level of service.

Just-in-time management (JIT), or more correctly, 'lean manufacturing', has been widely adopted by companies with large purchasing power who impose stringent delivery conditions on their suppliers (see Hutchins, 1988). This system involves carrying only a few hours' stock of raw materials and component parts that has to be replenished regularly to keep production running. These companies demand a high level of service from suppliers. JIT has been extensively taken up by the automotive industry, where large companies operate strict delivery controls. They make large financial savings in stock-holding costs. The logistical process involves more than just transportation. PDM covers the movement of goods from the receipt of an order to delivery to the customer. It involves close liaison between production planning, purchasing, order processing, material control and warehousing. These areas work together to serve the customer efficiently.

How valid is the analogy between military logistics and total business logistics? Explain your position by using examples to illustrate the points made.

This question should be answered by first explaining what is meant by the term 'military logistics'. This is best illustrated by means of example. You can then make the comparison between the role and importance of logistics in military campaigns and in commercial campaigns. You need to compare and contrast the two situations and clearly state your opinions. In the twentieth century, modern wars have been fought either globally, for example the First and Second World Wars, or in distant lands, for example the Korean War, the Vietnam War and the Gulf War. In the Second World War, the UK had severe resource

constraints, so great effort was expended in trying to find more efficient methods to organise inward transportation of raw materials for
the production of war supplies, usually munitions. In addition, outward
distribution of a whole range of products, including rations for troops
at the front line, ammunition and small arms, transport, bridges, clothing and a host of other materials, was necessary. Military operations
today have to be meticulously planned using the latest operations
research and management science techniques, aided now by the use of
powerful computers.

Many businesses are global and competition is extensive. Component
parts are often made throughout the world and then assembled in one
particular country. Such products are marketed and distributed worldwide. In a sense, firms operating in the global marketplace really are at
war with one another and are fighting for their survival. Production
and distribution complexities are just as difficult and important in
today's commercial war as they have been in past military conflicts.
The same basic principles apply and scientific techniques that were
used with great effect in military campaigns can be just as effectively
employed in helping to solve logistical problems in peace time commercial 'conflicts'.

▶▶ Definitions

As we have discussed, management theory and practice takes a holistic
approach to physical distribution and today this managerial function is
often referred to as 'total business logistics'. The five main elements are:

1. Order processing
2. Stock levels/inventory
3. Warehousing
4. Transportation
5. Service levels.

Business logistics management integrates these functions, ensuring each
element is used to maximum effect towards a common objective. This is
known as the 'systems approach' to distribution management.

As PDM has a clearly defined scientific basis, we now present some
of the analytical methods that are employed by management when
developing a logistics system. A clear understanding of the two core
themes is important.

1. The attainment of an effective distribution system is based on solidarity of effort. The overall service aim can be achieved, even though it may look as if some individual elements of the system are not working to optimum efficiency.
2. The best service cannot be provided at the lowest cost, since costs increase with the level of service offered. After deciding on the level of service that should be offered to customers, the company must explore ways of keeping costs to a minimum without jeopardising the agreed level of service.

▶▶ The distribution process

A supplier initiates the distribution process on receipt of an order. The customer placing the order has no practical interest in how the supplier's distributive system is structured, or in problems the supplier might have. The customer's concern is that the distribution system is effective, resulting in the goods ordered being in the right place at the right time. The period of time between the placing of the order and receipt of the goods is known as the 'lead time', and this varies for different types of products and type of market and industry. Two extreme examples are the shipbuilding industry, where lead time is measured in parts or multiples of years, and the retail sector, where days or hours are more prevalent measures. The lead time quoted by the supplier is the base used by the customer when planning production. Customers expect the quoted delivery time to be met. Suppliers not adhering to quoted lead time run the risk of customer dissatisfaction.

▶ Order processing

This is the first stage of the logistical process, and an effective order-processing department has a direct influence on lead times. Orders come from the sales department, with most companies preferring to build up regular supply routes, with an efficient supplier, that remain stable over a period of time. Contracts are frequently set up and regular repeat orders are made throughout the duration of the contract.

Fast and accurate order processing systems are essential so other departments in the company are aware of the order and can pass on rapid confirmation to the customer, along with an exact delivery time. Company image depends on a high level of office efficiency and slow reaction to orders leads to dissatisfaction. Effective order processing often makes the difference when buyers are making decisions about preferred suppliers.

Order processing has been made more efficient by the use of computerised systems, which allow automatic updating of stock levels and delivery schedules, thus accurately illustrating the sales position. Such accuracy is essential in order processing, and it must be combined with speed of processing.

❱ Inventory

This is a critical area of PDM as customer satisfaction depends on a company not running out of stock and being able to deliver. An optimum stock level must be operated, whereby stock-out situations do not happen. However, stock levels should not be too high as this is costly to maintain. Techniques for ascertaining optimum stock levels are examined later.

Stocks mean cost – the 'opportunity' cost that exists through competition for the company's resources. If a high stock level has to be maintained the profit contribution must be larger than the costs associated with carrying extra stock. Some companies may have to carry high stock levels to meet short lead times in a particular market, and these companies must then look to reduce costs in other areas of the PDM mix.

❱ Warehousing

Many firms send goods direct to customers from their own on-site warehouse. However, if a company sells goods that are taken off regularly, but in small quantities, strategically located warehouses around the country may be used. Large retail chains use this type of system, in which goods are transported in bulk from manufacturer to retail warehouse, where stocks are stored before being distributed to individual stores belonging to the retail chain. Levels of service and costs will increase with the number of warehouses used and, again, an optimum strategy should be laid down which enables operation of a desired level of service. Factors that must be taken into consideration are the location of customers, the size of orders, frequency of deliveries and desired lead times.

▮▮▮ Vignette 10.2

The Fife Warehousing Group offers a full spectrum of warehousing services within central Scotland.

The Fife Warehousing Group was founded in 1963 to provide professional warehousing services to companies within central Scotland. The firm now has nearly 24,0000 square metres of warehousing space of which 40 per cent is racked. The firm offers clients a full spectrum of integrated warehousing services which includes storage, materials handling, order processing and fulfilment, stock control, forecasting and management, packaging, physical distribution and information services. The general trend amongst many firms today is to concentrate on their core business, for example manufacturing, and outsource non-core activities to specialist providers. The Fife Warehousing Group gives firms in the central Scotland area the opportunity to outsource their warehousing and distribution operations to a specialist company with many years' experience in the area of warehousing management. Fife Warehousing is a family owned business and prides itself on the close customer relationships and level of service it gives to its customers. Specialist consultants establish customer's individual requirements and tailor-made solutions are found to meet the requirements of each individual customer. The company tries to build a mutually beneficial partnership with its customers and practices the principles of long-term relationship marketing with great emphasis on customer retention. The Fife Warehousing Group is associated with the Russell Group of companies and the combined group is one of the largest transport, warehousing and distribution organisations in Scotland. The group as a whole has over 160,000 square metres of warehousing space and offers a total warehousing service and a transport and distribution service to firms throughout Europe.

▶ Transportation

This is usually the greatest cost in distribution, and is calculated according to number of units or weight. Management of transportation means that costs must be carefully controlled along with type of transport chosen and these must be kept under review. Many companies now have individual transport managers, illustrating the importance of PDM.

Road transport, with its advantages of speed and door-to-door delivery, has become the most popular method of transportation over the past fifty years. Its flexibility is essential for many companies operating on low stock-holding and short lead times. Some firms purchase their own fleet of vehicles instead of using subcontractors where large volumes of goods are moved. Some large retailers like Tesco, Sainsbury's and Marks & Spencer now leave their warehousing and transportation arrangements to logistics specialists such as BOC, Excel Logistics and Tibbett & Britten.

Rail transport is often used when lead time is not of such paramount importance, or when attempting to bring down transport costs. Hazardous or bulky goods are often transported by rail, but it is also suitable for light goods which must be delivered quickly, for example letter and parcel post who use an integrated system of rail for transport over longer distances and then road for shorter distances.

Air transport is not widely used for distribution within the UK, although overseas long-distance routes justify the cost. It is used for transporting goods that are highly perishable or valuable in relation to their weight. It also has the advantage of being less of a problem in terms of packaging as less is needed than for ocean transport, coupled with the fact that insurance premiums are less costly for airfreight than for sea freight. Airfreight is popular in the USA because of the great distances involved.

Whatever mode of transportation is selected, goods should be protected during transit and this applies particularly to ocean transport where longer times and more robust handling methods mean that more protection is needed.

▶ Service levels

When we aggregate the effects of the four elements of the logistics system we arrive at the total output of the system and the total output of the system in the eyes of customers is the level of service they receive. Customers are likely to view the products and services they buy in their entirety, as a 'total bundle of attributes'. Stock availability, speed at which purchase orders are processed, stock control, storage, materials handling procedures employed, location of warehouses and delivery reliability are rarely examined individually by customers. The logistics component of the 'bundle of product attributes' is seen as a level of service. Customers or market segments are likely to attach varying levels of importance to the level of service they receive. Some will be more service sensitive or service 'elastic' than others. From this viewpoint marketing management, as a base for market segmentation, can use service sensitivity. Burbridge (1987) has given recommendations as to how levels of service to customers can be provided optimally. He recommends a total cost philosophy. Management must first of all communicate overall distribution objectives to all staff and ensure that they are understood properly. The systems approach to physical distribution management should include production and production planning, purchasing and sales forecasting. Included in the systems approach is the concept of total cost, because individual costs are less important than the total cost. The cost of holding large stocks may appear too high when considered in isolation, but if large stocks provide a service that leads to higher sales and profits, then the total cost of all the PDM activities will have been effective. Costs are a reflection of distribution strategy, and maximum service cannot be provided at minimum cost. It is the optimisation of the total integrated distribution system for a given level of optimum service that is important, not necessarily the individual costs of each element making up the system.

▶▶ A systems approach to PDM

We have emphasised that various marketing activities need to be combined to form a single marketing effort. Managers are now more conscious of the potential of PDM and that logistical systems should be designed with the 'total' function in mind. A disconnected approach to PDM will result in a firm failing to provide satisfactory service and involve it in excessive costs. It should also be noted that within the PDM structure there might be conflict between individual managers aiming to achieve their personal goals to the detriment of the overall PDM objectives. For example, production managers will favour long production runs and standard products, whilst sales and marketing will look towards high stock levels, special products and short production runs. At the same time, transport managers may want to lower costs by selecting a slower transportation method or waiting for a full load, and financial managers will prefer reduced inventory and dislike extensive warehousing networks. Each department may appear efficient when they can realise their individual goals, but marketing strategy might not be effectively served.

Companies aim to provide customers with an acceptable level of service at optimal cost. Essentially, senior management must ensure that overall distribution objectives are communicated and understood throughout the management structure, making it clear that company objectives should be considered before departmental objectives. If management fails to make objectives clear, this can cause organisational problems when implementing the systems approach. This should include production and production planning, purchasing and sales forecasting and the concept of total cost, where individual costs are held to be less important than the total cost. For example, the total cost of holding high stocks may look unacceptable, but if it enables a company to provide a service leading to higher sales and profits, then the total cost of all the PDM activities will be justified.

PDM is now recognised as a marketing tool in its own right. In a market where products are similar and price variations small, service counts as a major force in competition. It may even be possible to command a higher price for products that are always delivered on time. A salesperson in a company that provides an effective spare parts and service facility for customers has an advantage in price discussions. It can be seen that far from being merely an adjunct to marketing, distribution has a full place in the marketing mix and is a fundamental part of marketing strategy. A well-coordinated business logistics system can help to discover marketing opportunities and improve the overall marketing mix.

Explain the 'total systems' approach to logistics management and examine how the position of the final output from such a system is perceived by potential and actual customers in 'level of service' terms.

To answer a question like this you need to explain the concept of a system and the fact that most systems are made up of a number of subsystems. The output from each subsystem contributes to the achievement of objectives for the system as a whole. Each subsystem must be fully integrated to achieve its individual objective. The objective for a logistics system is likely to be a particular level of customer service. You need to explain this service concept and how an integrated logistics system can help to deliver customer service. The marketing mix has been variously described over the years, but perhaps the most widely used definition is that of McCarthy's 4Ps. It is a simple model, but it serves its purpose. One of the Ps is of course 'place'. The place component is made up of two separate, but nonetheless highly interrelated subcomponents, channels of distribution and business logistics that are often referred to as physical distribution management. The 4Ps marketing mix system can and should be viewed as a total system. Many management scientists have been working on ways to optimise the marketing mix in terms of resources allocation and marginal return by using a systems approach. Each P of the marketing mix can be viewed as a subsystem and treated as a system in its own right. Each system can then be split further, for example the logistics system can be viewed as a system in its own right. The objectives set for each subsystem are not set in isolation, but in terms of how they contribute to the achievement of objectives for the marketing mix system as a whole. For example, the objective for a logistics system is likely to be a given level of customer service. This service level is likely to have been

set by marketing management, as the level of service offered to customers is an intrinsic part of the product or service offering and hence
an important marketing variable.

▶▶ Monitoring and control of PDM

Getting the right goods to the right place at the right time for least cost is
the objective of PDM. The basis of monitoring and control is to provide
measures of operational effectiveness, giving management objectives
that point to criteria allowing useful assessment of performance.

▶ The output of a physical distribution system

The level of customer service is the key output from any system of
physical distribution and this is a competitive benefit that can be
offered to customers to sustain existing business or attract new
business. The level of service offered should be at least comparable to
that of major competitors. Level of service is often seen as the time it
takes to deliver a customer's order or how many orders can be met
from stock. Technical assistance, training and aftersales service is also
involved. The two most fundamental areas are reliability and frequency
of delivery and the ability to meet orders quickly from stock. If a
company sets a service policy of delivering a certain percentage of
orders within a set number of days from the receipt of the order, this is
a useful and specific objective that offers strict criteria for evaluation.
From this, a simple delivery delay analysis, showing number of orders
received, days late and relating this to the percentage of total orders,
can be prepared, making clear whether such objectives are being
reached or whether any adjustment of service level is needed. This
analysis can be updated upon receipt of a copy of the despatch note and
will indicate any over- or under-provision of service.

▓▓▓ Vignette 10.3

McCain Foods Limited optimises its North American delivery operations with food logistics specialists Logility Voyager Solutions.

McCain Foods Limited, the world's largest manufacturer of oven chips and an international producer of pizzas, appetisers and other frozen foods, has chosen the spe-

cialists food logistics firm Logility Voyager Solutions in an effort to improve trans-portation operations throughout the company. McCain Foods will use Logility Voy-ager Fulfill, a specialist system offered by Logility, to gain greater visibility into supply chain execution processes including customer order status, purchase order payment status, load tendering and freight payment. With Voyager Fulfill, McCain Foods can plan with Logility both inbound and outbound transportation of shipments with their trading partners. The company will also have the ability to send orders to their carri-ers on a real-time basis in order to accelerate shipment planning to meet customer service objectives with their retailers. McCain Foods will also implement Logility Voy-ager Transportation Planning and Management to optimise shipments of orders to all customers. Voyager is designed to optimise transportation costs and improves cus-tomer service by consolidating orders based on destination, required delivery date and carrier. In addition, Voyager will facilitate the complex processes of tendering loads to carriers, tracking shipments with real-time status information, auditing all carrier invoices, and tactical planning with reporting, modelling and simulation tools. McCain Foods Limited, with international headquarters in Florenceville, New Brunswick, Canada, has annual sales of more than C$5 billion and manufacturing operations in 13 countries on five continents.

▶ Elasticity of service

The cost of providing service is measured in time and money, especially in industrial markets where service can often take precedence over price when potential customers are deciding on a supplier. Companies oper-ating lean (JIT) manufacturing are particularly conscious of this factor.

Marketing firms wishing to raise their service levels can face dimin-ishing returns. Figure 10.1 shows a hypothetical example. Here, 80 per

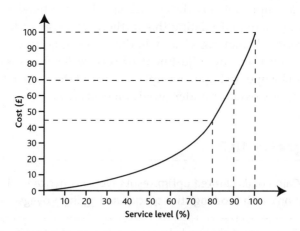

Figure 10.1 An illustration of possible diminishing returns to service level provision

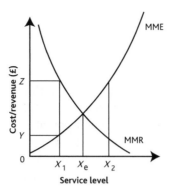

Figure 10.2 Service level versus cost/revenue

cent of the total possible service can be provided for about 45 per cent of the cost of 100 per cent provision. An increase of 10 per cent in general service levels, means a cost increase of approximately 25 per cent.

For a company to offer 100 per cent service provision, every eventuality would have to be covered, which is costly. Maximum customer satisfaction and minimum distribution costs are not compatible and there has to be some compromise in other areas. This depends on the degree of service sensitivity or service elasticity in the particular market. Two industries that use the same product from the same supplier may have different criteria for choosing that supplier. As an example, both the oil exploration and the sugar processing industries use large high-pressure 'online' valves in their process. The oil industry is highly service sensitive because of the high cost of operations and potential breakdowns. Therefore, price is not as important as service, whereas the sugar processing industry is more price sensitive. Much of the processing is done within two months and as long as service levels are adequate to avoid disruption during this period, they can be given a lower priority for the rest of the year.

Service levels should be increased to the point where marginal marketing expense equals marginal marketing response. This follows the economist's profit maximisation criterion of marginal cost being equal to marginal revenue. Figure 10.2 illustrates this point. The marginal expense (MME) of level of service provision X_1 is Y, and the marginal revenue (MMR) is Z. It would pay the firm to increase service levels since the extra revenue generated by the increased services (MMR) is greater than the cost (MME). At service level X_2, however, the marginal expense (Z) is higher than the marginal revenue (X) and service provision is too high. Clearly, the theoretical point of service optimisation is where the marginal marketing expense and the marginal marketing response are equal, at service level X_e.

❱ Inventory management (stockholding)

Inventory gives cover against what may happen tomorrow. Inventory is kept to increase profitability with the support of manufacturing and marketing. Manufacturing support comes through two types of inventory, that of the materials for production, and that of spare and repair parts for maintaining production equipment. Marketing support is provided through an inventory of the finished products, and of spare and repair parts which support the products. Stocks are accumulated because supply and demand cannot be perfectly coordinated, and because of the uncertainty of future demand and reliability of service. They ensure that raw materials, spare parts and finished goods are available when needed.

Inventories are kept as they act as a hedge against such events as unexpected demand or machinery failure. They assist production, transportation and purchasing economies. They also act as a hedge against inflation, price or exchange rate fluctuations. In addition, inventories can enhance customer service levels by providing greater stock availability.

Different types of cost need to be balanced when planning inventories, weighing the cost of holding stock and procurement, against the cost of running out of stock that could result in stopping production and loss of business and goodwill. Larger inventories reduce the possibility of this happening, but it means that more money is tied up in working capital. However, if quantity discounts are offered for large orders, then fewer orders being placed will reduce purchasing administrative costs.

When these conflicting costs are combined, the total cost thus

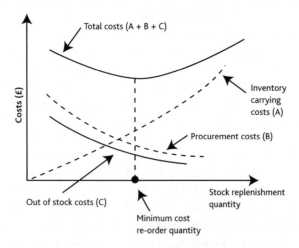

Figure 10.3 Cost trade-off model

formed can be plotted as a 'U-shaped' curve. Management must establish a plan of ordering which results in an inventory level involving the lowest possible total costs. This is illustrated in Figure 10.3.

Economic order quantity (*EOQ*) assumes that total inventory costs are minimised at some definable purchase quantity. This method assumes that inventory costs are a function of the number of orders processed per unit of time, and the costs of maintaining an inventory over and above the cost of items included in the inventory (for example warehousing). It takes no account of transportation costs (which may greatly increase for smaller shipments) or the effects of quantity discounts. These factors limit the usefulness of the *EOQ* concept in inventory management, but increasing use of computing applications has allowed the operation of more sophisticated versions. To give a general understanding of the principles there follows an example of the traditional *EOQ* method.

EOQ can be calculated using the following formula:

$$EOQ = \sqrt{\frac{2AS}{I}}$$

where: A = annual usage (units)
S = ordering costs (£)
I = inventory carrying cost as a percentage of inventory value

For example for: Annual usage = 2000 units
Ordering costs = £10
Inventory carrying cost = 15% (= 0.15)
Unit cost = £1.50

$$EOQ = \sqrt{\frac{2 \times 2000 \times £1.50 \times £10}{0.15}}$$

$$= \sqrt{\frac{60,000}{0.15}}$$

$$= \sqrt{400,000}$$

$$= £632.46$$

The *EOQ* concept and its variations basically seek to define the most economical lot size when considering the placement of an order. The order point method can be used to determine the ideal timing for placing an order. The relatively simple calculation uses the following equation:

$$OP = DL + SS$$

where: OP is the order point
         D is the demand
         L is the lead time
         SS is the safety stock

For example for: Demand   = 200 units per week
                  Lead time   = 4 weeks
                  Safety stock = 400 units

$$OP = (200 \times 4) + 400$$
$$= 800 + 400$$
$$= 1200 \text{ units}$$

A new order should be placed when inventory levels decrease to 1200 units. The size of the order placed when stock reaches this level can be computed using the *EOQ* formula.

This order point method assumes fixed lead times that can be evaluated accurately, which is not often the case. Despite certain limitations, *EOQ* and order point methods are basically valid and form the basis of the more meaningful computer-based inventory models.

SELF-CHECK

Why is a specialist area such as physical distribution management of such strategic concern to marketing management?
Physical distribution or logistics provides 'time' and 'place' utility to the customer that is contained in the 'level of service'. Delivery of a certain 'level of service' is an intrinsic part of the product or service offering, that is it is part of the marketing mix. Success or failure in meeting agreed service levels can impact on customer perception of the firm's product offering. As such, logistics is of vital strategic concern to marketing management.

Why is the physical distribution function often referred to as 'total business logistics'?
The concept of 'logistics' has been derived from the military. There is a strong similarity between running military campaigns and running equally complex commercial campaigns. The military developed a total systems approach to procurement, storage, equipment supply and transportation. Firms have adopted this integrated systems approach to their purchasing, warehousing, materials handling and transportation needs.

Explain the concept of 'service elasticity' and show how management can apply this concept when setting levels of service or pricing strategies in different sectors.
A firm may be supplying similar products to different industries. Product offerings might be more or less the same, and what differentiates the needs of one industry or sector from another using similar products is the level of service demanded. This service level is part of the total product or service offering and contributes to what is often called the 'augmented product (or service)'. The marketing firm can offer different service levels and different pricing structures to reflect this difference in line with the service sensitivity of different customers.

Examine the idea that 'diminishing returns' might face marketing firms when attempting to raise their level of service to certain customer groups.
People, whether in the capacity of individual consumers or as part of an organisation, will only pay for something if they consider that the utility they receive from the purchase is

at least equal to the price they are prepared to pay. If the perceived utility for a particular good or service is less than the utility to be gained, a purchase is unlikely to result. If a high level of service is important (for example for a contractor operating in the North Sea for an oil company) then the contractor might be prepared to pay a premium price for an enhanced level of service. If it is a less service sensitive industry then a level of service offered in excess of what a company would be prepared to pay for has little value. As marketing firms increase their service levels they are likely to approach a level that some customers regard as being adequate. Any further increase will have little or no effect. In this way the marketing firm may experience diminishing returns when increasing service levels.

Explain the concepts of 'time and place utility' with respect to the output of the total logistics concept.

Where and when a product or service is used or consumed has a value to the customer. For example, if you are going out to the pub for a drink with friends you expect to be able to get a beer when you arrive. The beer should not be somewhere else or only available at a different time. Consuming beer at the right place and at the right time is part of the 'consumer value' of consuming the beer. If you use a special delivery firm such as TNT, Group 4 or Parcel Line to get an important package to the USA for next day delivery, it is of no use if it arrives, say, in France three days later. For the service to be of any value, the package needs to be delivered in the right place at the right time. If flowers are purchased through Interflora for a funeral two days later, the flowers must be there on the correct day and in the correct cemetery. Owning a product can give 'possession utility', but 'time' and 'place' when products or services are purchased or used also has significant value to the customer.

▶▶ Summary

An understanding of physical distribution is important to suppliers and purchasers. As well as understanding the distribution tasks facing the supplier, the purchasing department should understand logistical techniques for inventory control and the order cycle. PDM is therefore closely associated with purchasing, as well as with operations management. A logistical system should not be inflexible, but should have established routines for certain functions that facilitate the distribution process.

PDM is linked to all marketing subfunctions, and in this way a coordinated marketing approach is offered to customers. The marketing manager should not necessarily have 'hands on' control of every element in the physical distribution system, as such expertise would probably be beyond the scope of many marketing managers. The logistics function has highly technical and specialised areas of expertise that necessitate the employment of specialist staff. Likewise, materials handling, warehouse management and transport and distribution are also specialist areas. The logistics function plays a vital part in delivering value and satisfaction to customers. It is a long-term strategic tool that can be used to gain competitive advantage. It delivers levels of service and 'time' and 'place' utility to customers. Because of this, it should form an important part of the marketing function. Specialist staff are needed to carry out the complex tasks that make up the logistics function, but strategy and policy formulation for logistics management should be woven into the fabric of a strategic marketing plan if logistics is to play its full part in achieving marketing orientation.

FURTHER READING

Adcock D. (2000) *Marketing Strategies for Competitive Advantage*, Chapter 12, 'Channel Management and Value Added Relations', John Wiley & Sons, Chichester.

Armstrong G. and Kotler P. (2000) *Marketing: An Introduction* (5th edn), Chapter 10, 'Distribution Channels and Logistics Management', Prentice Hall, Englewood Cliffs, NJ.

Blythe J. (2001) *Essentials of Marketing*, Chapter 8, 'Distribution', Pearson Education, London.

Cateora P.R. and Ghauri P.N. (2000) *International Marketing: European Edition*, Chapter 15, 'The International Distribution System', McGraw-Hill, Maidenhead.

Christopher M. (1986) *A Strategy of Distribution Management*, Butterworth Heinemann, Oxford.

Davies M. (1998) *Understanding Marketing*, Chapter 8, 'Distribution', Prentice Hall, London.

Keegan W.J. and Green M.S. (2000) *Global Marketing* (2nd edn), Chapter 13, 'Global Marketing Channels and Physical Distribution', Prentice Hall, London.

Lancaster G.A. and Reynolds P.L. (1999) *Introduction to Marketing: A Step-by-Step Guide to All The Tools of Marketing*, Chapter 13, 'Logistics Management', Kogan Page, London.

Plamer A. (2000) *Principles of Marketing*, Chapter 15, 'Physical Distribution and Logistics', OUP, Oxford.

Rosenbloom B. (1991) *Marketing Channels: A Management View*, Dryden Press, Chicago.

Stern L.W. and El-Ansary A.I. (1977) *Marketing Channels*, Prentice Hall, Englewood Cliffs, NJ.

◗◗ References

Burbridge J.J. (Jr) (1987) 'The Implementation of a Distribution Plan: A Case Study', *International Journal of Physical Distribution and Materials Management*, **17**(1): 28–38.

Gilbert X. and Strebel P. (1989) 'From Innovation to Outpacing', *Business Quarterly*, Summer, pp. 19–22.

Hutchins D. (1988) *Just in Time*, Gower, Aldershot, pp. 27–47.

11 MANAGING SELLING

▶▶ Importance of personal selling in the organisation

Selling is part of the promotional, or the communications mix. Other elements in the communications mix are: above-the-line promotion (for example advertising) below-the-line promotion (for example sales promotion) and public relations as it applies to marketing. These areas are the subjects of Chapters 12 and 13, where they are explained in further detail. However, personal selling is a very important element of marketing and categorising it as a subfunction of promotion devalues its importance. The way personal contact is managed with customers is critical to the success of an organisation, and it can only be carried out well by people who adopt a professional attitude towards their training and their approach to the business of looking after customers in a caring manner. As a consequence, opinions about a company's products are often based on the impression the salesperson has left after meeting a prospective customer. The importance of leaving a good impression is particularly emphasised nowadays when customer retention is often viewed as being as important as the task of seeking out new customers.

The task of selling differs according to the products or services being marketed. In some situations the task of selling is more a case of keeping customers satisfied and the task will then call more for skills of personality and 'caring'. In other situations, contractual negotiations might be the main emphasis of selling where skills of prospecting, negotiating, demonstrating and closing a sale will be crucial elements for success.

In organisational (including industrial) marketing, great reliance is placed on personal communication. For FMCG products a lot of faith is placed on above- and below-the-line communication. In organisational selling the proportion of selling within the total market budget often outweighs all other marketing expenditure.

Personal selling plays a major part in the commercial process of any country. Within the ever-expanding European Union, the place of selling is increasingly important in establishing contact and bringing about contracts in an ever-more competitive marketplace. Markets are continuously being opened up and barriers to free competition are being broken down. This is a two-way process so the UK is also subject to equal competition coming in from companies within the EU. In a modern economy without selling, business transactions would simply not take place. Indeed it is effective selling on the part of international salespeople that contributes to the positive side of the balance of payments.

Where the marketing of products or services involves more complex decision processes, personal selling assumes a critical role. Techniques of negotiation and sales skills plus good product knowledge are required to negotiate the sale of major items, particularly in the industrial marketplace. This calls for highly developed skills of personality as well as sales technique.

Think of a product or service that requires the sales skills just referred to. Examine the kinds of skill that the salesperson should possess in this situation.

The purchase of a new computer system for a company involves much negotiation. The buyer, or, more appropriately in this case, the DMU, demands that salespeople should have an in-depth knowledge of computer systems. This will reduce the perceived risk that members of the DMU might feel before making their purchasing decision. Familiarity will be expected of the seller's own system as well as the systems of competitors. The salesperson should recognise customer requirements in relation to performance of the system, and should focus on appropriate arguments when making the sales presentation. This might consider such factors as performance of the system, the likely price ceiling within the DMU, delivery, credit and after-sales service. The salesperson should be able to apply appropriate points of view when dealing with different members of the DMU.

Personal selling can be costly because it does not simply include a salesperson's salary. On top of this must be added the expenses of a motor car, an expense account including hotel accommodation and support from head office. Such additional costs are normally larger than a salesperson's salary. Salespeople are authorised to spend the company's money in achieving sales, so this should be done responsibly.

Marketing effort is designed to achieve long-run satisfaction on the part of customers. Personal selling is about personal communication of information with a view to persuading customers to purchase, so it is a major communications tool. Therefore, how well an organisation manages its sales force will have a bearing on the ultimate success of the company.

 **Vignette 11.1**

Sales Information Systems Inc. of Pennsylvania, USA deliver good quality sales leads to the personal sales profession.

Sales Information Systems Inc. (SIS) was founded in 1985 as a part of the TMR Group, a provider of telephone market research. TMR, Inc. is a multidimensional marketing research organisation founded in 1985. Originally, TMR operated as a telephone data collection company, but has since expanded to cover all facets of quantitative data collection. This ranges from simple mail surveys to sophisticated web-based studies. Later the company expanded its services to include lead generation/database management systems for high profile, business-to-business clients. The company's objective is to use the collective experience and expertise of its staff in the tele-services industry to provide client firms with effective and professionally developed marketing support systems. SIS Inc. specialises in business-to-business lead generation, lead qualification, customer satisfaction surveys, and database management. The firm is market research based and their goal is to produce a thorough 'qualified lead' by using long-standing market research principles. General leads cost about £7 each whereas leads with an exclusive right to the clients cost around £15 each. Set-up costs are around £110 and there is a minimum order of 100 leads. The firm's consultants are experts in identifying the primary decision-makers first, then fact-find for vital prospect intelligence specifically tailored to clients needs. SIS Inc's leads will contribute to producing a higher conversion rate with a higher value, and give the client company more time to close more sales instead of sourcing leads. SIS Inc. offers clients the knowledge and support of managers and supervisors who work with tele-service programs and database management systems every day. They offer the availability of professional tele-qualifying personnel to offer recommendations and support quickly where and when needed.

▶▶ Benefits of personal selling

When compared to more impersonal elements in the communications mix, selling has a lot to commend it:

▶ It is a flexible medium in that salespersons can adapt their sales presentations to the individual circumstances of the purchasing situation and respond to the prospect's reactions as the sales interview progresses.

▶ Each sales presentation can be different and parts of the presentation can be cut out or adapted to suit individual circumstances.

▶ Perhaps the biggest advantage it has over other forms of promotion is that it usually results in a sale, unlike other elements of promotion that simply move the prospect towards the final sale.

The personal approach afforded by selling is particularly appropriate in circumstances that relate to organisational purchasing:

▶ *Situations of perceived high risk* – which might involve an expensive purchase that carries a certain degree of risk on the part of the purchaser. Good sales presentation can anticipate buyer behaviour and overcome any potential fear the purchaser might feel in relation to a major purchase not being value for money.

▶ *Technically complex products* where customers might be confused as they are not necessarily product experts. Careful explanation will be needed on the part of the salesperson so as not to confuse, but at the same time reading the selling situation such that the level of technicality of the potential buyer can be assessed and the sales presentation adjusted accordingly.

▶ *Commercially complex negotiations* might involve special servicing or training arrangements on the part of the seller. Such complexity means that the situation might be one of high risk on the part of the buyer, and the approach afforded by the personal salesperson can help to alleviate this perception of risk.

▶▶ The broader task of selling

All selling jobs are different and this is what makes selling unique. 'Formula' approaches to the selling task have never been successful in building long-term relationships. Such formula approaches were a facet of sales orientation, and techniques such as putting the customer in the position where they can't say no through the clever use of questions designed to give affirmative reactions, might be alright for short-term transactions, but for long-term customer loyalty they are counterproductive. As we move towards customer satisfaction and retention as being long-term goals, the task of selling is becoming more expansive than it was in the past. Salespersons are spending less time on the task of selling and more time acting as a liaison between their host organisations and key clients. To illustrate what this means we now consider some of these broader obligations:

Activity

Think about this problem before you move on to the suggested solution. It is designed to make you think and understand. What do you think these broader obligations of the modern salesperson might be? Can you add any more to the list that has been suggested?

- Technical advice in relation to product performance. Arranging an aftersales service visit for a maintenance problem.
- Short-term financial problems that the client might be facing might mean arranging the extension of a credit arrangement.
- Progressing delivery of an order with the manufacturing plant in relation to an order the client needs urgently.
- Following up sales leads that have been provided, although this is of course a function of every salesperson's job.
- The task of gathering information from the marketplace is now an important part of a salesperson's broader job remit. As we saw in Chapter 5, the marketing information system inputs market intelligence, and the principal source of such intelligence can come from data gatherers in the field, and what better source than the people in an organisation who work there every day? By the very nature of their work, salespeople have close contact with customers and are well placed to accumulate information and market intelligence on competitive activity and in fact in relation to the marketplace as a whole. This information can then be used, for instance, in terms of providing strategic advice within the organisation in the areas of forecasting sales and new product development through providing research and development with information on competitors' products and how these are viewed by buyers.
- Another task of the salesperson is the use of personal communication when liasing with customers. In the past this tended to rely mainly upon face-to-face contact and 'smooth talking' was a prime requirement for selling success. However, the modern salesperson has many other means at his or her disposal as a result of advances made in information technology. For instance, laptop computers can be quickly set up and used at the client's office to display diagrams, spreadsheets and reports. There is a plethora of IT devices that can help to communicate the company's message and image in a modern manner thus building confidence on the part of the client towards the salesperson and the company being represented.

■ Marketing is a philosophy that aims to give customers exactly what they require when they require it. However, there are times when raw materials might be in short supply either for natural reasons or because of something such as an industrial dispute hitting a major production component. For whatever reason, the salesperson might then have to consider customer loyalty in the past and, based upon this, assess future potential before providing support in the form of supplying raw material or parts during the period of shortage.

Selling is dynamic and has acclimatised to its more professional role in the world today. A number of recent developments are cited that reflect this adaptation:

▷ *Systems selling* refers to the selling of a total package of related goods and services and not just the piece of equipment or basic service itself. Companies offer solutions to problems rather than attempting to sell individual products.

▷ *Relationship selling* stems from the notion of relationship marketing, whereby selected important customers are singled out for special treatment in terms of developing longer and deeper relationships. This is also called 'key account selling' whereby important customers are dealt with by a senior salesperson (often the sales manager). In relationship selling the persons chosen to do this work are hand-picked salespeople who have the right personality and are able to nurture customers with a view to building up their long-term trust and business commitment.

▷ *Selling centres or team selling* have grown as a result of the development of more professionalism on the part of purchasing people. A team of people are drawn not only from sales, but also from areas such as production, research and development and finance. The services of non-salespeople are called upon when required, but the team remains constant. The objective is to meet and demonstrate to customers that they are being visited and serviced 'in depth' with different views being put, rather than just the sales view.

▶▶ Different types of selling task

A classification of different types of selling task was suggested by McMurry in 1961 and this classification is still appropriate. He classified selling positions into categories ranging from simplistic to the most complicated level of negotiating ability:

▶ *Mainly delivery* where the job is concerned with the distribution of, say, milk to individual homes or bread to retail outlets. This type of salesperson will possess little in the way of sales skills and responsibilities and continued sales are more likely to come from a pleasant attitude and good service. In some situations, such as the delivery of branded soft drinks, a small amount of merchandising work might be required, such as setting up display material at the point-of-sale.

▶ *Inside order taker* where the task consists of clerical duties and the opportunity to sell is limited, typified by sales work in a catalogue store like Argos. Customers have normally made up their minds, so the process is simply one of processing the order and only occasionally offering advice when requested to do so by customers.

▶ *Outside order taker* is similar to the above, but here the salesperson goes on a repeat round of regular customers. Most negotiation is conducted at higher levels, typically between the sales manager of a range of grocery products and the purchasing manager of a large chain of food outlets and it is the task of salespersons to service the account. This task sometimes includes merchandising activity or introducing and demonstrating new products.

▶ *Missionary selling* is where salespeople are expected to build up goodwill, educate and ultimately influence the actual or potential user rather than simply soliciting orders. Occasional service work can be undertaken, as can sales promotional activities.

▶ *Technical selling* involves the task of explaining the function of a product to a prospect as well as adapting it to individual customer's needs. The job entails expert knowledge on the part of salespersons in terms of product capabilities and design, the likelihood being that salespersons negotiate with technically expert personnel within a decision-making unit.

▶ *Creative selling* is the final category and this calls for the greatest amount of sales 'skills'. Often customers do not realise that they have a 'need' for certain product or service and it is up to the creative salesperson to communicate with, and demonstrate and convince the buyer of such a need. A good illustration might be a new type of production line system that will save the company money in terms of the new system having greater speed and less wastage of material.

 In relation to each of the classifications cited, think of a product or service example that fits each of the categories.

- Mainly delivery – coal or solid fuel merchant
- Inside order taker – a stores person in a builders' merchant's store

- Outside order taker – a salesperson who sells products to pet shops
- Missionary salesperson – somebody who represents a pharmaceutical company
- Technical selling – a computer salesperson
- Creative selling – a life insurance salesperson

▶▶ Selling skills and qualities

A good salesperson is a good listener. Only by listening to customers and recognising their needs and fears can the effective points of the goods being offered for sale be put before the customer in the form of a sales presentation. This is a matter of appreciating and understanding buyer behaviour. Once this has been understood, the task of selling is much simpler because irrelevant sales points can be discarded. One of the commonest reasons for customers not purchasing is the fact that they are overwhelmed by information. A problem that experienced salespeople face is that they have developed a degree of sophisticated technical expertise, so product points and features which might appear simple to the salesperson may not be clear to the customer. It is only by listening to customers that salespersons can assess levels of technical competence and guide the sales discussion accordingly. This is perhaps the most important quality a salesperson must develop.

Vignette 11.2

A von Cosmetics pioneered developments in the direct personal selling industry by emphasising the need for developing interpersonal skills.

Avon Products Inc. is the world's largest direct seller of beauty and related products. Its 'core' business is direct selling door to door, although today it offers Internet ordering services alongside its traditional selling format. Avon can be found in 139 countries on six continents and is widely acknowledged as being among the pioneers of the direct selling movement. Avon started as an American company but has grown to become a global player. The latest countries to receive the Avon treatment are Bulgaria, Latvia, Lithuania, Slovenia, and Hong Kong. Most of the firm's business is carried out in the USA, UK and the rest of Europe although there is tremendous profit potential in all of the developing countries. As emerging economies develop the population has greater disposable income and a larger middle-class segment comes into being. People in this segment, particularly woman, are prepared to spend a large amount of their disposable income on personal grooming and on beauty products in particular. There are parts of the developing world where the use of cosmetics by women is discouraged for cultural and religious reasons. But otherwise developing nations hold out wonderful future prospects for the firm as Avon moves towards becoming a truly global organisation. Like many global companies Avon has diversified and extended its product range to include a wide range of items related to perfume and beauty products. As the world's leading direct seller of beauty and related products, with $5.7 billion in annual revenues, Avon also markets an extensive range of fashion jewellery, apparel, gifts and collectibles. Avon's international management team looks after business operations in 51 different markets. The company uses a network of three million independent representatives and handles over a billion customer transactions a year. Great emphasis is placed on finding the right sales team and so selection is very important. So also is training and especially the development of interpersonal skills amongst the sales force. All Avon agents benefit from extensive sales training in this area. Traditionally representatives make direct contact with customers, often friends and relatives in the first instance. Word of mouth is very important and clients soon start being recruited from the friends of friends and so the network of clients grows. Using network marketing principles, representatives are also rewarded for introducing other representatives and get financial rewards based on downstream commissions earned. It is also possible to be an e-commerce representative for the company. Most of these positions can be run on a part-time basis although there are opportunities to join Avon on a full-time basis as part of their management team. Avon offers excellent employment opportunities for people who want to work on a part-time basis, especially woman who may need to look after children. It also offers good full-time prospects. The key to the company's success worldwide is careful sales force selection with the emphasis on good training, particularly the development of network and interpersonal skills on which the continuation of the business depends.

There are a number of other qualities that it is felt are needed in order to become a good salesperson. These qualities were the basis of a research exercise conducted amongst salespeople, and were put forward by Jobber and Lancaster (2000). These qualities in descending order of importance are:

▶ Communications skills
▶ Personality
▶ Determination
▶ Intelligence
▶ Motivation and self-motivation
▶ Product knowledge
▶ Educational background

- Confidence
- Appearance
- Resilience and tenacity
- Business sense
- Integrity
- Ambition
- Acceptability or personality
- Empathy
- Initiative
- Self-discipline
- Experience
- Adaptability
- Persuasiveness.

Interestingly persuasiveness comes last, so the role of the modern salesperson is not seen to be to 'win arguments'. We have interpreted these factors into qualities to be included in a job specification for an outside sales position:

- Physical prerequisites – good speech, presentable appearance that will be acceptable to buyers with whom contact will be made.
- Attainments – reasonable education and qualifications that match the degree of knowledge required for understanding the product or service for which representation is sought. Previous experience in the specific product or service area will probably be essential for a senior position as will demonstration of previous success as a salesperson.
- Qualities and aptitudes – the ability to communicate effectively and a high degree of personal drive and self-motivation.
- Disposition – a mature personality and a strong sense of responsibility in terms of always representing the company's best interests.
- Interests – social activities expected that reflect a sociable nature.
- Personal circumstances – in terms of family commitments and responsibilities. This can be argued in a number of ways and it should be looked at in terms of how it suits the particular sales position. If, for example, family commitments are large and remuneration is based upon some kind of incentive, then the will to earn more will be strong. If, however, the task entails long periods away from home then family life might suffer.

▶▶ The sales routine

The sales routine or sales sequence is the term used to describe the processes and stages through which a typical presentation to a buyer proceeds. The process described is too sophisticated for the sale of FMCG to typical customers. In this situation most buyers will have made up their minds before they purchase and buying is simply a matter of routinely choosing and paying for the goods. Indeed, in many products that are sold in organisational buying situations, the same will apply.

In which type of organisational buying situation in particular will a simplified purchasing procedure pertain?

In the case of 'routine rebuy' products or services.

It is important to realise that the sales routine we describe should be treated flexibly in terms of salespeople being able to adapt it to suit individual purchasing situations, and in some cases miss out certain parts of the sequence. Pre-planning before each sales interview is very important and if the potential customer is known to the salesperson then the interview plan must be tailored and adapted with the customer's needs in mind. Such adaptation also takes place during the sales routine, as the salesperson listens to cues and signals given by the buyer.

Having such a sales routine assumes that the salesperson has a buyer to meet. Before such a meeting can take place 'prospects' must be identified and 'qualified'. A 'prospect' is a potential purchaser and 'qualified' means that the prospect has authority to make a purchase decision. However, the fact that the prospect might not be qualified does not mean that a meeting should not take place; in many organisational purchasing situations the first meeting a salesperson has with a company is not with the actual buyer.

In a 'first time' organisational buying meeting, what member of the DMU might the salesperson meet first before meeting the buyer at a subsequent interview?'

A 'gatekeeper' who might be a junior purchasing assistant, might meet the salesperson and then report this meeting to the buyer. If the possibility of doing business exists, the buyer will probably arrange a full presentation at a subsequent interview. In this case the 'gatekeeper' will also have an 'influencer' role to play. It might also be that the salesperson might meet an 'influencer' first, or even a 'decider' (other than the buyer) who could be somebody who has authorisation over specifications (perhaps a designer or somebody from research and development). A later meeting might then be set up with the buyer. In most cases a first meeting with a 'user' would not be appropriate.

Think for a moment before going to the answer, or make enquiries from friends and colleagues, and then list the means through which you think 'prospects' can be identified with a view to potentially arranging a sales interview?

- Writing to named buyers in trade directories
- Purchasing a list of named buyers through a database 'broker' and then using a mailing house to canvass them directly
- Through referrals or sales leads you may have had from colleagues or other market intelligence sources
- Through potential customer enquiries
- Through past sales records to identify buyers who might have been 'dormant' for some time

Figure 11.1 describes the process of the sales routine and each stage is dealt with in more detail afterwards.

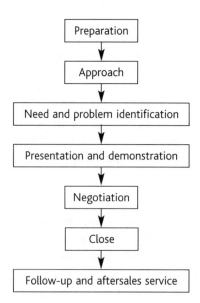

Figure 11.1 The sales routine or sales sequence

▶ Preparation

At this stage the sales interview has been arranged and the prospect has been qualified. However, before the interview takes place, there are a number of matters in which the sales representative must be versed. Most of this will be information that is known already as part of the salesperson's general knowledge of the marketplace or it will be information that has been acquired through formal training. Essential information at this stage is:

▶ *Company knowledge* about the latest commercial procedures relating to such matters as price, payment terms, complaints and returned goods.

▶ *Product knowledge* in relation to technical performance and specifications of current and proposed products and services. This should also include knowledge of the limitations of products in order that false claims will not mistakenly be made.

▶ *Market knowledge* relates to activities and product offerings of competitors including the terms and conditions they are giving. In addition, such information should also extend to general sales trends in the marketplace. If a salesperson has this kind of information, then authority is immediately conferred on any subsequent negotiation procedures. In addition, it is the salesperson's job to find out such information and this all forms part of market intelligence. This can be gained by talking to buyers during or after a sales interview, so the better salespeople will establish a lasting rapport with buyers and so be in a position to acquire this kind of knowledge during the course of their visits to regular customers.

▶ *Customer knowledge* relates to knowledge of the customer's organisation, spending patterns and type and volume of purchases and personal knowledge in relation to the buyer. A manual or electronic 'customer record card' can be used which details knowledge of the customer and details of the sales visit. This is usually filled in directly after the sales interview, but not, of course, in the presence of the buyer. It also provides a record for any other member of the company who might have to make a visit to the same buyer, so commercial data like delivery times or price negotiations can be picked up straight away. The information on this record can relate to general information about the company including any future contracts that the company might be anticipating, or any promises that were made in relation to future orders or contracts. At a personal level, details in relation to the buyer should also be entered. In any organisational selling situation, if the salesperson has established an appropriate rapport, then personal matters might be discussed in addition to business matters, and this is the kind of thing that builds up long-term customer relationships. However, how far this goes is usually a function of the personality of the buyer, some of whom regard personal friendships with salespeople as being a hindrance to successful commercial negotiations.

What kind of personal data do you think should be recorded in relation to a buyer and why?

Hobbies ... does the buyer, say, play golf and at what handicap? Details in relation to family – sons or daughters at school – perhaps about to take examinations. This kind of detail is important to the buyer, and it would take a feat of memory to remember such detail about every buyer visited. An examination of the customer record prior to a sales interview will quickly allow the salesperson to recall the last interview and the personal details. Moreover, the salesperson can relate to what was said last time and perhaps ask if the golf handicap has been reduced, all of which leaves a good impression of long-term caring in the mind of the buyer.

▶ *Aids to selling* include sales literature describing the company's products or services, current price lists, samples or models. A sales demonstration might utilise spreadsheets or other supporting material delivered through a salesperson's computer and can be demonstrated in the buyer's office as part of the sales presentation. Anything that supplements the face-to-face verbal part of the sales interview process adds to the variety and quality of the presentation.

▶ *Journey planning* relates to a plan for calls to regular clients who expect such calls as a matter of course in terms of keeping personal lines of communication open between sellers and buyers. A calling cycle should include a variety of regular customers in addition to calls to prospective customers. A method of planning such journeys is what is known as 'differential call frequency' where more important customers deserve more frequent calls than other customers do. The system is sometimes referred to as the 'sales journey cycle' and here the normal situation might be to visit most customers say once every eight weeks when the cycle will be complete. However, some customers might be visited twice in a cycle and others every other cycle. The kind of organisation involved here is sometimes termed 'cloverleaf', whereby the salesperson covers a closely defined geographical area over a period of time and then another similar area when this has been completed, and so on until the sales journey cycle has been completed – in a clover-leaf type pattern.

At a more detailed level, each journey should be planned in terms of a definite appointment that will most probably be through some prior email or telephone arrangement.

▶ *Dress and demeanour* includes matters of personal hygiene and clothing. Dress and behaviour that suit the client is what is appropriate, but it might not be possible to satisfy all customers if, say, eight are being visited in a single day. In organisational purchasing situations the temptation to overdress should be avoided as this might upstage the buyer so the best guide might be to be soberly smart and also avoid extremes of behaviour like gushing comments or affectations.

▶ Approach

This is sometimes termed 'the opening' and an inherent skill in selling is the ability to size up a situation quickly. How this initial approach, especially to new customers, is handled could determine the outcome of the sales interview. Opening remarks are important, and should try to address the circumstances at a very general level, even if only to comment on the weather. A point worth remembering in the case of a first-time visit is to be the first to speak by introducing yourself by your Christian name and surname (both of which should be cited on your visiting card). You will then know very quickly if the buyer operates on a familiar or a formal basis, by whether he or she refers to you by your Christian name or by your salutation then surname.

▶ Need and problem identification

What the salesperson should attempt to do here is to discover purchasing motives or buyer behaviour, especially when making a call to a new buyer. In the case of an organisational buyer purchasing motives will probably revolve around general economic value for money criteria, but there might be other motives.

What underlying motives can you think of in relation to an organisational purchaser?

A regular supplier might have let the company down in being unable to meet the quality criteria called for, and they might now be looking for a replacement supplier. Their current supplier might have put prices up to an unacceptable level and they are seeking to change.

A few probing questions, that demand more than straight 'yes' or 'no' answers before the presentation stage are desirable in order to attempt to determine buyer behaviour. This will affect the course of the presentation and the salesperson will be able to focus on points that the buyer has made clear are a particular issue. It is also the time when listening skills are appropriate. This is an illustration of how selling is still important at a face-to-face level in terms of being able to adapt to individual circumstances.

▶ The presentation and/or demonstration

Effective communication is needed here and what are known as USP (Unique Selling Proposition) points can be highlighted. These USPs are product or service features that competitive products do not possess. A common phrase in selling is: 'You don't sell products; you sell benefits', so the benefits that the customer will gain should be communicated effectively as part of a logical sequence within the presentation, which should have been rehearsed in many different ways before the sales interview.

If the presentation can include a demonstration then so much the better as this provides hard evidence. If the buyer is able to participate in this demonstration (even if just to handle the product) then this is good because the potential buyer is being seen to empathise with the product and can see its benefits at first hand. Demonstrations can also be shown on video or laptop computer, and well-produced brochures showing the merchandise and describing its technical detail will also be very effective.

The presentation should focus on those points that the buyer regards as important and this relates to buyer behaviour which should have been assessed by this stage. The level of technicality of the sales presentation should be adjusted to suit the buying situation.

What different kinds of emphasis do you feel there can be?

Price – especially in relation to a buyer with an eye for value for money. Quality – especially for somebody who is more concerned with production. Specification – especially for somebody who is concerned more with function and design.

It is at this stage that testimony can be presented which might include letters from satisfied customers. If guarantees over and above statutory guarantees are available then these should be mentioned. Objections from the buyer are possible at this stage, but an experienced salesperson should be able to anticipate the nature of these and even forestall them by raising them as part of the sales presentation. A principal objection in an organisational purchasing situation is one of price, so the good salesperson is able to prepare for this in terms of 'value for money' points as part of the presentation.

What the salesperson should guard against is over presentation and the needs of the prospect should be kept in mind to avoid giving too much overwhelming detail. What is looked for at this stage are buying signals and once these are apparent it is time to bring the presentation and demonstration to a quick conclusion.

▶ Negotiation

The topic of negotiation is complex. In this context, negotiation usually relates to price that is normally the final hurdle to overcome before a sale is made. Negotiation is not totally about price. It can involve matters like service arrangements, credit terms and penalty clauses in relation to late delivery. The essential element is that both parties should aim for an accord that benefits them both. In relation to price negotiation, the 'room for manoeuvre' concept is illustrated in Figure 11.2.

When negotiating price, sellers and buyers have ideas as to what they would like to receive or pay for their merchandise. Only in rare circumstances are these figures identical, and market pricing suggests that prices should be set at what the market will bear. The likelihood is that a higher price will be stated by the seller with a view to reducing it through negotiation. This philosophy is at the centre of market trading. After the sales presentation, matters like credit and delivery will be discussed and agreed as part of negotiation, but price is normally the final item on this part of the agenda. The concept is simple and starts with the

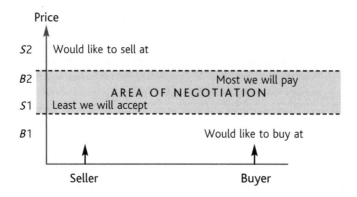

Figure 11.2 'Room for manoeuvre' concept of negotiation

supposition the seller is normally the first person to state the price required (price S2). The buyer will counter with the price he or she would like to pay (B1). Gradually, negotiation brings the two together and once B2 and S1 are reached from both the buyer's and the seller's respective points of view then the area of negotiation has been reached, but the buyer will not know S1 and the seller will not know B1. It is then a matter of proposal and counter-proposal, coupled with concessions on either side before a final price is agreed.

▶ Close

The aim and fundamental objective of selling is to reach the closing stage resulting in an agreement to purchase. However, it is sometimes the most difficult stage and a number of techniques exist relating to closing a sale. Some of the more common methods are:

▶ *Basic close* is the simplest as it consists of filling out an order form, but it presumes that the buyer wishes to buy. If, however, the seller is unsure of the buyer's purchasing decision at this stage, then this might be a high-risk strategy that could well frighten off the buyer in the case of a major purchase.
▶ *Trial close* is perhaps better than basic close because it attempts to test the buyer's willingness to purchase by asking an either/or question such as: 'If you were to purchase, would you be paying cash or credit?'
▶ *Alternative choice* is where the salesperson, having received buying signals, attempts to close the sale by offering an alternative choice, for example 'Would you like it in black or white?'

▶ *Assumptive close* is another variation that assumes the purchaser will buy and the salesperson asks questions like: 'Where and when would you like the goods to be delivered?'

▶ *Puppy dog technique* springs from the idea that if you give a puppy to somebody to look after for, say, two weeks, then they will not want to part with it when you go to collect it. The same philosophy is adopted for tangible goods that might be offered on free trial for a short period.

▶ *Sharp angle* is a technique the salesperson uses when the customer asks for information like: 'What is the delivery period?' The sales-person would then respond with something like: 'What delivery are you looking for?' and upon being told, would then say: 'If we can supply it by then will you place the order?'

▶ *Summary question* is a technique that is used when caution is being exercised on the part of the buyer prior to placing the order. The salesperson then attempts to isolate causes of resistance by asking questions like: 'Is it quality?' – 'No!' 'Is it price?' – 'No!' 'Is it deliv-ery?' – 'No!' ... and so on, until the cause of resistance is isolated. This can then be concentrated on as part of the sales erosion process in attempting to win the order.

▶ *Similar situation* is where the salesperson listens to what the pur-chaser is saying and if this relates to an experience (normally a bad one) relating to the product for sale, the salesperson then brings in, as part of the conversation, another story that relates to another experience (a good one).

▶ *Concession close* is normally kept until towards the end as a final negotiating and closing tactic. This means keeping a final concession in reserve before agreement is reached in the expectation that this should conclude the sale.

Apart from those mentioned, cite an example of a close under each of: trial close; alternative choice; assumptive close; puppy dog technique; sharp angle; similar situation; concession close.

- Trial close – 'If we can offer free servicing for a year will you be interested?'
- Alternative choice – 'Are you thinking of the basic or de-luxe version?'
- Assumptive close – 'Will it be cash or credit?'
- Puppy dog technique – 'Try this video recorder free for a week'
- Sharp angle – to buyer's query about colour – 'If we have it in that colour do you want it?'

- Similar situation – to buyers who are relating an experience that shows that house contents insurance policies are expensive and a waste of money – 'Mr and Mrs Cundy in the next street were burgled last week and they didn't have house contents insurance'
- Concession close – 'I can offer a final 2% discount if you place the order now'

▶ Follow-up and aftersales service

The order process is not fully completed once the sale has been closed. This final area is more prominent now where customer retention is seen as being a long-term strategy of marketing. 'Customer care' is now the principal theme of a number of marketing texts. Follow-up can simply be a telephone call to the buyer to ascertain whether or not the goods were received in a satisfactory condition at the time promised. This kind of act gives reassurance to the buyer that the sale was in the interests of the customer. Aftersales is more than just this as it concerns a number of post-sale activities that can be designed to build long-term goodwill on the part of customers and help to ensure repeat purchases. Such activity can also reduce what is known as 'cognitive dissonance' which, in the case of a major purchase, is a nagging fear of doubt on the part of the buyer that what has been purchased might not be value for money. A feeling of caring can be generated through follow-up, and aftersales service can help to reduce these feelings of doubt.

 Give an example of aftersales service.

In the case of a motor car, through the provision of a dealership network that customers know will be able to provide virtually any part from stock anywhere in the country and which has the ability to repair or service the car at short notice.

Without selling and its associated tactics, commerce would not exist which is why this critical area of marketing has received thorough attention in terms of the techniques involved. The next section looks at the way this activity is managed through the process of sales management.

▶▶ Sales management

The function of sales management is to devise and implement a sales plan and evaluate and control it during the course of the planning

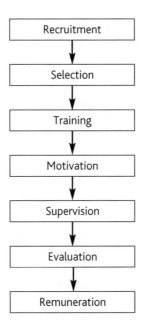

Figure 11.3 Responsibilities of sales management

period. The sales plan is part of the marketing plan and this is dealt with in more detail in Chapter 15. The starting point for business planning is the sales forecast which is the responsibility of sales management in conjunction with marketing management. The techniques involved in forecasting have been covered in Chapter 5 which examined forecasting in conjunction with marketing information systems. Evaluation and control of the plan are more to do with the tactics of sales management and the remainder of this section covers these specific areas. Figure 11.3 describes these activities in chronological sequence.

Each of the elements in Figure 11.3 is discussed as part of the sales management process.

▶ Recruitment

The first consideration is to establish the size of the sales force. In any organisation there are competing demands on company funds, so consideration has to be paid to balancing financial resources against other criteria.

What factors should be taken into consideration when establishing the size of the sales force?

- Number of current customers plus number of potential customers
- The period between calls (for example weekly, monthly, quarterly)
- The number of calls to be made in a typical selling day (for example in certain sales tasks covering tight geographical locations it might be a lot, whereas in geographically dispersed locations it might be less)
- Whether calls are being made to end-users or to distributive intermediaries like wholesalers or distributors

Prior to recruitment a job description should be written for each sales position and this should be agreed with and given to human resource management (HRM) who conduct the initial recruitment and then pass on suitable shortlisted candidates to the sales manager for interview. A typical job description contains a number of elements:

- ▶ Job title
- ▶ To whom responsible
- ▶ Duties and responsibilities, including selling tasks which typically include frequency of visits to customers, after-sales service activities and feedback of market intelligence
- ▶ Technical ability in terms of knowledge of products or services and their applications and specific sales abilities
- ▶ Geographical area to be covered
- ▶ Degree of autonomy in terms of reporting to the sales manager and being responsible for the territory (some sales jobs are tightly controlled and others leave it to the individual salesperson to develop the territory).

 What sources are most suitable when recruiting field sales-force personnel?

- From inside the company – perhaps certain members of staff who are in the sales office might show an aptitude for selling
- Sales recruitment agencies – some employ 'headhunter' services whereby they canvass potential individuals directly
- From competitive companies – but probably via the recruitment press
- From recommendations from existing sales personnel

▶ Selection

At this stage, HRM will have shortlisted appropriate candidates for interview by sales management and sifted out those who do not match the criteria laid down in the job description. Asking candidates to fill in an application form makes it easier to provide a standard comparison. However, in some cases, candidates are asked to submit a curriculum vitae on the basis that a CV will demonstrate imagination of the part of the potential candidate and perhaps highlight some areas that the standard application form might not cover.

It now remains for sales management to pick an appropriate candidate in an interview situation. There are a number of ways of tackling interviews; one method, that tends to be less favoured nowadays is the 'stress' interview whereby an aggressive stance is taken by the interviewer and the candidate must 'defend' him or herself and put forward reasons why they should be chosen. This type of interview might be appropriate if the sales task involves high pressure selling – which is, of course, more a facet of sales orientation. However, most interviews now tend to put interviewees at their ease on the basis that what is ultimately needed is a harmonious partnership. There are two ways in which interviews can be tackled – either on a formal question and answer structured basis or on an unstructured basis whereby the interviewee is encouraged to discuss the position and the interviewer only interjects occasionally to probe certain points. The qualities looked for are some of those listed earlier under the heading Selling skills and qualities, but what is required is somebody who will be an effective member of a team. Research suggests that for selling, the following factors should be considered during the interview process, bearing in mind the selling job for which the interview is being conducted:

▶ Demographic factors in terms of location for which representation is required
▶ Background and experience in selling and in the product or service to be represented
▶ Current domestic and financial status and lifestyle
▶ Intellectual and perception abilities
▶ Interpersonal and presentation skills.

▶ Training

This can be an expensive component of the marketing budget, allied to the fact that during training, the salesperson has to be paid whilst not being involved in sales activity. Sales training should be carried out professionally to gain maximum value for money. Programmes can be conducted in-house or through outside sales trainers.

In-house programmes relate to matters such as product knowledge – perhaps in terms of a member of the product development team conducting a session on a new product that is about to be launched or a modification being planned for an existing product. An initial training programme might be conducted by HRM that explains the company and its associations. The marketing manager might input into a programme in terms of market developments and competitive activities. The sales manager might input on organisational matters such as work routines and preparation and presentation of reports and how these are used within the company.

Vignette 11.3

Management at Sun Microsystems uses its new knowledge network to enhance the organisation's selling skills and improve its customer relationship management (CRM).

Sun Microsystems Inc. has launched a powerful new knowledge system which management of the £6 billion organisation hopes will enhance the firm's selling skills and improve its relationship marketing and customer relationship management capabilities. Sun, based in Mountain View, California, USA, uses its Sun WEB intranet system to link over 20,000 employees around the world and allows the firm to become a truly 'learning organisation'. The new system not only saves the company over £318 million on intranet distribution of documentation but it also enhances its long-term relationships with customers and suppliers by putting catalogues, pricing information and technical information online. The new system is contributing to the firm's relationship marketing policies and customer relationship management (CRM) procedures. Part of the system is used for sales-force training and is called SunTAN. The firm's learning and training needs are extensive. Sun is a constant innovator of new products and processes and is operating in a global market that is moving very fast technologically. Salespeople and other staff (and suppliers and intermediaries operating in the firm's 'task' environment) have always to keep up to date with what is going on in the market and constantly keep abreast of new product information and applications. As a major global provider of hardware, software and services for intranet and Internet business operations, the company now gets around 90 per cent of its sales revenue from new products and services that are less than one year out of development. This gives a clear indication of the fast pace of the market and the sales force's training needs. As a result of the firm's constantly widening product lines and shorter and shorter product life cycles the company found that under the old system of doing things it could not train its sales force and other staff fast enough or thoroughly enough. Because of the huge requirement for knowledge and learning amongst the firm's staff, management found that it could no longer simply use conventional classroom teaching and group seminar work. Such methods worked well when carried out properly but they tended to necessitate key staff having to be away from their customers for days or sometimes weeks at a time for training sessions. Such sessions often resulted in information overload for staff and high costs in travel and accommodation. Sales training at the company's head office costs on average £2,000 per week, not counting the opportunity costs of lost sales because the sales person is not interacting with customers during this time. Whereas other top competitors such as IBM and Hewlett-Packard were giving new staff six weeks of training in their first six months, Sun was only giving its staff one week. Compared to competitors, Sun's staff were underprepared. The new network consolidates sales training information, sales support resources, product updates, competitive intelligence and much more which is available to staff online using the intranet. The new system will hopefully considerably enhance management's provision of key sales training and related information to its staff and also help to forge mutually beneficial relationships with customers, suppliers and intermediaries.

External programmes conducted by sales trainers can be provided to new staff or through refresher programmes for existing staff. Such training can concentrate on specific sales techniques such as closing or dealing with objections or the general sales routine. Training programmes can be conducted by the sales manager, but this will depend on his skills of delivery and knowledge of modern techniques. Certainly, an in-house programme might be cheaper than one that is conducted elsewhere and many companies employ a skilled outside trainer to conduct programmes in-house. The advantage of sales programmes that are conducted outside involving sales personnel from other companies is the breadth of knowledge obtained from the training sessions themselves in addition to the indirect knowledge gained through sharing experiences with salespeople from different organisations.

▶ Motivation

Selling is a lonely job. A common misconception of the field salesperson is of a garrulous individual, shallow thinking and with a joke for every occasion. From what has been discussed it can be seen that field selling is an individualistic task often involving long hours driving and then meeting buyers on a formal basis. Quite often buyers reject a salesperson's offer after the sales presentation which can be demotivating. Selling often means periods away from home, staying in hotels with no close colleagues for company. In many sales situations, the salesperson looks after an area or territory that is distant from the head office. This makes personal relationships with colleagues difficult, as the salesperson might only visit head office once a week or less to meet and report to the sales manager.

It is of prime importance to ensure that field salespeople do not feel neglected and that they receive appropriate support and motivation from head office.

What factors or activities do you feel might be used to motivate members of the field sales force?

- accompanied visits to customers by the sales manager or regional manager with the salesperson
- financial incentives through commission or some other type of compensation plan
- some kind of promotional structure within the organisation — although in some cases sales representatives do not make good sales managers, because of the individualistic, and perhaps selfish, nature of the sales job
- job enrichment in terms of praise or recognition through some sort of award. This award might be a prize offered as part of a sales competition that might be based on criteria such as highest value or volume of sales in a period or most new accounts opened in a period
- sales meetings where opportunities are extended to members of the sales team to meet each other, although it can be costly in terms of non-selling time. Sometimes such meetings can be prefaced with a face-to-face meeting with the sales manager, the prime purpose of which might be to listen to the salesperson's view of the job in terms of points of dissatisfaction and then act upon these
- sales conferences that are held periodically and which provide an opportunity for the sales force to get together, usually in a social setting. Usually, such conferences have a theme, but they are costly to mount, particularly if they are in a hotel and include invitations to partners
- fringe benefits such as using the company car for social purposes or a holiday sponsored by the company — often related to sales performance

---

▶ Supervision

Selling in the field is an individualistic activity. It tends to be a geographically dispersed operation. Only in large companies can there be a structure, headed by a sales manager, that divides the country into regions, each controlled by a regional manager. Each region is then split into areas each of which is controlled by an area manager. Each area contains a number of field sales representatives. For some companies, however, there is a sales manager with only a single tier of either area or regional managers with groups of field sales representatives reporting directly to each area or regional manager. In many companies the situation is even more modest than this with the country being geographically divided and there being a single field sales representative in charge of each region reporting directly to a sales manager at head office.

On the subject of individual salesperson supervision, this is largely a function of the product or service being sold and the culture of the parent organisation. In geographically dispersed markets close supervision might not be possible or desirable, for one of the attractions of a field sales position is the amount of freedom it offers in being able to control one's own destiny. It also allows an individual to solve customer problems in a creative manner, so if close supervision is maintained from head office this might negate feelings of independence on the part of salespersons.

Performance measures are perhaps the best way of providing supervision of salespeople who work away from the head office. Such measures can be qualitative ones through criteria such as the quality of sales presentations as assessed by the field sales manager or the degree of product or market knowledge that the salesperson possesses. This can be assessed by the field sales manager on an accompanied call to customers during the normal course of selling activity, so supervision is effected at the time the assessment is being made. Quantitative measures are more tangible and these relate to sales volume, number of orders secured, number of new accounts opened, number of sales and service calls made or amount of market intelligence gathered.

▶ Evaluation

Evaluating performance of salespeople is the result of supervision and this is perhaps the most important aspect of sales management. Performance measures must be set before evaluation can take place and these measures should be agreed at the appointment stage. Measures of evaluation can relate to sales volume, number of orders secured and number of calls made. Using these measures as an incentive is linked to sales remuneration.

❱ Remuneration

Remuneration is a prime motivator in field selling positions and this is why it is normally linked directly to the volume the salesperson sells. However, it is not that simple in many selling situations. In cases when securing an order is part of a team effort it is then difficult to measure the input of an individual salesperson to the negotiating process and in such cases a shared commission or a bonus might be more appropriate.

Basically, there are three options when considering compensation plans:

❱ *Straight salary* is more appropriate when the principal component of selling is calling on regular customers and customer care and where retention of existing customers is of prime importance. Quite often such situations call for technical advice being given during sales visits, and it is in this category that we tend to find many sales engineers. A facet of the type of industry in which this is appropriate is in high-value/low-volume market situations. Straight salary can provide security, but such a situation will not attract those whose main motivation is money, and who, because of this, might be more successful individual salespersons. Straight salary arrangements can be incentivised through the use of a bonus that in some way is linked to the success or otherwise of the company over a previous period.

❱ *Straight commission* is the other extreme and here the sole incentive is to sell. This has drawbacks in that salespeople might be reluctant to spend time on matters that do not directly relate to sales. They will also be reluctant to spend time away from selling in order to meet the sales manager or attend sales training programmes. If customer care is a company aim then this type of remuneration system will not encourage it on the part of salespersons. It is, however, an efficient system from a company viewpoint as it is a straight variable cost that only increases as sales increase. The downside is that it is often used for these very reasons by financially insecure companies.

Give an example of a product and a service that tend to utilise a straight commission remuneration system.

Home improvements – burglar alarms, double glazing, security screens. Life assurance arrangements that attempt to sell a single policy to an individual. In such situations it is quite common for the salesperson to have another form of employment apart from the sales job.

▶ *Salary plus commission* brings together the advantages of both systems and this is why it is termed the 'combined plan'. As income is not solely dependent on commission, management has a greater degree of control over the salesperson's time, yet sales costs are only generated through increased sales revenues. It is a system that can attract ambitious salespersons wishing to combine security with greater earning power through enhanced personal efforts. At its simplest, payment can be based on a basic salary plus a fixed percentage on all sales. However, in most organisations a more incentive related system operates. Such a system usually operates on the basis of an 'escalator', where commission increases once a certain level of sales has been reached. Another system is the 'sales target' or 'sales quota' system, when commission is only earned after an agreed target or quota has been reached for a specified period. This target is usually for a short period. If the period was long (say one year) and if during the course of that year it seemed unlikely that the target would be reached, there might be a temptation on the part of the salesperson to simply give up, on the basis that the commission level could never be attained. Such a target or quota is agreed with the sales manager beforehand and it normally reflects sales for a period of not longer than three months.

SELF-CHECK

Selling is part of the communications mix. What are the other elements?
Above-the-line promotion, below-the-line promotion and public relations as it affects marketing.

In which organisational selling situations is personal selling most appropriate?
Situations of high perceived risk; technically complex products; commercially complex negotiations.

What is meant by team selling or selling centres?
People are drawn into a team from other departments such as production, research and development and finance and they jointly conduct negotiations with customers.

McMurry quoted a list of sales tasks ranging from the simple to the most complicated. What were these?
Mainly delivery; inside order taker; outside order taker; missionary selling; technical selling; creative selling.

What elements are contained in the sales routine?
Preparation; approach; need and problem identification; presentation and demonstration; negotiation; close; follow-up and after-sales service.

In sales preparation what information and planning are essential?
Company knowledge; product knowledge; market knowledge; customer knowledge; aids to selling must be organised; the journey plan must be organised and personal grooming should be appropriate for the purchasing situation.

What is a USP?
A unique selling (or sales) proposition relates to product or service features that your product or service has, but competitive products lack.

> *List four closing techniques.*
> Four from: basic close; trial close; alternative choice; assumptive close; puppy dog technique; sharp angle; summary question; similar situation; concession close.
>
> *What are the responsibilities of sales management?*
> Recruitment; selection; training; motivation; supervision; evaluation; remuneration.
>
> *What are the basic forms of field sales remuneration?*
> Straight salary; straight commission; combination plan.

▶▶ Summary

Along with products and services, selling is an essential element of the marketing process, for without it products would never reach their intended markets. This chapter has covered a large and important part of the process of marketing.

It has examined the importance of personal selling within an organisation and how it relates to the communications mix and marketing in particular, as well as to the economy in general. Personal selling has been discussed in terms of its advantages over other elements in the communications mix. Different market situations have been identified, and selling arrangements most suited to each of these has been discussed. At a more individual level, skills appropriate to selling have been examined followed by what is known as the sales routine.

Sales management is an important element of the sales process and this was examined from the point of view of recruitment, selection, training, motivation, supervision, evaluation and remuneration.

FURTHER READING

Armstrong G. and Kotler P. (2000) *Marketing: An Introduction* (5th edn), Chapter 13, 'Integrated Marketing Communications: Personal Selling and Sales Promotion', Prentice Hall, Englewood Cliffs, NJ.

Blythe J. (2001) *Essentials of Marketing*, Chapter 9, 'Marketing Communications and Promotional Tools', Pearson Education, London.

Cateora P.R. and Ghauri P.N. (2000) *International Marketing: European Edition'*, Chapter 17, 'Person Selling and Negotiations', McGraw-Hill, Maidenhead.

Coner J.M. and Dubinsky A.J. (1985) *Managing the Successful Sales Force*, Lexington Books, Lexington, MA.

Davies M. (1998) *Understanding Marketing*, Chapter 9, 'Marketing Communications 2: Public Relations, Personal Selling and Direct Mail', Prentice Hall, London.

Day R.L. and Bennett P.D. (1964) 'Should Salesmen's Compensation be Geared to Profits?', *Journal of Marketing Research*, May.

Keegan, W.J. and Green M.S. (2000) *Global Marketing* (2nd edn), Chapter 15, 'Global Marketing Communications Decisions 2: Sales Promotions, Personal Selling, Special Forms of Marketing Communications, New Media', Prentice Hall, London.

Lancaster G.A. and Reynolds P.L. (1999) *Introduction to Marketing: A Step-by-Step Guide to All The Tools of Marketing*, Chapter 7, 'Personal Selling', Kogan Page, London.

Mancrief W. (1986) 'Selling Activity and Sales Position Taxonomies for Industrial Salesforces', *Journal of Marketing Research*, August.

Plamer A. (2000) *Principles of Marketing*, Chapter 18, 'Selling and Sales Management', OUP, Oxford.

Raiffa H. (1982) *The Art of Science of Negotiation*, Harvard University Press, Cambridge, MA.

Rubin J.Z. and Brown B.R. (1975) *The Social Psychology of Bargaining and Negotiation*, Academic Press, New York.

▶▶ References

Jobber D. and Lancaster G. (2003) *Selling and Sales Management*, Prentice Hall, London.

McMurry R.N. (1961) 'The Mystique of Super Salesmanship', *Harvard Business Review*, March–April, p. 114.

ABOVE- AND BELOW-THE-LINE PROMOTION

▶▶ Introduction

In terms of public perception of the marketing mix elements that a firm employs, it is promotion which is the most high profile and prominent P in the four Ps and to many people promotion is marketing. Promotion is a part of a firm's overall effort to communicate with consumers and others about its product or service offering. The company and the consumer both have needs to fulfil in that the profit-making company wishes to improve or maintain profits and market share and gain a better reputation than its competitors, and the consumer has personal goals. The 'total product offering' allows each party to move towards these goals, offering a 'bundle of satisfactions' that fulfil needs in an instrumental and psychological sense. The phrase 'marketing communications' is generally preferred to the term 'promotion', this latter term often being reserved for a division of communications called 'below-the-line promotion'.

In a sense, all marketing communication activity is a form of promotion that in one way or another attempts to promote the interest of the brand, product range and/or company. What differentiates 'above-the-line' activity from 'below-the-line' activity is a somewhat arbitrary division. There is no universally accepted definition of either. Below-the-line activity has been described as non-media advertising. If a formal advertisement is submitted to a publication and a fee paid to feature this advertisement then this is deemed 'above-the-line' communication. If no commission has been paid, for example in the case of a public relations press release, a trade exhibition or a sponsored sports event, this is referred to as 'below-the-line' communication. This distinction is accepted by many and is the distinction adopted in this chapter.

▶▶ Real and implied product attributes

The role of marketing communications is to communicate the benefits of the product, service or firm to potential consumers. The same process is undertaken in 'not-for-profit situations' such as a political party. In such a situation the party publicity team (which often includes a professional marketing communications firm such as Saatchi & Saatchi) attempt to convey the benefits of a particular political ideology or even the personality of the party leadership. Many of the benefits marketing communicators try to convey are 'real' for example a Jaguar car really can go from 0 to 60 in 6.8 seconds, but many attributes are implied and have been created through marketing communications. For example Perrier water is basically gaseous water, but in the minds of consumers it is much more than this. It is the implied attributes of Perrier that have made the product a major global brand. Nike training shoes are another example. About 70 per cent of people who buy Nike shoes and clothes are not athletes or even sporty. Most people buy the brand as a fashion item so they can be seen to be wearing the right brand to impress friends and colleagues.

Products and services have been described as a 'total bundle of attributes' that consumers perceive in a holistic manner. Potential consumers see the product or service offering as a unified whole, rather than separate component parts such as price, packaging, shape, and so on. In this way, marketing communications conveys the meaning of the company's total product offering, helping consumers attain their goals and moving the company closer to its own goals. Many products, especially FMCG are similar to other products in their class, for example toothpaste is basically a commodity for cleaning teeth and no matter what brand is selected it is still just toothpaste. In times of shortage, as in the war years, goods are treated as homogenous commodities, and basically soap is soap. Many FMCG are perceived as commodities rather than differentiated branded products with added perceived value.

As an illustration we have taken two different products, one from the consumer market sector and one from the industrial sector. The consumer product is an FMCG like Perrier water. The industrial product is a heat-treated steel bar used in manufacturing industrial products and produced by the industrial firm Guest, Keen & Nettlefold (GKN). Even an industrial firm such as GKN uses marketing to create a favourable image in the minds of customers so the products it produces will have an 'implied attribute' component because the reputation of the firm will, to a certain extent, be reflected in its products. Figure 12.1 compares the two products in terms of the ratio of their real to implied attributes. It can be seen that the FMCG has a higher proportion of implied attributes.

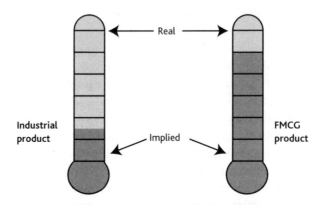

Industrial product

FMCG product

Figure 12.1 Comparison of the degree of implied attributes making up product concepts in consumer and industrial markets

All commercial forms of communication are a form of promotion. Do you agree or disagree with this statement?

We can use the terms 'promotion' and 'marketing communication' interchangeably. All forms of marketing communication are purposeful communication, that is designed to achieve a specific commercially relevant effect. Some marketing communications attempt to bring about a sale, for example an advertisement for a record company showing a particular album that cannot be purchased in the shops, and inviting you to use a freephone number at the end of the advertisement to purchase the record using a credit card, is a form of direct marketing and is trying to elicit a sale from those watching the advertisement. The majority of marketing communications, however, are not of this type, and usually have a more intermediate objective such as communicating product attributes to consumers. They do not try to elicit a sale directly but make a contribution to the communication process at the end of which a sale may take place. Whether the communication 'tool' being used is public relations, direct mail, telephone marketing, trade journal advertising, sponsorship or corporate advertising all of these forms of communication, whether they be direct or indirect, are promoting either the product, service or firm. In this sense all forms of commercial marketing communications are types of promotion.

▶▶ The marketing communications mix

'Promotion' as an element of the four Ps describes the communication activities of advertising, personal selling, sales promotion and publicity.

Advertising is a non-personal form of mass communication, paid for by an identified sponsor. Personal selling involves a seller persuading a potential buyer to make a purchase. Sales promotion encompasses short-term activities such as coupons and free samples that encourage quick action by buyers. The company has control over these three variables, but little control over the fourth, publicity. This is another non-personal communication method that reaches a large number of people, but it is not paid for by the company and is usually in the form of news or editorial comment regarding a company's product or service. Companies gain publicity through the release of news items.

▮▮▮ Vignette 12.1

Crosby Marketing Communications offers a fully integrated marketing communications mix service to clients in the Washington DC and Baltimore region.

Crosby Marketing Communications (CMC) is based in Annapolis, Maryland, USA. The firm's marketing communications philosophy is based on the principle of integration. The firm's motto is 'Success goes to those who see the goal clearly – and aim steadily'. CMC was established in 1973 and the mission of the firm is to keep its clients' marketing communications focused on success. It does this by creating results-driven programmes that combine CMC's expertise in marketing strategy, advertising, direct response, public relations, corporate identity, promotions, interactive multimedia and event management. CMC uses as few or as many elements as needed in the marketing communications mix, each focused right on target and all delivered with cohesion, clarity and maximum impact. CMC call their approach a synchronised process known as 'integrated marketing communications.' And as one of its leading practitioners, CMC has brought its benefits to organisations in all arenas, from regional start-ups to international corporations. Today, CMC's pursuit of communications excellence has placed the firm among the top agencies in the Washington and Baltimore regions. As an integrated marketing communications firm, CMC acts as more than just an agency. Their aim is to become a client's strategic marketing partner, a participant in their client's total marketing success.

Put together, these promotional activities make up the 'communications mix' with varying emphasis on each element according to the product, characteristics of consumers and company resources. Company size, competitive strengths and weaknesses and style of management are influences on the promotional mix used.

Other communications elements with which promotion must be coordinated are the product, price and distribution channels used. Product communication, including brand name, design of packaging and trademark are product cues, conveying a message about the total product offering. Price can communicate, for instance, 'prestige appeal' for buyers who perceive that a high price equals quality and prestige. The place in which products are found has communication value. Retail stores have 'personalities' that consumers associate with the products they sell. Products receive a 'halo effect' from the outlets in which they can be found and two stores selling similar products can project entirely different product images, for example perfume sold through an up-market store will have a higher quality image than one sold through discount stores and supermarkets.

Promotion is one of a number of activities used by companies to communicate their product or service offerings. The combination of these variables as perceived by consumers is the 'marketing communications mix'. This is really a submix of the overall marketing mix. Figure 12.2 illustrates the overall marketing budget as a circle. The marketing communications budget is shown as a shaded segment. How big the segment will be differs between firms, as varying percentages of the overall marketing budget will be devoted to marketing communications.

If we take the shaded area from Figure 12.2 and expand it into a 360 degree pie chart we show the idea of the marketing communications mix having been derived from the overall marketing mix as shown in Figure 12.3.

It can be seen from the pie chart in Figure 12.3 that it has been divided into segments. Each segment shows the proportion of the overall marketing communications budget allocated to each communications 'tool' in the mix. The way in which the pie chart is segmented will differ amongst firms even in the same industry. It will certainly differ between firms in different industries and between firms operating in different market sectors, for example consumer markets and industrial

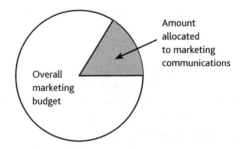

Figure 12.2 Marketing communications as a proportion of the total marketing budget

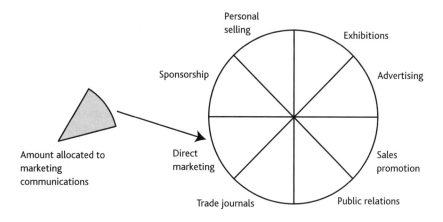

Figure 12.3 Marketing communications mix

markets. Figure 12.3 shows a typical marketing communications mix for FMCGs such as branded packaged grocery products. The majority of the communications budget is allocated to non-personal forms of communications especially below-the-line sales promotions and conventional media advertising with relatively little spent on personal forms of communications such as personal selling. Contrast this with Figure 12.4 that shows a typical marketing communications mix of a company involved in marketing industrial products. Contrasting Figure 12.3 with Figure 12.4 you will see that this time the majority of the communications budget is allocated to personal selling which is the most important communications tool in industrial markets and often represents 90 per cent of the marketing communications budget. Trade exhibitions and trade journal advertising is also used extensively in industrial marketing as reflected in the mix shown in Figure 12.4.

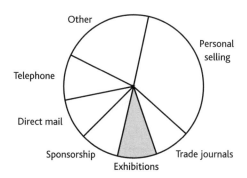

Figure 12.4 Typical marketing communications mix for an industrial product

'The marketing communicator is rather like a chef who has a finite array of ingredients. It is the creative way in which these ingredients are used to produce the desired outcome that determines the reputation of the chef and the marketing communicator.' Discuss this viewpoint.

The comparison of marketing communicator and chef is an interesting analogy. In fact the two professions have many things in common. An imaginative, innovative, original and creative chef will have as customers people willing to pay high prices, eager for a table at that restaurant. Such a chef is able to think of imaginative outcomes, and has the skill to put a complex array of ingredients together in the right quantities and cooked in the right way to achieve the desired outcome. The marketing communicator is in a similar situation and has a finite array of marketing communication 'tools' or 'ingredients' at his or her disposal. A good marketing communicator is able to think of imaginative outcomes for a communications strategy that may be for a brand, a corporation or a political party. In the same way as the chef, the gifted marketing communicator will possess the necessary skills to be able to formulate the communications mix in the right way to achieve the desired outcomes for the campaign.

▶▶ The marketing communications process

The amount and type of information received influence customer perceptions of market offerings. There should be a good flow of information between seller and buyer to help in the decision-making process that precedes a purchase. Decisions are made as to the optimal combination of resources and setting up of control systems. An effective marketing communications system allows feedback from the consumer to the seller and it must be remembered that marketing communications is a dialogue between buyer and seller. The basic communications process is shown in Figure 12.5.

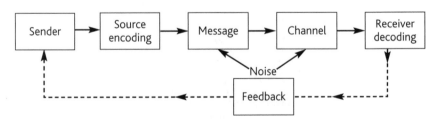

Figure 12.5 Simple model of marketing communications

In this model the sender is the marketing firm. The firm develops a message and sends this via a communication channel to the receiver or the target audience the marketing firm is trying to reach. The marketing message has been encoded. The marketing firm may have used visual images, comedy, music, guilt and so on to encode the message for maximum effect. When the message reaches the receiver (potential and existing customers) it is decoded. The marketing firm needs to ensure that the message that has been creatively and carefully encoded is decoded in the way intended and that the recipients have understood it. In order to find this out and obtain on-going feedback from the market as to the effectiveness of the communication, some form of post-communication research has to take place. This is shown in Figure 12.5 as a feedback loop.

▶ The two-step flow model of communications

When a firm deals with new products or services a simple model of marketing communications shown in Figure 12.5 may not be appropriate. A model of communication, known as the 'two-step flow' model, has more validity in the case of new products. This model of communication was not developed for marketing. Like many theories and models in marketing the two-step flow came from a different academic discipline, in this case political science. Research was conducted in the USA in the 1950s into the effects of political communication. The research was known as 'The People's Choice' and the research team found that the majority of voters were not strongly influenced in their choice of political candidate by political literature, direct mail shots and political broadcasts on television and radio. This form of political marketing communication has been used in the USA for many years, unlike the UK where it has only relatively recently taken off. Most voters, the research found, tended to be influenced by other people, friends, relatives, sporting personalities or actors and singers who they had seen on television and in the press and for whose views they had some respect. Friends, relatives, personalities and so on having such a strong leading influence were referred to as 'opinion leaders'. The general idea was that political communication had to be targeted at the opinion leaders if the campaign was to be effective. The opinion leaders would then pass on their own views and opinions, influenced by political marketing communication, to the mass of regular voters. In this respect communication to the mass of voters took two distinct stages or steps. The key thing for political communicators was to identify and reach the group of politically aware people known

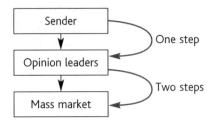

Figure 12.6 The two-step flow model of communication

as opinion leaders who had to be effectively targeted through media scheduling and planning and have the desired message communicated to them. The basic idea of the two-step flow model of communication is shown in Figure 12.6.

The two-step flow model of communications and the related idea of opinion leaders began to be applied in a marketing context in the launching of new products and services. The two-step flow model is related to another marketing model developed by Rogers in 1962 and known then as 'The diffusion of an innovation through a population'. Because this model had a long title, marketers referred to it as the 'diffusion model'. This model has already been discussed in a different context in Chapter 7 under the heading Product diffusion and adoption and the model was described in Figure 7.5.

Rogers stated that people have a predisposition to buy new products and services. This could be modelled using a normal distribution. Some people derive pleasure from acquiring new products and being first in the market. Such people have low levels of perceived risk and positively like risk and excitement associated with the purchase of new, innovative products. These people are 'innovators' and according to Rogers account for 2.5% of the population. Subsequent groups, as discussed in Chapter 7, are 'early adopters' (13.5%) 'early majority' (32%), 'late majority' (32%) and finally 'laggards' (16%).

A key question for marketing communicators is: Are the innovators and early adopters also opinion leaders? If they are, then we can apply the two-step flow concept of communication. The majority of potential customers are too risk averse or too disinterested to be first in the market for an innovation. They are largely unaffected by media communication about the innovation. Instead, people they know, whom they regard as opinion leaders, influence them. Some people might be innovators of early majority types across all products and services. It is more likely, however, that people will be classified as such for only one or a limited range of products. For example, a computer enthusiast might be regarded as an innovator for new computer products. Likewise, someone who is interested in photography or cars may be regarded as an opinion leader in relation to these products, but not others.

Of course new products have different degrees of newness. A new brand of toothpaste containing baking soda is not really that new to people, because after all it is just toothpaste. A vacuum cleaner for a garden is, on the other hand, quite a radical innovation. This latter product has recently come onto the market, although many people, including keen gardeners, seem a little unsure as to whether they should buy one or not. At present less than 2·5 per cent of households own such a product. If these products are good then the message will soon circulate by word of mouth and soon most households will own one, just as most now own a garden strimmer which was considered to be a radical innovation only 10 years ago. For new product developments the two-step flow model and the diffusion model appear to have some application, and can help marketers plan their communication campaigns when dealing with product or service innovations.

These models are usually discussed in the context of consumer products and services. However, they might also have applications in fields of industrial and business-to-business marketing communications. Larger firms tend to be financially stronger than small ones. They also tend to be technologically more advanced and hence more likely to adopt new innovations related to production equipment or administrative systems and so on. Smaller firms may look up to, say, Ford, ICI or Pilkingtons. These larger, well-respected firms might act as opinion leaders to the rest of the market.

What method might you use to encode a message for a political marketing communication?

Whenever you see a party political broadcast on the television or a political advertisement on a poster or in a newspaper, try to analyse it and discover for yourself what encoding techniques the sender of the message has employed. Political messages on television, for example, often use patriotic music by Handel or Elgar to convey the gravity of the message and the fact that the political party concerned is the natural party of Britain. Fear and insecurity, whether about jobs, pensions, health or education are used to convey what might happen if the other party is elected. Pictures, comedy, music and playing on fear, aspirations and hopes for the future are all used in political broadcasts in much the same way as they are used in advertisements for products. The only thing that is really any different is the subject matter that is, message content.

❱ Marketing related messages

Marketing communications can be defined as the process of:

1. presenting an integrated set of stimuli to a market target with the aim of raising a desired set of responses within that market target
2. setting up channels to receive, interpret and act on messages from the market to modify present company messages and identify new communications opportunities.

As both a sender and a receiver of market-related messages, a company can influence customers to buy its brands in order to make profits. At the same time the company can stay in touch with its market so it can adjust to changing market conditions and take advantage of new communications opportunities.

❱ The source of the message

Receivers of a message are often influenced by the nature of its source. If an audience perceives a communicator as credible, they will be more likely to accept his or her views. If the audience believes the communicator has underlying motives, particularly ones of personal gain, then he or she will be less persuasive than someone the audience perceives as being objective. Some advertisers use candid television interviews with homemakers in order to enhance their credibility, sometimes asking these homemakers to explain why they buy a particular brand or asking them if they would trade their chosen brand for another.

Another method used to increase credibility is to have the product endorsed by an expert on a given subject and this source will have more success in changing audience opinions. Specialised sources of information are often perceived as expert sources and are successful due to the fact that messages are aimed at selected audiences, for example the use of sporting professionals as promoters for brands.

The higher the perceived status of a source, the more persuasive it will be. If a receiver likes a source, it will be more persuasive. It is clear that age, sex, dress, mannerisms, accent and voice inflection all affect source credibility and subtly influence the way an audience judges a communicator and the message. A source high in credibility can change the opinion of receivers, but evidence suggests that this influence disperses in a short time after the message is received. It has also been observed that where people initially receive a message from a low-credibility source, their opinion change increases over time in the direction promoted by the source. This is referred to as the 'sleeper effect'. Another aspect of this is when a high-credibility source is reinstated, for example by a repeat advertisement, it has been found that audience agreement with the source is higher after a period of time than if the source had not been reinstated. For a low-credibility source, however, reinstatement results in less agreement with the source than with no reinstatement, that is reinstatement negates sleeper effect.

Explain the difference between a need and a want.

Everyone needs certain items and genuine needs are basic ones. Maslow's hierarchy of needs suggests that our real needs are mainly basic physiological needs. For example, none of us can live without water and sufficient food. We need appropriate clothing to keep us warm. Likewise with shelter, we need somewhere dry and warm to live and sleep. However, although we need water, we might want Coca-Cola or 7-Up. We need appropriate clothing, but we want Calvin Klein branded clothing. Our needs may be genuine, but marketers explore the way that we may satisfy our needs and turn these into wants. This is how we satisfy our needs through the purchase of goods and services that marketing people suggest will fill these needs.

▶▶ Above-the-line promotion

Marketing communications can be divided into two broad categories, above-the-line promotion and below-the-line promotion. These terms are the jargon used in the communications industry. There is no unified definition as to what constitutes above- or below-the-line promotion activity and different writers include different items under each heading. Generally speaking the term 'above-the-line' refers to paid for media advertising. If advertising space is bought in a newspaper or magazine, on television or radio or on a poster site the person that sells the space usually earns a commission. If an advertising agency places an advertisement in a magazine on behalf of a client this attracts a commission. In a sense the marketing firm rents space on the television, in the newspaper and so on and whoever buys that space on their behalf or sells them the space directly may be entitled to a commission. Above-the-line might, therefore, best be summed us as being the line above which commission is paid by the media. Most mass marketing communication campaigns using conventional media advertising are above-the-line campaigns. Below-the-line communication is defined as non-media advertising. Media are used to communicate a message where no commission is paid or space rented out to the client as in the case of conventional media advertising. Above-the-line promotion is concerned with conventional media advertising, and this is now explained.

▶ Media advertising

Media advertising communicates information to a large number of recipients paid for by a sponsor and its aims are:

1. To impart information
2. To develop attitudes
3. To induce action beneficial to the advertiser (generally the purchase of a product or service).

An advertisement for washing powder is paid for by the manufacturer to achieve greater sales; a party political broadcast aims to increase votes. It must be remembered that advertising is only one element in the communications mix, but it does perform certain parts of the communications task faster and with greater economy and volume than other means.

How large a part advertising plays depends on the nature of the product and its frequency of purchase. It contributes greatest when:

1. Buyer awareness of the product is low
2. Industry sales are rising rather than remaining stable or declining
3. The product has features that are not obvious to the buyer
4. Opportunities for product differentiation are strong
5. Discretionary incomes are high
6. A new product or new service idea is being introduced.

▶ Advertising models

These are drawn from psychological sources and from advertising practitioners to explain how advertising works. The stimulus/response formula was used at first, later models taking into consideration the environment in which the decision to buy is made. Daniel Starch said in 1925 'for an advertisement to be successful it must be seen, must be read, must be believed, must be remembered and must be acted upon'. This model assumed that the advertisement is the main influence on the state of mind of the consumer with respect to the product and makes no allowance for the combined or multiple effects of advertisements. Starch entered the burgeoning advertising field with his landmark *Advertising: Its Principles, Practices & Techniques* in 1906. He pioneered measuring actual advertisement readership by using current advertisements in interviews and analysing copy appeal and how it related to purchasing decisions, media usage and budgets. Starch introduced economic, sociological and demographic data to define the market environment. He founded Daniel Starch & Staff in 1923 and served as the first head of the American Association of Advertising Agencies' research department.

The DAGMAR philosophy

Colley's (1961) DAGMAR model (defining advertising goals for measured advertising results) allows for the cumulative image in advertisements and also maps out the states of mind consumers pass through:

1. From unawareness to awareness
2. To comprehension
3. To conviction
4. To action.

This is described as the marketing communications spectrum. Advertising, along with promotion, personal selling, publicity, price, packaging and distribution, move the consumer through various levels of the spectrum as follows:

▶ *Unawareness/awareness* The advertisement attempts to make potential customers aware of the product's existence.
▶ *Comprehension* The customer recognises the brand name and trademark and also knows what the product is and what it does; knowledge gained from the advertisement or from an information search prompted by it.
▶ *Conviction* The customer has a firm attitude, preferring a particular brand above others. Preferences may have an emotional rather than rational basis.
▶ *Action* Some move is made towards purchase; thus the advertisement has been acted upon.

This illustrates the concept that the purpose of advertising is to cause a change of mind leading towards purchase, but it is rare for a single advertisement to have the power to move a prospect from complete unawareness to action. Effectiveness is judged by how far an advertisement moves people along the spectrum.

A study reported by Majaro in 1970 established, by means of questionnaire replies, that companies adopting a systematic advertising-by-objectives process had an advantage over those who did not, but it did not prove conclusively that an increase in market share or financial performance follows directly from advertising.

The Lavidge and Steiner model

This consists of a hierarchical sequence of events on six levels:

1. Awareness
2. Knowledge
3. Liking
4. Preference
5. Conviction
6. Purchase.

These steps divide behaviour into three dimensions: cognitive (the first two), affective (the second two) and motivational (the third two). Although the two models discussed differ in the number and nature of stages, there is general agreement that purchase is the result of the persuasion elements, with the assumption that changes in knowledge and attitude towards a product and changes in buying behaviour form a predictable one-way relationship.

Dissonance theory

This illustrates a two-way relationship, with behaviour influencing attitudes as well as attitudes influencing behaviour. After making a decision to purchase, the prospect will be involved in cognitive dissonance and will actively seek information to reinforce the decision, focusing on attractive features and filtering out unfavourable data. The major implication of this is that advertising for existing brands in the repeat purchase market should be aimed at existing users to reassure them in the continuation of the buying habit at the expense of competition.

The unique selling proposition

Rosser Reeves (1961) who reported the principles his agency had worked to for 30 years developed this. This states that the consumer remembers one key element of an advertisement – a strong claim or concept. This proposition must be one that the competition does not offer that will be recalled by the consumer and will result in purchase at the appropriate time.

The brand-image school

Led by the famous advertiser David Ogilvy (1961) this focused on non-verbal methods of communication to invest a brand with agreeable connotations aside from its actual properties in use, such as prestige and quality.

An advertisement is the channel through which the sponsor communicates a message. The encoded message reaches recipients, through advertising or salespersons, and recipients then decode and absorb it either fully or partly. The quality of the transmission can be distorted by 'noise', occurring because the receiver does not interpret the message in the way the source intended (due perhaps to differences in cultural backgrounds of the two parties) or because of cognitive dissonance that occurs when the recipients' receipt of the message does not agree with what they previously believed.

Dissonance may cause a number of different reactions by the receiver:

1. Rejecting the message
2. Ignoring the message
3. Altering the previous opinion
4. Searching for justifications.

The first two reactions are negative, and from this feedback the source may change the message or stop communicating altogether with a particular receiver who is not receptive to the source's ideas. It can therefore be seen that advertising does not always convert people into users of a product. It can, however, have a positive effect in preventing loss of users, and increasing their loyalty.

▶ Advertising objectives

Advertising situations are so varied and unique that it is not possible to generalise about how advertising works. Any potential advertiser should adopt an advertising-by-objectives approach that makes clear what they are trying to achieve, how they will achieve it and how they are going to measure its effects.

Few companies give detailed thought to exactly what they are trying to achieve through advertising. Clear objectives are needed to aid operational decisions including:

- The amount to be spent on a particular campaign
- The content and presentation of the advertisement

- The most appropriate media
- The frequency of display of advertisements or campaigns
- Any special geographical weighting of effort
- The best methods of evaluating the effects of the advertising.

Setting and evaluating objectives provides a number of benefits:

1. Marketing has to define in advance what each element in the programme is expected to accomplish
2. An information system can be set up to monitor performance with
   the nature of information required clearly defined
3. Marketing will learn about the system from accumulated experience
   of success (and failure) and can use this knowledge to improve
   future performance.

Majaro's (1970) study on objective setting revealed that most managers saw increasing sales or market share as their main advertising
objective, but in fact this is a total marketing objective and it is unrea-
sonable to expect to achieve this objective through advertising alone
(unless it is the only element of the marketing mix being used, as in
direct mail and mail order businesses). The study also revealed that
methods of evaluation used by most companies were not relevant, and
that clear, precise advertising objectives, known to all involved, would
rectify this situation. The following advantages of the advertising-by-
objectives approach became clear:

1. It helps to integrate advertising effort with other ingredients of the
   marketing mix, thus setting a consistent and logical marketing plan
2. It facilitates the task of the advertising agency in preparing and evaluating creative work and recommending the most suitable media
3. It assists in determining advertising budgets
4. It enables marketing management to appraise the advertising plan
   realistically
5. It permits meaningful measurement of advertising results.

People who have an interest in, and influence on, advertising
decisions have different ideas about the purpose of advertising. The
chairman may be concerned with building a corporate image, whilst the
advertising manager may see it as an investment towards building
brand image and increasing market share. Marketing objectives have to
be separated from advertising objectives. Overall marketing objectives

should be defined and the next step is to determine the contribution that advertising can efficiently make to each of these. An advertising objective is one that advertising alone is expected to achieve.

Advertising objectives should be set with the following in mind:

1. They should fit in with broader corporate objectives
2. They should be realistic, taking into account internal resources and external opportunities, threats and constraints
3. They should be universally known within the company, so people can relate them to their own work and broader corporate objectives
4. They need to be flexible, since all business decisions have to be made in conditions of partial ignorance
5. They should be reviewed and adapted from time to time to take account of changing conditions.

Setting advertising objectives should not be undertaken until relevant information on the product, the market and the consumer is available. Consumer behaviour and motivation must be thoroughly assessed, particularly that of the company's target group of customers. The statement of an advertising objective should then make clear what basic message is intended to be delivered, to what audience, with what intended effects and the specific criteria to be used to measure success.

Five key words have been suggested to summarise the elements of setting advertising objectives:

1. *WHAT* role is advertising expected to fulfil in the total marketing effort?
2. *WHY* is it believed that advertising can achieve this role? (What evidence is there and what assumptions are necessary?)
3. *WHO* should be involved in setting objectives; who should be responsible for agreeing objectives, coordinating their implementation and subsequent evaluation? Who are the intended audience?
4. *HOW* are advertising objectives to be put into practice?
5. *WHEN* are various parts of the programme to be implemented? When can response be expected to each stage of the programme?

 Define the term 'above-the-line promotion'.

There is no unified definition of the term 'above-the-line promotion'. Generally it is used in the marketing communications profession to denote paid-for space in conventional advertising media for which some form of commission is earned from sale of the space or placing

the order for space on behalf of clients. All conventional media advertising falls into this category, for example TV, newspaper and magazine advertising, cinema and commercial radio advertising and
advertising hoardings, that is poster advertising. Other non-media
advertising would be classified as below-the-line promotion because
media space has not been rented and commission has not been paid
by media owners.

▶▶ Below-the-line promotion

Below-the-line promotion or communications, refers to non-media
communications, examples being exhibitions, sponsorship, public
relations and sales promotions such as competitions, banded or
'limpet' packs and price promotions. Such promotions are important
within the communications mix, not only of FMCG companies, but also
industrial products. For example, dealer incentives, exhibitions and
sponsorship activities are growing in popularity. All forms of non-
media communications are a form of 'promotion' if we use the word in
the broadest sense. A specific form of below-the-line activity is known
as 'below-the-line sales promotion' and relates to short-term incentives, largely aimed at consumers but also aimed at the trade, for example wholesalers, retailers, distributors, factors, and so on, as well as
members of the sales force. There is now great pressure on marketing
budgets and on marketing management to achieve marketing
communications objectives more efficiently. Hence, marketers have
been searching for more cost-effective ways to communicate with their
target markets than conventional media advertising. A move to below-
the-line promotion is the result. Davidson (1987) provided a definition
of below-the-line sales promotion:

> An immediate or delayed incentive to purchase, expressed in cash or in kind and
> having a short-term or temporary duration.

This definition highlights the important characteristic of its short-
term nature. Most conventional advertising campaigns are medium to
long term in nature. Some campaigns are very long term, sometimes
lasting for 20 years or more. Below-the-line sales promotions on the
other hand are short term in nature. Rarely does a promotion last more
than six months and most last for much shorter periods.

▍▍▍ Vignette 12.2

Palgrave, Macmillan's global academic publishing company, uses a price promotion to increase sales of its academic book titles.

Palgrave, the academic book publisher, reduced the price of many of its academic books during the 2001–02 period, as part of a major international below-the-line sales promotion in order to increase sales. The company handpicked over 1000 book titles and offered them at a special promotional price from November 2001 until March 2002. Many of the hardbacks were usually priced at up to £60 a copy but Palgrave made them available at less than half price at £19.99 with paperbacks at £9.99 or less. The sale included books for students, lecturers, researchers and professionals and covered all key subject areas in the humanities, social sciences and business. The promotional campaign was staged and targeted. Palgrave authors were in the first wave of targeting. As a Palgrave author they were given a unique price promotional offer. Not only could they take advantage of the catalogue price reductions but were offered an additional 35 per cent author discount on top of the sale price. This meant that Palgrave authors could get a reduction of up to 85 per cent off the normal retail book price. Authors were encouraged to order within 10 days of receipt of the offer. The sales promotion had been timed to coincide with the Christmas period and many authors took advantage of the offers both for themselves and to use as Christmas presents for family and friends. This was a major international sales promotion to not only Palgrave authors but eventually also to bookshops, library suppliers and researchers.

▶ Elements of sales promotion

All promotions are variations of each other, but since they are dynamic, new types of promotion will probably be developed in the future. Table 12.1 shows the primary types and their possible uses.

The scope of sales promotions includes:

▶ Display materials (stands, header boards, shelf strips, 'wobblers')
▶ Packaging (coupons, premium offers, pack flashes)
▶ Merchandising (demonstrations, auxiliary sales forces, display arrangements)
▶ Direct mail (coupons, competitions, premiums)
▶ Exhibitions.

Industrial promotions include these elements, but with modifications to suit individual circumstances.

Table 12.1 Guide to the effective use of consumer promotions, showing objectives that certain promotions might achieve depending on circumstances

Objectives	Self-liquidating premiums	On-pack premiums	In-pack premiums	With-pack premiums	Container premiums	Continuing premiums	Trade stamps/gift vouchers	Competitions	Personalities	Coupons	Samples	Reduced-price pack	Banded pack	Related items
Product launch/relaunch							√			√	√	√	√	
Induce trial										√	√		√	
Existing product, new usage										√	√	√	√	√
Gain new users						√	√	√	√	√	√	√	√	√
Increase frequency of purchase						√	√							
Upgrade purchasing size		√	√		√	√						√		
Increase brand awareness									√		√			
Expand distribution								√	√			√	√	√
Increase trade stocks				√								√	√	√
Reduce trade stocks										√				√
Expand sales 'off season'								√		√		√	√	√
Activate slow-moving lines										√		√	√	√
Gain special featuring in store	√	√	√	√	√			√				√	√	√
Increase shelf space		√		√									√	√
Retain existing users						√	√					√	√	

▶ Sales promotion planning

A plan is needed to ensure that each stage of a promotion is reached:

1. Analyse the problem task

2. Define objectives
3. Consider and/or set the budget
4. Examine types of promotion likely to be of use
5. Define support activities (for example advertising, incentives, auxiliaries)
6. Testing (for example a limited store or panel test)
7. Decide measurements required
8. Plan timetable
9. Present details to sales force, retailers, and so on
10. Implement the promotion
11. Evaluate the result.

▶ Advantages and disadvantages of sales promotions

Advantages
- ▶ Easily measured response
- ▶ Quick achievement of objectives
- ▶ Flexible application
- ▶ Can be extremely cheap
- ▶ Direct support of sales force.

Disadvantages
- ▶ Price-discounting can cheapen brand image
- ▶ Short-term advantages only
- ▶ Can cause problems with retailers
- ▶ Difficulty in communicating brand message.

It is difficult to know which marketing expenditures can be attributed to sales promotion. For example price reduction can cause confusion where 3p off a packet of biscuits is a sales promotion, but what about price discounting by manufacturers?

Define the term 'below-the-line sales promotions' and use examples to compare and contrast it with conventional media advertising.

Below-the-line sales promotions can be defined as immediate or delayed incentives to purchase, expressed in cash or in kind and having only a temporary or short-term duration. The key phrase is 'short-term duration'. There are two important factors that distinguish below-the-line from above-the-line media advertising. Unlike conventional media advertising, no space is bought in the media, for example television, newspapers, magazines and so on, and no commission is paid by the marketing firm or earned by persons selling advertising space or placing clients' orders for advertising. Secondly, conventional media advertising tends to be at least medium term and often long term in both its effects and duration. For example, the advertising for Guinness tends to be on the same theme for 1 to 2 years. There are small variations between advertisements, but the underlying theme of the campaign is the same. We can compare this with Guinness below-the-line sales promotions such as a competition (duration about six months) or 'extra product' promotions, for example at one point Guinness offered 13.5 per cent more 'product' for the same money and this offer was 'flashed' across the can for extra impact, this lasted for about two months.

▶▶ Direct marketing

Direct marketing is broadly defined, in media terms, as any direct communication to a consumer or business recipient that is designed to generate a response. This may be in the form of an order (direct order), a request for further information (lead generation), and/or a visit to a shop or other place of business to purchase a specific product or service. The emphasis is on marketing communications; in fact direct marketing could equally be called direct marketing communications, although direct marketing has other marketing mix implications, especially for distribution decisions because it is also a form of direct distribution. A leading trade magazine *Direct Marketing* goes further and defines direct marketing as a process that is:

> An interactive system of marketing that uses one or more advertising media to effect a measurable response and/or transaction at any location, with this activity stored on a database. (Institute of Direct Marketing official definition, 2003)

Direct marketing manifests itself in a variety of forms and utilises a variety of methods. It is one of the fastest growing areas of marketing and one of the most important. It is being driven by technical developments, particularly in the field of computer technology and especially database technology and systems. The term 'direct marketing' is used to refer to a group of methods, which, when applied, enables firms to market their goods and services directly to their customers, hence the name. It is a proactive approach to marketing that takes the product and/or service to the potential customer rather than waiting for them to come to the marketing firm. It can be classified as a method of 'non shop' shopping as customers often order from catalogues or over the telephone or Internet and it is sometimes referred to as 'precision marketing' or 'one-to-one' marketing. Instead of the marketing firm sending out a general communication or sales message to a large group of potential customers, a typical above the line mass campaign, direct marketing allows management to target a specific individual or household. Some writers call it a 'rifle' approach rather than a 'shotgun' approach because of its increased accuracy. In a business-to-business context this would be an individual member of staff such as the sales director or a specific organisation or firm, for example Asda. Direct marketing does not simply deal with marketing communications, it is also concerned with distribution and is in fact a method of distribution. In using direct marketing the firm is making a policy decision not to use marketing intermediaries but to market the product or service in question direct to the customer themselves. This has important implications for both channels of distribution decisions and physical distribution decisions.

▶ Development in direct marketing

Direct marketing has been used by firms for a long time, many firms having sold their products direct to the public for years. Direct mail through the post or even mail order catalogues have been around for a long time and are all a form of direct marketing, as is door-to-door selling. Direct marketing originated in the early 1900s and in fact the Direct Marketing Association (DMA) was established in America in 1917. Direct marketing became a strong force in the UK in the 1950s but at this stage in its evolution the industry was generally concerned with direct mail, mail order and door-to-door personal selling – basically the traditional direct selling type of techniques. Of course technology was in its infancy in those days compared to modern times. Today the scope of direct marketing has expanded dramatically largely due to the use of the telephone and related technologies and in particular the use of the World Wide Web and the Internet. Direct marketing includes all the marketing communications tools that allow the marketing firm to communicate directly with a potential customer. This includes direct mail, telephone marketing, direct response advertising, door-to-door personal selling and of course the use of the Internet. Party plan companies have been selling products directly to customers in people's homes for many years, for example Ann Summers Ltd, and Tupperware Ltd. The telephone has been used for business-to-business sales for a long time, particularly for the regeneration of routine orders and for making sales appointments. Most firms have a telephone and business people often prefer to be telephoned rather than be sent a letter or form. On the telephone the task or job is over with quickly whereas with written communication the order form or whatever it is may be lost or forgotten and adding to an already increasing pile of paperwork for the beleaguered manager. The telephone is now being used increasingly in domestic direct marketing programmes often to 'follow up' a posted personalised mail shot as part of an integrated programme.

▶ Telephone marketing

Telemarketing is defined as: 'any measurable activity that creates and exploits a direct relationship between supplier and customer by the interactive use of the telephone'.

Telephone marketing can take the form of both 'in-coming call' and 'out-going call'. In-coming call telephone marketing usually makes use of special numbers such as the 0800 free-phone number or numbers that allow calls from anywhere in the country or overseas for the price of a local call. In-coming call telephone marketing campaigns are usually used in conjunction with other communications tools.

▶ Direct mail

This is the use of the postal service to distribute promotional material directly to a particular person, household or firm. Direct mail is often confused with the following related activities, which all fall under the general heading of direct marketing:

1. *Direct advertising* is one of the oldest methods of reaching the consumer, with printed matter being sent directly to the prospect by the advertiser, often by mail but sometimes by personal delivery, handed out to passers-by or left under the windscreen wiper of a car. *Direct mail advertising* uses postal services, and this is a form of direct mail.
2. *Mail order advertising* aims to persuade recipients to purchase a product or service by post, with deliveries being made through the mail, by carrier or through a local agent. Thus it is a special form of direct mail, seeking to complete the sale entirely by mail and therefore being a complete plan in itself. Mail order is a type of direct mail, but not all direct mail is mail order.

3. *Direct response advertising* is a strategy of using specially designed advertisements, usually in magazines or newspapers, to invoke a direct response, such as the coupon-response press advertisement that the reader uses to order the advertised product or request further information. Other variants offer money-off coupons and incentives to visit the retail outlet immediately.

The usage and acceptance of direct mail is continually increasing. One reason for this is that the media has become increasingly fragmented, with three terrestrial commercial TV channels along with satellite and cable channels and the growth of 'freesheets' and special interest magazines. This means that advertisers have to spend more money to reach their audience, or spread the same amount of money over a wider range of media. Improvement in the quality of large mailshots has attracted increasing numbers of large advertisers. Direct mail, with increasing use of computerisation, enables advertisers to segment and target their markets with flexibility, selectivity and personal contact. Direct mail can be used to sell a wide range of products or services, and its uses are varied.

 **Vignette 12.3**

The Fortune 1000 Database: the ultimate resource for direct mail, telemarketing and research.

The Fortune group is perhaps best known for the business publication *Fortune* magazine and the business index of America's top companies the Fortune 500. Both *Fortune* magazine and information about the Fortune 500 index are available on the Internet. Fortune also offers details of the firms it has on its files to the direct marketing industry, for example those communication firms involved in direct mail and telephone marketing. The official Fortune 1000 database gives users instant access to all the data they will need on America's largest companies. The Fortune 1000 database provides key contact and financial information on the top 1000 US businesses. The Fortune 1000 database can be downloaded, sorted, researched, and incorporated or mail-merged into firms' mailing lists. With more than 40 columns of data, users can prospect clients, and customise direct mail and telemarketing initiatives. The cost per user is $899 or about £600. Fortune sells a suite of databases, which it calls the Datastore Collection. This collection puts the power of three Fortune databases to work. Customers can get the Fortune 1000, the Global 500, and the Fastest-Growing Companies, complete with more than 7000 key contacts and valuable financial information on the world's biggest and fastest growing companies for the total price of $2399.

Some of the more common uses of consumer-targeted direct mail are:

1. *Selling direct* where direct mail is a good medium for selling a product directly to the customer by a company that has a convincing sales message. It provides a facility for describing the product or service fully and for an order to be sent back, cutting out the middlemen.

2. *Sales lead generation* is used for products such as fitted kitchens or central heating that require a meeting between the customer and a specialised salesperson, and direct mail can be used to acquire good, qualified leads. A mail shot that has been well thought through can reveal the best prospects and rank other leads in terms of potential, enabling interested respondents to be followed up by a salesperson. An invitation can be made for the customer to view the product in a retail outlet, showroom or exhibition. *Cordial-contact mailings* create a receptive atmosphere for salespeople by building on the reputation of the company and creating a good impression that can be converted into buying action by a later mailing.

3. *Sales promotion* messages such as special offers can reach specific targets through direct mail. In the same way, prospects can be encouraged to visit showrooms or exhibitions.

4. *Clubs*, such as book clubs and companies marketing 'collectibles', find direct mail a convenient method of communication for dealings between club and members.

5. *Mail order* is a form of direct selling and recruitment of new customers and agents is possible.

6. *Fundraising* makes use of direct mail to communicate personally with individuals and it is a good method of raising money for charitable organisations. Large amounts of information can be included to induce recipients to make a donation.

7. *Dealer mailings* are where dealers or agents use direct mail to reach the prospects in their own areas.

8. *Follow-up mailings* help to keep the company's name before customers following a sale, for example checking that the customer is satisfied with a purchase. New developments, products and services can be communicated or invitations issued, thus maintaining contact and increasing repeat sales.

In a business context, direct mail is more effective than mass advertising for identifying different market sectors and communicating to each an appropriate message. Some of the more common uses are:

1. *Product launches* where direct mail is able to target small but significant numbers of people who influence buying decisions.
2. *Sales lead generation* where direct mail provides qualified sales leads, as well as doing some initial selling.
3. *Dealer support* in terms of dealers, retail outlets and franchise holders who can be kept informed of marketing promotions and plans.
4. *Conferences* where delegates in specific business sections can be issued with invitations through direct mail.
5. *Follow-up mailing using the customer base* where mailing existing customers regularly can encourage repeat sales.
6. *Market research/product testing* especially amongst existing customers is possible through direct mail, using questionnaires as part of a regular communication programme. Small-scale test mailings give an accurate picture of market reaction with low risk. A successful product can later be mailed to the full list.

When direct mail is added to a television or press campaign the effectiveness of the overall campaign can be significantly raised. The media reach a broad audience and raise general awareness of the company and its products, while the direct mail campaign is targeted specifically at the groups of people or companies most likely to buy. Mailing lists of respondents to coupon-based press advertisements or television or radio commercials with 'phone-in' numbers can be used for direct mail approaches.

Outline some of the major benefits of using direct mail as part of an integrated marketing communications campaign.

An important part of this question is 'integrated marketing communications campaign'. Direct mail, or any other marketing communications tool, is rarely used in isolation. It usually forms part of a multi-media mix that is made up of both above- and below-the-line promotional tools. There are examples of marketing companies using predominantly one communication tool. Cornhill Insurance uses predominately sports sponsorship (cricket) but also uses direct mail and media advertising. In terms of direct mail a well-known user of this medium is *Reader's Digest*. *Reader's Digest* not only markets its own magazine by direct mail and attempts to get people to agree to a subscription, but also uses this technique to market related products such as gardening books, DIY manuals, cookery books and language courses. Here, direct mail is often linked with below-the-line sales promotion activity. Many direct mail shots contain promotional material, usually some form of competition where one can win a new car or a large amount of money. Direct mail can be personalised and hence sent to specific individuals. Direct mail is a flexible medium that is controllable in terms of the amount and types of material to be included. It is also flexible in terms of time and can be coordinated with telephone marketing and conventional media advertising campaigns. It is relatively cheap compared to other media. Response rates make this form of marketing communications a highly effective tool that has grown in importance over the last 20 years and continues to grow in terms of use, sophistication and applications.

▶ Exhibitions

These are a form of below-the-line activity. As with other below-the-line methods, exhibitions are growing in popularity. They come in three basic forms: exhibitions aimed at the consumer, those aimed solely at the trade and those aimed at and open to both. The third category is the most common. Most exhibitions start off as trade exhibitions and then after a period when 'trade' business has been conducted they are often opened to the public. The public usually pays an entry fee that brings in revenue for the exhibition organiser and helps to pay for the costs of staging the exhibition. The general public might have an interest in the products and services being exhibited, for example the Clothes Show, Motor Show and Ideal Homes Exhibition. Sometimes products and services are of little direct interest to the public in terms of wanting to buy any of products on show, but attendance at an exhibition makes for a good day out and the public is prepared to pay for the privilege of visiting an exhibition such as the Royal Agricultural Exhibition held near Warwick each year. This is concerned with livestock, feedstuffs, agricultural equipment and so on, but is nonetheless popular with the general public.

Trade exhibitions tend to attract a high quality audience including managing directors and company chairmen and thus offer the marketing firm an opportunity to come into personal contact with high status decision-making unit (DMU) members. They also attract a wide range of influencers like technical staff and purchasers.

▶ Sponsorship

Like other below-the-line activities this is growing in popularity. In some ways sponsorship achieves many of the functions of exhibitions especially in terms of audience quality. We have already established that in business-to-business (B2B) marketing environments, high status DMU members are difficult to contact on a personal basis. The firm sponsoring an event can invite members of a prospective customer company DMU to an event enabling personal contact to be made.

Explain how both above- and below-the-line promotional tools can be used in such a way as to result in an integrated marketing communications programme.

Some communications tools are long term in nature such as conventional media advertising, corporate image, product brands and so on and some of these tools are short term in nature, for example below-the-line sales promotions such as competitions, banded pack and price reductions. Some tools are direct like telephone marketing and direct selling, for example Avon Cosmetics, and direct mail, for example *Reader's Digest*, and some are indirect, for example conventional television or radio advertising. Each communication tool in the mix has specific qualities. Each element in the mix has a specific part to play in the overall scheme. Each element in the mix builds on and interacts with each other element. The effectiveness of any marketing communications mix is derived from how successfully all these mix elements mesh and reinforce with each other in achieving the overall marketing communication objectives of the firm.

How are the below-the-line communication tools of exhibitions and sponsorship similar in terms of attracting a high audience quality and facilitating personal contact with important prospects?

In B2B markets, buying decisions are usually made by groups of people that marketers call the decision-making unit. The DMU is made up of various people within the purchasing organisation and these people will have different roles, different vested interests and different levels of seniority. Senior people such as managing directors and chairmen often play an important role in purchasing decision-making processes for many products and services. However, it is difficult for the marketing firm to arrange personal contact with important, high status DMU members. Such people rarely see salespersons.

Exhibitions and sponsored events, whether concerned with sport such as golf, or the arts, may often attract such high status people and thus provide an opportunity for the marketing firm's team to at least make personal contact.

How does 'marketing' differ from 'marketing communications'?

Some texts argue that the marketing mix is a communications mix. The rationale for this position is that virtually everything in the marketing mix whether it be price, distribution (place), product (or service) as well as, of course, promotion all communicate something. Other texts differentiate between marketing and marketing communications by considering marketing communications as one of the later stages of marketing within the overall marketing process.

What does marketing communications communicate?

Communications is the process of establishing a commonality of thought between a sender and a receiver. Communications is therefore a process, and as such has elements and interrelationships that can be modelled and examined in a structured manner. There must also be a commonality of thought developed between senders and receivers if the communications process is to occur in a true sense. Commonality of thought implies that a sharing relationship must exist. In its simplest form the communications process can be modelled as a simple flow diagram like that shown in Figure 12.5. The sender designs a commercial message using encoding techniques. This is then sent via a channel to a receiver who decodes the message. Research is needed to ensure that the message is being decoded (understood) in the way intended by the sender. Marketing messages are purposeful and are intended to generate some form of response or change in thinking in the receiver.

SELF-CHECK

▶▶ Summary

The marketing communications mix is made up of personal selling, a range of conventional advertising media and an equally impressive range of non-media communication tools. Conventional media tools involve renting space on television, in newspapers, on posters, radio and so on, and are referred to as above-the-line promotional techniques. Other marketing communications techniques, such as sales promotion, sponsorship and exhibitions do not involve the commissioning of space or airtime in conventional media. These techniques are referred to as below-the-line techniques. Marketing effectiveness depends significantly on communications effectiveness. The market is activated through information flows. The way a potential buyer perceives the seller's market offering is heavily influenced by the amount and kind of information he or she has about the product offering and the reaction to that information influences the market offering. Marketing therefore relies heavily upon information flows between the seller and prospective buyer. To many people, marketing communications, such as television advertising, direct mail and poster advertising is marketing, because marketing communications is the most visible aspect of marketing activity and it impacts daily on our lives. Marketing communications is collectively one of the conventional four Ps of the marketing mix. However, it is a very important part. No matter how good a firm's product or service offering, the benefits to consumers need to be communicated effectively. Marketing communications, in the form of above- and below-the-line promotion lie at the centre of marketing planning activity.

FURTHER READING

Armstrong G. and Kotler P. (2000) *Marketing: An Introduction* (5th edn), Chapter 12, 'Integrated Marketing Communications: Advertising and Public Relations, Consumer and Business Buyer Behaviour', Prentice Hall, Englewood Cliffs, NJ.

Blythe J. (2001) *Essentials of Marketing*, Chapter 9, 'Marketing Communications and Promotional Tools', Pearson Education, London.

Broadbent S. (1983) *Spending Advertising Money*, Business Books, London.

Cateora P.R. and Ghauri P.N. (2000) '*International Marketing: European Edition*', Chapter 16, 'The International Advertising and Promotion Effort', McGraw-Hill, Maidenhead.

Coulson-Thomas C.J. (1983) *Marketing Communications*, Heinemann, London.

Davies M. (1998) *Understanding Marketing*, Chapter 9, 'Marketing Communications 1: Advertising and Sales Promotion', Prentice Hall, London.

Hart N. and O'Connor J. (1983) *The Practice of Advertising*, Heinemann, London.

Keegan W.J. and Green M.S. (2000) *Global Marketing* (2nd edn), Chapter 14, 'Global Marketing Communication Decisions 1: Advertising and Public Relations', Prentice Hall, London.

Lancaster G.A. and Reynolds P.L. (1999) *Introduction to Marketing: A Step-by-Step Guide to All The Tools of Marketing*, Chapter 8, 'Above the Line Promotion' and Chapter 9, 'Below the Line Promotion', Kogan Page, London.

McIver C. (1984) *Case Studies in Marketing, Advertising and Public Relations*, Heinemann, London.

Plamer A. (2000) *Principles of Marketing*, Chapters 16–20. These chapters cover all the elements of the marketing communications mix, OUP, Oxford.

◗◗ References

Colley R.H. (1961) *Definitive Advertising Goals for Measured Advertising Results*, Association of National Advertisers, New York.

Davidson H. (1987) *Offensive Marketing or How to Make Your Competitors Followers*, Penguin, London.

Majaro S. (1970) 'Advertising by Objectives', *Management Today*, January.

Ogilvy D. (1961) *Confessions of an Advertising Man*, Atheneum, New York.

Reeves R. (1961) *Reality of Advertising*, A.A. Knopf, New York.

Rogers E.M. (1962) *Diffusion of Innovation*, Free Press, New York.

Rogers E.M. (1983) *Diffusion of Innovations* (3rd edn), Free Press, New York.

Starch D. (1906) *Advertising: Its Principles, Practices & Techniques*, University of Iowa, Iowa.

13 Public Relations

▶▶ Introduction

Public relations (PR) is a communications tool that can be employed both within and outside the organisation. It is usually viewed as an external marketing tool, where the organisation attempts to communicate with a wide range of external publics to cast the organisation in a favourable light. This is a limited view that fails to appreciate the value of PR as an internal communications tool. Good internal marketing, that is, achieving the right internal organisational culture so everyone pulls in the same direction in terms of marketing effort, is an important prerequisite to effective external marketing, particularly in those companies who engage in long-term relationship marketing with their customers. In this context PR has seen a dramatic increase in its importance as a strategic internal marketing communication tool.

PR is versatile and is used by many types of organisations including charities, the police, political parties and commercial organisations. PR is concerned with the management of information in such a way that certain publicity objectives are achieved. Positive publicity is not always the outcome of a managed PR campaign, as this is a theoretical outcome, for example PR has a particularly important role to play in crisis management scenarios. Where a catastrophe has occurred, especially where people have been injured or lost their lives, for example a ferry or aircraft disaster, it is often a case of containing the situation, putting a fair and balanced account of events forward to the general public and mitigating the adverse effects of the disaster to the organisation.

PR is not new. Its modern day origins in the United States can be traced back to 1807 with President Jefferson's address to

Congress, although evidence suggests that the ancient Greeks and Romans used it to influence public opinion. PR in the UK began as a government information and propaganda tool during the First World War and it was used more extensively for this purpose in the Second World War. Industry seemed to show little interest in PR as a commercial communications tool until 1945, after which its use increased considerably. PR's poor reputation over those early years was a result of generally bad practice. By the late 1960s the PR profession was referred to as the 'gin and tonic brigade', typically made up of smooth-talking fixers with the right connections, who carried considerable social influence and were able to open doors. A major function was wining and dining important clients. This has changed out of all recognition and PR professionals now come from a wider background and are often trained in communications management, some with degrees in journalism or even public relations itself. Unfortunately, the profession still carries the stigma of its immediate post-war image.

PR has spread through industry and commerce, although overall PR strategy is often commissioned from consultants, marketing research firms or advertising agencies. The slow adoption of PR practitioners internally into industry and commerce has meant that external PR firms have developed quickly and many have lacked expertise, and have simply taken advantage of the boom in the PR profession. This happened particularly towards the end of the 1980s when total quality management (TQM) was the latest business emphasis, and many consultants became TQM experts overnight. Because of the rapid expansion of PR firms, particularly in London, the poor reputation of PR in the eyes of journalists, businesspeople, politicians and the general public that persists even today, can be traced back to this period of uncontrolled growth. In the past 20 years many agencies have built reputations for marketing oriented PR. In more recent years some have built a reputation for strong relationship marketing oriented PR. Some firms specialise in consumer PR, trade relations, corporate PR, financial, political, industrial, service and technical PR. A growing number of firms now offer services in PR for not-for-profit organisations such as tax-exempt charities.

 Examine the view that professional PR is just as valuable when it is employed within organisations as it is outside them.

PR is concerned with communicating desirable information to a wide variety of publics and not just customers. One important group is employees of the organisation.

In order for management to be able to create a genuine marketing orientation within the firm they must have full cooperation and assistance from people working within the firm. After all, a commercial organisation is simply made up of the people that work within it.

Many progressive marketing oriented firms follow what has come to be known as a relationship marketing strategy, where the emphasis is on customer retention rather than on acquiring new customers, and on building long-term, profitable relationships with customers.

PR employed internally can assist management in achieving the right internal culture and cooperation which is a prerequisite for genuine external relationship marketing behaviour towards customers.

▶▶ Recent developments

From the mid-1970s a change occurred in the role and perceived value of PR leading to a growth in this form of marketing communications. Explanations for this upsurge in PR activity are varied. Many in the PR business identify the late 1970s recession as a major turning point. Companies were desperate to reduce costs to stay in business. As often happens in times of economic downturn managers of firms look to marketing budgets as a first strike and view marketing expenditure as a luxury and a cost rather than an investment. Managers found that PR, with a much broader base and cost effectiveness, was preferable to maintaining a conventional advertising budget.

The cost saving aspect of PR is a major reason for its growth in popularity. Other factors include the increasing complexity of business that has produced a need for more complex communications to get corporate messages across. Another factor is the growth of fast-developing new business sectors such as IT, financial services, travel and leisure which has lead to a new breed of marketing manager who is conversant with, and appreciates the value of, PR as a marketing communications tool. A further factor is a recognition by management, especially those working in business-to-business (B2B) firms, of the importance of creating and maintaining relationships with a wide range of people and groups. There is recognition that in industrial and organisational marketing situations there are complex buyer–seller interactions in the marketing process. Some of these take place within the official channels of communications, for example between salespersons and buyers or at least the purchasing team or committee within the buying organisation. However, interactions also take place on a less formal basis, amongst technical personnel from both marketing and buying firms. It was recognised that these informal buyer–seller interactions were just as important as more formal contacts and that these too had to be managed effectively. The recognition that organisational, or B2B, marketing involved an often complex web of formal and informal, but no less important, commercial interactions become known as the 'interactive approach' and was basically the precursor to what is now referred to as the 'relationship marketing approach'. Throughout its development as a communications tool PR has always been primarily an instrument for establishing, crystallising, cementing and maintaining mutually beneficial relationships with various groups of people or publics. It is, therefore, no surprise that as the recognition of the importance of the interactive and relationship-driven nature of modern marketing practice became accepted and practised by firms, the adoption of PR as a key communications tool grew in stature and importance, particularly in the area of corporate communications. The role of PR in achieving sound relationship marketing practices as well as its contribution to achieving good internal marketing is now examined.

Vignette 13.1

The Institute for Public Relations, based at the University of Florida, supports the PR profession worldwide through training, research and dissemination of professional practice to its members.

The Institute for Public Relations, based at the University of Florida in Gainesville, northern Florida, USA, is the only independent foundation in the field of public relations focusing on research and education. Since it was first established by a group of senior public relations practitioners as the Foundation for Public Relations Research and Education, the Institute for Public Relations (IPR) has distinguished itself for pioneering involvement in the field of public relations all over the world. Through publications, lectures, awards, symposia, professional development forums and other programmes, IPR has been at the leading edge of efforts to promote and encourage academic and professional excellence to the PR profession worldwide. Equally important, IPR has supported more than 200 separate research projects covering everything from what PR students should study to an analysis of how new technologies are affecting the profession. Through the years, IPR has made impressive contributions to the sum and substance of modern PR through the following:

- Non-proprietary research has led to breakthroughs in improving the teaching and understanding of PR.
- Practice-oriented programmes and publications help to strengthen the effectiveness of PR in profit-making and non-profit institutions.
- The Commission on Public Relations Measurement and Evaluation is the lead-

ing provider of information about, and advocate for, PR and related communication research and evaluation.

■ The IPR's distinguished awards and competitions serve as incentives for students and scholars to build the body of knowledge in the field.

Research and education are so critical to the future of PR that IPR attempts to assist
everyone in the field. More practically, they try to serve everyone with better programmes and activities to improve the knowledge and practice of PR. IPR's mission is
to improve the effectiveness of organisations by advancing the professional knowledge and practice of PR through research and education. Everything they do, whether
publications, awards, competitions, or research is open to students, educators and
practitioners regardless of their organisational affiliations.

▶▶ Role and nature of PR

▶ Defining PR

A plethora of definitions exists, each emphasising a different approach
and each attempting to arrive at a simple, brief and accurate form of
words. The difficulty in developing a single acceptable definition reflects
the complexity and diversity of the profession. For the purposes of this
discussion we look at two definitions. Firstly, the official definition of the
Institute of Public Relations (IPR) (2003) in the UK:

> Public Relations practice is the deliberate, planned and sustained effort to establish
> and maintain mutual understanding between an organisation and its public.

The essential features of this definition are that PR practice should be
deliberate, planned and sustained and not haphazard; and secondly that
mutual understanding is necessary in order to ensure that the communication between the organisation and its public is clear that is, the
receiver perceives the same meaning as the sender intends.

An alternative definition provided by the late Frank Jefkins (1988) is:

> Public Relations consists of all forms of planned communication, outward and
> inwards, between an organisation and its publics for the purpose of achieving spe-
> cific objectives concerning mutual understanding.

This definition is a modified version of the Institute of Public Relations'
definition and emphasises 'publics' in the plural as PR addresses a
number of audiences. It also includes 'specific' objectives, making PR a
tangible activity.

▶ Achieving marketing orientation

In marketing literature we read about how it is important for an organisation to become 'marketing oriented', 'customer focused' and adopt the 'marketing concept'. Achieving a true marketing orientation is not easy. In a sense, achieving a marketing orientation amongst the entire workforce is similar to achieving a religious conversion. How does senior management achieve this change in attitude and bring about the right customer-focused spirit within an organisation? PR alone cannot achieve this, but it can certainly make a significant contribution.

▶ Communications and PR

Communications is central to PR and its purpose is to establish two-way communication to resolve conflicts by seeking common ground or areas of mutual interest. If we accept that this is the primary function of PR, then we must also accept a further implication. PR exists, implicitly or explicitly, whether an organisation likes it or not. Simply by carrying out its day-to-day operations, an organisation communicates certain messages to those who interact with the company who then form opinions. PR needs to orchestrate as far as possible the behaviour of the organisation and the messages that result from such behaviour, to help develop a corporate identity or personality.

PR is not paid for like advertising, although the marketing firm will have to pay fees if it employs a PR consultant or a salary for an internal specialist. Because PR is not paid for it tends to have greater source credibility. That is because write-ups in the press, television or radio programmes are seen as emanating from an independent third party rather than a paid for advertisement. It does of course originate from press releases that are generated by PR on the company's behalf. The mark of good PR is that the receiver of the message does not realise that PR has been employed. If it is clear that a message has been cooked up by spin doctors then the message loses its intended effect. Good PR is analogous to good security. If a firm, film star or politician employs security personnel to look after them, a key criterion for success is that no one knows that they are anything to do with security. They simply melt in to the background and are indistinguishable from members of the public. It is this anonymity that makes them so effective. The role of PR within the overall marketing communications mix is shown in Figure 13.1.

Figure 13.1 The role of public relations within the overall marketing communications mix

▶ Corporate identity

Corporate identity is inextricably linked to public relations. All PR activities must be carried out within the framework of an agreed and understood corporate personality. This personality must develop to reflect the style of top management since it controls the organisation's policy and activities. Corporate personality can become a tangible asset if it is managed properly and consistently. However it cannot be assumed that managers will consider the role of corporate personality when they make decisions. Therefore, PR needs to be managed in terms of being aware of issues, policies, attitudes and opinions that exist within the organisation, and that have a bearing on how it is perceived by outsiders.

▌▌▌ Vignette 13.2

Tiffany & Young create world-renowned corporate identity by using blue as a colour of distinction and quality.

- -

On September 18, 1837, Charles Lewis Tiffany and John B. Young established Tiffany & Young, stationery and fancy goods emporium at 259 Broadway in New York City. Every article was marked with a non-negotiable selling price, a revolutionary policy that made headlines. The first day's sales totalled $4.98. Soon after Tiffany & Young was founded in 1837, a distinctive shade of blue was chosen to symbolise the company's renowned reputation for quality and craftsmanship. The colour was adopted for use on Tiffany & Young boxes, catalogues, shopping bags, brochures, as well as in advertising and other promotional materials. Over time, this lustrous colour became so closely identified with Tiffany & Young that it is today universally recognisable as the trademark Tiffany Blue. Tiffany Blue® boxes and shopping bags evoke images of elegance and exclusivity. True to the vision of Charles Lewis Tiffany, the Tiffany Blue Box® was to become an American icon of style and sophistication. As early as 1906, The *New York Sun* reported, '[Charles Lewis] Tiffany has one thing in stock that you cannot buy off him for as much money as you may offer; he will only give it to you. And that is one of his boxes. The rule of the establishment is clear, never to allow a box bearing the name of the firm, to be taken out of the building except with an article which they have sold and for which they are responsible.' The tradition of the famed Tiffany Blue Box® has endured for one essential reason: its contents are unsurpassed in quality and design. The Tiffany catalogue upholds a long tradition that continues to the present day. Tiffany's can today be found on 5th Avenue, near Central Park South in New York City.

The use of the term 'personality' rather than 'image' is deliberate. An image is a reflection or an impression that might be too polished. True PR is more than skin deep. This is important because colloquially a 'PR job' implies that somehow the truth is being hidden behind a false facade. Properly conducted PR emphasises the need for truth and full information. The PR executive, as a manager of corporate personality, can only sustain an identity that is based on reality. Corporate PR is concerned with image that is based on a long-term, carefully planned, programme designed to achieve maximum recognition and understanding of the company's objectives and performance, which is in keeping with realistic expectations.

▶ International public relations

Many firms are involved to various degrees in international business, even if it is only importing raw materials or exporting a proportion of finished goods. In the same way that PR can assist marketing effort in the home market, so similar techniques can provide aid to exporters in their efforts to enlarge the scope of overseas trade. PR in international markets can be targeted at various levels. For example an individual country such as the UK has a vested interest in projecting a favourable image overseas.

PR is employed overseas to represent particular industries. For example, the British Meat Federation represents the interests of British beef farmers overseas and representatives of this body give papers at conferences, speak on behalf of the beef industry at the European Parliament and design press releases for the European press. The British wine industry, cheese industry and defence industry, to name but a few, are actively involved in international PR, attempting to build good commercial relationships overseas.

Examine the view that good communications is central to effective PR.

PR is a form of marketing communications and forms an intrinsic part of the marketing communications mix.

The purpose of PR is to establish an effective two-way communications link with a whole range of publics including internal publics, that is those working for the organisation.

An organisation carries out activities that result in publicity. This publicity may be good or bad.

The role of PR is to manage events as far as possible, so that resulting publicity is good, and to effectively communicate this good publicity to various publics in an appropriate manner.

Hence PR is basically concerned with communications and good communications lies at the heart of effective PR.

◗ What PR is not

Misunderstanding as to the nature of PR has led to it being confused with other disciplines and activities. It is appropriate at this point to clarify certain distinctions:

PR is not 'free' advertising

1. Advertising emphasises 'selling' whereas public relations is 'informative', 'educational' and creates understanding through knowledge.
2. PR is not 'free'. It is time consuming and costs in terms of management time and expertise.
3. Editorial space and broadcasting time are unbiased and have more credibility than advertisements.
4. Every organisation necessarily has PR.
5. PR involves communications with many groups and audiences, not just consumers.

PR is not propaganda

Propaganda is designed to indoctrinate to attract followers. It does not necessarily call for ethical content, so facts are often distorted or falsified for self-interest. PR seeks to persuade by securing the willing acceptance of attitudes and ideas. The former Soviet Union authorities lied to their own people. They showed them untypical and biased pictures of the West to try and make the population believe that the Soviet system was superior to democracy and capitalism. They exaggerated the claims made for the output of their economy and progress in equality and health. All of these 'official' communications were propaganda designed to deceive people.

PR is not the same as publicity

Publicity is a result of information being made known. The result may be uncontrollable and either good or bad. PR is concerned with the behaviour of the organisation, product or individual that leads to publicity. It will seek to control behaviour if possible in such a way that publicity is good. Sometimes actions or events that lead to adverse publicity are outside the control of the organisation. The role of PR in such circumstances is to mitigate the effect of possible adverse publicity. For example, the firm Eurotunnel had to deal with a serious fire in the channel tunnel in 1996. Nobody was seriously injured although the people involved were afraid that they were going to die. A damming report into the incident was published in May 1997 highlighting weaknesses in the company's safety procedures. Eurotunnel has since had a struggle convincing a wide range of publics including the press, government, banks and customers that the firm behaved in a responsible manner and that such an incident is unlikely to happen again. Many holidaymakers were initially put off crossing the Channel by tunnel as a result of this fire.

How might receivers of messages created as a result of PR activity regard these messages with a greater degree of 'source credibility' than other forms of commercial messages?

The mark of good PR is that it is in a sense 'invisible' to the various groups, individuals or publics to which it is directed. If it is obvious to everybody that a particular commercial or corporate message is a PR concoction, then the message loses its impact.

The behaviour, events, publicity and messages resulting from PR activity are powerful as they appear to the receiver to be unsolicited. The favourable mention of a firm on a financial television programme, or a favourable piece on the future commercial prospects of an organisation in the business press, or coverage of a charity event sponsored by an organisation on the local radio news, should appear to have been delivered by unbiased third parties, with no vested interest in the nature or the content of the message being delivered, who were simply doing their job as journalists, television programme editors or whatever.

It is the impression of spontaneous, unsolicited messages delivered by unrelated and commercially independent and disinterested parties that gives PR its unique quality and extraordinary power as a marketing communications tool.

▶▶ The need for PR

As PR is a process of communication it is often needed when conditions are such that normal communications are strained and some people are left uninformed. In a modern industrial economy commercial organisations have a genuine need for sophisticated communications that can be accurately tailored and targeted at specific groups of people. In a real sense, especially in areas like political campaigning, communications itself has become a twenty-first-century skill. With the development of communication there has been a parallel development in the sophistication of the audience. Generally people are better educated and hence are better able to make objective judgements about the messages they receive. The very word 'communications' is a buzz word and the terms 'effective communications' and 'inadequate communications' are postmodernist. The subject of communications is agonised over by managers in commercial and non-commercial organisations, by trade union leaders, by political spin doctors and even media advisers to the Royal Family. Failure to communicate can be identified as part of the cause, even the principal cause of many commercial and non-commercial problems. PR is by no means a universal answer for every situation, but at least it is a formal system of communications and as such employs concepts of analysis, action, review and control that can provide structure and suggest a way forward in many situations.

Changing social attitudes have forced a new responsiveness and sense of responsibility in public and commercial life. A belief that people are entitled to be told is becoming matched by a sense of accountability, which was missing thirty years ago. For example, Boards of Directors can no longer dispose of ordinary shareholders' money, or pay themselves large amounts of money and other benefits like share options, without adequate explanation. It is in this social climate that an appreciation of PR as a management and advisory function is being recognised.

▶▶ Publics of PR

PR incorporates tracking, reviewing and where possible influencing the type of publicity communicated to various sections of the public through the media. In so doing the organisation anticipates being able to cultivate and maintain a positive corporate image. The strategic management of publicity through the employment of PR is referred to as 'corporate communications'. PR is concerned with communicating to a wide range of publics and not just to customers or clients.

The PR practitioner has to conduct activities that concern every public with which the organisation has contact. In order to exist, succeed and survive an organisation depends on many individuals and groups of people. Even in the distribution of products, for example, a manufacturer must communicate with salespeople, delivery staff, servicing staff, wholesalers, mail order houses, agents, importers, exporters, overseas agents and many different kinds of retailer including chain stores, cooperatives, department stores, supermarkets and smaller independently owned shops. There are many other people or groups who may shape the success or failure of a commercial enterprise. These include printers, package manufacturers, transport contractors, media owners and advertising agents. To these we can add others such as journalists who may write about the company's products, television producers of consumer affairs programmes and technical news programmes such as 'Tomorrow's World'. Business analysts, professional bodies, trade associations, government departments and other organisations are also important 'publics'.

The publics of an organisation are those groups of people with whom it needs to communicate. The exact nature of these groups and individuals will vary from organisation to organisation. These can be broadly described under the following categories and are subsequently discussed:

1. *The community*
2. *Employees*
3. *Government*
4. *The financial community*
5. *Distributors*
6. *Consumers*
7. *Opinion leaders*
8. *Educational world.*

▶ The community

Good community relations are important for every organisation. An organisation should act as if it were a member of the community and not abuse its power. It should behave as a responsible citizen just like any member of the community. The situation is one of interdependence; industry needs the support of the community and the community must understand industry. It is important for an organisation, through its PR function, to establish a community relations programme that both deals with complaints and involves itself in community activities. This may include local press relations, special visits to the workplace, open days, sponsorship and community projects.

On a broader scale, companies such as Levi Strauss have a voluntary committee in every factory that involves itself in local charities. BP sends 1 per cent of its workforce out on community projects at any one time. Firms such as Citybank and Marks & Spencer are involved in local business, employment and housing creation. The general public tends to judge commercial organisations by the way they conduct themselves, in the same way that individuals form a good or bad impression of the people that they come in contact with. Commercial projects like the building of new plant or the processing or storage of waste materials may affect or interfere with local conditions and amenities, and care should be taken by the firm to anticipate such resentment and attempt to mitigate this resentment as far as possible. An increasingly important aspect of community relations is the subject of pollution, particularly with the rise of environmentalism and 'green politics'. Increasingly firms have to take environmental management issues into account when planning their commercial operations. It is politically and socially unacceptable and commercially less profitable to disregard aspects such as pollution. This greener, cleaner marketing movement has had a big impact on the PR industry. The first task of PR is to help industry become aware of environmental issues and the potential consequences for the environment, public opinion and the commercial consequences of their actions. The second is to persuade both management and the public to see the whole problem in perspective and to recognise that environmental problems can be avoided. The third responsibility of PR is to make industry and its customers recognise that the firm is conducting its business in an environmentally responsible and socially ethical manner.

▶ Employees

Internal, or employee, PR is a neglected area in the study of PR. Worker/management relations are often 'them' and 'us' and confrontational. Poor industrial relations are basically a PR problem of poor communications within the firm. The solution to such problems often lies in involving employees in areas of decision making, in setting organisational goals and establishing mutual understanding. Appropriate objectives for management to set for PR in the area of employee relations could include increasing awareness of company policy, improving safety standards and determining the cause of, and helping to reduce, high staff turnover. High staff turnover is symptomatic of problems within the organisation and unhappiness amongst the work force. A disaffected workforce can be damaging for an organisation. Marketing orientation within an organisation requires the cooperation of staff. It is impossible to achieve marketing orientation with a disaffected workforce. The role PR is of strategic importance.

Internal PR encourages employees to make their maximum contribution to productivity and the prosperity of the organisation. It overlaps with personal welfare, industrial relations, education, staff development and marketing orientation and it should be integrated with these facets of management. PR can contribute to the creation of an atmosphere in which people work more effectively. It can initiate a suggestion scheme, a safety campaign, lessen waste, carelessness, absenteeism, and so on and enables management to communicate more effectively with employees.

▶ Government

Perhaps the biggest growth and development in PR over recent years has been in the areas of government relations and political lobbying. This form of activity has two main purposes, first to keep companies informed of legislative changes that may affect their business, and second to attempt to influence government or local government in favour of their industries. Political PR is often misunderstood, particularly with such matters as 'cash for questions' in the House of Commons and occasional allegations of corruption and sleaze in government. The success of some businesses depends heavily on decisions made in parliament which is the reason for the existence of certain pressure groups. Some companies have politicians as directors who keep management abreast of political happenings and who can put forward in parliament a case for the company or the industry in which the company operates.

Personal contact is the best way of establishing mutual respect and many organisations invite members of all political parties to informal meetings where matters of interest can be discussed.

❱ The financial community

The number of takeovers and mergers in UK industry over the past 25 years illustrates the need for financial PR. Commercial organisations need to communicate with a diverse range of interested parties such as investors, and city institutions such as pension funds, share analysts and financial journalists. Effective financial relations will produce benefits to the firm. Those companies that have established good reputations and relations will have less difficulty in raising additional capital that may be needed for future investments. Many companies rely for their existence on the support of banks. Such organisations might be highly 'geared' where much of their capital structure is made up of bank debt. Bank finance supporting this capital structure is often short or medium term. Finance arrangements are continually under review. Short-term loans are repaid and then a further set of loans is often negotiated. Good relations with banks might be fundamental to an organisation's financing strategy. Holding companies often hold shares in their own subsidiary companies. These shares might be offered as collateral in support of bank loans. Clearly the holding company has an interest in keeping the price of such shares at an appropriate level otherwise the value of their collateral on which loan finance is based falls in value. PR is used to communicate the commercial health of an organisation and favourable future prospects that investors can expect over the medium term. This information is aimed at key groups with the intention of helping to support market sentiment for the company and support the share price, and so assuage any doubts that potential lenders may have about the commercial robustness of the firm.

❱ Distributors

Distributors handle goods between producers and consumers. They include an array of businesses, wholesalers, retailers, dealerships, agencies and factors. It is essential that these marketing intermediaries are informed and educated about the company's products, services and methods of carrying out their business. The more staff working for marketing intermediaries know about the manufacturing company and its products and services the greater will be their confidence and expertise in marketing the firm's product or service offerings. Marketing intermediaries are often independent businesses with their own set of commercial needs and want. The manufacturing or service firm who markets through a distribution network relies on these marketing intermediaries to achieve their own commercial goals. There are many PR techniques that can be applied to create greater knowledge and understanding amongst the staff of marketing intermediaries including videos, talks, training courses and works visits.

A manufacturer can be affected by the behaviour and efficiency of marketing intermediaries so assessing and influencing their attitudes is important. The goodwill of dealers or distributors can make the difference between success and failure for a manufacturer. Much activity on advertising, sales promotion, merchandising and packaging can be wasted if a bad partnership exists. Effective use of marketing intermediaries can be a key factor in the success of their business, and PR can play a key role in creating and maintaining long-term commercial relationships.

◗ Consumers

'Consumer relations' is often considered to be the only public that concerns PR. As can be seen from the list of publics in this section this is not the case. However, it is an area of great significance because although other groups of publics are important, customers are especially important in that the purpose of the profit-making firm is the generation of satisfactory returns through the satisfaction of customers' needs and wants more effectively and efficiently than competitors.

Large retailers have most dealings with end customers and this group has done much in the way of PR activity. Stores are conveniently laid out, service is good and products represent fair value for money. Littlewoods distribute brochures to members of staff to show them how to improve the image of their store as well as creating better customer relations. Retail chains such as Sainsbury's, Tesco and Asda attempt to show that they are 'live' organisations listening and responding to customer views and opinions. Firms such as Kwik Fit have ongoing staff training schemes to inculcate proper customer awareness amongst staff.

A major aspect of customer relations is the subject of complaints and returns and Marks & Spencer was the first multiple to introduce an unequivocal policy of 'money back without question' in this respect. This subject is especially applicable to mail-order firms. Here purchasing is carried out at a distance and the organisation is not physically seen in the sense that a customer can visit a shop so it is essential that complaints and returns be treated carefully. Large mail-order catalogue businesses all pay particular attention to this aspect of business.

PR can be used for product and service support and can help to educate the market before and during a product launch through press involvement via conferences, demonstrations and interviews with key personnel. PR can also maintain consumer interest by publishing articles describing the use of the particular product or service.

▶ Opinion leaders

As the name suggests an opinion leader may have a particularly strong influence on the opinions of others. Such people might be held in high esteem. From an individual product point of view consumer affairs programmes and consumer magazines such as *Which* are held in high esteem by the general public who believe them to produce fair and unbiased views on various products, services and organisations and to act in the best interests of the consumer. Firms attempt to achieve favourable reports from such programmes and publications, as they know that positive messages will be more readily accepted and believed by the market. Other opinion leaders include professional bodies, trade associations, pressure groups and government.

The concept of opinion leaders was discussed in Chapter 12 when the two-step flow model of marketing communications incorporating the idea of opinion leaders was shown in Figure 12.6. It is shown again in Figure 13.2 in a slightly altered form and expressed specifically in the context of PR.

It can be seen that the organisation's PR message is targeted at individuals or groups, for example trade associations that have been identified as opinion leaders. These opinion leaders then diffuse the message to wider groups of publics.

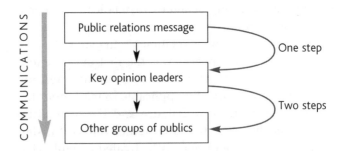

Figure 13.2 The two-step flow model of marketing communications applied in the context of public relations

▶ Education

Some companies pay particular attention to this area of activity to assist recruitment, especially graduate recruitment, and to improve general community relations. For example, the main high street banks place importance on exhibiting at colleges and universities at the beginning of the academic year with a view to persuading new students to open an account with them. They offer a number of special benefits such as zero interest overdrafts as well as giving away T-shirts and other merchandise. ICI issue charts and diagrams to schools and colleges on how their compounds are made from basic raw materials, and how they are made into products like paint and solvents. Companies invite parties of school children and students to visit their plants or factories to see how manufacturing takes place. Cadburys invite schoolchildren to visit their plant to see how chocolate is made and present each with a special commemorative tin of chocolates, which many children use as a pencil case when empty.

When considering the various groups of publics that PR activity is concerned with, why do PR practitioners consider that customers are the most important group?

PR can be applied by organisations in many different contexts that require communication to various groups of publics. These are not just profit-making organisations. For example, a charity requires donors and the support of the general public as well as government. A political party requires votes in order for its candidates to be elected as Members of Parliament and form a government. A museum or art gallery requires visitors in order to prove to grant awarding bodies that they are worthy of being supported with public funds. They also require benefactors and patrons to donate money in order to acquire works of art or other historical artefacts. All of these organisations make use of PR targeted at various key groups in order to help them achieve their objectives.

In a profit-making organisation the retention and acquisition of customers is a necessary requirement for survival. Other areas of a business might be running smoothly, for example purchasing, HRM and production and PR might be being used effectively on other key groups such as government, the financial community or the local community. However, if the firm has no customers, these other activities do not really matter because it is customers who provide revenues. All groups of publics are important, but as far as the profit-making firm is concerned customers are paramount.

▶▶ Media used in public relations

▶ Personal communication

This is the strongest and most persuasive means of putting across a message. It is aided by the personality of the communicator who can adapt both matter and manner to the reactions of the audience. A polished speaker can do much to enhance the image of the company, particularly at press conferences. The job of the PR officer (PRO) is not necessarily to appear on a public platform, but to organise events so that an appropriate representative of the organisation can address the audience.

▶ Printed Communication

Direct mail
This is a very versatile medium suitable for direct marketing, general advertising and PR. Direct mail can be used to send copies of press releases to interested parties, and to despatch house magazines to employees, customers, distributors and agents. It can be used to send invitations to sponsored events, exhibitions, conferences, demonstrations, film shows and corporate hospitality events.

Literature
This is related to the above because direct mail is often used to target certain pieces of information to the desired audience. Literature for direct mail usually consists of leaflets, folders, booklets, books and other print items including wall charts, diaries, postcards and pictures for exhibiting and framing. PR literature tends to be explanatory and educational, providing information or telling a story rather than trying to persuade or sell. Literature can be distributed to visitors, customers, dealers and members of the local community, while handouts and press kits are used at conferences. PR efforts of this nature can inspire confidence and trust in an organisation which can result in long-term commercial benefits.

Press relations
The press release is regarded as the most important form of PR. Two important factors in press relations are timing and distribution in terms of choosing the correct moment to release news and seeing that it reaches the right people. The aim of press relations is to gain maximum publication or broadcasting of PR information through newspapers, magazines, radio and television, to achieve specific communication objectives with clearly defined target audiences. The most common method of achieving this is a press release sent to relevant editors and journalists.

◗ Visual communications

Photography
Good photographs have an impact and appeal that is lacking in printed media. To see a photograph of some event lends more credence to the report as it provides proof in the mind of the audience that what has been reported actually happened. Photographs are rarely used in isolation, but normally in conjunction with a press release, one form of PR supporting and augmenting the other.

Films and videos
These were once the domain of larger organisations as they were expensive to make. Professional film/video production is still costly. If material is to be distributed overseas or shown in cinemas it needs to be produced to a high standard, otherwise it will give the wrong impression about the organisation and might be counterproductive. The development of camcorders has meant that a documentary, which might be suitable for certain PR purposes, can be produced by non-professionals relatively cheaply. However, if visual communication is to a wide audience it needs to be of a high, professional quality.

Television
Television is a high visual impact medium. Not only can points be explained verbally on TV, but products can be shown. Sometimes footage of a company's participation in a sponsored event or some other organised PR event is shown on TV programmes. BBC policy is not to mention company or brand names. However, the involvement by commercial firms in sponsored events in sport and the arts has increased dramatically over the past 20 years or so and it is now difficult not to mention the sponsoring company's name, or show a shot of a company or brand name, when reporting events like motor racing or football. The BBC and ITV also show science and technology programmes, such as 'Tomorrow's World' that introduces new products. Representatives from the companies that developed the products participate in the programme discussing details. There is growing demand for company personalities to appear on TV and give interviews on radio, especially local radio. There has been an increase of interest in anything to do with business, and there are now many programmes on TV and radio concerning business and money. This offers opportunities for organisations to capitalise on the PR opportunities available from this increasingly popular, important and sophisticated medium.

Exhibitions

There has always been a strong PR dimension to exhibitions. They offer marketing communicators a rare opportunity to come into face-to-face contact with high status decision-making unit (DMU) members. Many exhibition visitors go to view a market offering in its entirety in a short space of time and under one roof and treat the exhibition as a shop window and opportunity to gather technical information. Often products are available for inspection along with working models and videos of the company and its products. There can be a strong entertainment component to exhibitions with stands offering complimentary drinks and food to potential clients. Networking is achieved by lunch and dinner engagements and if the exhibition is overseas, or in London, firms often give complementary tours or tickets to local events, such as a concert or play. All media mentioned can be used in exhibitions including personal contact, literature, video and the event itself may even be reported on radio or TV and in the business press.

Sponsorship

Sponsorship has a strong PR component and firms use it in many ways. Being associated with the arts, for example, gives a strong sense of supporting, and being part of the fabric of, society. It also has a strong entertainment appeal. Clients and individuals from other publics can be invited to sponsored events such as concerts, plays and opera. They can mix with artists, such as conductors and opera singers, over drinks or dinner. In this way key individuals are entertained and long-term relationships are built and maintained.

 Explain the contribution direct mail can play when marketing plans an integrated PR programme.

Direct mail is a versatile marketing communications tool that is very precise. With the exception of personal contact and perhaps telephone marketing, which are also precise marketing communications tools from a targeting and delivery point of view, direct mail offers an unparalleled degree of precision.

Like sponsorship, direct mail has many PR applications and contributions to make. Direct mail messages can be highly personalised and can be made to fit individual communication requirements. Direct mail can contain product, service or corporate literature and invitations to sponsored events, conferences and exhibitions.

Imaginative use of direct mail and database marketing can make a valuable contribution to an integrated programme of PR.

▶▶ Internal and relationship marketing

Internal marketing is the process of applying the general principles of marketing to the staff and workforce of the organisation. Marketing as a business philosophy is about achieving the right internal company culture that will result in the company becoming marketing oriented.

The process of internal marketing involves more than the application of PR inside firms. In fact internal marketing operates at the interface between marketing and human resource management and involves both disciplines. As we have discussed already the application of internal PR has a salient role to play in the overall process of achieving a good internal marketing culture. The most common means of achieving internal PR objectives is through company publications. If these are to be effective, they must be more than paternalistic house journals. They should provide a forum for open, two-way discussion on company issues. Whatever methods are employed, the important requirement is that they represent a genuine desire to communicate on behalf of both the workforce and management. This reinforces the point that PR can only reflect reality. The contribution of internal and external PR to relationship marketing practices is now discussed. Figure 13.3 shows the relationship between PR and internal and relationship marketing.

Relationship marketing is based on the premise that existing customers are a valuable asset and must be cultivated and looked after properly. Relationship marketing applies to some firms more than others, but many are now adopting a more long-term relationship marketing approach. This philosophy looks beyond the next sale or transaction and views customers as a value stream of income stretching over decades. The true capital value of a customer is the net present value of a discounted stream of revenue attributable to the customer over their lifetime. Some consultancy firms specialising in relationship marketing now use investment appraisal techniques such as discounted cash flow

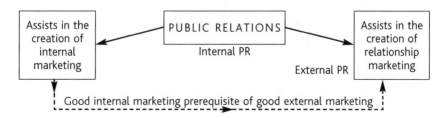

Figure 13.3 The relationship between public relations
and internal and relationship marketing

to value a customer portfolio. It is contended that it costs five times as much to acquire a new customer as it does to retain an existing customer and existing customers provide higher margins, need less marketing resources and are more profitable.

▌▌▌ Vignette 13.3

O gilvy Public Relations Worldwide is voted 'Agency of the Year' for its outstanding contribution to the PR profession.

Started by David Ogilvy, the advertising expert, in 1996, Ogilvy Public Relations Worldwide has made rapid progress and was voted the 'Agency of the Year' for 2001 by both *PR Week* and *The Holms Report*, a US publication which covers the PR industry worldwide. The firm operates in the USA, Europe, Africa and the Asia/Pacific region including Australia. The management of Ogilvy claim that their distinctiveness and success stems from following the business philosophy of their founder David Ogilvy. This philosophy has enabled them to grow in size by a factor of three over the past five years, a growth rate that is truly impressive any business sector and not just in the world of PR. The firm's management claims that their staff and their philosophy of concentration on providing excellence in client services fosters an environment that enables strategic thinking and creativity. This is the key strength of the organisation – clients know that they will get imaginative and innovative solutions to their PR problems. The firm is committed to developing and sharpening their staff's professional knowledge about the PR industry and public relations skills. They are a learning organisation, which attaches great importance to staff development and training. With their staff's commitment, knowledge, drive, energy and enthusiasm Ogilvy Public Relations continues to provide help to clients, which results in generating repeat business and acquiring new clients through word of mouth. The firm's commitment to client services is grounded in their pride in making themselves partners with their clients and developing a truly relationship marketing focus. Their clients include Coca-Cola, Unilever, Pfizer, Sun Microsystems and BP, to name but a few.

Relationship marketing is based on forging long-term relationships based on customer satisfaction, exceeding expectations and mutual trust. For this to happen everyone working in the marketing firm must adopt a relationship marketing mentality or it simply will not work. Good internal marketing is a prerequisite for effective relationship marketing, and internal PR can make a contribution to the achievement of an internal marketing culture. Internal PR contributes to relationship marketing. External PR, aimed at customers, marketing intermediaries and other important groups, makes a direct contribution to fostering long-term, commercially beneficial relationships.

SELF-CHECK

Misunderstanding as to the nature of PR has led to it being confused with other disciplines and activities. Many see it as a form of 'free' advertising. Do you agree?

PR is not 'free' advertising and there are a number of key differences between the two.

Advertising emphasises 'selling' whereas public relations is informative, educational and creates understanding through knowledge.

PR is not 'free'. It is time consuming and costs in terms of management time and expertise.

Editorial space and broadcasting time are unbiased and have more credibility than advertisements.

Every organisation necessarily has PR.

PR involves communications with many groups and audiences, not just consumers.

Account for the popularity of PR as a marketing communication tool in recent years.

The cost saving aspect of PR is a major reason for the growth in its popularity.

Other factors include the increasing complexity of business that has produced a need for more involved communications to get corporate messages across.

Another factor is the growth of fast-developing new business sectors such as IT, financial services and travel and leisure which has led to a new breed of marketing manager who is conversant with, and appreciates the value of, PR as a marketing communication tool.

A further factor is the recognition by management, especially in business-to-business (B2B) firms, of the importance of creating and maintaining relationships with a wide range of people and groups.

▶▶ Summary

PR is an important and versatile marketing communications tool. It is rarely used in isolation, but forms an intrinsic part of an organisation's marketing communications mix. There is a PR application to most marketing communication variables, whether this is personal selling, sponsorship, exhibitions, direct mail or telephone marketing.

PR can be applied both within and without the organisation. The process of achieving a true marketing orientation within organisations is a vital prerequisite to effective external marketing, particularly strategies based on relationship marketing principles. PR has a vital contribution to make to the creation of an effective internal marketing culture and to creating, fostering, nurturing and maintaining mutually beneficial long-term relationships with customers and other key groups. In this respect, PR has seen a dramatic increase in prominence and importance as both a strategic internal and external marketing communications tool.

The Institute of Public Relations defines PR as 'the deliberate, planned and sustained effort to establish and maintain mutual understanding between an organisation and its publics'. Each element in the organisation's communications mix, for example advertising, sponsorship, direct mail, exhibitions, above- and below-the-line promotion has a part to play in the marketing firm's communications strategy. Likewise, PR has a specific role to play in the overall scheme. The role of PR is to help build an understanding between a company and the publics with whom it communicates. This has the effect of augmenting and increasing the source credibility of marketing messages from other elements in the communications mix by improving the image and reputation of the company and its product and services. An organisation is judged by its behaviour. PR is about goodwill and reputation. At best, PR is the discipline that determines the content of messages that companies send to customers and other target audiences.

Whether consciously achieved or not, the organisation's customers and other publics hold particular points of view about the company and its products and services. Company image and corporate identity are of vital importance to the marketing effort. What is communicated by the marketing organisation should not simply be left to chance but should be planned and managed by the professional application of PR.

FURTHER READING

Armstrong G. and Kotler P. (2000) *Marketing: An Introduction* (5th edn), Chapter 12, 'Integrated Marketing Communications: Advertising and Public Relations, Consumer and Business Buyer Behaviour', Prentice Hall, Englewood Cliffs, NJ.

Blythe J. (2001) *Essentials of Marketing*, Chapter 9, 'Marketing Communications and Promotional Tools', Pearson Education, London.

Broadbent S. (1983) *Spending Advertising Money*, Business Books, London.

Cateora P.R. and Ghauri P.N. (2000) *International Marketing: European Edition*, Chapter 16, 'The International Advertising and Promotion Effort', McGraw-Hill, Maidenhead.

Coulson-Thomas C.J. (1983) *Marketing Communications*, Heinemann, London.

Davies M. (1998) *Understanding Marketing*, Chapter 9, 'Marketing Communications 1: Advertising and Sales Promotion', Prentice Hall, London.

Hart N. and O'Connor J. (1983) *The Practice of Advertising*, Heinemann, London.

Keegan W.J. and Green M.S. (2000) *Global Marketing* (2nd edn), Chapter 14, 'Global Marketing Communication Decisions 1: Advertising and Public Relations', Prentice Hall, London.

Lancaster G.A. and Reynolds P.L. (1999) *Introduction to Marketing: A Step-by-Step Guide to All The Tools of Marketing*, Chapter 8, 'Above the Line Promotion' and Chapter 9, 'Below the Line Promotion', Kogan Page, London.

McIver C. (1984) *Case Studies in Marketing, Advertising and Public Relations*, Heinemann, London.

Plamer A. (2000) *Principles of Marketing*, Chapters 16–20. These chapters cover all the elements of the marketing communications mix. OUP, Oxford.

▶▶ Reference

Jefkins, F. (1988) *Public Relations Techniques*, Butterworth Heinemann, Oxford.

14

INTERNATIONAL MARKETING

▶▶ Definitions

▶ The term 'multinational marketing' applies to a number of very large companies whose business interests, manufacturing plant and offices are spread throughout the world. Although their strategic headquarters might be based in the original parent country, they tend to operate autonomously in individual countries. Multinationals can be exporters and importers, but the main point is that they produce and market goods within the countries in which they have chosen to develop.

▶ 'International marketing' is the term commonly used to describe all international activity and is used as the title for this chapter for this very reason. It is a term used to describe companies whose overseas sales account for more than 20 per cent of their total turnover, where a strategic decision has been taken to enter foreign markets and where product mix and communications mix adaptations are considered when supplying goods or services for a particular overseas market.

▶ 'Exporting' describes the commercial activity involved when international transactions take place. In an international marketing sense it refers to those companies who consider overseas business as being marginal to their main activities. They simply accept export orders, rather than engage in active manipulation of their marketing mixes to suit the needs of customers in specifically targeted countries.

▶▶ Significance of international marketing

The economic theory of comparative advantage states that

each country should specialise in the production of those goods it can most efficiently provide, which should encourage unrestricted trade, international specialisation and increased global efficiency.

This is a common-sense yet idealistic view. Individual countries, for a variety of political and economic reasons, erect barriers to the free movement of goods and services between countries. Agreements are formed which encourage free trade within defined geographical regions, but which tend to erect barriers against those who are not in this 'club'.

▶ World trading blocs

The largest of these blocs is the Common Market or, more correctly, the European Union (EU), sometimes referred to as the European Community (EC) and previously the Economic Community (EEC). The title 'EU' reflects changes that have taken place since its inception when it was known as the 'EEC'. In the early days it was seen as a trading bloc, whereas the current title reflects its trading and political role as a kind of United States of Europe. This is an issue often debated among member nations of the EU in terms of those wishing for more federal control from Brussels (the headquarters) and those wishing to keep their autonomy. Currently the membership of the EU is as follows: Belgium, France, Germany, Netherlands, Luxembourg, Italy, Ireland, United Kingdom, Denmark, Greece, Spain, Portugal, Finland, Sweden and Austria, and this is about to be extended to include a number of former Eastern bloc countries.

Other organisations exist throughout the world, but such organisations are not as politically integrated as the EU. These organisations are:

▶ North American Free Trade Association (NAFTA) comprising the USA, Canada and Mexico.
▶ Organization for Petroleum Exporting Countries (OPEC) comprising Saudi Arabia, Kuwait, United Arab Emirates, Qatar, Iran, Iraq, Libya, Algeria, Nigeria, Venezuela and Indonesia.
▶ Association of Southeast Asian Nations (ASEAN) comprising Singapore, Thailand, Malaysia, the Philippines, Indonesia and Brunei.
▶ European Free Trade Association (EFTA) has lost most of its membership to the EU, but those remaining in this trading block are Norway, Switzerland and Iceland.

International business continues to rise worldwide as barriers to trade slowly come down. This has been principally due to incremental agreements sought by the General Agreement on Tariffs and Trade (GATT) organisation which was formed in 1948 to develop fair trading practices amongst its members who now total over 100 countries.

▶ Reasons for international trading between companies

Most companies recognise there is a need for them to expand their markets into the international arena for a number of reasons:

- To increase overall levels of profit
- The home market might be saturated
- With the general freeing up of trade, this has meant that more foreign competition now exists in the home market, so to counteract this, there is an equivalent need to enter foreign markets
- To take advantage of an innovative product or service
- To satisfy corporate management goals that might dictate that the company be committed to international operations
- To enjoy the corporate tax advantages offered overseas
- To take advantage of funding benefits from setting up manufacturing and assembly bases in certain overseas countries which might also offer access to the trading bloc to which that country belongs
- To obtain economies of larger scale operations
- Freer trade in general as a result of GATT accords.

Against these positive factors there are a number of negative factors (see also Kotler, 1997 p. 405):

- The company might wish to enter international trade to escape competition in the home market. One reason that has spurred a number of UK companies to unwillingly enter EU markets is because UK markets have now been legitimately opened up to other EU member countries.
- To dispose of surplus production or utilise surplus manufacturing capacity. This is a negative factor, but a number of companies dispose of their surplus production overseas at cost or even below cost rather than cut prices on the domestic market. In the case of selling below cost there is international law under 'anti-dumping and countervailing measures' that prohibits dumping, as it constitutes unfair competition against domestic manufacturers. The USA in particular is sensitive to products being 'dumped'.
- Import tariffs that impose a percentage duty on the cost of landed

products are a negative constraint to exporting, as are import quotas which impose numerical values on the number of products that can be imported. Some foreign governments demand payment to issue import licences for certain goods.

▶ Political unrest militates against companies wishing to trade in a foreign country. Sometimes an overseas government might stop payment for goods supplied on the basis that it seeks to preserve its foreign exchange. In the UK the Export Credits Guarantee Department (ECGD) was set up to insure companies against such risks, and this is available to insure against non-payment. This service of course costs money which all adds to the cost of trading competitively.

▌▌▌ Vignette 14.1

AOL Time Warner Inc. seeks to strengthen its position in Northern India through direct investment in Zee Telefilms, India's largest media company.

AOL Time Warner has a strong presence in the south of the Indian subcontinent through its so-called 'Turner unit', a group of media companies which include TNT, HBO and the mighty CNN. Turner Broadcasting System, Inc. operates many of the most powerful and well-established brands in entertainment and news. These include TBS Superstation, TNT, The WB, Cartoon Network, Turner Classic Movies, Turner South, CNN/US, CNN Headline News, CNN*fn*, CNN/SI, CNNRadio, and Boomerang, as well as the Atlanta Braves, Atlanta Hawks, Atlanta Thrashers, the Goodwill Games, and the Company's many international language-specific networks and other businesses. Although AOL Time Warner has strength in the south of the country through Turner, the company is weaker in northern India, which is an important and potentially lucrative market. In order to strengthen its position the firm is considering purchasing about 26% of the premier Indian media company, Bombay (Mumbai) based, Zee Telefilms. Zee is strong in the northern part of India and has been looking for a strategic partner for some time due to its own financial weakness. Zee's management regards an overseas partnership as crucial in order to stabilise the group, which has faced a number of problems during 2001. Zee's sale of a 26% share of the company should raise about $400 million dollars, but there is a price to pay. Under Indian law a 26% stake is enough for the holder to block decisions of the board. It is important for Zee's management to choose a company they feel they can work with for any future collaboration.

▶▶ A macro overview of international trade

Foreign exchange is important to pay for goods and services a country imports. We must export to pay for imports, as we are not self-sufficient in food, raw materials and many manufactured goods. However, we are a free-trading nation and traditionally have put up few barriers to countries wishing to market their goods and services here.

The gap between a country's total exports and total imports is known as the balance of trade and in monetary terms it is the balance of payments. If a country imports more than it exports then the balance of payments will be in deficit, but if exports are higher than imports then the balance of payments will be in surplus.

Two types of trade are considered. 'Visible' trade is the trading of physical commodities, ranging from raw materials to finished goods, that is accounted for separately in Government statistics and quoted as the visible trade balance, which, in the case of the UK, is usually in deficit. The other account is for what is called 'invisible trade' and this is for trading less tangible services between countries. In the case of the UK the trade in invisibles is usually in surplus. The total of visible and invisible trade is the balance of payments.

Consider invisible trade and quote three different examples.

- Insurance earnings from remittances from abroad to pay for insurance risks covered by UK companies
- Earnings of UK pop stars from overseas venues
- Earnings from overseas visitors on holiday in the UK in terms of money they spend here

▶ Help for exporters

Organisations exist to help UK companies engage in international trade. Some companies belong to trade associations which reflect the corporate views of subscribing members. Such trade associations often provide significant advice in relation to export markets. Many public libraries now have special sections devoted to information on export trade. However, the most significant organisation that gives advice is the British Overseas Trade Board (BOTB) which is a branch of the Department of Trade and Industry (DTI). The BOTB helps exporters by providing support in a number of ways to individual companies who are working with a recognised agency, such as a Chamber of Commerce:

▶ Financial support when exhibiting at overseas trade fairs or exhibitions.

▶ Subsidies for air travel and accommodation when travelling as part of an overseas trade delegation to a specific part of the world.

▶ Low interest loans for a substantial amount of the costs involved in entering new export markets on the basis that if the venture is unsuccessful the loss is shared.

▶ Help in general in terms of putting exporters in touch with markets (for example Computerised Export Intelligence which is a subsidised scheme through which companies receive regular updated reports in relation to export opportunities).

▶ Export intelligence gathering in a more general way in terms of investigating the commercial viability of doing business in certain countries and making this information available to the business community.

▶ Help through contacts with British Embassies in overseas countries. In recent years embassies have become more commercially proactive in terms of helping the interests of British overseas businesses. Services provided by such consular offices can include the preparation of shortlists of potential agents or distributors of a company's products.

▶ Stages of economic development

An international classification exists in relation to individual countries to denote the stage of development status in which they are placed. This classification is as follows:

▶ *Undeveloped countries* (sometimes termed 'subsistence economies') have subsistence living and engage in barter trade for the exchange of goods largely in central markets. There is no specialisation and no modern marketing activity.

▶ *Less developed countries* have a self-sufficiency philosophy with a predominance of small-scale cottage industry (see also Cateora and Ghauri, 2000 pp. 173–201 for a more detailed treatment of emerging markets and market behaviour). Agriculture and manufacturing are labour intensive. Producers tend to be marketers (production orientation).

▶ *Developing countries,* sometimes referred to as 'newly industrialising countries' (NICs), have specialisation of labour and manufacturing. There is separation of production from marketing.

▶ *Developed countries* (sometimes termed industrialised countries) engage in regional, national and international marketing. There is specialisation of manufacture and mass distribution.

▶ *Affluent countries* have reached developed country status, but additionally their people demand high quality, sophisticated consumer goods.

Cite a country that fits each of the categories listed.

- Undeveloped countries – Ethiopia
- Less developed countries – Uganda
- Developing countries – Malaysia
- Developed countries – Greece
- Affluent countries – Sweden

▶▶ The four Ps of the international marketing mix

A marketing policy for international markets should be developed on the basis of an integrated marketing mix, rather than simply selling products designed for the domestic market on an international scale. Marketing mix elements for international operations are no different to those used for domestic marketing, the principal difference being the range of options. Marketing management should decide, on the basis of what marketing research indicates, how the marketing mix should be adapted for each target area which the company considers entering. When international marketing is sufficiently mature and starts to produce adequate returns, consideration should be given to the appointment of an international marketing manager.

Each marketing mix element is now considered in turn from the viewpoint of issues that are at stake in the context of international marketing.

▶ Product

Due regard must be given to whether to market the entire product range or part of the range and whether to modify products to suit local demand, standards and regulations that might pertain in the overseas market. This might mean high modification costs, packaging, labelling and product or brand name considerations.

A policy of standardisation ('we sell what we make') is typical for a passive company that has found itself in international trade by accident. This is akin to simple exporting in terms of fulfilling unsolicited export orders. Such orders might come from an advertisement in a domestic journal that has some circulation overseas, but the company's philosophy tends to be that it will export if it has surplus stocks or production capacity. When selling to countries with a similar culture to that of the United Kingdom (for example Ireland, Canada, Australia, New Zealand and the USA) there will be few problems because of similarities in culture and language.

Some companies adapt their products to promote sales in particular countries ('we make what we can sell') and engage in market segmentation. Instead of simply attempting to sell domestic product overseas, attempts are made to adapt products in terms of design, function and size.

Where a company is committed to continuous, rather than ad hoc, overseas sales and takes on the notion of international marketing activity as being central to its existence then it can be regarded more truly as an international marketing company (ecological approach).

The notion of the three strategies mentioned above was first put forward by Thorelli and Becker (1980). International marketing decision making must consider the organisation's resources and its corporate objectives, and if the company is seriously to consider the international marketing route (the ecological approach) then it should have the backing of the board of directors and active support from top strategic level management.

||||| Vignette 14.2

McDonald's, the fast food chain, uses a global franchising network to achieve its business success.

McDonald's, the fast food chain, is an excellent example of the international application of the principles of business format franchising. With business format franchising the owner of the business idea, the franchisor, puts a complete business package together, which is then sold to the individual owner of the business, the franchisee. The system operates on a 'on your own but not alone' principle. Motivated people can get started in business using, in the case of McDonald's, an internationally known corporate brand name. McDonald's has always been a franchising company and has relied on its franchisees to play a major role in its success. Franchisees are owner-managers and tend to be more motivated than regular employees. Also, by selecting local entrepreneurs in different countries around the world, McDonald's can capitalise on the local knowledge of their franchisees. Many people think a 'hamburger is a hamburger' wherever you may be in the world. In fact there is considerable variation in the product offering. In Canada the burgers are far bigger than they are in the UK. In India and Pakistan the firm offers a range of vegetable-based burgers to the Hindu community and a range of Halal-based meat products to the Moslem community. In Israel the burgers are 'kosher'. In France customers can obtain alcohol with their meal and a range of salads are available for starters. Whereas the basic concept of burger-based fast food is the same wherever McDonald's operate in the world, the firm has taken a lot of care to ensure that the original USA-based fast food concept is acceptable to the tastes and religious sensitivities of local populations. Local entrepreneurs understand the local tastes and customs. In fact McDonald's achieves its own business objectives through its network of carefully selected franchisees.

McDonald's remains committed to franchising as a predominant way of doing business although it does have some corporate owned outlets as well as franchised outlets. Approximately 70 per cent of McDonald's worldwide restaurant businesses are owned and operated by independent businessmen and women. A recognised premier franchising company, McDonald's continues to be respected around the world.

▶ Price

Price considerations

Whether the company pursues a strategy of differentiated, undifferentiated or concentrated marketing in relation to its chosen market segments will depend upon the price levels to be charged overseas. Considerations relating to chosen market segments will affect decisions as to whether to adopt a skimming or penetration approach. The method of pricing international sales will largely depend upon how important overseas price will be in the overall marketing mix.

Extra factors in terms of costs to be considered include tariffs and logistics. In addition, there is the added uncertainty of extending credit for goods supplied to an overseas customer whom the company may not know well. However, this need not be a problem, as part of the sales agreement can include payment through a letter of credit or an irrevocable letter of credit, which means that the buyer's and the seller's banks exchange agreed funds at a certain point in the export delivery cycle.

Consideration should be given to the currency in which payment will be made. Most export orders arrangements stipulate 'hard' currency payments in US dollars or pounds sterling. However, there are circumstances in which an order can only be obtained if payment is made in the local currency. Consideration should then be given to the strength of the currency and the fact that it might devalue by the time the contract is paid. Occasionally, for exports to less developed countries, the government of that country might insist on some kind of barter deal, whereby in return for a company's products, some other products of that country must be taken as payment, thus saving the country foreign exchange. There is also the probability that, in order to be competitive, margins on products destined for overseas markets will carry less profit than those manufactured for home consumption. Such added costs and potential uncertainties are the reason why some manufacturers prefer to remain with the domestic market rather than becoming involved internationally. In some situations, companies are content simply to break even on international business simply to achieve higher sales volumes.

Price quotations

At a practical level, price has to take into account the extra costs of packing and freight charges. Quotations in export markets often include freight charges rather than being simply ex-factory cost. The principal quotations used are:

- *Ex-works* means that the purchaser bears all costs of packing, freightage and insurance, plus other liabilities like import duties after the goods have left the supplier's factory.
- *Free alongside ship* (FAS) means that the exporter is responsible for transporting the goods to the point where they are being loaded onto the ship.
- *Free on board* (FOB) extends the responsibility to the exporter until the goods have been loaded on the ship. The ship's master will then give the goods a 'clean bill of lading' which means that they have been accepted as being in good condition for the sea journey. If the goods are not received in good condition by the ship's master a 'foul bill of lading' will be issued which is not to say that the goods are damaged, but that the way they are packed might be not sturdy enough to stand the sea journey, in which case any subsequent insurance claims might pose problems. Assuming a clean bill of lading, from that point the importer pays the costs of carriage insurance and freight.
- *Cost insurance and freight* (CIF) means that as well as placing the goods on board the ship the exporter is also responsible for the freight to the end port destination plus any freight insurance charges. A variation of this quotation is 'cost and freight' (C&F) which is similar, but the importer pays the insurance premium.
- *Free delivered* or 'franco rendu' as it is sometimes termed means that the exporter has responsibility for all costs of freightage to the customer's premises which includes payment of any import duties, obtaining import licences where appropriate plus all other administrative details right up to organising foreign exchange where necessary. Clearly, this option is the most complicated one for the seller and the least complicated one for the buyer. However, companies that engage in regular international marketing have departments specifically established to deal with these kinds of transactions so the transaction is routinely dealt with.

Activity

The types of quotation that have been considered range from simple to complicated on the part of the supplying company. Which price quotation will best suit a small supplier and which would suit a large supplier?

- Small supplier – ex works or perhaps FOB
- Large supplier – any, but certainly a complex quotation like free delivered should not pose a problem

Transfer pricing

There is a consideration relating to international pricing decisions that is of benefit to multinational and international companies with overseas manufacturing or assembly bases. This is the subject of transfer pricing which is applicable to companies transferring components and finished products between their plants in different manufacturing countries.

The basis of transfer pricing is that prices of components and finished products moving between manufacturing or assembly locations can be manipulated to minimise import duties or corporation tax to the benefit of the enterprise as a whole. It works as follows:

▷ Component parts or completed products can be transferred into a high-duty country in which the company has a manufacturing/assembly base at an artificially low transfer price to minimise duties payable
▷ Components or finished products can be transferred into high corporation tax countries at high transfer prices so that profits in this country are minimised
▷ Components or finished products can be transferred at high prices into a country from which dividend repatriation is restricted or subject to additional government taxes.

It is more complicated than it seems and there are more possibilities in this respect. For example, in countries with high inflation rates where devaluation of the currency is feared, it is possible, through transfer pricing, to avoid the accumulation of funds in that country, and thus largely avoid the effects of devaluation. The corollary is that national governments are interested in the possible abuse of such arrangements. Naturally, the government of the exporting country will want to see that the transfer price is not artificially low, and will endeavour to see that appropriate profits are made and fair levels of taxes are paid. In the importing country, the government will want to see that goods are not being transferred at unreasonably high prices, which will reduce local profits and corporation tax liability. At the same time customs and excise might well investigate to enquire whether artificially low transfer prices might be seen as an attempt to minimise duty liabilities.

▶ Promotion

The company has a number of courses open to it in terms of promoting itself internationally, including forms of representation, media advertising, point-of-sale (POS) promotion, trade exhibitions, trade fairs, brochures and direct mail. The availability and quality of media are important considerations, as are factors such as foreign language considerations for translations of promotional literature. Promotion as an element of the marketing mix involves selling, and in an international marketing context the main concern is the type of representation that will be adopted. Selling takes on a wider remit than it does in a domestic marketing situation. It includes the type of distribution to be employed because, in most situations, the seller plays a critical part in the distribution and often the stocking of goods. This aspect is considered in more detail later.

An important aspect of international promotion is the policy that will be adopted in relation to standardisation. Keegan (1993) put forward five strategies for international marketing in terms of promotion and products as shown in Table 14.1.

Think of a product or service that best fits each of the strategies listed in Table 14.1.

1. Famous brands of cola (termed **straight extension**)
2. Famous brands of petrol using an international logo and advertising theme, but adapting the product to suit different climatic conditions (termed **product adaptation**)
3. Bicycles – leisure promotion in Western countries and means of transportation promotion in less developed countries (termed **communications adaptation**)
4. Clothing – different clothing to suit different tastes and different promotion to reflect fashion in certain countries and functionality in others (termed **dual adaptation**)
5. In some countries **product invention** might be necessary to meet customer needs at affordable prices. Keegan cites an example of a hand-cranked manual washing machine for subsistence level countries

---

Table 14.1 Five strategies for international marketing

Strategy	Promotion	Product
1	Same	Same
2	Same	Different
3	Different	Same
4	Different	Different
5	Invention	

Source: Adapted from Keegan (1993)

▶ Place (or distribution)

This is probably the most critical decision for the international marketer and the principal choice is between direct representation from the company or through some kind of commission agent or distributor. If the decision is to use direct representation from the company, then this can be expensive in terms of costs and expenses, especially if the representative is required to live permanently in the overseas country. There is the problem of culture and in some countries it would not be possible for a 'foreigner' to conclude negotiations single-handedly, as some kind of local intermediary would be required. Many local companies offer their services as commission agents working simply on commission for the goods they sell, leaving commercial transactions to the supplying company and the customers they sell to. At the other extreme there are distributors who purchase and stock products and then resell them in the overseas market as well as providing service facilities.

This aspect of international marketing is an important part of the organisation's representational and selling arrangements and is considered next under the heading Sales channels.

Place has logistics implications and the process is more complicated than for domestic sales. Goods must be packed for seafreight if they are bulky and cannot be transported in containers. Containerisation has made the task of international trade easier and cheaper, because an individual company's goods can often go in a container that is shared with other companies exporting to the same destination. The shipping company or shipping agent organises logistics, so it is not a question of the company having to locate another company to share a container load. Airfreight is a possibility and packing costs are much cheaper as it does not have to be at a standard to withstand a lengthy sea journey. Freight insurance charges by air are also cheaper as there is less likelihood of damage than with sea transport. Airfreight is still more expensive than sea, but it is a rapidly growing international transport medium that is particularly suited to perishable goods and goods that have a high value in relation to their weight as it means that they can be in the hands of the customer in a matter of days rather than weeks by sea freight.

▶▶ Sales channels

Before a company establishes marketing arrangements in an overseas country it should research appropriate distribution possibilities and export marketing research should suggest the best distribution arrangement among the following alternatives.

▶ Direct exporting

The company that chooses this route rather than marketing through a distributor has a number of choices:

▶ Setting up an *overseas branch* or *subsidiary company* has the advantage of offering fewest organisational changes, allowing management to think in more global terms of its responsibilities and commitments and giving it more control over its selling and marketing efforts. The downside is the high cost and greater risk, plus the fact that in such circumstances the physical distance between the overseas branch and head office is greater and this might lead to opportunities for misunderstanding and misinterpretation of policies put forward by head office as well as a feeling of isolation that can lead to motivational problems.

▶ A *joint venture* can take the form of an overseas arrangement with an indigenous firm. In some markets this is the only way in which the exporting company can legitimately do business. In other instances two or more companies with complementary products or services might form a joint venture to collectively enter an overseas market. This is of particular advantage to small manufacturers who can defray some of the costs of performing such a venture on their own. In the case of a joint venture with a local company, entry to the overseas market is often made easier because of their knowledge of trading and ways of doing business in that marketplace. It can be particularly attractive when the manufacturer sees such a partner as becoming an assembler or stockholder, who might be more committed to the success of the venture than say a distributor who distributes other manufacturers' products as well as those of the exporting company. Against this is the possibility that the partner to the joint venture might eventually become a competitor and also the possibility of friction between the parties in relation to matters of financing, profit sharing and control.

▶ Licensing

A company may negotiate a licence for a foreign company to produce and market its products overseas or simply market the goods. Alternatively, the company might grant a franchise to an overseas company that involves granting rights to sell certain goods or services in defined markets using methods agreed by the supplier. The advantage of licensing is that it is a low risk option with low investment costs and speedy entry to the overseas market. The disadvantages lie in the fact that it will be less profitable in the long term than direct exporting and the company's international reputation may suffer if the licensee produces inferior products. Also, legal aspects for such arrangements are often complex, lengthy and costly.

▶ Use of intermediaries

A number of possibilities exist for this kind of arrangement and it is the means through which the majority of trade by small and medium-sized companies is done:

▸ *Export houses* are export merchants based in the home country who buy goods from the home producer and sell to their clients overseas. In this type of arrangement risks are reduced, but there is no control over exports.

▸ *Confirming houses* are similar to export houses, but they act on behalf of overseas buyers of goods, finding sources of supply in return for a commission from the buyer.

▸ *Buying offices* are used by some large overseas companies and their function is to arrange initial contacts between overseas companies and prospective suppliers. They will then arrange any contract that might result to its completion as far as export documentation and final settlement if necessary.

▸ *Agents* are a popular type of intermediary in international marketing. A commission agent acts on behalf of a principal (the exporting company). The agent secures orders, and receives an agreed percentage commission on these orders. How far the agent becomes involved in the distribution of goods depends upon the agency agreement. In some cases the agent receives goods directly and forwards these to customers, but sometimes the agent's responsibility ends when the contract has been agreed. In other instances the agent might be on an agreed retainer as well as a percentage commission on orders obtained. In the event of this latter arrangement, it is probable that the agent might be an exclusive agent acting only for the principal's organisation in relation to particular goods or services. Agents often carry complementary lines and occasionally competing lines from other manufacturers. In such circumstances there might be a danger of competing lines, and not the principal's lines, being 'pushed' in the marketplace. Agents are a convenient way of doing business at relatively low cost through an intermediary who knows the local market and local conditions of trading. However, the principal loses control in terms of how goods are marketed. If the agent is carrying other complementary lines then the commitment to market the principal's product lines will not be as urgent as would be the case if only the principal's products were being represented.

▶ *Distributors* represent the most complicated end of a continuum that starts with the simple commission agent. They purchase goods from the manufacturer and market them, in some cases carrying out functions such as packaging and producing promotional material plus follow-up duties such as provision of service facilities and ensuring spare parts availability. The main disadvantage for the principal is lack of control in how the product is being marketed. Such arrangements are likely to be done on tighter profit margins, as the distributor does far more than an agent would do in terms of providing payment when the goods are received (if this forms part of the contract) and then carrying out additional warehousing and service functions. However, the right distribution arrangement in one country might mean that the manufacturer will have more time and resources to concentrate on other world markets.

▌▌▌ Vignette 14.3

BlueSky International Marketing Inc. provides comparative Internet use research between the USA and Europe.

Two entrepreneurs from the USA, Suzan Nolan and Walter Bazar co-founded BlueSky International Marketing, Inc. in early 1997. This was after more than a year of acting as

Internet marketing consultants to major European firms. The company has grown rapidly and has offices in the USA and Paris, France. The founders' extensive experience as advisors to large firms and their appreciation of the Internet as the first truly cross-border medium led them to identify a need for Internet market research, facts and market information that was comparable across international frontiers. Internet focused and international in outlook and focus from the beginning, BlueSky™ started by comparing European Internet users and activities to those in the USA. Other countries and regions were added as BlueSky directed clients into new markets. The founders have covered Internet marketing advances in the USA since 1994, both Europe and USA since 1996, focused on the financial services sector, an area in which the company specialises, in Europe and USA since 1997 and in South America and Asia-Pacific since 1998. This extensive online experience together with years of general international marketing experience gives the BlueSky staff the knowledge and means to succeed in this consultancy area. BlueSky's mission is to help clients leverage their Internet and international and/or marketing know-how by providing comparable facts and insight into international markets so they can reach their business objectives more rapidly and cost-effectively as they expand into new markets. The firm's objective is to assist clients in understanding what is the same and what is different between countries and regions and what matters in the international Internet market.

▶▶ Cultural and environment factors

- *Language* should be considered from the viewpoint of both the written and spoken language in terms of sales literature and sales presentation. There might also be a language hierarchy as in some countries it is not expected that translations will be made from English (the major international language) into the local language.
- *Attitudes and values* may be different in some countries in relation to matters like timekeeping in respect of appointments. In some societies it is deemed discourteous to be late for an appointment, yet in other cultures lateness is the norm. In some societies there is a strong feeling of kinship between members of the population and particularly towards an individual's family, whereas in some cases it is disrespectful to question the word of the head of the family.
- *Religion* is an important consideration in terms of the observance of matters such as prayer times, religious rituals, sacred objects, taboos and religious holidays.
- *Aesthetic considerations* cover matters such as what is good taste and design criteria such as colours, shapes and even brand name considerations. Some international brand names have unfortunate translations in other languages.
- *Standard of Education* in a country is important as levels of understanding and literacy must be considered when compiling instructions for use with complicated products.

> *Law and politics* should be considered particularly in the light of potential disputes in relation to the products being supplied. Does the home country's law take precedence over the supplier country's law, or does international law apply? Here, consideration must be given to drawing up a clear contract of sale.

> *Internal organisation* within the country is important in terms of its commercial infrastructure that can range from the way business is conducted to the state of roads and the transport system.

SELF-CHECK

Explain the difference between multinational marketing and international marketing.

Multinational marketing refers to organisations whose manufacturing and business activities are scattered throughout the world and which tend to function autonomously from their areas of operation. International marketing describes companies who have made a strategic decision to enter foreign markets and they adapt marketing mixes to suit the marketplace in their chosen areas of operation.

What is the theory of comparative advantage?

Each country should specialise in the production of those goods it can most efficiently provide that should encourage unrestricted trade, international specialisation and increased global efficiency.

Name six member states of the EU.

Any six from Belgium, Germany, Luxembourg, Ireland, Greece, Spain, Portugal, Sweden, United Kingdom, France, Netherlands, Italy, Denmark, Finland or Austria.

What is NAFTA?

North American Free Trade Association.

Give four reasons for trading internationally.

Because the home market is saturated; because top management has made a policy decision to enter international markets; to enjoy better corporate tax advantages offered in an overseas country; to obtain economies of larger scale operations.

Which UK organisation is the main provider of assistance to exporters?

The British Overseas Trade Board (BOTB) – a subdivision of the Department of Trade and Industry.

Cite the classification system used to denote the stages of development that countries have reached.

Undeveloped countries (subsistence economies); less developed countries; developing countries (newly industrialising countries or NICs); developed countries; affluent countries.

What are the three different product policies that a company might adopt in relation to its overseas activities?

Standardisation – 'we sell what we make'; adaptation – 'we make what we can sell'; ecological approach.

Name four different price quotations in relation to different responsibility levels for delivery.

Any four from free alongside ship (FAS); cost insurance and freight (CIF); ex-works; free on board (FOB); cost and freight (C&F); free delivered.

What is transfer pricing?

Where prices of components and finished goods can be manipulated between manufacturing/assembly plants in different countries to take advantage of different customs and excise duty or corporation tax rates in different countries.

Explain Keegan's five strategies for international marketing.

Permutations of 'same' and 'different' against 'promotion' and 'product' give four and the fifth is 'invention'.

Which form of international transport offers the most economical rate for the insurance of goods being transported – air or sea freight?

Airfreight.

Overall, which form of transport is cheapest – air or sea?

Generally sea, but in the case of high value/low weight goods the cheapest might be air because the goods will be in the hands of the importer much quicker resulting in quicker payment which can be used to fund more export work more quickly.

Name two options that a company has available to it when engaging in direct exporting.

An overseas branch/subsidiary company; a joint venture.

What is licensing?

Where a company negotiates to licence an overseas company to produce and/or market goods.

Name three methods of exporting through the use of intermediaries.

List any three from confirming houses; buying offices; export houses; agents; distributors.

Cite four factors that should be considered under 'cultural factors' when marketing internationally.

List any four factors from attitudes and values; law and politics; language; religion; education; aesthetic considerations.

▶▶ Summary

International marketing is a broad subject and many textbooks are devoted solely to this subject. In this chapter we have considered its importance to a country and to individual companies. We have examined the broader aspects of international trade in terms of difficulties encountered when trading internationally, including how countries are structured in terms of their economic development and some of the world's trading blocs. Practical problems have been considered from a company's standpoint and in this respect each of the elements of the marketing mix has been considered in the context of how it should be manipulated when marketing internationally.

FURTHER READING

Armstrong G. and Kotler P. (2000) *Marketing: An Introduction* (5th edn), Chapter 15, 'The Global Market Place', Prentice Hall, Englewood Cliffs, NJ.

Blythe J. (2001) *Essentials of Marketing*, Chapter 11, 'International Marketing', (Pearson Education, London.

Davies M. (1998) *Understanding Marketing*, Chapter 11, 'International Marketing', Prentice Hall, London.

Keegan W.J. and Green M.S. (2000) Global Marketing (2nd edn), Chapter 1, 'Introduction to Global Marketing', Prentice Hall, London.

Lancaster G.A. and Reynolds P.L. (1999) *Introduction to Marketing: A Step-by-Step Guide to All The Tools of Marketing*, Chapter 14, 'Macro Issues in Marketing', Kogan Page, London.
Plamer A. (2000) *Principles of Marketing*, Chapter 23, 'Global Marketing: Underlying Principles' and Chapter 14, 'Pricing: Applications', OUP, Oxford.

▶▶ References

Cateora P.R. and Ghauri P.N. (2000) *International Marketing: European Edition*, Chapter 9, 'Emerging Markets and Market Behaviour', McGraw-Hill, Maidenhead, pp. 173–201.
Keegan W.J. (1993) *Global Marketing Management*, Prentice Hall, Englewood Cliffs, NJ.
Kotler P. (1997) *Marketing Management, Analysis, Planning, Implementation and Control* (9th edn), Prentice Hall, Englewood Cliffs, NJ, p. 405.
Thorelli H.B. and Becker H. (eds) (1980) *International Marketing Strategy*, Pergamon, London.

15

MARKETING PLANNING

▶▶ Marketing planning in the context of corporate planning

Corporate, or strategic company planning, comprises the following sequential steps:

▶ *Company mission statement* has an influence on all planning throughout the organisation, for it is a statement of the company's overall business philosophy. It is normally a set of guidelines, rather than something that is stated in quantitative terms.

▶ *Situational analysis* means evaluating external and internal factors that affect the planning process and asks the question 'Where are we now?' This means researching and analysing all information that might have a bearing on the organisation and its operations, from internal factors such as individual departmental company resources, to external factors such as current political events that might impinge on company activities.

▶ *Set organisational objectives* requires that company management puts forward guidance as to how the company should fulfil its mission and this clarifies where the company wants to be. Unlike the mission statement, this should be expressed in achievable quantitative terms.

▶ *Choose strategies to achieve these objectives* are concrete ideas that set about achieving company objectives and relate to how the mission will be accomplished.

It is from this latter point that we can plan strategically and tactically for marketing, as can other major divisions of the organisation including: finance, production, human resource management and distribution. The function that brings these planning operations together is corporate planning, and it is the person entrusted with corporate planning who ensures that departmental plans are in harmony with other each other and that they all work towards achieving overall organisational objectives.

Think up an appropriate mission statement for an organisation.

Pepsi Cola's mission statement, for example, is: to be an outstanding company by exceeding customer expectations through empowering people guided by shared values.

In forward-thinking organisations it is the chief executive who is responsible for corporate planning, and strategic planning is at the core of managerial activity and drives the organisation.

It is often the case that as strategic planning concerns the long-term future it can be put to one side in the interests of dealing with everyday tactical matters. This being so, in larger organisations, corporate planning is often set up as a separate function reporting directly to top management, with the remit of bringing together and synergising individual departmental plans into the final corporate plan. It is placed directly under top management in what is called a 'staff' relationship, but it is not a 'line' relationship, that is, in the line of command of the company from the board of directors downwards (for example it is not alongside marketing management in terms of the hierarchical structure).

Figure 15.1 provides a practical idea of how the corporate planning process works in practice.

Figure 15.2 shows how top management formulate general strategic plans which then progress to more practical levels as they are implemented.

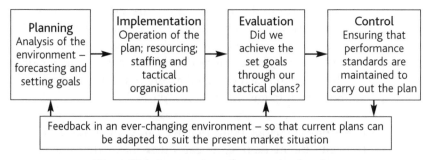

Figure 15.1 An overview of corporate planning

Figure 15.2 Planning hierarchy

At top management levels, these plans for the longer term can be anything from one year to five or ten or even more years, depending upon the planning horizons in the particular industry. It is at this level also that strategic business units (SBUs) are created with a view to carrying out the general plans decided upon by top management. An SBU is a group or unit within an organisation that comprises separately identified products or market divisions with a specific market focus. An SBU manager has responsibility for integrating all of that SBU's functions into a marketing programme so it can then be measured in terms of its success at the end of an accounting period.

Plans become more practical and shorter term in nature as they are translated into tactical action plans further down the organisational hierarchy. Planning horizons at a functional level tend to be for one year, and throughout that year plans are spelt out on a periodic basis – usually on a month by month or quarter by quarter basis. Figure 15.2 shows how marketing plans stem from the more general corporate level and move down the planning hierarchy to sales and advertising where they become more tangible.

 Vignette 15.1

Volkswagen plans to place its portfolio of car brands into two strategic groups.

Volkswagen is Europe's largest car manufacturer and a major brand within the global motor car industry. For some time the company has been troubled by its existing branding strategy. The strategy lacks any real rationale and has come about through accident rather than through logical planning. Over the years Volkswagen has expanded by acquisition but the car brands brought on board through this strategy have never been convincingly placed into workable strategic business units. Many of the brands are in fact competing with one another and share similar features in the eyes of potential customers. The car giant has decided to address this problem and is planning to place all its car brands into one or other of two strategic groups. The company's seven car brands will be placed into two new groups, oriented around the VW and Audi marques. Management have agreed that the Lamborghini and Seat brands from the firm's Italian and Spanish subsidiary companies respectively, will be placed into a new 'sports oriented' division based around the Audi marque. The other group based on the VW marque will be more traditional in its orientation and will include Skoda, Bugatti and Bentley. Basically the company is trying to reduce internal competition between brands. Volkswagen shares several basic chassis platforms between different brands but is trying to avoid too much duplication and similarities between brands in the future. Industry experts welcome the reorganisation, which they see as leading to a much more logical and cohesive branding strategy.

▶▶ An overview of marketing planning

Strategic marketing planning is the application of a number of logical steps in the planning process. There is no single formula that must always be applied as such a model would not suit all marketing planning situations. Most textbooks cite slightly different models that are a variation on the same theme. Kotler's (1997) definition is:

> The managerial process of developing and maintaining a viable fit between the organisation's objectives, skills, and resources and its changing market opportunities. The aim of strategic planning is to shape and reshape the company's businesses and products so that they yield target profits and growth. (p. 63)

Figure 15.3 is a relatively comprehensive model that gives an overview of the strategic and tactical marketing planning process. The early part shows how marketing planning fits into the corporate framework and then more detailed activities take place resulting in a practical marketing plan.

▶ Situational analysis

This stage, relating to an analysis of the current situation, has two inputs. The first input relates to the organisation's macroenvironment and are factors over which the company has little or no control. They are listed under four separate headings – political, economic, sociocultural and technological – and are known by the acronym PEST. Some marketing planners also include 'legal' (the acronym then being SLEPT) and some add 'competition' if it is felt to be a specific issue that should be considered separately. This is the external audit part of what is called the company audit. From this external audit a number of very short state-

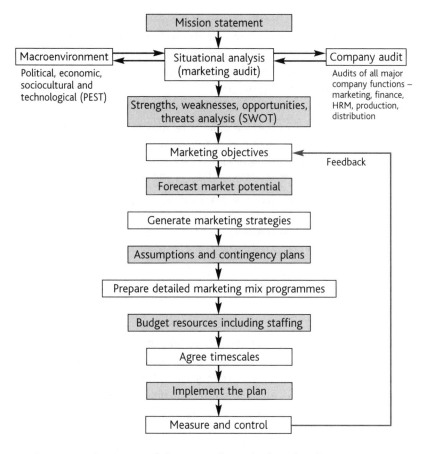

Figure 15.3 Summary of the strategic marketing planning process

ments are made in respect of each of the PEST + C + L subdivisions. Recently, another E has been added to the equation (minus the C) standing for 'environmental' and making the acronym PESTLE, and more recently still, yet another E has been added for 'ecological' making the acronym STEEPLE. However, it is now questioned whether this degree of subdivision is really necessary as the original PEST contains all the necessary subdivisions of the external audit. Statements under each of the subheadings need not be justified, as they are observations that help formulate more detailed plans at a later stage.

The next part of the situational analysis concerns what is called the company audit or, in corporate planning terms, the internal audit. This looks at the individual capabilities of the company, SBU by SBU, and department by department. Again, short statements or observations are made that do not have to be justified. These two actions – both at an external and internal level – are what are called the corporate audit process and form the situational analysis. Marketing's part of this total corporate auditing procedure is termed the 'marketing audit' and it is included here as part of marketing planning because it is the beginning of the marketing planning process.

Think of the kind of areas relating to marketing to be considered as part of the marketing audit process under 'situation analysis procedure' concerning both macroenvironmental factors and company specific factors.

Economic factors such as inflation, unemployment levels and taxation. Sociocultural factors such as eduction, environment and consumer life-styles. At a company level, factors such as reviewing marketing activity like pricing and discounts and the range and quality of products or services that the company markets.

❱ SWOT analysis

SWOT analysis (strengths, weaknesses, opportunities, and threats) is an attempt to translate company specific factors from the company audit into company strengths and weaknesses plus external environmental factors (from the PEST analysis) into external opportunities and threats. As was the case with the PEST analysis, no attempt should be made to justify points being placed in each of the categories as they are meant as mere statements to assist marketing planning at later stages.

SWOT analysis is usually presented as a four box matrix with internal strengths and weaknesses being listed in the top two boxes and external opportunities and threats being listed in the lower two boxes. Experience has shown that for most companies, whether they be large or small, the number of strengths and weaknesses is around 10–15 each and the number of opportunities and threats is about 5–12 each. Anything less normally indicates that the SWOT is not complete and any more indicates that a number of points are being repeated in a different form of words.

Vignette 15.2

Cable & Wireless finds strength in technological expertise and plenty of cash.

Cable & Wireless is a large global telecommunications organisation, with expertise in the provision of high-performance global Internet protocol (IP) and data services to business customers. Communications over the Internet make larger firms faster and enable smaller businesses to operate globally and compete with larger enterprises. The Internet can make firms more efficient by lowering costs, cutting response times, opening new channels of distribution to market and offering new ways of doing business to customers and suppliers. Cable & Wireless is committed to maximising business performance and minimising costs for its customers through the provision of fast, secure and reliable communications solutions, in any form, anywhere in the world. One of Cable & Wireless' main competitive advantages lies in its strong presence in the key business markets around the world – Europe, Japan and the United States. The firm is also very strong from a financial base point of view. So strong in fact that it has decided to return approximately £1.75 billion of its £4.7 billion cash pile back to shareholders in the form of a special dividend and a buy back of 15% of its shares, thereby strengthening the remaining share price. The strength of the firm's balance sheet is a real competitive advantage in these economically uncertain times. It allows the firm to invest for the future without the need for borrowing. The firm is capitalising on this and focusing its growth strategy on the services that are in increasing demand from the business community – data and Internet Protocol (IP) based services. Over the past year, Cable & Wireless has reinforced its strong position in these markets by acquiring 100 per cent control of its operations in North America, the United Kingdom, Europe and Japan. This has enabled Cable & Wireless to integrate its activities across these regions. To implement its global strategy in these regions, the firm is investing $500 million to develop global IP products and $3.5 billion to build the most advanced, single-hop architecture infrastructure in the world.

▶ Marketing objectives

Objectives are concerned with what is to be achieved, unlike strategies which are the means of achieving objectives. These objectives are obtained from corporate level strategies and such objectives should be very specific. An acronym used in this context is that marketing objectives should be SMART, standing for, specific; measurable; achievable; realistic and time constrained. An objective must have some kind of measurable characteristic that might relate to a standard of performance such as a percentage level of profit or a situation that has to be achieved such as penetrating a specific market.

Think of a marketing objective for a service organisation of your choice.

A large insurance company might decide to enter the annuities market and achieve a 5 per cent share of this market by the end of the year.

▶ Forecast market potential

This is a stage that many marketing planning texts seem to forget. This is illogical, for without a forecast of market potential a company does not know for what it should be making its plans. As was shown in Chapter 5, medium- and long-term forecasting are at the very basis of all company planning.

▶ Generate marketing strategies

Strategies are the means through which marketing objectives can be achieved. They are meant to detail selected approaches that the company will use to achieve its objectives. Determining strategies leads to a series of action statements that are clear sets of steps to be followed to achieve objectives. Operational decisions then come from these marketing strategies and form the tactical foundations of the detailed marketing mix programmes.

▶ Assumptions and contingency plans

Assumptions relate to external factors over which the company has little control. These should be stated as a series of points that relate to, and which preface, the make-up of the detailed marketing mix plans in the next stage. Assumptions should be as few as possible and if they are not needed then they should not be introduced. For each assumption a directional contingency plan should be formulated so, in the case of an assumption being wrong in practice, an appropriate contingency plan can be brought in. At this stage, contingency plans should not be detailed. They will probably only consist of a sentence or two that are merely directional plans to be implemented if assumptions are incorrect in practice.

▶ Detailed marketing mix programme

This enables the organisation to satisfy the needs of its target markets and achieve its marketing objectives. It is what comprises the greater part of an organisation's marketing efforts. The first part of the programme is to determine the marketing mix where detailed consideration is given to each of the areas of the four Ps plus segmentation, targeting and positioning considerations. The ingredients of the marketing mix should be combined in an optimum way so that they work together to achieve company objectives. This part of the plan is concerned with who will do what and how it will be done. In this way responsibility, accountability and action over a specific time period can be planned, scheduled, implemented and reviewed.

As this is an action plan, the time period must be realistic. Most plans are for a period of one year which is the conventional medium-term planning period. A plan must contain timescales detailing marketing activities normally on a month-by-month or quarterly basis.

This is not to say that marketing planning should not be for longer than one year as long-term issues are also addressed in a more general long-range marketing plan. Long term has different meanings for different industries. In the case of modern electronics long term is probably not longer than three years, whereas in steel production long term can mean 10 years or more.

When long-term planning is addressed as part of a marketing plan, then all that can be realistically considered is a directional marketing plan, because to plan in terms of month-by-month expectations for, say, five years hence would cause the plan to be viewed as being spuriously unrealistic. If reality proved the plan to be hopelessly incorrect, confidence might well be lost in the usefulness of the planning process. Many companies, however, have rolling plans that are modified in the light of what actually happens. As one planning period finishes (one month, one quarter, one year) the rolling plan is modified in the light of what has happened, and a further planning period is added onto the end of the plan.

What criteria do you think should be considered in relation to 'products' when designing a detailed marketing mix programme?

Quality; features; style and design; services and warranty; packaging; range of products in terms of width and depth; new product development.

Strategic planning tools such as the matrices discussed in Chapter 7 are also appropriate to use for planning analysis purposes.

Consider what planning tools relating to products might be appropriate in this context?

BCG matrix; GE matrix; Shell directional policy matrix; Ansoff's matrix.

An important area of marketing planning is that of attaining sales revenues that have been forecast as part of the planning process. Put in practical terms, the sales forecast has predicted the amount of sales that are possible, and budgeting determines the expenditure available towards achieving this forecast. It does not follow that forecast sales will be achieved in practice. Individual members of the field sales force will each have been given sales targets or quotas and the summation of these should equate to the budgeted sales target for the marketing plan. This is why some salespersons refer to their sales target or quota as their sales budget. This is not an expenditure limit as the 'budget' description might infer, but it is the amount each must sell in order to satisfy the sales volume requirements of the marketing plan.

We have only considered product in these activities, so similar considerations need to be made in relation to other elements of the marketing mix. Indeed, this part of the marketing plan is the largest section, and in many cases this section, plus its various marketing mix subsections, is bigger than the rest of the plan put together.

▶ Budget resources and staffing

Now that detailed decisions have been made in relation to different elements of the marketing mix, the next stage of the programme is to budget. Organisations have many demands on limited resources, and this final balancing act is the responsibility of corporate planning. Budgeting covers not only general marketing expenditure, but also salaries and expenses. If the plan calls for an increase in sales and market share, then this normally has resource implications for the marketing department, perhaps in terms of greater representation or increased advertising costs.

It is at this budgeting stage that plans are sometimes modified in the light of reality, and the initial marketing objectives might well have to be modified. Practical financial considerations could cause the organisation to downgrade its original marketing objectives.

▐▐▐ Vignette 15.3

C&N Touristic changes to Thomas Cook to reflect the pan-European nature of the group.

C&N Touristic, the German leisure group, has doubled in size over the past two years through a policy of acquisition, most notably the UK Thomas Cook Holdings Ltd. The group is jointly owned by Lufthansa, the airline, and Karstadt Quelle, the retail group. In view of the pan-European orientation of the group, C&N Touristic AG was renamed Thomas Cook AG at the end of June 2001. In addition, the Thomas Cook brand has since been used worldwide also in the travel agency and destination management field as the name has global recognition. As a result of the acquisition of the British leisure group, Thomas Cook Holdings Ltd., London, and the French travel group Havas Voyages, Paris, Thomas Cook AG has become the second largest European leisure group and the third largest travel group in the world, with a revenue of DM 17 billion. The group has around 17 million customers, some 30 tour operator brands, about 4000 travel agencies world-wide, a portfolio of more than 73,000 controlled hotel beds (including approximately 12,000 beds in hotels under construction), a fleet of 85 aircraft and it did have around 30,000 staff before cutting the workforce by 10 per cent in the light of what happened on 11th September 2001. Thomas Cook AG is represented in the sales markets of Germany, Great Britain, France, Benelux, Austria, Hungary, Poland, Canada, Egypt and India. The firm is planning to expand into Cuba. It has an agreement with the Cuban government to develop hotels on the island. Cuba is an attractive holiday destination for both Europeans and Americans. The group has also acquired a majority 60 per cent stake in Thomas Cook India; it already had a 40 per cent stake. The strategy of the group is to go global and it is looking for other non-European acquisition opportunities.

▶ Timescales

This often takes the form of a Gantt chart that places time along the top and activities down the side as illustrated in Figure 15.4.

▶ Implement the plan

This means precisely what the heading says. The plan is now put into action within predetermined budget and resource parameters, and along the timescale that has been agreed. More importantly, those who will carry out the plan should be informed of its details and know the part they must play within its implementation to ensure its success. This sec-

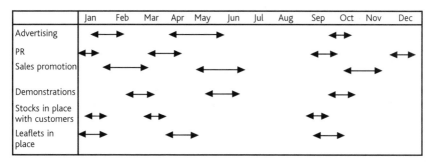

Figure 15.4 Gantt chart showing timescales in a marketing plan

tion is not addressed in the actual planning document as it is self-evident, but it is mentioned now as this is the 'doing' part of the planning process.

▶ Measure and control

A marketing plan cannot be operated without some measure to monitor, measure and control its progress. A system of controls should be established whereby the plan is reviewed on a regular and controlled basis and then updated as circumstances change. Such controls can address tactics in terms of sales analyses which will commence with a comparison of budgeted sales revenue against actual sales revenue. Variations might be due to volume or price variances, perhaps an unfavourable variance due to having to cut prices to match the tactical actions of competitors.

The marketing information system provides essential inputs to the marketing planning system as shown in Chapter 5. This information comes from market intelligence, marketing research and the organisation's own internal accounting system and inputs into the marketing plan. It is a control mechanism as well, as customer reactions are fed into this marketing information system from market intelligence through the field sales force or from marketing research. Information on sales analyses is fed into the system so assessments can be made as to whether or not forecasted sales are being achieved.

As the planning horizon unfolds, if plans do not go exactly as anticipated (they rarely do) action can be taken as required, and this is the reason behind the feedback loop in Figure 15.3. These measures of performance thus allow the planner the opportunity to adjust and fine-tune plans as necessary during the planning period.

SELF-CHECK

What are the sequential steps in the strategic corporate planning process?
Mission statement; situational analysis; set organisational objectives; choose strategies to achieve these objectives.

What are the stages in a strategic corporate planning model?
Planning; implementation; evaluation; and control.

How does the planning hierarchy work from the top downwards?
Corporate planning; functional planning; subfunctional planning.

What are the stages in a typical marketing planning framework?
Mission statement; situational analysis; SWOT; marketing objectives; forecast market potential; generate marketing strategies; assumptions and contingency plans; detailed marketing mix programmes; budget resources and staffing; agree timescales; implement the plan; measure and control the plan.

What are PEST factors?
Political; economic; sociocultural; technological.

▶▶ Summary

In a well-ordered company, managers have a duty to plan, organise, direct and control the activities of those for whom they have taken responsibility. In this chapter we have investigated the meaning and relevance of strategic and tactical marketing planning in an ordered framework of structures. This has shown that planning is a practical activity that should be approached in a professional manner as such plans give guidance not only to top management, but to those whose task it is to carry out such plans. More to the point, an ordered system of planning gives security to an organisation in terms of its vision and the image it presents to its internal employees and to the outside world.

FURTHER READING

Armstrong G. and Kotler P. (2000) *Marketing: An Introduction* (5th edn), Chapter 2, 'Strategic Planning and the Marketing Process', Prentice Hall, Englewood Cliffs, NJ.

Blythe J. (2001) *Essentials of Marketing*, Chapter 10, 'Marketing Planning, Implementation and Control', Pearson Education, London.

Davies M. (1998) *Understanding Marketing*, Chapter 2, 'Marketing Planning, the Environment and Competitive Strategy', Prentice Hall, London.

Dibb S. and Simkin L. et al. (1994) *Marketing Concepts and Strategies* (2nd European edn), Houghton Mifflin, London.

Hofer C.W. and Schendel D. (1978) *Strategy Formulation: Analytical Concepts*, West Publishing, New York.

Hussey D.E. and Langham M.J. (1979) *Corporate Planning – The Human Factor*, Pergamon Press, London.

Keegan W.J. and Green M.S. (2000) *Global Marketing* (2nd edn), Chapter 16, 'Leading, Organising and Controlling the Global Marketing Effort', Prentice Hall, London.

Lancaster G.A. and Massingham L.C. (1994) *Essentials of Marketing* (in particular, Part 5), McGraw-Hill, Maidenhead.

MacDonald M.H.B. (2002) *Marketing Plans – How to Prepare Them, How to Use Them*, (5th edn), Butterworth Heinemann, Oxford.

Plamer A. (2000) *Principles of Marketing*, Chapter 11, 'Developing a Sustainable Competitive Advantage', OUP, Oxford.

Stapleton J. (1982) *How to Prepare a Marketing Plan*, Gower, London.

Steiner G.A. (1979) *Strategic Planning (what every manager **must** know)*, Free Press, New York.

▶▶ Reference

Kotler P. (1997) *Marketing Management, Analysis, Planning, Implementation and Central* (9th edn), Prentice Hall, Englewood Cliffs, NJ, p. 63.

16

MARKETING AND THE USE OF INTERNET TECHNOLOGY

▶▶ Introduction

In this penultimate chapter we are going to be examining and discussing some of the more important developments and advances in computer-based technology that are of interest to the marketing firm. In particular we shall be examining the use of the Internet and the World Wide Web, which has formed the platform for the new e-marketing revolution. Today technology is all around us and influences every area of our lives and we have to live with it because we cannot possible escape from it. This is particularly true of computer-based technology which seems to be coming a part of everything we do from making a telephone call to writing and sending a letter. In this chapter we shall be looking at developments in marketing-related technology such as the World Wide Web, the Internet, e-commerce in general, e-marketing in particular, databases and their applications such as data mining and data fusion and the way these new developments and techniques have changed the face of marketing practice over the past ten years and are continuing to bring about change in the world of marketing practice.

The Internet (or simply the Net) is a vast and continually growing web of computer networks that links computers around the world. The World Wide Web (or simply the Web) is a development of the Internet where the accessing of information has been designed using systems that have made it relatively easy and user friendly for ordinary people to use. The term 'electronic commerce' is a general term for the buying and selling process that is supported by electronic means. Advances in technology are having a tremendous impact on all areas of business, including marketing. This chapter cannot make you an expert in the subject of electronic commerce because there has been an explosion of information on the subject, which would take many books to cover. However by reading this chapter you should nonetheless be able to appreciate the main issues involved with the use of electronic commerce in general and e-marketing specifically.

As marketing students or professionals it is important that you understand what some of these key technological advances are and how they are affecting the marketing firm and are impacting on marketing activities. After all they are impacting on your job and on your future. It is also important to have some understanding of the main trends and how the continual development of technology is likely to affect marketing firms in the future. Although the Internet has become an important communication tool, it has recently suffered a public relations crisis because of the fall in the stock value of many dot.com firms, with many experts questioning its credibility and promised ability to revolutionise the way we do business. Many people believe the importance of the Web in marketing is overexaggerated and that it is simply yet another direct marketing tool. It makes a useful contribution but is hardly revolutionary. In fact many firms are reviewing the significance of the Web for their businesses. Despite the changes in market conditions, businesses are still successfully using the Internet to increase revenue and reach a wider, sometimes even global audience. E-business has become a must for any company wanting to keep up with the competition. And one of the biggest impacts the Internet has had on business is in its role as a crucial marketing tool.

▶ Marketing in the new millennium

Human history is an unfolding story of technological innovation. Each generation develops technology which astounds the previous generation. The twentieth century saw astonishing technological developments in space travel, communications, computers and genetic engineering. However the developments of the last century were only the start and the full impact of these developments will be seen in the present century. As we enter the twenty-first century we enter a millennium of advanced technology. People living in this century are going to see staggering advances in the application and development of technology, which at present they would scarcely recognise or believe possible. The product life cycle of many products is moving ever faster as technological advances supersede existing product types and forms. Some people and firms cannot cope and are experiencing what Toffler (1981) called 'future shock' or an inability to come to terms with the future invading the present. In his book of the same name Toffler examines the effects of rapid industrial and technological changes upon the individual, the family, and society. However we must do more than cope if, as marketing professionals, we hope to capitalise on and fully exploit the tremendous business opportunities that this new technology brings. It does no good for businesses to ignore the technological revolution. Denial will get them nowhere at all. Marketing firms have to be proactive and fully embrace the new marketing technology because, even if they do not, their competitors probably will.

▶▶ Development of e-marketing

In its official definition (2003) the Chartered Institute of Marketing (CIM), the main marketing professional body in the UK, described e-marketing as '... the way in which marketers increase sales or build brand awareness via the Internet, be it over their PC, TV, mobile phone or some other mobile device'. Business in general and certainly marketing in particular has become more and more affected by, and dependent upon, technology. Furthermore, technological progress itself is altering and accelerating, for example the Internet and Web page design and content is developing all the time. Technology seems to be developing at an exponential rate, that is, at an ever-increasing rate. The rate of development increases because scientists and technologists can learn from what has happened in the past, in a sense they are 'standing on the shoulders of giants'. For example the digital computer was developed in a laboratory in Manchester University, England and since then other people have developed the basic technology to what we see today. Some experts go so far as to say that the traditional marketing model or 'paradigm' is no longer applicable in the world of the Internet and that a new model is called for. Certainly at the very least, the modern-day marketer needs to be familiar with the key advances in technology, which are at this time impacting on the marketing process. Some of these developments are discussed below.

Smaller firms in particular benefit from Internet-based business technologies as it reduces their size disadvantage. Electronic commerce has no geographic boundaries; it is just as easy to interact with consumers in New Zealand from the UK as it is to interact with consumers in the next town. Many firms, in order to both differentiate their products and reduce their costs are increasingly using computer-based technology. Just-in-time ordering and stock holding systems save firms millions in inventory and logistics costs compared with the traditional way of doing things. Computers have facilitated the use of these new systems and processes.

New technology increasingly facilitates the ease with which information, so vital to effective marketing planning and decision making, can be collected, analysed and used. Marketing information systems and the ability to tap into internal and external databases have revolutionised the planning process in marketing in terms of detail and speed. Data mining and data fusion are techniques which allow marketing research professionals to engineer information from a wide variety of sources and even create virtual consumer models from such information. Competitive success is increasingly based on the application of advances in technology. Consider mobile telephones – it is no longer enough to simply produce a product that is capable of making a telephone call. Today people want telephones that can send text messages, answer emails, play computer games and have a host of other functions such as a video capability. Advances in technology enable the marketing process to be carried out not only more effectively but also more efficiently – computer-aided questionnaire design for marketing research and the computerisation of measuring instruments for advertising research being two such examples.

The examples given above are not intended to be exhaustive but are merely indicative. However they do demonstrate that marketing management must not only be aware of, but understand, the advances in technology which are taking place, otherwise they will not be able to do their job. Some marketing firms may even contribute to these changes, for example the now defunct Napster.com pioneered the marketing of music on the Internet and many other e-marketing firms such as Music-Net which is part of AOL Time Warner (see Vignette 16.3) are likely to follow its lead in one way or another. Amazon.com leads the way in the marketing of books and compact discs on the Internet and is one of the most high-profile names in the whole of e-marketing. Napster.com and Amazon.com are two examples of how the marketing firms making use of the new technology are themselves contributing to the development of the Internet as a mainstream commercial medium. These companies are rather like Procter & Gamble Limited as they were back in the 1950s and 60s when they pioneered many of the fast-moving consumer goods marketing techniques used today particularly in the field of branding and sales promotions.

Moreover, the marketer must also be aware of, and be prepared for, future advances in technology. Marketing is all about staying ahead of the competition. This in turn means that the marketer must also have the required skills to use the new technologies of today and tomorrow to help assist the marketing process. Similarly, those organisations whose management and marketers are unaware of, or unable to, use advances in technology will become increasingly uncompetitive. The marketing manager of the future will need an understanding of the use of technology within the discipline. He or she may not need to be a technical expert, after all they can be employed, but he or she must be able to appreciate how they can factor the use of new technology into all aspects of their marketing plans and operations.

According to the Chartered Institute of Marketing's official policy (2003) there are two types of company that will use e-marketing:

1. An online company, (for example Amazon, Lastminute.com), or online arm of an offline company (Thomascook.com, WHSmith Online) which wants to encourage customers to visit their website, or a particular promotion on the website. In a sense the Internet is the firm and the only way customers interact with the company is through the Internet. The website is both transactional and informational in content.

2. An offline company (for example Vauxhall, Boots) using the Internet to build its brand message, but not necessarily to encourage online transactions (although that can be incorporated too if necessary). Such firms use the Web as another form of advertising and the website is usually just for information purposes rather than transactional.

Figure 16.1 indicates how marketing firms can have different orientations when using e-commerce. At the one extreme firms may use their Web pages for purely informational reasons. This is shown in the top

	Low	High	
Role of e-commerce in information provision	Information focus orientation	Integrated e-commerce orientation	High
	Low involvement orientation	Transaction focus orientation	Low

Role of e-commerce in supporting
the purchase transaction

Figure 16.1 E-commerce orientation matrix
Source: Based on Jobber (2001)

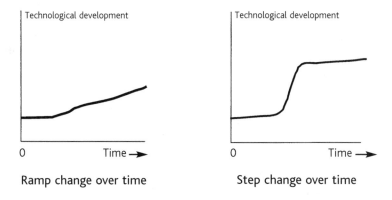

Figure 16.2 Graphs showing examples of ramp and step changes in the effects or impact of technological development

left-hand box as 'Information focus orientation'. At the other extreme firms may provide low informational content and high transactional content in their Web page. This case is shown in the bottom right-hand box as 'Transaction focus orientation'. Firms in the right-hand top box would have both high transactional content and high informational content in their Web page and are referred to as 'Integrated e-commerce orientation'. Low involvement orientation describes those firms who have not fully grasped the idea of e-commerce.

Not since the Industrial Revolution has the marketing firm been affected so much, down to the very core of its business, by changes in the technological environment. Sometimes this change is gradual, representing a ramp change or steady change in the firm's technological environment. At other times technological change is very rapid representing what can be called a step change or sharp change in the environment. This step change is what results in the 'future shock' discussed by Toffler and referenced earlier. Examples of the ramp- and step-change concepts are illustrated in Figure 16.2.

Those firms that are not fully aware of technological advances and developments will fall behind in the commercial race and will probably cease trading. There is a significant change in the technological environment of marketing firms; this is not a minor technological change but a huge step change in the way marketing firms do business. If they do not react and adapt to the new environmental factors there is a danger that they will become like the proverbial dinosaur – extinct. It is a cliché, but one that is highly applicable in today's rapidly changing technological environment.

▌▌▌ Vignette 16.1

The Alexandria Library hopes to become the largest online facility in the world.

The Alexandria Library hopes to take up where its legendary forerunner left off a millennium ago. The legendary library of Alexandria boasted that it had a copy of virtually every known manuscript in the ancient world. This bibliophile's fantasy in Egypt's largest port city vanished, probably in a fire, more than a thousand years ago. But the dream of collecting every one of the world's books has been revived in a new arena – online. The directors of the new Alexandria Library, a steel and glass structure christened with 250,000 books in October 2002, have joined forces with an American artist and software engineers in an ambitious effort to make virtually all of the world's books available at a mouse click. Much as the ancient library nurtured Archimedes and Euclid, the new Web venture also hopes to connect scholars and students around the world. Of course, many libraries already provide access to hundreds or even thousands of electronic books. But the ambitions of the Alexandria Library appear to surpass those of its rivals. Its directors hope to link with the world's other major digital archives and to make the books more accessible than ever with new software. To its supporters, the project, called the Alexandria Library Scholars Collective, could ultimately revolutionise learning in the developing countries, where libraries are often nonexistent and access to materials is hard to come by. Cheick Diarra, a former NASA engineer and the director of the African Virtual University, said he plans to begin using the Alexandria software this year at the university's 34 campuses in 17 African countries. Still, the idea faces staggering logistical, legal and technical obstacles.

▶ Permission marketing

The phrase 'permission marketing' has been coined by Internet pioneer Seth Godin (1999). The basic idea behind permission marketing is the fact that most people receive far too many commercial messages each day for the vast majority of them to have any real effect. In many cases having too many commercial messages becomes rather annoying to many people and instead of paying attention to the message people either ignore them or do something to try and avoid them. For example they may use the hand control 'zapper' to fast forward advertisements when watching a pre-recorded television programme. Godin and his colleagues are working to persuade some of the most powerful companies in the world to reinvent how they relate to their customers. His argument is as stark as it is radical (1999, p. 6): Advertising just doesn't work as well as it used to – in part because there's so much of it, in part because people have learned to ignore it, in part because the rise of the

Net means that companies can go beyond it. 'We are entering an era,' Godin declares, 'that's going to change the way almost everything is marketed to almost everybody' (1999, p. 7). If we take the standard marketing communication model then 'permission marketing' gets over the problem of the 'noise' in the system (1999, p. 132).

The communication model (Figure 16.3) introduces *encoding, decoding, channel, feedback* and *noise* elements. *Encoding* is the process of putting thought into symbolic form and is controlled by the sender. The encoding process might use music, visual art or a psychological message containing sadness, guilt and so on. Similarly, *decoding* is the process of transforming message symbols back into thought and is controlled by the receiver. Both encoding and decoding are mental processes. The message itself is the manifestation of the encoding process and is the instrument used in sharing thought with a receiver. The *channel* is the path through which the message moves from the sender to the receiver. The noise element is basically interference by a host of other marketing communications from other firms crowding the original communication out of the receiver's attention span. It is this noise element that Seth Godin's 'permission marketing' paradigm attempts to overcome. The *feedback* element recognises the two-way nature of the communications process; in reality, individuals are both senders and receivers and interact with each other continually. Feedback allows the sender of the original message to monitor how accurately the message is being received. Thus, the feedback mechanism gives the sender some measure of control in the communication process. In marketing, it is sometimes acknowledged that customers do not receive an advertising message as originally intended. Based on market feedback, the message can be re-examined and perhaps corrected.

The key feature of all the conventional, simple models of mass-media communications is that there is no interaction taking place between the sender and the receivers of the message.

The biggest problem with mass-market advertising, Godin says, is that it fights for people's attention by interrupting them, for example a

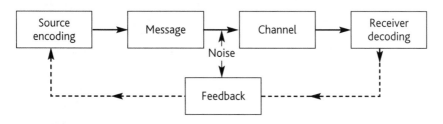

Figure 16.3 A more detailed model of the communication process

30-second advertising spot interrupts a *Coronation Street* episode or some other programme on commercial television. A telemarketing call interrupts a family dinner or may get you out of the bath or a print advertisement may interrupt an interesting magazine or newspaper article. The 'interruption model' as Seth Godin calls it, can be extremely effective when there is not an overflow of interruptions but there is often too much going on in our lives for us to enjoy being interrupted anymore. The new model, he argues, is built around permission, you only receive the marketing communication because you have asked for it and given your permission for the marketing firm to send it to you. Because of this you are much more likely to read the message and respond to it. Much of this permission type of communication is sent via the Internet. The challenge for marketers is to persuade consumers to volunteer their attention – to 'raise their hands' (one of Godin's favourite phrases) – to agree to learn more about a company and its products. 'Permission marketing turns strangers into friends and friends into loyal customers,' he says. 'It's not just about entertainment – it's about education' (1999, p. 9). Seth Godin is regarded as something of an Internet 'Guru' and the use of the Internet is central to his concept of 'permission marketing'.

Activity

- **What do understand by the term 'permission marketing'?**
- **Why do some commentators claim that permission marketing can overcome the 'noise' problem in the firm's marketing communications process?**

Most marketing communication takes place when a sender, usually the marketing firm, sends an encoded commercial message, to the receiver, that is potential customer, usually without permission. The marketing communication message usually has to interrupt the receiver in some way. For example a television advertisement might interrupt your favourite programme. As the name suggests, permission marketing gets the potential receiver's permission to send the message first. So, for example, if you want DIY tips and product information from AMAZING.com everyday via the Internet you have to request it first. Permission marketing has to be compared and contrasted with the more traditional form of marketing, especially advertising, which for want of a better phrase could be called 'interruption marketing'.

Because people receive many commercial messages every day they have to be selective otherwise all they would be doing all day is reading advertisements. When an individual firm sends a marketing message it has to compete with many other messages for the prospect's attention. Other competing messages are a form of interference or, to use an engineering term, 'noise'. Many commercial messages do not get through because of the noise in the system. Some say that permission marketing overcomes this noise. Because the receiver has given permission for the message to be sent they are much more likely to read and respond to the message than with other forms of more conventional unsolicited communications.

▶ Ways of using the Internet in marketing

There are many methods of marketing over the Internet but here are some of the main ones listed by The Chartered Institute of Marketing in the UK on their 'Understanding E-Marketing' website:

- *Sales promotions:* The Internet is an excellent vehicle for communicating promotions and special offers to specific customers. Scratch cards, lotteries, loyalty schemes and bulk-purchasing offers are much more interesting when applied to the Internet. With online loyalty schemes such as iPoints and Web Rewards, online gift vouchers, online lotteries, give-aways and viral marketing promotions, the possibilities are legion. Viral marketing describes any strategy that encourages individuals to pass on a marketing message to others, creating the potential for exponential growth in the message's exposure and influence. Like viruses, such strategies take advantage of rapid multiplication to explode the message to thousands, even millions, of receivers.
- *Short Message Service (SMS):* SMS is the ideal platform to distribute important information instantly to multiple cellular users. Uses include:
    1. Dissemination of product or financial information to valuable clients and members.
    2. Communication with mobile support staff and site staff.
    3. Communication with club, society and workgroup members.
    4. Notifications of meetings, sales and new products.
- *WAP (Wireless Application Protocol):* WAP provides information on the mobile internet for consumers. An internet and WAP portal, the site provides reviews and news and other information on the mobile internet for consumers. WAP does contribute something new to the marketing mix. For example many travel sites, such as ebookers.com and Lastminute.com, notify users when a holiday meeting their stated criteria comes up.

▶ *Interactive TV (iTV):* Emerging interactive television technologies are shaping the future of entertainment. New technologies may be threatening the viability of current TV advertising models, but they simultaneously present new and lucrative opportunities. Cable and satellite television operators, as well as TV programmers, are leveraging new advertising technologies to realise additional revenue streams. A quarter of UK homes have access to iTV, and one in five iTV users have already bought over it. As it is most often viewed from the living-room sofa it is more conducive to rash purchases than the office. Add that to the scope for product placement and this is one to watch.

▶ *A website:* A website address has become as important as a telephone number. Firms of all sizes can have a website for a modest cost. In fact it is one of the areas where small firms can compete with larger firms just as effectively. Many websites began life as nothing more than online brochures for a company and have evolved to include e-commerce, competitions, promotions and what is known as 'sticky' content (the material that keeps people returning to the site). For many purely Internet-based companies the website is often all the consumer has to identify the company, in the absence of a physical store or headquarters. For an offline company, it can act as an interactive brochure which not only promotes the company but also encourages direct feedback, captures customer data and offers personalised content.

▶ *Advertising:* Internet advertisements can be targeted to the individual who receives them. Different advertising serving systems have differing capabilities, but it is technologically possible to deliver an advertisement to that one individual who you know is interested in buying your product. Commonly these advertisements are in the form of banner adverts on websites, either to help build a brand message, rather as a billboard or TV ad would, or more specifically to attract users to go immediately through to the website by clicking on the banner (called a click-through and a method that is often used to measure the success of online advertising campaigns).

▶ *Email:* Many product and service providers such as the New York Times or AMAZING – Your Home Front Tip asks you if you want to subscribe free to their information service. If you do they will email you every day. The New York Times on the Web not only contains free news but many other commercial messages. AMAZING too offers you daily DIY tips but also 'banner advertising' usually related to DIY products or at least products for the home. Email is an inexpensive way of reaching an existing database of customers who have visited and registered on a website. Permission-based email campaigns can take the form of one-off promotions, or regular newsletters.

▶ *Search engines:* Search engines use software robots to survey the Web and build their databases. Web documents are retrieved and indexed. When you enter a query at a search engine website, your input is checked against the search engine's keyword indices. The best matches are then returned to you as hits. There are two primary methods of text searching – keyword and concept. Many people's first port of call on the Internet is a search engine (for example AltaVista, Google or AskJeeves.co.uk). Having a site listed on a search engine, or indeed several search engines, is not only free but is also considered to be the most effective method of attracting visitors to a website.

▶▶ Database marketing

▶ Database marketing defined

The world of sales and marketing is changing all the time. The Internet, e-commerce, the continuing rise of direct marketing and the increasing marketing emphasis on customer retention over customer acquisition (covered in more detail in Chapter 17) are only a few of the salient factors affecting the way firms carry out business in the modern world. Firms have to move fast, keep up with the latest developments and trends and invest in the most relevant software and systems to stay ahead of the competition. You will notice that 'database marketing' is two words. The first word implies that data is organised and stored in a computer system. The second word implies that firms use this data in their marketing and sales programmes.

Database marketing is a marketing and sales system that continually gathers, refines, and utilises information and data that then drives relevant marketing and sales communications programmes. Examples of this are sales calls, direct mail pieces, and advertising to selected companies in order to acquire new customers, retain customers, generate more business from existing customers, and create long-term loyalty. Database marketing is much more than just a data retrieval system. While direct marketing describes a collection of marketing communication tactics (such as direct mail, telemarketing, response advertising and so on), database marketing describes a way of organising a company's total marketing and sales process. It is very broad and can have impact from market research and product development all the way through customer service. Information about customers that is accurate and available to everyone can truly transform a company's market capacity.

▶ What does database marketing allow you to do?

Database marketing is all about focusing and targeting. Databases take the guesses out of marketing programmes. They do not necessarily provide perfect accuracy but they do allow for significant improvements in both accuracy and efficiency if used properly. Many companies do a sort of hit-or-miss marketing, for want of a better phrase. That means that management often makes decisions based on intuition or instinct rather than on hard facts based on clear scientific evidence. Hence, instead of predicting their target audience based on hard facts they make their best guesses about whom their target audience is and what they want. This process of best guessing can be very expensive in terms of wasted direct-mail shots and other forms of communication, and wasted time and effort. As already stated, database marketing lets you work more intelligently and it gives you the tools to make more accurate assessments. It lets you take the information you already have in your customer or sales-lead databases, analyse it to find the patterns in it, such as purchasing associations and relationships, and use the information you gained from your analysis to produce and instigate better marketing and sales programmes. Running better marketing and sales programmes simply means targeting specific groups with specific messages about products that are important to them rather than giving them irrelevant and uninteresting information. If you are able to target the right industries with the right messages about the right products, you will spend less sales and marketing resources marketing to companies and/or individuals that are never going to buy. Thus, you will have more resources to spend on the prospects who are most likely to buy, thereby increasing the return on your marketing and sales investment. Basically the proper use of databases gives the marketing professional the tools to do a more accurate and professional job. It improves the effectiveness of marketing campaigns and saves time and money. It allows for the more effective allocation and utilisation of valuable marketing resources. Database marketing is sometimes referred to as precision marketing. It is analogous to a commercial 'smart bomb' in its ability to accurately hit its target. Directing a marketing programme from a well-constructed and managed database is analogous to shooting a riffle at a target using an advanced precision telescopic sight rather than a conventional sight.

▶ Basic principles of database marketing

Below are some illustrations of the possible applications and basic principles of database marketing. They are not intended to be exhaustive or definitive but they do serve to illustrate the main principles:

- First of all find out what characteristics your best customers have in common so you can target your next programmes to prospects that have those same characteristics. See exactly which market segments buy from your firm. You might think that you already know your best market segments, but through analysis you could uncover market segments that you have sold a significant amount of product to but did not realise it. This process may enable the firm to improve its segmentation of the market by refocusing and redefining existing segment or may highlight totally unexpected new segments.
- Ascertain whether different market segments buy different products from you. This information will allow you to spend your marketing and sales resources more effectively by marketing each of your products to their best potential industries, individual firms or individual people. Learn which market segments bring you the most revenue and which ones bring you the highest average revenue. This is what differentiated marketing is all about. Dividing the total market into segments and then having a slightly different marketing strategy for each segment.
- Find out what types of industries, firms or individuals respond to what types of marketing communications so you can decide where to spend your advertising and marketing resources the next time. Find out which market segments not only respond to your programmes but also actually buy and which buy from you repeatedly. Again, these might have very different demographic profiles or be different in some other way which may be commercially exploitable, and you might decide to modify your targeting tactics and only market to the segments that buy repeatedly or at least reasonably frequently.
- Calculate the average lifetime value of your customers. This can be done using discounted cash-flow procedures. You can use this information to find out which customers are not living up to their potential and devise marketing and sales programmes to encourage them to buy more. Identify new customers and create programmes that will encourage them to buy again. Reward your most frequent buyers and the buyers that bring you the highest revenue. The concept of 'lifetime' value is central to the idea of customer retention

and long-term relationship marketing. The subject of relationship marketing is covered in more detail in Chapter 17.

▶ Data mining

Database marketing is a process that enables marketers to develop, test, implement, measure and modify marketing programmes and strategies more accurately and more efficiently than non-database methods. By applying data mining techniques, marketers can fully harvest data about customers' buying patterns and behaviour, and gain a greater understanding of customer motivations. Data mining and customer relationship management (CRM) software allows users to analyse large databases to solve business decision problems. Data mining as the name suggests, involves 'interrogating' a database in order to discover interesting and hopefully commercially exploitable associations, patterns or relationships in the data. Modern data analysis software such as SPSS allows the user to manipulate, group and correlate data variables and sets. CRM related computer software is also examined in more depth in Chapter 17.

▶ Basic principles of data mining

In order to implement successful database marketing solutions, management needs to know how to carry out certain basic tasks. The list given below is once again not intended to be prescriptive and certainly not exhaustive, however is does serve to illustrate some of the basic principles:

- ▶ Identify and gather relevant data about customers and prospects to construct the database in the first place.
- ▶ Use data warehousing techniques, which are systems of data storage and organising, to transform raw data into powerful, accessible marketing information. This adds value to the data collected by putting it into a format that can be retrieved and analysed effectively.
- ▶ Apply statistical techniques to customer and prospect databases to analyse behaviour and attempt to establish patterns, associations or relationships in the data that may be commercially exploitable.
- ▶ Establish meaningful market segments that are measurable, reachable, viable and hence commercially valuable.
- ▶ Score individuals in terms of the probability of their response. This will involve prioritising prospects in terms of the probability of purchase and long-term commercial value.

Data mining is, in some ways, an extension of statistical analysis. Like statistics, data mining is not a business solution; it is just a technology. CRM, on the other hand, involves turning information in a database into business decisions. For example, consider a mail order retailer who needs to decide who to send a new catalogue to. The information incorporated into the customer relationship management process is the historical database of previous mailings and the features associated with the (potential) customers, such as age, postcode, their response in the past and so on. The software uses this data to build a model of customer behaviour that can be used to predict which customers are likely to respond to the new catalogue – rather like building a 'virtual customer'. By using this information a marketing manager can target the customers who are likely to respond with much greater accuracy and saving time and money.

▶ Data fusion

Data fusion is in many ways similar to data mining. Again, as the name implies, data is obtained from a range of different sources and put together, rather like a jigsaw puzzle, to form a complete profile of an individual. For example you may fill in a loyalty card at a supermarket which means a lot of your personal information is now on a company database. You may apply for a bank account or credit facilities with the same or related company (supermarkets such as Sainsbury's offer bank and credit facilities to their customers) and fill in another form and give further personal details. This data may be merged and integrated with data held about you on other personal databases, for example those run by Equifax or Experien which supply personal data to firms, including financial data such as credit history.

Data from all these sources will be fused together, cleaned using a filtering system and will basically form a complete picture of you as a person and as a consumer. Sometimes data will be fused together from fragments held on different databases on different people. These people may share similar characteristics and form part of the same market segment. There may be associations between key variables that link a particular consumer to a particular segment. If you have the right value on one or two of these variables you are then treated as if you have the characteristics of the virtual consumer built up from the fused data fragments. Using these techniques firms can attribute a probability to you that you will behave in a certain way as modelled by their virtual consumer profile (Figure 16.4). Data fusion is a formal frame-

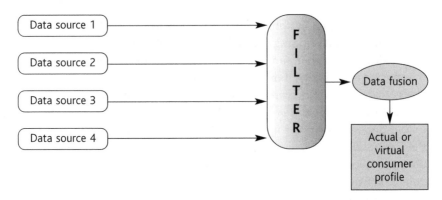

Figure 16.4 Schematic flow chart representing the data fusion process

work in which are expressed means and tools for the alliance of data originating from different sources. It aims at obtaining information of greater quality, the exact definition of 'greater quality' depending upon the application.

- **What is the principle behind data fusion? Explain using examples.**
- **What are the main sources of data marketing firms could use to create a 'virtual' consumer?**

The process of data fusion involves collecting data on an individual from a wide variety of sources and fusing the data together to create a more comprehensive profile or picture. Sometimes research and direct marketing firms use data from people who are similar to one another to 'fill in the gaps'. Because people have similarities, for example education or income, they may purchase in a similar way.

Whenever we fill in a form for a credit card such as American Express or Barclaycard or a loyalty card such as Nectar, we provide personal information to marketing firms. Whenever we apply for credit, or even make a credit payment, this information is logged by credit reference agencies such as Experian and Equifax – again more personal information. Even when we purchase something from a supermarket such as Sainsbury's and hand over our loyalty card for points, data about our purchases is being recorded. In addition to our own personal data marketing firms also hold personal data on people like us, for example the same age or income level and so on. Because other people have similar profiles to us the chances are they may purchase similar things to us. This is the basis behind marketing segmentation. By fusing data together in this way firms can create 'virtual consumers'.

▶▶ The Internet

The technology involved in setting up the Internet has demonstrated to management that it will significantly change the way people interact with each other, particularly in the sphere of business. The Internet crosses the boundaries of geography, politics, race, sex, religion, time zones and culture. Technology, of any kind, helps to make possible and, hopefully, improve the way we work. Without it many of the things we do – and often take for granted – would be at best difficult, and often impossible. For example, much of advertising relies on communications technology; effective distribution and logistics rely on transport technologies; marketing research and analysis increasingly rely upon computing technology. Admittedly, this reliance on, and use of, technology in marketing is not new but the extent to which it is used and the way it is used today is new. Think for a moment how different your life would be without, say, the calculator, email or even television. What would the lives of some of us be like without the technology to, say, telephone a relative or deliver electricity and power to our homes and offices? Perhaps less noticeably, but in context perhaps no less significantly, technology also affects and helps aid marketing and the marketing process. So much so that some areas of marketing and marketing techniques are almost totally underpinned by technology and its application.

E-business, based on Internet technology and the variations that have been developed from the original Internet concept such as intranet and extranet, connects and links employees, customers, suppliers and partners. The Internet has reduced the planet into a global village, accelerated the pace of technology, opened up tremendous possibilities for marketers and altered the way they think about doing business. It has started the new revolution in marketing which some say is the most important revolution since the invention of commercial advertising – the 'e-commerce revolution'. It is the revolution people can no longer ignore. Some experts say that this new revolution will rebuild the existing economy and change the way business is conducted. Others say the likely effect of the new technology is over blown and that many people will stop using it once the initial novelty has worn off.

▶▶ World Wide Web

The World Wide Web market will reach a staggering £1.2 trillion by the year 2004 according to many experts on the subject and publications such as the *Financial Times*. The World Wide Web has unique features, which differentiate it from other forms of business communications. Because the Web is so different from the more traditional media, such as television and radio, its use is revolutionising the manner in which some marketing activities are carried out. In fact they could not be carried out at all without the use of Web-based technology.

Some writers see the Web as the innovation that will totally transform the whole marketing concept. Many argue that for firms' marketing activities to be successful using the new technology a totally new model of marketing is required for the Web-based society in which these firms will be doing business. In the USA, more than two thirds of firms are setting up computer-based systems such as intranet and/or extranet facilities. As with many other technological innovations, the USA seems to be leading the way and acting as a driving force for the diffusion around the world of the new technology and the new marketing methods that go with it. These are tools that have the potential to increase profits by cutting costs, improving productivity, efficiency and communications and reducing paper work. E-commerce helps to improve all areas of business including bringing in new customers, improving service levels, creating growth potential, tracking customers, data mining of databases, better targeting of marketing communications, reducing distribution costs and speeding up growth. The so-called e-commerce revolution, of which the World Wide Web is at the very epicentre, has been hailed as one of the most important developments ever to occur in the world of business. These developments will affect every area of firms' business operations but particularly marketing. Some experts are calling the new developments in marketing a 'paradigm shift'. This means that the new technology is not simply resulting in marketing firms doing basically the same thing but with more up-to-date technology but that we have to change the whole way we think about doing marketing. We need a new model or 'paradigm'.

Vignette 16.2

Kellogg Foundation finances the 'Creating Community Connections Project' in Boston, Massachusetts – a programme to get low-income residents online.

Camfield Estates, a rebuilt 102-unit public-housing development, has trimmed bushes and groomed grounds. What also sets it apart from other low-income complexes lies hidden behind its walls, atop its roof and in the airwaves. For the past two years, Camfield has been the site of a project aiming to span the 'digital divide' between impoverished Americans and those with easy access to technology. Called the Creating Community Connections Project, it has given residents free computers to connect to the Internet using high-speed cable lines wired into every home. Residents gather at a community computer room to take free classes on everything from how to plug in a mouse to setting up websites. The project, mostly paid for with a $200,000 grant from the Kellogg Foundation and supported by companies such as Hewlett-Packard and Microsoft as well as public and non-profit entities, is taking another step. Now that Camfield's Internet provider has ended its two-year commitment to offer discounted cable-modem access, the project's organisers will soon give residents the option of replacing their wired Internet access with a wireless connection. The high-speed Wi-Fi system transmits and receives data from four barely visible antennas atop the development's main building. Residents can buy wireless cards for their desktops or laptops. The cards, which can cost up to $100 retail, will be given away to the elderly and sold for $60 to others. After that, residents will be able to log on – for free – from anywhere within Camfield. While wireless zones are popping up around the country in airports, coffee shops and universities, technology experts say it's unusual for such a network to explicitly serve the poor. 'It's something that's going to be replicated elsewhere, but this is, I think, the first example of a project like this emerging out of the community, rather than being required by a grant,' said Anthony Townsend, a New York University professor and a co-founder of NYCwireless, an advocacy group. US Department of Commerce data from 2001 indicated that 78.9 per cent of people in families making $75,000 or more had Internet access, compared with 25 per cent of people from households earning less than $15,000 a year. While the federal government says the divide is narrowing, consumer and public-interest advocates say it remains a problem. High-speed access often remains out of reach for the poor and low-cost wireless Internet access could be a remedy. Many people point to issues of democracy and public participation and dialogue, and having access to what the Internet brings is really important.

▶▶ The World Wide Web: a new model for electronic marketing

The World Wide Web is a form of hypermedia computer mediated environment (HCME) which is networked on a global scale. This is a bit of a mouthful but basically an HCME is a networked system which allows the users of the system to interact in some way with the system. Both the sender and the receiver of the message can supply information to, and interact with, each other and other users, and with the system itself. This makes the World Wide Web very different from other systems used in marketing, and in particular in marketing communications, at the present time. The telephone and other media allow for a certain amount of interaction. For example people can telephone in to the local radio channel and be heard by listeners to the programme. However the interactivity provided by the World Wide Web goes much further than this.

As mentioned earlier, users can not only interact with the sender of the commercial message but with other users of the system and also contribute material to the system itself. It is this person interaction and machine interaction that differentiates the Web from other commercial media and has led to its widespread use and adoption as a marketing media (see Hoffman and Novak 1994).

▶ Models of communication

Models of the communications process may be verbal, non-verbal or mathematical. Regardless of form, they share three basic elements – *sender*, *message* and *receiver*. The message may be sent to one receiver or, as is more common in marketing communications, the message is sent to multiple receivers simultaneously. The basic model is shown below in Figure 16.5.

Hoffman and Novak, 1995, have constructed a new model of communications which is more suitable for an HCME such as the World Wide Web. In this model customers/receivers can actually interact with the medium and both marketing firms and the receivers of the message can provide actual content to the medium. In this mediated model Hoffman and Novak show that the primary relationships are not between the sender and receiver so much as with the HCME itself with which they interact. Hence in this new model, information or content is not simply transmitted from sender to receiver, but actually mediated environments are created by all parties using the system and then experienced by them. Figure 16.6 is based on Hoffman and Novak's model.

Figure 16.6 is also based on traditional models of mass communication although the model incorporates a feedback view of interactivity between the firm and customers and customers and customers. Interactivity is the feature which really differentiates Figure 16.3 from the two

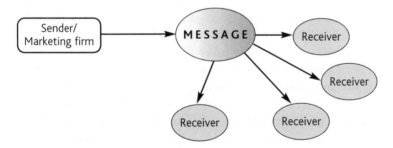

Figure 16.5 A simple communications model

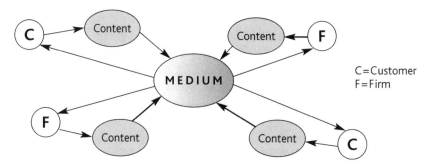

Figure 16.6 A communications model for a hypermedia computer mediated environment (HCME) such as the World Wide Web
Source: Adapted from Hoffman and Novak (1995)

earlier figures. Figure 16.6 represents a 'many to many' communications model for HCMEs such as the World Wide Web. Hoffman and Novak show through their work, on which this model is based, that interactivity can be with the medium, that is machine interactivity and through the medium, that is person interactivity.

▶▶ E-commerce: opportunities

As we have seen, one of the most important areas affected by advances in technology has been the growth of electronic commerce, sometimes referred to as electronic marketing or e-marketing, or more generically, as e-business or e-commerce. E-commerce is a collective term to describe a variety of commercial transactions which make use of the technologies of electronic processing and data transmission. The majority of these are based on the Internet and its hybrids such as extranet and intranet.

> *Electronic commerce* – the use of electronic technologies and systems so as to facilitate and enhance transactions between different parts of the value chain.

This definition focuses on the fact that all e-commerce is designed to improve the business transaction processes. E-commerce would not have grown to the extent it has, and will continue to do, had it not provided the potential for improvements to the marketing process. Often these potential improvements, as already stated, will be in the form of cost reductions for the marketer, but much more important are those improvements that can be passed on to the customer. Put another way, the growth of e-commerce would not have been possible without the growth of the e-customer. For example, it will be some time before e-commerce becomes a major mass force in carrying out business transactions in developing countries such as India. That is because the majority of the rural population in India does not even have electricity, gas or telephone yet. Even if such people can make use of cyber café or Internet facilities provided by local authorities, most would not have an acceptable credit card in order to facilitate such commercial transactions.

The marketing concept states that marketing is about identifying and satisfying customer needs and wants more efficiently and effectively than the competition. If customers did not want to become e-commerce customers the technology would have never have been adopted by so many people in the first place. Finally, our definition points to the fact that e-commerce and the technologies which underpin it can, and do, relate to the total value chain including not only customers but also intermediaries, suppliers, and other external agencies such as advertising and market research companies. In fact, as we shall see, the ability to link and coordinate all the members of the so-called value chain is one of the primary reasons for the growth of e-commerce.

▌▌▌ Vignette 16.3

A OL offering music catalog for downloads.

In the strongest attempt yet to create a legitimate alternative to free music-trading sites, America Online will introduce a service today that lets users download and listen to a large catalogue of songs. For $8.95 a month (about £6), users will be able to listen to a catalogue of music, now at 250,000 songs and growing, on their computers. Moving songs to CDs or portable players will cost more. MusicNet is a consortium of RealNetworks, the BMG unit of Bertelsmann, EMI, and Warner Music which, like America Online, is a unit of AOL Time Warner. AOL refused to introduce MusicNet's first product a year ago, arguing that it was too hard to use and did not have enough music. Now AOL says that the service has improved enough to offer it to its 27 million members. That represents the most important test yet for the concept of selling music as a subscription service rather than as discrete discs. For AOL, MusicNet also represents a crucial part of its strategy to increase its tiny share of the market for Internet users who connect over high-speed, or broadband, connections. AOL is already promoting its free music content, which includes hundreds of songs, videos and original recordings of musicians. The standard $8.95 version of the service will allow users to listen to an unlimited number of songs on demand while they are connected to the Internet through a technology called 'streaming'. They can also download the songs to their computers for higher sound quality and the ability to listen to them when not on the Internet. Unlike music downloaded from Napster, the defunct free music sharing service, and its successors such as KaZaA, a subscriber can listen to MusicNet's downloads on no more than two computers. The downloads also cannot be copied to other devices or sent to other people. But a premium version of the service, for $17.95 a month (about £12), gives users the right to burn 10 songs a month onto a recordable CD. These will be in the standard, unprotected format used by all music CDs, and thus those songs could be copied, converted to a popular format like MP3 and sent over the Internet at will. So far, legitimate music download services have not been a success with consumers, not only because they charge a fee but also because the first versions had very limited numbers of songs and even more draconian rules about what users could do with them.

E-commerce enables small businesses to market their goods globally, with minimum cost and without travelling overseas, thus allowing small and medium-sized enterprises to market their products and services internationally without being disadvantaged by their size. E-commerce can save enormous expense, time and effort on marketing, accounting, financing and billing. There is no need for printed catalogues or price lists. Leading publishers of newspapers, magazines and books are doing lucrative business on the Internet. E-commerce is serious business and attracting money. Of total on-line business, retailing accounts only for approximately 10 to 15 per cent of business, the rest is made from business-to-business commerce.

◗◗ Principles of successful Internet marketing

The Internet offers unique opportunities for companies and customers to communicate with each other via a mass medium on a new mediated environment. Business firms and customers are now in positions to build relationships with one another effectively and cost efficiently. They can learn on an individual basis how to satisfy needs and wants of their customers by using Internet technologies. At the same time, the new medium also challenges business, because the Web and its relationship-marketing business model may conflict with more established marketing methods. Using an HCME, which is what the Internet and the World Wide Web actually are, is very different from conventional marketing media and ways of carrying out the marketing task.

Firms will need to redefine their businesses in terms of organisational structure, production, marketing, communications, sales, after-sales services and overall strategic planning processes. Successful Web strategies can only be achieved by embracing the medium proactively and from a complete organisational point of view. The Internet should be part of overall and comprehensive corporate strategies formulated by the top management. Internet marketing strategies should be integrated within the entire organisation and not viewed simply as an additional marketing and advertising channel. The Internet has provided immense opportunities for business people to reach global sourcing, and will be the most cost-effective business place.

Firms must seriously consider the following points when thinking about using the Internet to market their goods and/or services:

- What value does your website add for your customers? Is it informative, interesting or valuable from an operational point of view? For example, can your industrial customers re-order their industrial consumables from your website?
- What goals and objectives do you set for your website and how are you going to measure, control and act on these metrics? How are you going to track truncations, enquiries and so on and what kind of analysis are you going to employ in the evaluation process?
- What purpose does the website have and how do you justify the website? Is the firm clear as to what the objectives for the website are? Is it to provide information and educate? Is it merely a backup for other more mainline marketing communications tools such as conventional media advertising?
- What is your site and what is in it? Are the contents correct for the type of business you are running? Is the amount and type of information on your site correct and suitable for the type of potential customer you hope to attract?
- How big is your Internet budget and is your organisation fit for web traffic? Is your firm taking the Internet venture seriously and does it have all the necessary facilities in place to handle both the volume and type of Internet traffic expected? Do you have support lines and product return strategies worked out? Are there people who can answer enquires online or offline?
- What do your website customers know about the Internet? how often they use the Internet. What do they want to know from your site and what Internet connection do they have?

▶ How to persuade visitors to return to the site

It is important not only to attract visitors once to the site but also to ensure that they keep coming back often. That is why it is necessary to update Web content regularly with information and articles. Visitors should be encouraged to return with regular articles, newsletters or even a story. It should be remembered that Web content and promotion is not a one-off affair but an ongoing process to market and build relationships. Your website should be a place of community atmosphere and have definite project goals resulting from the corporate marketing plan.

▍▍ Vignette 16.4

Ratings agency underestimated website use by basing figures on workplace panel data.

ComScore Media Metrix, one of the leading companies that measure website audiences, has discovered flaws in the methodology that it introduced in October, and it has restated its measurements for the last three months of 2002. Web ratings services have faced questions about accuracy since they began trying to estimate audiences by projecting the behaviour of a panel (a sample of people) of presumably representative users. Despite their limits, ComScore's ratings, and those of its main competitor Nielsen/NetRatings, are widely used by advertisers, investors, journalists and the websites themselves. The biggest differences in ComScore's ratings, announced last week, come in its estimates of Web use at the workplace, always the most difficult to measure. Big companies in particular do not want employees to install the software that the ratings companies use to track website usage. When ComScore adjusted its formulas to account for the underrepresentation of big companies, its audience projections increased, in some cases sharply. In response to complaints by its clients, the company has discovered some flaws in its new system. It decided to publish restated data for last autumn rather than change its formulas from now on. Marketers and advertising experts agreed that ComScore's approach ultimately improves the quality of the data available. Furthermore, these audience measures are not used to set Internet advertising rates, as they are in radio and television. Since broadcasters have no way to tell how many people are watching a given programme, they must use Nielsen's television ratings to determine how much to charge advertisers. On the Internet, websites charge to display an advertisement a certain number of times. Still, some industry executives worry that the restatement will add further doubt about the online medium, which is still trying to establish its credibility with marketers.

▶▶ Basic principles in website construction

Think of a website as being analogous to a television programme. It has to have some of the same qualities of creativity and interest, be intriguing, beguiling and so forth. Web surfers have similar characteristics to television channel surfers, the difference being that there are hundreds of millions of channels on the Internet, so an individual website has to stand out if it is to be noticed. There is so much material on the Internet that most of it just passes us by. Try a little exercise and ask yourself what method does your most popular website currently use to capture the attention of web surfers? What stimulates your interest, while providing information about products or services? There are no definitive rules, although the following general principles should prove useful.

A firm's website must consider the following elements:

- Ensure visitors will revisit
- Promote word-of-mouth communication
- How does a website communicate with potential customers?
- Do you use traditional marketing methods on the Internet?
- How do you use Internet-based technologies to increase sales?
- Attract people to your website otherwise there is little point in having one
- Retain their interest long enough to sell your product or service. Again this is usually the whole point of a commercial website.

A commercial website has a single objective, to stimulate visitors into taking some form of desired action, such as placing an order. This key motive is behind every element of a commercial website design and content. Firms should start with the idea that they have one chance to reach their customers. They will never return to a site unless the marketing firm makes it worth their while, and they will not buy unless they are encouraged to.

▶▶ Improving Web sales

A business website may get a lot of visits or hits, but are these visitors buying anything? Attracting visitors to a site is half the battle, but visitors do not always mean sales, quite the contrary. The majority of people visiting a site will buy nothing. Many of these will simply be having a look around or surfing the Web. Also, attracting attention in today's loud, crowded business culture is difficult. No business should bother attracting lots of visitors to its site if it does not know what to do with them once they are there. Instead, it needs to turn all those Web surfers into dedicated Web buyers if the site is to be commercially viable.

▶ Provide the possibility for communicating with people

Look around any particular website, and see if you can tell that it involves human beings in any way. Could it just as easily be a front-end for a database or search engine? Many e-commerce sites are unwelcoming and need to do substantially more to make visitors feel at home and welcome them to the site. That is no surprise as their focus is on the sale, not the customer. However the key thing to remember is that the Web is a communication tool directed at human beings. Marketing firms have to give customers what they want and this means a user friendly and attractive website, which reassures them and allows them to contact people from the marketing firm if necessary. The key is to create opportunities for visitors to interact with actual human beings – or at least to get the sense that there is someone behind all those bits and bytes. A free telephone number that lets customers talk to an actual person is an invaluable addition to any website. If you were an Internet marketing company would you not rather have customer's telephone in their orders or call for help than have them leave your website with nothing? Even listing the address of your physical location will reassure customers. Consider offering live, instant customer service through the Internet, using a chat-like interface. Several companies are now offering this service at very little cost – or even for free. It adds a valuable human dimension to a medium that can sometimes appear cold and unfriendly to some customers.

▶ Instil confidence in your visitors

Many potential website customers are worried about carrying out transactions on the Internet for security and other reasons. We have all read horrendous newspapers stories about unethical marketing companies operating on the Web and fleecing the general public. People want reassurance. Customers want to know a site is legitimate and that they can trust the people behind it. They also want to know who they can contact if something goes wrong. A firm will never get business if they cannot instil confidence in their customers. One idea that many successful Internet-based firms use is to include a 'Comments from our customers' page to show newcomers that others like to buy at that that site. Some sites also have customer chat facilities where they can discuss products and related issues. Others, like Amazon.com and Napster.com, allow visitors to post their own product reviews. If your firm's site feels like a comfortable place to come to, your visitors will – and they will be more likely to purchase and tell other people about the site and their experience. Join a trade association, a professional organisation or an industry group – and abide by the rules they set. For example franchisees can display the logo of the British Franchise Association which tells the user of the site that the company is ethical and abides by a code of practice. The Direct Marketing Association has a similar scheme that its members can use to instil confidence in their business practices in the minds of potential customers. When you display the logos of such nationally or internationally recognised bodies, customers know your firm has put its name and reputation on the line and you will not suddenly be going out of business or, worse, running off with their money. If someone distrusts the privacy of their transaction, they probably will not start one.

Another important point is that e-marketing firms should create and prominently display a return policy. If customers buy a product from a conventional retail store they can usually take the product back and have it replaced if it turns out to be faulty. Many potential Internet customers are worried that they may not be able to do this if they purchase from a website. A clear returns policy will give customers information needed to make informed purchasing decisions and save your company a lot of time and effort when items are returned. Customers often leave sites because they are too slow or difficult to navigate. It may be easy to keep much of the business your firm may be losing now simply by making the shopping experience more convenient for users. We have all been on websites that take far too long to load and when we have eventually got on to them things do not work or it is difficult to get the information we want. People who have had that experience learn from them. The next time they come across a slow loading or difficult website they immediately exit.

▶ Include a search option and a frequently asked questions (FAQ) list

Firms should provide e-mail links for users to ask questions – and provide answers effectively and efficiently. Many sites accept only Master-Card and Visa credit cards for example. Some users may find this inconvenient so the firm should consider offering other payment options such as American Express, Discover, online checks, money orders and cash on delivery (COD) (as companies such as Gateway Computer do).

Finally, firms should try to identify the reasons customers abandon transactions on their sites. This may be a relatively simple question to answer (for example, your firm may be receiving a lot of e-mail about your returns policy or some other aspect of your business that customers are not happy with) or it may be incredibly difficult. There are Internet consultants who will track the behaviour of customers and get an idea of when and why they are backing out of transactions. These services can be expensive, but are worth it if you are ready to commit seriously to your e-commerce site. Alternatively your firm can carry out the tracking and analysis of customers exit behaviour in-house if you have staff with the right expertise and the time to do it.

▶ Leveraging profit from existing customers

Recently businesses have started to calculate what they spend to get each new customer. Existing customers are more profitable and cost less to retain than new customers cost to attract. This illustrates one of the biggest problems businesses have. Generally, when firms think of building bigger profits, they think about getting more customers. For bigger, quicker profits, also market to the customers you already have. It would be good if your marketing impacted on the new potential consumer and instantly persuaded him or her to buy from your firm's website right away, but the process is almost always more complicated. Here is why focusing entirely on new customers can seriously deplete your marketing budget with little in the way of sales to show for it.

▶▶ Steps to a successful sale

Before anyone buys from your firm's website, they have to step through at least four stages:

1. You get their attention (the hardest stage of all since we are bombarded with hundreds of marketing messages every day and people are very selective in what they choose to look at).
2. Get the prospect to think about your offer, which has to be interesting to the prospect and give them some value. There has to be some unique selling proposition (USP) which is intriguing to the prospect and at least makes them consider the possibility of placing an order with you.
3. Have the prospect decide to buy from you; this is one of the key stages. The material on the website must be sufficiently enticing to make the prospect decide to buy. Security and other commercial safety issues will come in to play in the prospect's decision-making process here. These must be addressed for the purchase to go ahead.
4. Then the prospect must take action to buy from you. This is the most important stage; if the prospect does not actually place an order then everything else is for nothing. Even in e-marketing you

still have to find a way of actually closing the sale with a prospect. The fundamentals are no different from traditional personal selling in this respect.

Even after someone buys, they may not come back to buy again. Studies show many people cannot accurately remember where they bought things several weeks after the purchase. Meanwhile, current and past customers are the easiest to sell to again. All this clearly leads to the need for you to stay in touch with customers you already have. A lot of Internet business is based on repeat business and customer retention. For example once someone has purchased a book online from Amazon.com that same person usually purchases a book again some time in the future. Also include in this group 'hot' prospects that have shown an interest in your business in the past. These are the most targeted and willing audiences you will ever find.

◗ Construct a prospect list

E-marketing firms should construct a list of people who have bought from the firm in the past week, during the past month, over the past six months, and within the past year. The idea is to develop different lists so management can send just the right offer to interest and motivate them. If you clearly see that a big group buys one product or service while another group goes for a different offer, divide your customers up along these lines. You can double, triple and quadruple your response rate by making advertising 'zero in' on just what a customer or prospect is truly interested in buying. This is where database marketing comes into its own. A well-constructed database will allow the marketing firm to analyse the data and prioritise customers in terms of their probability to purchase and allow effective segmentation of the firm's customer base. You can use any database program to keep your lists organised. Most word processing programs include a basic database feature, or you can use a more specialised program, such as Microsoft Access.

◗ Actively 'work' the prospect list

The main reason for working your in-house list of customers and 'hot' prospects is to keep your business in people's minds. If you do not do this they will forget you and turn elsewhere. Today people have many options to spend their money on, even when buying specialised products and services. If you live in a city of any size, there are ar least a few and possibly dozens of businesses marketing more or less the same things as your firm does. There may be thousands more firms on the Internet that can take your customer's credit card order and deliver the product within a few days. If you do not work to stay in the minds of your customers, others will. But how do you work your list without incurring too much expense? Many e-marketing firms have found their best low-cost marketing tools for working an in-house list are postcards and email. Postcards are cheaper than letters to send and do not require the customer to open an envelope. Many people throw away enveloped direct mail material without even opening it. Many firms put a colour photograph or graphic on one side of their postcard, which adds interest and brings the communication to your customers' and prospects' attention. The other side should have the main offer in a bold, black headline, again so it can be noticed and make an impact. It should be followed with a deadline for the offer. Busy people may put off buying and soon forget about your firm's offer. The postcard offer will never be more powerful than it is right at the moment when the customer has it in his or her hands. Many firms use these simple techniques and in principle they seem to work well and get results. Finally, make sure the information on the card briefly tells people how to buy from your firm and make the process as simple as possible. List your firm's website, phone number, store location if appropriate, and email address. Building an email list is even easier and almost free. Unlike a postcard, email messages can contain just as much information as you want them to. Make sure to collect prospects' addresses. Forms can be put on your website to gather email addresses from prospects wanting to be sent information. You can also place a printed form in your office or store if you have one, so those customers can request to get on your list. Make sure you keep the form they filled out in case there is ever a question. Some specialist Internet management firms will offer you a list management service for a fee.

◗ Increasing the number of visitors to a website

◗ Include your URL (site address) in every print advertisement or other advertising media that you use. Print advertising can be quite effective in getting more profitable visits. People may see your website address on posters, newspaper advertising, direct mail shots, van livery and all sorts of other communications. They will then be able to visit your site and explore what you have to offer.

▶ Make sure your graphics communicate who you are as a business. The type of business you are and what you have to offer customers must be clearly communicated and to the point. Choose graphics with a specific purpose, according to your overall colour themes and page layout structures. Always be clear about the brand image(s) that you are portraying via your site.

▶ Find out where (on the Web and elsewhere) the people who want your products like to go, and actively communicate there using Internet and non-Internet communications such as conventional direct mail, posters and advertising.

▶ Get your site registered with as many search engines and link exchange services as you can. Re-register yourself monthly to make sure you are on them. You can list your site with well over 2,000 search engines monthly. If you are too busy to do it yourself then specialist management companies can provide this service for your firm.

▶ Track the number of visits you receive to each page of your website at least once a month, this includes repeat visits. This is one way to track the effectiveness of your advertising campaigns and establish what works best. If your firm has an e-commerce site, then track the money generated by your site at least once monthly. Find out what works (in terms of site marketing) in your particular industry, and do more of it. If something does not work, then this is valuable information also. At least you can learn from your mistakes.

▶ Market very specifically to your target audience, in order to get 'high quality' visits to your site. These are the customers who are most interested in your product or service, and are most likely to buy from you. Segmentation and targeting are of paramount importance here. Prioritise and concentrate on marketing to those prospects that represent the highest probability of success.

▶ Exchange links with everyone you can find who has the same target audience that you do. This can be a great source of 'high quality' and profitable visits. For example if you are targeting academics have hotlinks to your site on other sites which may also be of interest to academics.

▶ Know the purpose for your site. What do you want it to do for you? Sell your product? Have people place orders? Gather data about your site's visitors? Sell advertisers' products so you can sell more ads on your site? Get people to call you for more information? Make sure your Web designer understands what your business is about, and make sure your Web page design effectively communicates who you are as a business.

▷ It is very important that your prospects know who you are and where to find you. As already mentioned, you should put your URL on every piece of paper that leaves your company. If you are not ready to print new stationery and cards, add a clear label with your URL printed on it to each of your pieces – this is a cost effective way of getting your Internet details in front of prospects without wasting the resources you already have.

▷ Make sure your site is a quality one. There is nothing worse than visiting a poor website that does not work properly or one that is poorly constructed and designed. A bad site is worse than no site at all, as having someone come to your site and then leave it completely frustrated can be devastating to the achievement of your site's purpose. Your site should be easy to use, attractive, and informative.

SELF-CHECK

Compare the Internet to the Intranet.
An intranet is an electronic system of internal communication throughout an organisation. Similar to the Internet but operating within an organisational system, the intranet connects functions and activities within an organisation thereby facilitating rapid and effective internal systems of communication. The intranet is similar to an internal management information system, which is open to all approved users within the firm.

▶▶ Summary

The world of sales and marketing is changing all the time. The Internet, e-commerce, the continuing rise of direct marketing and the increasing marketing emphasis on customer retention over customer acquisition are only a few of the salient factors affecting the way firms carry out business in the modern world. Firms have to move very fast, keep up with the latest developments and trends and invest in the most relevant software and systems to stay ahead of the competition. Business in general and certainly marketing in particular has become more affected by, and dependent upon, technology. Furthermore, technological progress itself is altering and accelerating. Technology seems to be developing at an exponential rate, that is, at an ever-increasing rate. The marketer must also be aware of, and be prepared for, future advances in technology. Those firms that are not fully aware of technological advances and developments will fall behind in the commercial race and will probably cease trading. There is a significant change in the technological environment of marketing firms; this is not a minor technological change but a huge 'step' change in the way marketing firms do business. Marketing means staying ahead of the competition and this means acquiring skills to use new technologies. Marketing needs an understanding of the use of technology.

The Web is seen as the innovation that will totally transform the whole marketing concept. Some writers argue that for firms' marketing activities to be successful using the new technology, a totally new model of marketing is required for a Web-based society. In the USA, more than two thirds of firms are setting up computer-based systems such as intranet and/or extranet facilities.

The World Wide Web developments will affect every area of firms' business operations but especially marketing. These new developments in marketing are seen as a 'paradigm shift', which means that the new technology does not simply mean that marketing firms do the same thing but with more up to date technology. It means we have to change the way we think about doing marketing, which requires a new model or 'paradigm'.

FURTHER READING

Anderson B. and Moore J. (1979) *Optimal Filtering*, Prentice Hall, Englewood Cliffs, NJ.

Armstrong G. and Kotler P. (2000) *Marketing: An Introduction* (5th edn), Chapter 14, 'Direct and On-Line Marketing', Prentice Hall, Englewood Cliffs, NJ.

Blattenberg R.C., Glazer R. and Little J.D.C. (eds) (1994) *The Marketing Information Revolution*, Harvard Business School Press, Boston.

Bornman H. and von Solms, S.H. (1993) 'Hypermedia, Multimedia and Hypertext – Definitions and Overview', *Electronic Library*, **11**(4-5): 259–68.

Hafner K. and Lyon M. (1996) *When Wizards Stay Up Late: The Origins of the Internet*, Simon & Schuster, New York.

Hardaker G. and Graham G. (2001) *Wired Marketing: Energising Business for e-Commerce*, John Wiley & Sons, Chichester.

Katz E. and Lazarsfeld P.F. (1955) *Personal Influence*, Free Press, New York.

Keegan W.J. and Green M.S. (2000) Global Marketing (2nd edn), Chapter 15, 'Global Marketing Communications Decisions Two', Prentice Hall, London.

Kotler P. (1994) *Marketing Management: Analysis, Planning, Implementation and Control* (8th edn), Prentice Hall, Englewood Cliffs, NJ.

Lasswell H.D. (1948) 'The Structure and Function of Communication in Society', in Bryson C. (ed.), *The Communication of Ideas*, Harper, New York.

Plamer A. (2000) *Principles of Marketing*, Chapter 20, 'Direct Marketing', OUP, Oxford.

Sorenson H. (1985) *Kalman Filtering: Theory and Application*, IEEE Press, New York.

Steuer J. (1992) 'Defining Virtual Reality: Dimensions Determining Telepresence', *Journal of Communication*, **42**(4): 73–93.

Wald L. (1998) 'A European Proposal for Terms of Reference in Data Fusion', *International Archives of Photogrammetry and Remote Sensing*, Vol. XXXII, Part 7, pp. 651–4, 1998.

▶▶ References

Chartered Institute of Marketing, www.connectedinmarketing.com/ece/cfml/ uemhomepage.cfm.

Godin S. (1999) *Permission Marketing*, Simon & Schuster, New York.

Hoffman D.L. and Novak T.P. (1994) 'Commercialising the Information Superhighway: Are We in For a Smooth Ride?', *The Owen Manager*, **15**(2): 2–7.

Hoffman D.L. and Novak T.P. (1995) 'Marketing in Hypermedia Computer Mediated Environments: Conceptual Foundations', Project 2000 Working Paper No. 1, Owen Graduate School of Management, Vanderbilt University, Nashville, Tennessee.

Jobber D. (2001) *Principles and Practices of Marketing* (3rd edn), Chapter 14, McGraw-Hill, Maidenhead.

Toffler A. (1981) *Future Shock*, Bantam Books, London.

17 CUSTOMER RELATIONSHIP MANAGEMENT

▶▶ Introduction

Customer relationship management (CRM) is not just about keeping your customers satisfied; it allows firms to attract customers with speed, accuracy, availability, creativity and flexibility. In today's ever-changing business and technology environment, CRM is more crucial than ever – ultimately a firm's ability to compete, survive and profit may depend on it. The subject of marketing is dynamic and evolving. Every year there seems to be a new conceptual, strategic or operational innovation within the field. The nature and direction of modern marketing has changed over the past 20 years. The basic definition of marketing as a business process concerned with satisfying customers' needs and wants more effectively and efficiently than the competition remains the same and probably always will do. The basic marketing concept is as valid today as it has always been. Businesses still need to put the customer at the very centre of their operations. In fact, in today's globalised and increasingly complex and competitive world, it is probably even more relevant to today's commercial enterprises. However the processes used by firms to achieve marketing goals have altered dramatically. If one were to compare a standard marketing textbook from the 1970s or even the 1980s with one from today one would see a number of topics in the more recent version which were not even mentioned in earlier versions. Topics such as 'internal marketing', 'relationship marketing', 'e-marketing', 'green marketing' and 'customer relationship management (CRM)', are all fairly recent additions to the marketing literature. In particular there has been what can only be described as a complete 'paradigm shift' in the way the management of marketing firms view their customers, look after them, nurture them and establish relationships with them over the long term. Basically the focus of marketing has shifted from the shorter term view of customers as the next transaction to seeing customers as a long-term income stream over many years, a so-called relationship marketing approach. CRM is a business strategy that integrates people, processes and technology to maximize relationships with a firm's day-to-day customers, distribution channel members, internal customers and suppliers. CRM is a comprehensive approach that provides seamless coordination between sales, marketing, customer service, field support and other customer-facing functions.

▶▶ Customer care

Today, the cost of acquiring new customers greatly exceeds the cost of retaining existing ones. As a result, in the age of the Internet, business is all about the customer. With increasing competition, companies need to unify customer communication across all functions. High levels of customer care are essential for firms operating in the increasingly competitive market environments of today. In the service sector particularly, customer service, rather than price, becomes the prime differentiator. It pays firms to take care of their customers. This principle is not only good business sense but it makes sound economic sense as well. Today the cost of acquiring new customers often greatly exceeds the cost of retaining existing customers. As a result, in order to be economically logical, businesses must focus their resources on effectively targeting and retaining their most attractive customers, nurturing their existing customer base of profitable customers, and on expanding their base of profitable customers. Good customer care means satisfied customers and satisfied customers usually mean a high level of customer retention.

The most valuable asset your company has is its customer. Two aspects of marketing in relation to new and existing customers are:

▷ *New prospects for customers.* This means high cost of sales and high sales resistance. New customers cost more money to persuade to switch suppliers. This extra cost may be in the form of advertising, direct marketing and other marketing costs and in terms of special price deals. For example many of the credit card firms have to offer cheap introductory rates to get new customers to switch. Existing customers just get charged the standard rate and are hence more profitable. Existing customers also take up less marketing time and money as the are already 'on board' so to speak. All the marketing firm has to do is to retain them.

▷ *Repeat business from happy customers*. This means low cost of sales, economies of scale for the seller and low risk for the buyer. Contented customers tend not to be too price sensitive, see the example above. They are therefore more profitable. They do not require special rates or a stream of expensive marketing communications. They do however have to be looked after as other firms are trying to make them switch to them.

Today's successful companies are totally focused. The truth is your customers don't care how much a firm knows about them until they know how that firm actually cares about them. The cost of replacing existing customers is much higher than the cost of keeping them; in fact it can cost five times as much. If those lost customers include some that firms can not afford to lose, that is, some of the more profitable ones, then the effect on profits can be grave. In *The Loyalty Effect*, (Reichheld and Teal, 1996) Frederick F. Reichheld provides information illustrating this principle. According to the research carried out by Reichheld a 5% increase in retention can lead to profit improvements of up to 85%. But he also warns of what he calls the 'satisfaction trap' which is an interesting concept, particularly for marketing researchers involved in carrying out customer service appreciation surveys. His research shows that 60% to 80% of customers who defect from firms had said in a satisfaction survey just prior to defecting that they were 'satisfied' or 'very satisfied' with the service provided by the company. Customer purchase patterns themselves seem to provide a more accurate basis for measuring satisfaction than customer surveys. Hence users of such surveys should be aware of this.

▌▌▌▌ Vignette 17.1

Delta Air Lines Inc. uses high levels of customer care as a strategic marketing tool to stay ahead of the competition.

Paying attention to the needs of customers and developing high levels of customer service has enabled Delta Air Lines to grow into one of the biggest airlines in the world. Delta Air Lines, Inc. provides air transportation for passengers and freight throughout the United States and around the world. As of September 1, 2002, Delta (including its wholly owned subsidiaries, Atlantic Southeast Airlines, Inc. and Comair, Inc.) served 234 domestic cities within the USA in 46 states, the District of Columbia, Puerto Rico and the US Virgin Islands, as well as 44 international cities in 32 countries. Delta mainline, domestic, and international service, Delta Express, Delta Shuttle®, Delta Connection®, Delta SkyTeamTM, and Worldwide Partners operate 5826 flights each day to over 437 cities in 78 countries.

Delta Air Lines spends a lot of time and effort on developing customer care programmes, and this attention to high levels of customer care has paid off. Based on calendar 2002 data, Delta is the second-largest airline in terms of passengers carried, and third largest as measured by operating revenues and revenue passenger miles flown. Delta is the leading US transatlantic airline, offering the most daily flight departures, serving the largest number of non-stop markets and carrying more passengers than any other US airline. Delta is a Delaware corporation headquartered in Atlanta, Georgia and is subject to government regulation under the Federal Aviation Act of 1958, as amended, as well as many other federal, state and foreign laws.

In response to the tremendous growth of air travel and the demanding need for excellence in customer service, Delta has joined other US airlines and the Air Transport Association (ATA) in an effort to provide passengers with a clear understanding of the industry's commitment to meet essential performance objectives. Delta has outlined its responsibilities and how the firm will fulfil them in 12 key points presented in the form of a customer care charter and given to every customer. Delta intends to ensure that its customer air travel experience will encompass, to the best of its abilities, the most comprehensive customer service possible. To emphasise the importance of meeting these essential performance objectives, Delta officially adopted the 12-point 'customer commitment' charter as part of its contract of carriage.

However customer satisfaction is actually measured, one thing is certain and that is that high quality customer care is the key to achieving many of the business objectives confronting all competitive firms, which include:

1. minimising customer turnover
2. attracting new customers
3. improving profitability
4. improving company image
5. enhancing customer and employee satisfaction.

The subject of customer care is really the starting point for understanding developments in customer relationship management (CRM). In a sense CRM is the current 'state of the art' in the marketing profession to provide superior customer care. In today's commercial environment of increasing competition and dwindling resources, companies need to integrate all forms of customer communication across all functions. One of the best ways to achieve this is to implement a customer care or, as we shall discuss later, a customer relationship management (CRM) programme. Customer care refers to the processes, software, hardware, and

Internet capabilities used to acquire, store, manipulate and manage information about customers and potential customers. Companies of all types and in all industries can use such information to help plan and implement marketing, sales, and customer service activities in order to identify, attract, and retain profitable customers.

Activity

- **Why it is important for firms to pay attention to customer care?**
- **What are the benefits of high levels of customer care to (a) the customer and (b) the marketing firm?**

Firms are operating in an increasingly competitive environment. Much of this competition is international as the globalisation of markets continues. Customers have greater choice and are more discerning. If a company does not give them what they want they will go elsewhere. Today, the cost of acquiring new customers often exceeds the cost of retaining existing ones. Satisfied customers tend not to argue about price and it takes less marketing and sales activities to service them than it does for new customers. As a result, particularly today in the age of the Internet, business is predominantly concerned with the customer. With increasing competition, companies need to unify customer communication into an integrated system which can be used to deliver customer satisfaction. Businesses must focus their resources on aggressively targeting and retaining their most attractive customers and on expanding their base of profitable customers.

- The benefits to the customer of high levels of customer care are fairly obvious. They experience a superior service and are completely satisfied with the level of customer care provided. Consequently they do not have to spend time and effort searching the market for alternatives. Price is not everything. Most satisfied customers will remain loyal even if other firms offer similar products and/or services at a lower price.

- The benefits to the individual marketing firm of providing customers with a high level of customer care is that a satisfied customer is likely to remain a customer. New customer acquisition is usually far more expensive than existing customer retention.

▶ Marketing's evolution

As we mentioned in our introduction, marketing is not a static subject but is evolving and changing over time. Some would say that the more recent changes are exponential. The drivers of such changes are legion but some of the more important factors have been technological developments and the globalisation of markets. Like life in general the world of marketing is full of dynamic change as it attempts to adapt to an ever-changing commercial environment. Even over the past ten years or so the world of marketing has changed significantly. Many people who have been working in the marketing field for years often feel alienated and find it difficult to keep up with the changes. Many people who trained in marketing in the 1970s or 80s find that their knowledge is out of date and the subject has changed considerably since that time. Today many people working in the field of marketing are young, often under 35 years of age. This is not because older people are incapable of holding down a marketing career but because changes are happening so fast in many areas of the marketing industry that only the very young understand what is going on. As we discussed in the last chapter, a lot of this change has to do with the adoption of new computer-based technology such as the Internet, extranet, intranet, database marketing, data warehousing and the World Wide Web. Today, marketing management must at least have some grounding in the commercial possibilities of these new marketing technologies. Management do not necessarily have to be technical experts themselves because specialist technical staff can be employed to do this side of the work. They do, however, need to be able to see the strategic implications and possibilities of the new technologies and be able to advise others how the technology can be employed to gain a strategic advantage over the competition and to improve marketing performance. However not all the dramatic changes in marketing thinking over this period have been due to technological advances and change. On the contrary in fact, many of the changes have been more philosophical in nature. The application of the new Internet-based marketing technologies may have facilitated some of these changes. Up until recently, for example, the concept of totally integrated customer relationship management systems remained just that in many firms, an idealised concept that was fine in the text books and academic papers but extremely difficult to put into practice in the day-to-day business world. The development of sophisticated computer software products and the increase in the memory available to systems to enable them to store, manipulate and retrieve large amounts of customer data have made the idealised concept a reality for at least the more progressive business firms. Industrial companies have practised this relationship building and management approach for some years in their business-to-business marketing, but it is a fairly new concept in business-to-consumer marketing. Of course the relationship marketing approach may not be appropriate in all situations.

▶▶ Relationship marketing

Relationship marketing is a business concept, which has developed from a growing body of literature expressing lack of satisfaction with conventional transactional marketing. This dissatisfaction applies to all areas of marketing but especially business-to-business and services marketing where the shortcomings of the more conventional marketing approach were first recognised. In 1954 Peter Drucker said 'there is only one valid definition of business: to create customers. It is the customer who determines what the business is' (Drucker, 1973, pp. 64–5). Hence customers are central to business and the underlying theme behind relationship marketing is the acquisition, satisfaction and retention of customers. Retention is the key word here and is the basic premise behind the CRM approach to business and the main rationale for employing a long-term CRM strategy. In a sense it is the basic marketing concept in principle but developed into a format in which it can be applied in an operational setting rather than merely being an idealised concept that management merely aspire to.

▌▌▌ Vignette 17.2

The Association for the Advancement of Relationship Marketing (AARM) of Canada pioneers the professionalism of customer relationships.

Since 1995 the Association for the Advancement of Relationship Marketing (AARM), based in Canada, has become one of the largest associations focused on the development, understanding and communication of the principles and discipline of marketing, managing, maintaining and enhancing customer relationships. This encompasses relationship marketing, customer management and direct marketing, technology, research and virtually any form or methodology of connecting with a prospect or customer in an ongoing and positive manner on an enterprise-wide basis. It goes without saying, it's simply good business to get closer to the customer. From an attending membership of 52 in 1996 to some 1800 plus currently, AARM has experienced exponential growth. Today the association comprises organisations from all industries across the Fortune 1000 companies as well as within the small and medium-sized enterprise category (SMEs).

AARM's members include major financial institutions, insurance companies, publishers, retailers, charitable organizations, agencies, relationship marketers, direct marketers and those involved in e-business and Internet marketing. The AARM industry breakdown shows a diverse membership following, with 52 per cent falling in the financial, telecoms, advertising, computer services and software, direct marketing, retail and the manufacturing industries and the other 48 per cent from many other industry groups. The AARM membership has 43 per cent in senior management, 49 per cent in middle management and 8 per cent in all other management areas. Senior representatives from organisations in a wide array of product and service industries believe that AARM provides a unique forum for those wishing to understand and apply key strategic and tactical dimensions of CRM. Today, AARM continues to promote industry growth, development and education through a network of people who provide a forum for the business community and offer networking opportunities for those involved in specific disciplines. AARM fulfils its educational role by providing conferences, seminars, workshops, executive briefings, networking sessions and other CRM educational content.

The concept of relationship marketing was introduced into the literature by early researchers into customer care such as Berry (1983). The subject of marketing had been developed largely from the experience of firms and university business school researchers involved in consumer markets and based in the USA. Marketing as a subject and business discipline was developed in the USA. These principles and theories seemed to have almost universal applicability in the consumer markets of developed economies throughout the world, especially in Europe where the concept arrived from the USA and was applied by firms as an overriding business philosophy much later. Some adaptation was of course necessary because of cultural and environmental differences in the markets, and this was covered in the international marketing literature.

However the principles and practices of modern marketing developed in the crucible of the USA consumer market sector did not work quite so well in business-to-business environments or for the increasingly important service sector. As the first world Western economies reconstructed and developed after the war, agriculture and manufacturing became less important and comprised a smaller proportion of these countries' GDP. Such countries are often described by economic commentators as being in the 'post-industrial' phase of development. In a post-industrial economy a lot of the jobs are of an intellectual or at least brain-based type. Services become the predominant economic activity carried out by human beings. Marketers looked to the conventional wisdom in the marketing literature and found that it no longer fitted so well in the new service-based economies and that some new thinking was required. In the growing business-to-business sector of the economy too, there developed a deep dissatisfaction with the conventional 'one sale ahead' transactional marketing approach. It had been recognised in industrial markets for some time that commercial relationships between buyer and seller organisations required a more long-term interaction approach rather than the short termism of the next sale. This new thinking resulted in the development of the relationship marketing model.

This has now been accepted by firms across the board, so to speak, and not only by firms involved in the marketing of services or involved in industrial markets.

Writing on relationship marketing Gronroos (1990) proposed a marketing strategy continuum, ranging from transaction marketing, which was regarded as more appropriate to business-to-consumer marketing particularly in the field of fast-moving consumer goods (FMCG), through to relationship marketing. This approach was seen as more suitable for business-to-business marketing and services marketing. However relationship marketing is now used in all markets, including consumer markets. Copulsky and Wolf (1990) used the term 'relationship marketing' to identify a type of database marketing. In their model the database is used by marketing firms to select suitable customer targets for the promotion of products and services. The message sent to customers is tailor made to fit in with their particular needs and wants. The response is monitored and used to produce various measures, including the projected lifetime value of the customer. McKenna (1991) linked relationship marketing to the organisational structure of a business. The whole business was organised to produce a relationship marketing approach rather than it being merely another business process. To summarise at this stage, the major concern amongst practitioners with the conventional marketing approach was that it was too short term and transactional in focus. This may have worked well over the years in a predominantly business-to-consumer environment but less so for service marketing, industrial and other forms of business-to-business marketing where the creation and maintenance of long-term relationships with customers was crucial for long-term commercial success. The modern usage of the term 'relationship marketing' describes a situation where the creation, satisfaction and retention of customers are at the very centre of marketing strategy.

■ **Explain the difference between transactional marketing and relationship marketing.**

■ **What do you understand by the term 'lifetime value of customers' in respect to the concept of relationship marketing?**

Transactional marketing, as the name suggests, is when the marketing or sales approach of management tend to be concerned with the next sale or transaction. Customers are viewed as the next potential sale in a rather short-term fashion. They are viewed in discrete terms rather than in a continuous sense. By contrast, relationship marketing takes a much longer term perspective. Customers are viewed not simply as the next sale, or even the one after that, but as a long-term potential income stream. A firm's existing customer base is the most valuable resource it possesses.

The concept of 'lifetime value' applies in consumer and business-to-business settings. In a consumer setting a person may open a bank account on leaving college and taking up their first job and may well keep the same account for the rest of their life. On buying their first house they may well stay with the same mortgage lender for the rest of their life. In a business-to-business setting a firm may use the same firm of accountants or consultants over many generations of managers. Profit from customers should be viewed as a flow over many years or even over the customer lifetime. It is the net present value of the customer income stream that indicates the true value of a customer to the marketing firm.

▶ TQM as the starting point

In the 1970s W. Edwards Deming, the well-known expert on quality issues, formulated a now seminal theory of quality based upon his intimate knowledge of Japanese manufacturing which concerned 14 key quality points and this revolutionised many aspects of production management (Deming, 1993). His ideas on quality have been termed 'total quality management' (TQM) and this philosophy now permeates thinking throughout entire organisations. Total quality management is a structured system for satisfying internal and external customers and suppliers by integrating the business environment, continuous improvement and breakthroughs in development, and maintenance cycles while changing organisational culture. One of the keys to implementing TQM can be found in this definition. It is the idea that TQM is a structured system. Describing TQM as a structured system means that it is a strategy derived from internal and external customer and supplier wants and needs that have been determined by management. Pinpointing internal and external requirements allows management to continuously improve, develop, and maintain quality, cost, delivery, and morale. TQM is a system that integrates all of this activity and information.

▶ Supply chain integration (SCI)

In 1994 a study was undertaken in the UK by A. T. Kearney, Management Consultants. It investigated the supply chain from end-of-line manufacturers right back up the supply chain to sources of raw materials. Its conclusions were that business improvements would be possible by simply not viewing dealings between purchasers and sellers as isolated transactions each time, but by seeking to involve everybody down the supply chain from which came the term 'supply chain integration' (SCI).

The study found that different supply chain relationships should be possible with some members being content merely to act as manufacturers and fabricators and supplying to a specification (that is, seeing their task as being good producers at the right quality and at the right time) but that others might like to become more involved in end-use applications and even proffer suggestions for improvement, even though they may be towards the beginning of the supply chain. By considering the entire supply chain new opportunities would present themselves and benefit everybody in the supply chain. This would improve overall effectiveness in the chain with regard to the elimination of waste and suggesting better ways of doing things, thus reducing overall costs.

The result would be that it would be possible to impel service standards to final customers to superior levels by concentrating the complete supply chain in this direction through mutual cooperation, rather than weakening the attempts of individual elements of the chain through conflicting objectives. The outcome would be the necessity for closer relationships between suppliers and customers. The task would not be easy because of the problems of such integration, and having to investigate the measures of sophistication that individual members of the supply chain wanted or expected.

Following the discussions relating to relationship marketing and SCI, it is appropriate now to consider the view put forward by Christian Gronroos in 1990 who argued that traditional views of marketing are unsatisfactory in a modern business environment. He emphasised the shortcomings of McCarthy's four Ps and went on to say that more Ps such as 'people' and 'planning' should be added as new marketing viewpoints. He believes that the basic concept of supplying customer needs and wants in target markets has always had relevance, but contends that this still views the firm as supplying the solutions and not receiving its ideas from the marketplace. He therefore attempted to redefining marketing in a way that applies the principles of relationship marketing.

▶▶ Service marketing

The concept of relationship marketing is particularly important in the area of services. Much of the UK's economy is service based in terms of GDP output. Service offerings are largely intangible. Most service offerings have some actual tangible product component and most products have some service component. What we are talking about here are service offerings that are predominately intangible. For example a financial service such as a bank account or a PEP scheme is largely intangible. Because services are largely intangible it is more difficult for the marketing firm to tell whether they are providing what the customer wants. Service satisfaction depends on the experience and the perception of the customer. It is a largely subjective thing. Hence it is vitally important for the marketing firm to monitor their service offering to the customer and to ensure that they are at least matching and possibly even exceeding the customer's service expectations. You provide a quality service to your customers when you either meet or exceed their expectations. Many companies make the fundamental mistake of assuming that they know what their customers expect and through that often lose customers.

Because of the nature of services the traditional marketing mix is extended from the four P paradigm to the seven P model. We retain the existing so-called four Ps of product, price, promotion and place and add to these processes, people and physical evidence. Processes are concerned with the efficiency of the process used in the delivery of the service, for example how well a travel firm booked and organised your holiday. People deliver the service, for example how well you were looked after by staff in a hotel. Physical evidence is the service firm's attempt to give some form of tangibility to what would otherwise be an intangible service, for example giving a brand name to a certain type of bank account along with special literature and so on to make the brand more 'physical' in the minds of consumers.

Research has shown that it is five times more expensive to win a new customer than it is to keep an old customer. And so it is very important for firms to retain existing customers, especially potentially profitable key accounts. Therefore it is essential that marketing firms spend time and energy to find out what customers really want. Also, people experience service in different ways and each customer has a particular perception of the service a firm provides. Therefore, if you are serious about determining the quality of your service, you should study at least a representative sample of your customer base. In certain service marketing situations when a firm loses a customer they are often lost for good. This can also be the case for products but is more common for services. For example a man in his 50s might have been with one of the high street banks since his university days. He may still hold his account in his old university branch. Such a person is likely to be inundated with direct mail and other personalised direct marketing messages, for example on the Internet, to try and persuade him to switch his account to another branch. If such a person ever did switch his account then he would be very unlikely ever to return to his original bank and from the bank's point of view the customer would be lost for good. On the other hand, if the same person switched his loyalty from, say, Sainsbury's supermarket to Asda because he thought Asda offered better sales promotions, it might be possible to get him back. Such a person is unlikely never to visit Sainsbury's again in his life. In such a situation such a customer would be classified by Sainsbury's as always a share. The concepts of 'lost for good' and 'always a share' type customer situations are listed below:

1. *Always a share:* low transaction and switching costs, if you lose a customer you can always get them back.
2. *Lost for good:* if transaction and switching costs high then when you lose a customer you are unlikely to get them back.

Relationship marketing is particularly important in 'lost for good' situations because once the firm has lost the customer it is highly unlikely that they will ever manage to get them back.

Research has shown that the quality of the service provided by a company or institution can be measured by determining the discrepancy or gap between what the customer wants (customer expectations) and how the customer experiences the service (customer perceptions). Expectations and perceptions are unlikely to be identical. It may be the customer is delighted by receiving a service experience far greater than they expected. This would be a good situation for the marketing firm as long as the service level was valued by the customer. If it was not valued then the overly high service provided would amount to an inefficient use of the firm's resources. Customer expectations are formed by a number of factors including word-of-mouth communications, personal needs, past experience and what and how you communicate to your customer. Customer perceptions are formed by the customer experiencing so-called moments of truth. 'Moment of truth' is the basic concept of service marketing and is used to describe each episode in which a customer comes into contact with any aspect of your organisation. Remember that a single negative experience at any point in the service cycle can spoil the entire experience. Parasuraman et al. (1990) developed the so-called SERVQUAL instrument which can be used to measure the quality of service. They developed the so-called 'gaps model' of service quality (see Figure 17.1). The most important gap, referred to as Gap 5, is the gap between customer expectations and customer perceptions. This gap is caused by the four other gaps, defined as follows:

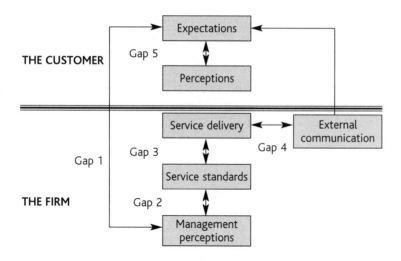

Figure 17.1 The GAPS model of service quality
Source: Parasuraman et al. (1985)

▶ *Gap 1:* represents the discrepancy between what the customer wants (customer expectations) and what management think they want (management perceptions).

▶ *Gap 2:* represents the discrepancy between management's perception of client expectations and service quality specifications.

▶ *Gap 3:* represents the discrepancy between the service delivered and the service quality specifications.

▶ *Gap 4:* represents the discrepancy between the promised service (external communication to customers) and the service provided.

Parasuraman et al. developed a methodology which is now widely used in the measurement of service delivery and customer satisfaction. The methodology is based on a series of standard questionnaires in order to determine whether the above gaps exist in an organisation. The general idea is to be able to close the gaps, especially GAP 5 which is the most important and really cased by the other gaps in the model. These questionnaires are applied to customers (gap 5), management (gaps 1 and 2) and service contact personnel (gaps 3 and 4). The questionnaires are based on five quality dimensions which were constructed by Parasuraman et al. when their research showed that customers use the following five criteria in judging the quality of service:

1. *Tangibles:* appearance of physical facilities, equipment, personnel and communication materials.

2. *Reliability:* ability to perform the promised service dependably and accurately.
3. *Responsiveness:* willingness to help customers and provide a prompt service.
4. *Assurance:* knowledge and courtesy of the employees and their ability to convey trust and confidence.
5. *Empathy:* caring, individualised attention the company provides its customers.

The standard questionnaires that they developed for measuring gap 5, are based on the above five dimensions. The questionnaires firstly measure the respondent's expectation of service quality and then his/her perception of an organisation's service quality. The difference between these two is then used as a measure of gap 5. After more research, the gap 5 concept was extended to what is called 'a zone of tolerance'. In this case, the customer's expectancy of service quality is measured on two levels:

▶ *Desired service:* the level of service representing a blend of what customers believe can be and should be provided.
▶ *Adequate service:* the minimum level of service customers are willing to accept.

Figure 17.2 depicts the zone of tolerance. The customer's perception of service quality is then compared to this zone of tolerance.

From the three measures of service (desired, adequate and perceived) two more measures are derived:

▶ Measure of service adequacy (MSA) = perceived service – adequate service
▶ Measure of service superiority (MSS) = perceived service – desired service.

The MSA measures the gap between perceived service and the minimum service the client will tolerate. If this gap is negative, then you have serious problems pertaining to the service you provide.

The MSS measures the gap between perceived service and the desired service level the client would prefer. This gap is comparable with gap 5.

The area of service marketing is large and only an introduction is given here in the context of the importance of relationship marketing to the marketing firm. If any organisation is serious about providing a

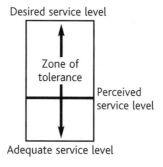

Figure 17.2 The zone of tolerance model

quality service to customers they must measure their service satisfaction. By monitoring and measuring the quality of their service marketing management can obtain the necessary information that will enable them to satisfy and retain existing customers. (Remember research has shown that it is five times more expensive to win a new customer than to keep an old customer.)

▶▶ Internal marketing

Internal marketing is the process of engaging the support and commitment of employees and other organisational members for the goals and objectives of the company. Successful businesses recognise the importance of internal communications. An effective system of cross-company communications is vital for keeping staff informed of what is happening throughout the company and for providing a feedback mechanism. Internal marketing takes place at the interface between marketing and human resource management and involves both of these management disciplines. The application of internal public relations has a salient role to play in the overall process of achieving an internal marketing culture because it too embraces both of these areas of management. In a very real sense internal marketing is actually an intrinsic part of the relationship marketing process – it would be difficult to have the latter before first achieving the former. Internal marketing is an important implementation tool. It aids communication and helps organisations overcome any resistance to change. It informs and involves all staff in new initiatives and strategies. It is simple to construct, especially if you are familiar with the traditional principles of marketing. If you are not, it would be a valuable exercise to spend some time considering marketing plans. Internal marketing obeys the same rules as, and has a similar structure to, external marketing. The main differences are that the firm's customers are staff and colleagues from the same organisation. In a sense they are 'internal customers'. If staff are not aware of and supportive of your marketing campaign, they may be unable or unwilling to provide the backing that will ensure your project or campaign is a success. Besides, it's important for everyone on the team to have the same information. What do you do if a staff member gets a call from the local newspaper and hasn't been told about your planned event? Get staff members involved in your planning. Ask their opinion about marketing materials and procedures. Treat them as another focus group. Finally, spend time selling your staff on the marketing concept. Make sure they understand and agree.

The staff represent the 'coal-face' of the corporate brand. They meet, greet and serve customers in a variety of different ways, face-to-face, online, via the telephone and so on. Customer relationships depend on their attitude and loyalty. In turn they build loyalty longer term for the company. The longevity of customer relationships is a continuing issue for many companies as it costs more to recruit a new customer than to serve a customer of longer standing. To motivate staff, it is necessary for communication to flow both horizontally and vertically to all staff levels. This process of communication should include the brand mission, philosophy and core values. Many organisations are unable to harmonise these communication flows to reach all staff levels; some do not achieve even one of these flows. For this reason, a new view may have to be taken of the classic human resources function in many organisations. In the future, the process of internal marketing will require an empowered human resource capability. Potentially, internal marketing could have a wide variety of applications, yet too few companies would be able to benchmark themselves against the holistic range of these three concepts. By ensuring that all members of staff are aware of the corporate vision, it becomes clearer what the organisational goals and priorities are, thus helping to avoid conflict within the organisation. A focus on development can help them to develop the skills and the knowledge that they need. Finally, rewarding them financially through salary packages as well as recognition for their individual and collective contribution towards the corporate strategy means that all three factors can work as a cohesive whole.

▶ Intranet technology

Intranet is a form of closed loop Internet. That is, it can only be accessed by people who have the authority to do so. Intranet is often used within organisations so that staff can access information and keep in touch with what is going on, sometimes on a 'need to know' basis. intranet technology is the fastest growing method of internal communications. Many companies are finding that it is the ideal tool for cross-company communications; it provides instant information and is more cost effective than producing a regular company newsletter. An intranet can be used to give employees access to company documents, distribute software, enable group scheduling, provide an easy front end to company databases, and it allows individuals and departments to publish information they need to communicate to the rest of the company.

Here are some tips for items to include in order to keep people interested in your intranet:

▶ A corporate directory
▶ Telephone lists
▶ Internal email lists
▶ Company structure
▶ Photographs of staff
▶ A calendar of events
▶ A policies and procedures manual
▶ The health and safety plan
▶ Company newsletter
▶ Price lists
▶ Customer order history
▶ A poll – vote on some of the pressing issues within your company
▶ Add a discussion board.

▶ Extranet technology

It is also possible to allow external companies to view some of your information. This selected sharing of information is known as an 'extranet'. Extranets can be used for maintaining ongoing business relationships while enabling privacy, security, and customised communication. It is very important that extranets are secure. The information on extranets is often sensitive and tailored for each user, for example supplier price lists, order history and so on. Extranets can be relatively simple and inexpensive to implement, but can deliver far-reaching benefits to your organisation and your business partners. Communication, collaborative working and shared applications already established within the corporate intranet can all be delivered to external organisations and business partners via an extranet.

▮▮▮ Vignette 17.3

Maracom Precision Marketing (USA) offers internal marketing advice and consultancy.

Maracom Precision Marketing (USA) is a consultancy firm, based in the USA, which offers consultancy services in many areas of marketing, via the Internet or the telephone, for an affordable up-front fee. The convenience of telephone and/or Internet delivery and the pay-as-you-go method of payment make this company's services particularly attractive to small and medium-sized enterprises (SMEs). Over the past ten years, Maracom's special focus has been in an area usually referred to as 'internal marketing' – the process of engaging the support and commitment of employees and other organisational members for the goals and objectives of the company. Goals might include broad strategic initiatives, as well as specific tactical marketing programmes and campaigns.

The company's internal marketing projects usually encompass five phases:

1. An assessment phase that uncovers management and employee attitudes and beliefs towards each other, the company, customers, and marketing mix components.

2. A review of communications activities and their effectiveness, including a mapping of communications channels. Instrumental in this map are the links among customers, employees, and marketing/management.

3. An assessment of employee performance systems, including goal-setting, measurement and rewards. The discovery with management and employees of realistic internal marketing goals and objectives.

4. The development of workable strategies to achieve internal marketing goals. These strategies usually include communications, behavioural and performance related outcomes across all organizational levels.

5. Using a combination of internal and external resources, the firm then 'follows-up' by helping clients to implement their internal marketing strategies.

The firm considers their intervention an opportunity to help clients learn how to practice effective internal marketing. In other words, while they are often called in to resolve existing issues, their goal is to leave clients with the skills and attitudes that they need to perpetuate the successes of their initial marketing consultancy work.

▶▶ Customer relationship management

Customer relationship management (CRM) is a comprehensive approach which provides seamless integration of every area of business that touches the customer – namely marketing, sales, customer service and field support – through the integration of people, process and technology, taking advantage of the revolutionary impact of the Internet. CRM creates a mutually beneficial relationship with your customers. The task of implementing and maintaining a CRM solution can seem overwhelming, but when the goal of cheaper, faster, better customer service is considered, the results far outweigh the challenges. At no time, has CRM been more crucial than it is today with heightened attention to cost cutting, revenue generation and customer retention. CRM is not just a software solution, but also a set of skills and competencies that will enable a company to better understand and profit from each and every customer relationship. In a tough economy, competition is more evident than at any other time, and the ability to compete on the basis of customer relationships is more important than ever.

CRM enhances a firm's contact with customers. It extends the reach of businesses, provides insight that improves service and helps drive new customer acquisition and optimises customer loyalty to boost the profitability of your business. CRM has developed from a synthesis of relationship marketing, internal marketing and customer care to form a fully integrated system. The ability of firms actually to use such a system owes a lot to the availability of the appropriate computer-based technologies, as was discussed in the last chapter. However CRM is much more than just a Web-based customer care programme or an enhanced database marketing programme. In fact CRM is evolving from a technology-centred scheme to a business-value enterprise as firms move from viewing customers as purely exploitable income sources to important assets that have to be looked after and developed – in fact the most important asset the company has.

▶ CRM is all about relationships

- ▷ CRM is about a march forward in the quest to find ways and means to connect people with people in a meaningful way in a world full of robots and electronic touch points
- ▷ CRM is about the tools, techniques and processes that are required to help make positive things happen as a result of our knowledge and deeper understanding of each other's needs
- ▷ CRM is about connecting people who need CRM tools and techniques
- ▷ CRM is about relationships with people. Connecting people with people. Relationships with customers, clients, vendors, suppliers and employees

▸ CRM is about the marketing aspects of relationships with all these constituents and more

▸ CRM is about the management aspects of relationships with all these constituents and more

▸ CRM is about knowledge enhancement, about how to manage the CRM process on an enterprise-wide basis

▸ CRM is about technology and the move forward to try to connect the customer's mind with our individual corporations.

Providing customers with ongoing value, satisfying their individual needs and ensuring that customers get what they want when and where they want it, is critical in today's dynamic and competitive market. If one company fails its customers, there is any number of rivals waiting to take over. With e-commerce, any company, anywhere in the world can take away customers. Retention is especially difficult with respect to commodity products when all it takes to move to another supplier is to type in a new Web address. CRM is a major part of many companies' e-commerce strategy and their long-term relationship marketing strategy. It is a business and technology discipline that helps firms in the acquisition and retention of their most important and profitable customers. Ideally, CRM systems help firms provide start to finish customer care, from initial acquisition of the customer right the way through to product delivery and aftercare services (Figure 17.3).

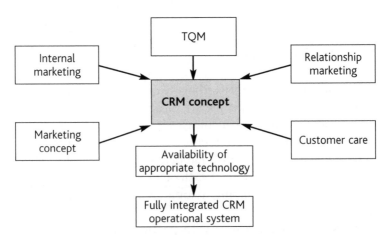

Figure 17.3 Factors contributing to the development of the CRM concept and its practical implementation

▶ CRM and the Internet

CRM is not just a technology, it is a business strategy that technology can help deliver. Businesses would do best looking not only at traditional customer service technologies to deliver on their CRM goals, but also making sure their strategies incorporate and leverage the customer-facing documents they're already generating. Society is changing at what seems to be an ever-increasing rate. More choice, less time to choose and to enjoy the results of our choice. Everyone seems to have less time even though the futurologists of only a few years back stated that new technology would give us all more time and lead to the leisure society. Customers have more products and services to choose from and more information available to them to help them make their purchasing decisions. Think about the task of purchasing a new mobile telephone for example. The products are so sophisticated today, there are so many different models and the information available on the capabilities of each model in magazines, on the Internet and in conventional advertising is enormous. Where do you start? Consumers wish to shop at all hours, even on a Sunday or bank holiday. Some people want to go to the supermarket in the middle of the night. People do their banking on their mobile telephone, research house purchases on the Internet and book their air tickets through the television offers using teletext. Seth Godin, author of the book *Permission Marketing* (1999), said that the average consumer sees 3000 marketing messages a day. So to reach its audience a message has to be relevant and well targeted. Godin and his colleagues are working to persuade some of the most important firms in the world to change the way they relate to their customers. His argument is both simple and radical – conventional marketing communications, particularly conventional media advertising, are not as effective as they used to be. This is partly because there is far more advertising for consumers to see and digest, and partly because people have learned to ignore it. Additionally the rise of the Net means that companies can go further than conventional communications would allow them to in the past.

Today's customer is more sophisticated – and more demanding – than ever before. Customers expect to be able to conduct product research, place orders, check order status, customise orders, and investigate new products and services, 24 hours a day, seven days a week. In this environment, customer loyalty is low. While companies can differentiate themselves from their competition with the scope and quality of their products and services and with their physical or virtual surroundings, the best way to generate customer loyalty is to ensure that customers have a positive, satisfying experience every time they interact with your company. Consider the following:

▶ A study at Harvard University by researchers Reichheld and Teal (1996) calculated that a mere 5 per cent reduction in customer defections increases company profits by 25 per cent to 85 per cent.

▶ Datamonitor projects that if companies continue to provide poor service levels on their websites, they could lose more than $63 billion in potential revenues in 2004. To meet this challenge, today's progressive companies are adopting a new business model – one that emphasises a customer's lifetime value. They are executing this model by integrating new Internet initiatives and Web-based applications, including:

　▶ Interaction technologies, which allow customers to interactively communicate with the enterprise (through co-browsing, chat, email management and legacy interactive voice response) and to capture, manage, and seamlessly transfer interaction from one media contact point to another.

　▶ Communication enablers, which permit data to flow physically and logically across multiple media. These enablers let companies migrate from voice-based time-division multiplexing operations to an Internet protocol-based model that supports all media (voice, data, and video) and from closed, proprietary architectures to open, standards-based platforms.

　▶ Network/intelligent network services, which provide a flexible, secure, reliable, and scalable network infrastructure that supports data, voice, and video communications across multiple environments.

Companies that incorporate CRM customer care solutions into fundamental business processes reap many benefits, including improved customer relations, internal workforce optimisation, and cost savings. Specifically, companies can:

▶ Integrate customer interactions across marketing, sales, e-commerce, fulfilment, billing and provisioning, service, learning, and online communities

▶ Create a flexible, effective channel for communicating with existing customers and reaching out to new customers

▶ React quickly to customers' changing needs and increase brand awareness

- Enable customers to do business at their convenience – let them order online, find technical information, check order status, or configure products online at any hour of the day
- Create online tools for the sales force that allow them to access product information, communicate with other groups, create proposals, and check availability
- Allow the sales organisation to focus on the customer, provide more value-added services, and pursue additional sales opportunities
- Maintain order processing and customer support at a steady headcount despite an increasing customer base
- Increase order accuracy
- Reduce the time for handling orders, resolving customer issues, and transferring knowledge to and from a customer or to partners across the supply chain
- Move transactions away from agents to automated fulfilment
- Eliminate redundant infrastructure.

There is a new group of products and services that relies on customers registering their interest in them with the company. Amazon.com encourages its customers to review books and publishes their comments on the website so both the firm and other users can read them and make use of them. A US airline invites customers to register their preferences for last minute offers via its website, and then emails potential customers with details of weekend breaks at their preferred resorts. Building high value, loyal, lifetime relationships is the most powerful competitive tool a firm possesses. Management should reward staff for doing it right and make sure that they ask the customers if they are satisfied with the service they are getting. Then check their purchasing behaviour to see if they remain loyal. For example The Leadership Factor is a marketing research firm based in Huddersfield, UK which carries out customer service satisfaction surveys for clients and monitors customer retention and loyalty. Some people take it very seriously indeed. Jeff Bezos (CEO of amazon.com) says 'I encourage everyone who works at Amazon to wake up terrified every morning. They should be afraid of our customers. Those are the folks who send us money. That is why our strategy is to say, "Heads down, focus on the customer", because the customer needs change at a slower rate.' (Interview with Jeff Bezos, www.annonline.com/interviews/970106/biography.html/realaudio). Control of the relationship lies in the hands of the customer. The marketing firm should help customers to train them to meet their needs.

▮▮▮ Vignette 17.4

Vignette is about to enter the overcrowded CRM market with Vignette Dialog, a product derived from its acquisition of Revino.

Vignette Inc. unveiled a new software program designed to help companies plan and keep track of interactions with their customers, a move that pushes the company into the highly competitive customer relationship management (CRM) software market.

The Austin, Texas based software company said the new product, called Vignette Dialog, can help companies convert prospects into sales by keeping prospective customers engaged through a succession of targeted emails, phone calls, text messages, direct mail or even pager messages – though it advises companies not to go overboard. 'We don't want to flood people with information they don't want to receive' said Darrin Wood, product manager at Vignette.

Vignette based the product on software assets it acquired from Revino Inc., another CRM software firm which had been based in Burlington, Massachusetts, before it went out of business. It plans to release a new version of Dialog that is more closely tied into its Web-content-authoring software. The Dialog product lets companies design standard responses to customer interactions. For instance, a company could set up the software to automatically send follow-up emails to people who called a customer service number. The company could then tailor follow-up email messages, offering new promotions, for instance, depending on the customer's profile and questions. The company does not mean to compete with other major CRM software makers such as Siebel. Instead, it views its new product as complementary to Siebel's sales, marketing and call centre applications. Dialog is unique in its ability to coordinate customer communications both online and off. The price of Vignette Dialog starts at $150,000 (£95,000). Vignette Dialog is a classic example of where the CRM software market is heading in term of its advanced integrated technology.

CRM is a major part of many companies' e-commerce strategy and their long-term relationship marketing strategy. CRM is a business and technology discipline that helps firms in the acquisition and retention of their most important and profitable customers. Ideally, CRM systems help firms provide start to finish customer care, from initial acquisition of the customer right the way through to product delivery and aftercare services. But CRM is rapidly evolving from being a technology-centred undertaking to a business-value endeavour. Organisations are moving away from seeing their customers as merely exploitable income sources to treating them as assets to be valued and nurtured. The value of customers is a long-term concept; lifetime value of customers is now what is important to many firms. This is an important trend that represents the use of knowledge-management practices, such as the use of databases to capture and store comprehensive information about the customer, to build long-term, mutually beneficial, customer relationships. Companies need a CRM strategy because it helps them to understand their customer-acquisition and retention goals, which is the whole basis of relationship marketing practices. CRM also helps companies retain customers and increase profitability.

▶ CRM computer software

CRM software reduces service costs and maximizes sales and marketing profits by organising a business around its customers. The heart of a firm's automation system is the CRM software. The way a firm's CRM software handles the rapidly changing data, with accuracy, and the instant responses to the varied needs of sales representatives and service technicians can mean the difference between the failure and success of a business. CRM software can bring together data from disparate systems and business units to provide a holistic view of customers and the company's relationship with them. It can help coordinate customer contact and relationships across channels (retail, channel, Web) by presenting a unified message regardless of where the contact point is.

CRM computer software allows marketing firms to undertake the following tasks:

- Extensive complaint/request tracking
- Corrective action tracking
- Compile comprehensive customer profiles
- Contact management/sales activity tracking
- Problem category, product defect and cause analysis
- Return authorisation (RMA) and field service tracking
- Letter and email integration
- Attachment of related documents and images
- Unlimited number of security levels
- Reports, charts and user-defined queries
- Scalable, flexible and customisable
- Fully integrated Windows® or browser-based Web interface
- Supplier, distributor and third-party issue tracking.

CRM strategies can be a defence against being the same as every other supplier and can allow the marketing firm to differentiate itself through superior service. For example, if you manufacture a commodity type product such as welding rods, you can differentiate yourself through better CRM and customer service. CRM is most effective when companies use proactive strategies to support the whole sales process through acquisition, retention and development. Most businesses are moving to Web-based CRM, but this does not do away with the need for the personal interaction that is so crucial to many companies' sales and marketing approach. Active CRM technology means that a customer contacting a website for information can be followed up immediately by a telephone call or some other form of communication. A mixture of communications can be used from the Internet, telephone, direct mail and even personal contact. In addition, modern CRM computer-based technology allows the firm to undertake the following tasks.

Complaint tracking

A framework enabling a customisable workflow with establishment of ownership, due date reporting and email reminders. Letter generation, email integration, and document attachments are powerful time-saving tools.

Corrective actions

Fully document and track all corrective actions that result from customer concerns or internal concerns, such as a quality review meeting or an audit. Instantly generate a summary report of a corrective action and email it to a customer or supplier, engaging them in your quality process.

Customer support

Involves front-line customer support representatives with crucial information. Detailed account profiles, past complaint history and search capability will empower your employees to communicate effectively with all of your customers. For each problem type, establish unique requirements in your workflow :

- default problem ownership
- pre-defined turn around times
- required action steps.

Quality improvement

Continuous improvement occurs within an organisation when problems are identified, root causes are determined and solutions are found. Use built-in reports and charts to track customer complaints, requests, product defects and corrective actions. Problem types, categories and three levels of defect codes are user-defined. Target the most prominent problems and product defects to ensure quality improvements make a positive impact on the bottom line.

Customer relations

Synchronises customer service, quality assurance, sales, marketing and management by providing a central customer information system, in addition to comprehensive concern and request tracking. For example, Vignette Dialog (see Vignette 17.4) includes contact management tools for sales activity tracking and customer equipment (or product) profiles.

 Vignette 17.5

Siebel Systems, Inc. develops CRM in your pocket.

Siebel Systems, Inc. is a leading provider of e-business applications software, enabling corporations to sell to, market to, and serve customers across multiple channels and lines of business. It is a company leading the way with many innovations and, especially in the field of CRM technology, mobile CRM applications for sales staff and other marketing personnel who need to access customer and company information whilst on the move. With more than 3500 customers worldwide, Siebel Systems provides organisations with a proven set of industry-specific best practices, CRM applications and business processes, empowering them to consistently deliver superior customer experiences and establish more profitable customer relationships. Siebel Systems' sales and service facilities are located in more than 28 countries. The company is working to encourage mainstream adoption of mobile CRM.

New products hit the market regularly, with later entrants challenging industry stalwarts for a piece of this sub sector. The value of mobile CRM applications is clear. Though they come in a variety of permutations, all of them offer salespeople or field representatives a way to take along, synchronize with, or have wireless access to corporate client data and information. For the most part, the mobile CRM products currently available allow a user to function with a common application either connected or disconnected. Basically, all the user is doing is storing and forwarding changes both to and from the corporate database. Siebel has been making a very aggressive play for the mobile CRM market. Its mobile application has modules specifically designed for field sales, field service, channel partners and customers, as well as some vertical industries. Siebel Systems, Inc. is developing the future for the next generation of CRM practioners with its innovative range of mobile CRM applications.

CRM projects are important projects and managers must have clearly defined objectives for their programmes. Measuring the return on investment is an important first step in determining the criteria against which success of the programme will be appraised. The main quality of any set of measures must be to tell management if each project requirement was achieved. Some common CRM measures include the number of new customers, the cost of acquiring those new customers, customer satisfaction, customer attrition, the cost of promoting products, profit margins, incremental revenue, and inventory turn over. Firms need to consider ways in which Web-based CRM will enhance relationships with their customers and where the service and information provided will be excellent but also where the relationship-management teams really utilise the data available to cement and nurture the relationship with their clients. At this point, the e-communication and e-interaction between a firm and its external customers will truly be dyadic.

SELF-CHECK

What was the contribution of organisational buying behaviour to the evolution of the relationship marketing concept?
It had been recognised in industrial markets for some time that commercial relationships between buyer and seller organisations required a more long-term 'interaction approach' rather than the 'short termism' of the next sale. This new thinking resulted in the development of the 'relationship marketing' model. This has now been accepted by firms 'across the board' so to speak, and not only by firms involved in the marketing of services or involved in industrial markets. Hence the subject of organisational buying behaviour has made a significant contribution to the subject of relationship marketing.

▶▶ Summary

The very nature and even the direction of modern marketing have altered. Marketing as a business process that satisfies customers' needs and wants more effectively and efficiently than the competition remains constant and the concept of marketing is still valid today. However the processes used to accomplish this have changed. Firms need to market the very concept of marketing to their own staff and others, the so-called 'internal customers'. Firms need to create the right spirit and internal culture before they can hope for success in their long-term external relationship marketing policies. The internal aspect of marketing is a little different from the external aspect. It has been shown that employees behave toward customers in very much the same way as the management behaves toward them. If they are treated badly they are more likely to treat customers badly. If they are treated well they are more likely to treat the firm's customers well. The whole area of customer care and CRM has evolved and developed substantially over the past 20 years. This has been the focus of this last chapter of the book. However the topic is also related to the subjects covered in Chapter 16 because so much of modern customer care and CRM systems are Internet based. The subject of totally integrated CRM has itself evolved out of the earlier, but related topic of relationship marketing. As with the subject of e-commerce, some commentators feel that CRM is just the latest management search for the perfect business philosophy – in a sense the latest management fad. Others see CRM as a significant change in the philosophy of business, one that incorporates and consolidates many of the earlier areas of new management thinking such as total quality management, internal marketing and relationship marketing. The task of implementing and maintaining a CRM solution can seem overwhelming. But, when the goal of cheaper, faster, better customer service is considered, the results far outweigh the challenges. CRM emphasises cost cutting, revenue generation and customer retention and it is not just a software solution. It is a set of competencies that enables a company to enhance customer relationships. Competition is increasingly evident. The ability to compete on the basis of customer relationships is very important.

FURTHER READING

Armstrong G. and Kotler P. (2000) *Marketing: An Introduction* (5th edn), Chapter 13, 'Relationship Marketing in Personal selling and Sales Promotion', Prentice Hall, Englewood Cliffs, NJ, p. 459.

Berry L.L. and Parasuraman A. (1991) *Marketing Services: Competing Through Quality*, Free Press, New York.

Berry L.L. and Parasuraman A. (1992) 'Prescriptions for a Service Quality Revolution in America', *Organizational Dynamics*, Spring 1992, pp. 5–15.

Berry L.L. and Parasuraman A. (1997) 'Listening to the Customer: The Concept of a Service-Quality Information System', *Sloan Management Review*, Spring 1997, pp. 65–76.

Berry L.L., Parasuraman A. and Zeithaml V.A. (1988) 'The Service-Quality Puzzle', *Business Horizons*, September–October, pp. 35–43.

Berry L.L., Parasuraman A. and Zeithaml V.A. (1990) 'Five Imperatives for Improving Service Quality', *Sloan Management Review*, Summer, pp. 29–38.

Berry L.L., Parasuraman A. and Zeithaml V.A. (1993) 'Ten Lessons for Improving Service Quality', *Marketing Science Institute*, May, Report No. 93–104.

Berry L.L., Parasuraman A. and Zeithaml V.A. (1994) 'Improving Service Quality in America: Lessons Learned', *Academy of Management Executive*, May, pp. 32–52.

Lancaster G.A. and Reynolds P.L. (1999) *Introduction to Marketing: A Step-by-Step Guide to All The Tools of Marketing*, Chapter 14, 'Macro Issues in Marketing', Kogan Page, London.

Parasuraman A. (1995) 'Measuring and Monitoring Service Quality', Chapter 6 in Glynn W. and Barnes J. (eds) *Understanding Services: Management*, John Wiley & Sons, Chichester, pp. 143–77.

Parasuraman A. (1998) 'Customer Service in Business-to-Business Markets: An Agenda for Research', *Journal of Business and Industrial Marketing*, **13**(4/5): 309–21.

Parasuraman A. (2000) 'Technology Readiness Index [TRI]: A Multiple-Item Scale to Measure Readiness to Embrace New Technologies', *Journal of Service Research*, **2**(4): 307–20.

Parasuraman A. and Grewal D. (2000) 'Serving Customers and Consumers Effectively in the 21st Century: A Conceptual Framework and Overview', *Journal of the Academy of Marketing Science*, **28**(1): 9–16.

Parasuraman A. and Grewal D. (2000) 'The Impact of Technology on the Quality–Value–Loyalty Chain: A Research Agenda', *Journal of the Academy of Marketing Science*, **28**(1): 168–74.

Parasuraman A., Berry L.L. and Zeithaml V.A. (1990) 'An Empirical Examination of Relationships in an Extended Service Quality Model', *Marketing Science Institute Research Program Series*, December, Report No. 90–122.

Parasuraman A., Berry L.L. and Zeithaml V.A. (1991) 'Perceived Service Quality as a Customer-Based Performance Measure: An Empirical Examination of Organizational Barriers Using an Extended Service Quality Model', *Human Resource Management*, Fall, pp. 335–64.

Parasuraman A., Berry L.L. and Zeithaml V.A. (1991) 'Refinement and Reassessment of the SERVQUAL Scale', *Journal of Retailing*, Winter, pp. 420–50.

Parasuraman A., Berry L.L. and Zeithaml V.A. (1991) 'Understanding Customer Expectations of Service', *Sloan Management Review*, Spring, pp. 39–48.

Parasuraman A., Berry L.L. and Zeithaml V.A. (1993) 'More on Improving Service Quality Measurement', *Journal of Retailing*, Spring, pp. 141–7.

Parasuraman A., Zeithaml V.A. and Berry L.L. (1994) 'Alternative Scales for Measuring Service Quality: A Comparative Assessment Based on Psychometric and Diagnostic Criteria', *Journal of Retailing*, Fall, pp. 201–30.

Parasuraman A., Zeithaml V.A. and Berry L.L. (1994) 'Moving Forward in Service Quality Research: Measuring Different Customer-Expectation Levels, Comparing Alternative Scales, and Examining the Performance-Behavioural Intentions Link', *Marketing Science Institute*, September, Report No. 94–114.

Parasuraman A., Zeithaml V.A. and Berry L.L. (1994) 'Reassessment of Expectations as a Comparison Standard in Measuring Service Quality: Implications for Future Research', *Journal of Marketing*, January, pp. 111–24.

Parasuraman A., Zeithaml V.A. and Berry L.L. (1998) 'SERVQUAL: A Multiple-Item Scale for Measuring Customer Perceptions of Service Quality', *Journal of Retailing*, Spring, pp. 12–40.

Plamer A. (2000) *Principles of Marketing*, Chapter 22, 'The Marketing of Services', OUP, Oxford.

Voss G.B., Parasuraman A. and Grewal D. (1998) 'The Roles of Price, Performance, and Expectations in Determining Satisfaction in Service Exchanges', *Journal of Marketing*, October, pp. 46–61.

Zeithaml V.A., Berry L.L. and Parasuraman A. (1988) 'Communication and Control Processes in the Delivery of Service Quality', *Journal of Marketing*, April, pp. 35–48.

Zeithaml V.A., Berry L.L. and Parasuraman A. (1993) 'The Nature and Determinants of Customer Expectations of Service', *Journal of the Academy of Marketing Science*, Winter, pp. 1–12.

Zeithaml V.A., Berry L.L. and Parasuraman A. (1996) 'The Behavioural Consequences of Service Quality', *Journal of Marketing*, April, pp. 31–46.

Zeithaml V.A., Parasuraman A. and Berry L.L. (1990) *Delivering Quality Service – Balancing Customer Perceptions and Expectations*, Free Press, New York.

▶▶ References

A.T. Kearney Management Consultants (1994) 'Partnership of Power Play', consultancy report, London.

Berry L.L. (1983) 'Relationship Marketing' in Berry L.L. et al. (eds) *Emerging Perspectives on Services Marketing*, American Marketing Association, Chicago, pp. 25–8.

Copulsky J.R. and Wolf M.J. (1990) 'Relationship Marketing: Positioning for the Future', *Journal of Business Strategy*, July–August, pp. 16–20.

Deming W.E. (1993) *The New Economics for Industry, Government, Education*, Massachusetts Institute of Technology Center for Advanced Engineering Study, Cambridge, MA.

Drucker P. (1973) *Management Tasks, Responsibilities, Practice*, Harper & Row, New York.

Godin S. (1999) *Permission Marketing*, Simon & Schuster, New York.

Gronroos C. (1990) 'Relationship Approach to Marketing In Service Contexts: The Marketing and Organisational Behaviour Interface', *Journal of Business Research*, **20**(January): 3–11.

McKenna R. (1991) *Relationship Marketing*, Century Business, London.

Parasuraman A., Berry L.L. and Zeithaml V.A. (1990) 'Guidelines for Conducting Service Quality Research', *Marketing Research*, December, pp. 34–44.

Parasuraman A., Zeithaml V.A. and Berry L.L. (1985) 'A Conceptual Model of Service Quality and Its Implications for Future Research', *Journal of Marketing*, Fall, pp. 41–50.

Reichheld F.F. and Teal T. (1996) *The Loyalty Effect: The Hidden Force Behind Growth, Profits and Lasting Value*, McGraw-Hill, Maidenhead.

Index